The Trial of Jan Hus

THE TRIAL
OF JAN HUS

Medieval Heresy and Criminal Procedure

THOMAS A. FUDGE

OXFORD
UNIVERSITY PRESS

OXFORD
UNIVERSITY PRESS

Oxford University Press is a department of the University of Oxford.
It furthers the University's objective of excellence in research, scholarship,
and education by publishing worldwide.

Oxford   New York
Auckland   Cape Town   Dar es Salaam   Hong Kong   Karachi
Kuala Lumpur   Madrid   Melbourne   Mexico City   Nairobi
New Delhi   Shanghai   Taipei   Toronto

With offices in
Argentina   Austria   Brazil   Chile   Czech Republic   France   Greece
Guatemala   Hungary   Italy   Japan   Poland   Portugal   Singapore
South Korea   Switzerland   Thailand   Turkey   Ukraine   Vietnam

Oxford is a registered trade mark of Oxford University Press in the UK
and certain other countries.

Published in the United States of America by
Oxford University Press
198 Madison Avenue, New York, NY 10016

© Oxford University Press 2013

Library of Congress Cataloging-in-Publication Data
Fudge, Thomas A.
The trial of Jan Hus : medieval heresy and criminal procedure /
Thomas A. Fudge.
pages cm
Includes bibliographical references (pages) and index.
ISBN 978–0–19–998808–2 (hardcover : alk. paper)—ISBN 978–0–19–998809–9
(ebook)   1. Hus, Jan, 1369?–1415.   2. Council of Constance (1414–1418)
3. Church history—Middle Ages, 600–1500.   I. Title.
BX4917.F83 2013
284'.3—dc23
2012040610

1 3 5 7 9 8 6 4 2
Printed in the United States of America
on acid-free paper

For Jiří Kejř and Lubomír Mlčoch
Czech colleagues and friends

Contents

List of Maps/Figures

Note on Maps

The map of Prague is based on the work of Vilém Lorenc, *Nové město pražské* (Prague: SNTL, 1973); Václav Vladivoj Tomek, *Dějepis města Prahy*, 12 vols., 2nd ed. (Prague: Řivnáč, 1892–1906); Anna Petitova-Bénoliel, *L'Eglise à Prague sous la dynastie des Luxembourg (1310–1419)* (Hilversum: Verloren, 1996); and František Ekert, *Posvátná místa král. hl. města Prahy*, 2 vols., reprint (Prague: Volvox Globator, 1996). The travel route to Constance draws on Hus's letters and the *Relatio* of Petr Mladoňovice. The map of Constance is modeled after a single-sheet woodcut, Überlingen City Archives, printed by Hamma at Constance in 1544; a copper engraving, 36 x 41 cm, in Georg Braun, ed., *Civitatis orbis terrarum*, 6 vols. (Cologne: Apud Godefridum Kempensem, 1575–1617), pt. 2; an engraving by Mattäus Merian der Ältere (1633) in *Topographia Sueviae das ist Beschreib* (Frankfurt: Merian, 1643), 32.2 x 36.2 cm; descriptions in the *Chronik des Konstanzer Konzils* by Ulrich Richental; and, most important, descriptions on a map designed by Konzilstadt Konstanz and generously made available to me by Jürgen Klöckler, head of the City Archives in Constance.

Abbreviations

AHC	*Annuarium Historiae Conciliorum*
AÖG	*Archiv für Österreichische Geschichte*
Bartoš, *Čechy*	František M. Bartoš, *Čechy v době Husově*
Brandmüller	Walter Brandmüller, "Hus vor dem Konzil"
Brandmüller, *Konzil*	Walter Brandmüller, *Das Konzil von Konstanz 1414–1418*
BRRP	*The Bohemian Reformation and Religious Practice*
Buck	Thomas Martin Buck, ed., *Chronik des Konstanzer Konzils 1414–1418 von Ulrich Richental*
Carraway	Joanna Carraway, "Contumacy, Defense Strategy, and Criminal Law"
Castle Archive	Prague Cathedral Chapter Library
CCL	*Corpus Christianorum, Series Latina*
Cerretano	*Liber gestorum*, in Finke, *Acta*, vol. 2, pp. 171–348
ČSAV	Československá akademie věd
CSEL	*Corpus Scriptorum Ecclesiasticorum Latina*
CV	*Communio viatorum*
De ecclesia	Jan Hus, *De ecclesia*, ed. S. Harrison Thomson
De Vooght	*L'Hérésie de Jean Huss*, 2nd ed.
Documenta	František Palacký, ed., *Documenta Mag. Joannis Hus*
Dondaine	Antoine Dondaine, "Le manuel de l'inquisiteur (1230–1300)"
Du Pin	Louis Ellies du Pin, ed., *Joannes Gersonii Opera omnia*
Eymeric, *Directorium*	Nicholas Eymeric, *Directorium inquisitorum*, 1595
Fillastre	*Gesta concilii Constanciensis*, in Finke, *Acta*, vol. 2, pp. 13–170

Finke, *Acta*	Heinrich Finke, ed., *Acta concilii Constanciensis*
Flajšhans, *Hus Sermones*	Václav Flajšhans, ed., *Mag. Io. Hus Sermones in Capella Bethlehem, 1410–1411*
Flajšhans, *Mistr Jan*	Václav Flajšhans, *Mistr Jan řečený Hus z Husince*
Flajšhans, *Odvolání*	Václav Flajšhans, "Husovo odvolání ke Kristu"
Flajšhans, *Sebrané spisy*	Václav Flajšhans, ed., *Mistra Jana Husi Sebrané spisy*
FRA	*Fontes rerum austriacarum*
FRB	*Fontes rerum bohemicarum*
Friedberg	Emil Friedberg, ed., *Corpus iuris canonici*
Fudge, *Jan Hus*	Thomas A. Fudge, *Jan Hus: Religious Reform and Social Revolution in Bohemia*
Fudge, *Memory and Motivation*	Thomas A. Fudge, *The Memory and Motivation of Jan Hus, Medieval Priest and Martyr*
Glorieux	Palémon Glorieux, ed., *Jean Gerson Oeuvres Complètes*
Grundmann	Herbert Grundmann, *Religious Movements in the Middle Ages*
Gui, *Practica*	Bernard Gui, *Practica inquisitionis heretice pravitatis*
Hardt	Hermann von der Hardt, ed., *Magnum oecumenicum constantiense concilium*
Hefele and Leclercq	Karl Joseph von Hefele and Henri Leclercq, *Histoire de Conciles*
Hilsch, *Johannes Hus*	Peter Hilsch, *Johannes Hus (um 1370–1415): Prediger Gottes und Ketzer*
HM	Matthias Flacius Illyricus, ed., *Historia et monumenta Ioannis Hus atque Hieronymi Pragensis*
Höfler	Konstantin von Höfler, ed., *Geschichtschreiber der Husitischen Bewegung in Böhmen*

Hostiensis, SA	Hostiensis, *Summa aurea*
Hus, *Opera omnia*	František Ryšánek, ed., *Magistri Iohannis Hus, Opera omnia*
Hussite Chronicle	Jaroslav Goll, ed. Vavřinec of Březová, *Hussite Chronicle*, in FRB, vol. 5
Jesenice, *Repetitio*	Jan Jesenice, *Repetitio...pro defensione causae Magistri Joannis Hus*, in HM, vol. 1
JSH	*Jihočeský Sborník Historický*
JWLW	*John Wyclif's Latin Works*, 20 vols, in 33 parts, 1883–1922
Kadlec, *Synods*	Jaroslav Kadlec, ed., "Synods of Prague and their Statutes 1396–1414"
Kaminsky, HHR	Howard Kaminsky, *A History of the Hussite Revolution*
Kejř, *Husův proces*	Jiří Kejř, *Husův proces*
Kejř, *Jesenice*	Jiří Kejř, *Husitský pravník: M. Jan z Jesenice*
Kejř, *Odvolání*	Jiří Kejř, *Husovo odvolání od soudu papežova k soudu Kristovu*
Kejř, *Počátků*	Jiří Kejř, *Z počátků české reformace*
KNM	National Museum Library, Prague
Lambert, *Medieval Heresy*	Malcolm Lambert, *Medieval Heresy*, 3rd ed.
Loomis	Louise R. Loomis, ed., *The Council of Constance*
Maisonneuve	Henri Maisonneuve, *Études sur les origines de l'inquisition*
Mansi	Giovanni Domenico Mansi, ed., *Sacrorum conciliorum nova, et amplissima collectio*
Martène and Durand	Edmond Martène and Ursin Durand, eds., *Veterum scriptorum et monumentorum amplissima collectio*
MGH	*Monumenta Germaniae Historica*
NK	National Library, Prague
Novotný, *Correspondence*	Václav Novotný, ed., *M. Jana Husi Korespondence a dokumenty*
Novotný, *M. Jan Hus*	Novotný, *M. Jan Hus: Život a učení*
ÖNB	Österreichische Nationalbibliothek, Vienna
Ordo procedendi	*Ordo procedendi*, in Novotný, *Correspondence*, pp. 225–234

Peter Pulka	Friedrich Firnhaber, ed., "Petrus de Pulka, Abgesandter der Wiener Universität am Concilium zu Constanz"
Pez	Bernard Pez, ed., *Thesaurus anecdotorum novissimus seu veterum monumentorum*
PG	Jacques Paul Migne, ed., *Patrologia Graeca*
PL	Jacques Paul Migne, ed., *Patrologia Latina*
Provvidente	Sebastián Provvidente, "Factum hereticale, representatio et ordo iuris: Le procès contre Jean Hus au Concile de Constance (1414–1418)"
Relatio	Petr Mladoňovice, *Relatio de Mag. Joannis Hus causa*
Richental, *Chronik*	Ulrich Richental, *Chronik des Konstanzer Konzils*
Sedlák	*M. Jan Hus*
Sedlák, *Miscellanea*	Pavel Klener, ed., *Miscellanea husitica Ioannis Sedlák*
Spinka, *Church*	Matthew Spinka, *John Hus' Concept of the Church*
Spinka, *Constance*	Matthew Spinka, ed., *John Hus at the Council of Constance*
Spinka, *John Hus*	Matthew Spinka, *John Hus: A Biography*
SRB	František Palacký, ed., *Scriptores rerum bohemicarum*
ST	Jan Sedlák, *Studie a texty k životopisu Husovu*
Summa theologiae	Jean Nicolaï and François de Bois, eds., *S. Thomae Summa Theologiae*
Tanner, DEC	Norman P. Tanner, ed., *Decrees of the Ecumenical Councils*
Vallerani	Massimo Vallerani, *Medieval Public Justice*
Wakefield, *Heresies*	Walter L. Wakefield and Austin P. Evans, eds., *Heresies of the High Middle Ages*
ZRG KA	*Zeitschrift der Savigny-Stiftung für Rechtsgeschichte: Kanonistische Abteilung*

Canon Law References and Citations

THE DECRETUM OF Gratian (*Decretum Gratiani* or *Concordia discordantium canonum*) is the fundamental medieval law book. It contains about four thousand canons or statutes extracted from recognized authorities from the early church to the later Middle Ages, including canons of councils, letters of popes (some forged), and excerpts from the church fathers. These were compiled by Gratian, an ecclesiastical lawyer, in the twelfth century. There are different citations in references to medieval canon law. The *modern form*, which dates from the time of Edward Gibbon, has only been widely used over the past one hundred years. It is generally approved by the Institute of Research and Study in Medieval Canon Law (*Traditio* 11, 1955, pp. 438–439). The citation begins with the *Distinctio* (distinction) or the *Causa* (case), followed by the *quaestio* (question), *capitulum* (canon), or *dictum* (comment). The Arabic numerical system appears throughout. For example, D.32 c.2 or C.3 q.1 c.5.

There are five other parts of medieval canon law. The contents are largely papal decretal letters and are mostly productions of the twelfth through fourteenth centuries, initially collected unofficially but then later officially. The *Liber extra* was issued by Pope Gregory IX (1227–1241), compiled by Raymond of Peñafort (ca. 1175–1275), and is cited as X 1.18.7. The *Liber sextus* was commissioned by Pope Boniface VIII (1294–1303), compiled by a group of canonists, and appears as VI 5.11.7 or as Sext. 5.11.7. The *Clementines* are almost all decretals issued by Pope Clement V (1305–1314) but were promulgated by Pope John XXII (1316–1334). These are cited as Clem. 3.14.2. The *Extravagantes Johannis XXII* is a small collection of decretals linked to Pope John XXII. It is referred to as Extra. Jo. XXII. The *Extravagantes communes* is a series of decretals that had been cited often but had previously not appeared in collections of canon law. These were brought together by canon law licentiate Jean Chappuis at the end of the fifteenth century. It follows the established pattern of Extrav. comm. 5.2.1. References to canon law are cited herein from the standard edition by Emil Friedberg, *Corpus iuris canonici*, 2 vols. Friedberg is the closest we possess to a critical edition, but its limitations are well known to all familiar with the texts of medieval canon law. Occasionally, I have dated a particular canon or identified its author only when it seemed to shed light on a point of significance. A fulsome explanation of the canonical citation system can be found in James A. Brundage, *Medieval Canon Law* (New York: Longman, 1995), pp. 190–205. The explanation of a canon law citation follows:

D.40 c.6	*Decretum* of Gratian, part 1, distinction 40, chapter 6
C.16. q.1 c.19	*Decretum* of Gratian, part 2, case 16, question 1, chapter 19
X 5.7.9	*Liber extra*, book 5, title or inscription 7, chapter 9
Sext. 2.15.8	*Liber sextus*, book 2, title or inscription 15, chapter 8
Clem. 5.3.1	*Clementines*, book 5, title or inscription 3, chapter 1
Extrav. comm. 5.2.1	*Extravagantes communes*, book 5, title 2, chapter 1

To these standard references I have made two additions. Each canon or statute has been given a title. This is taken from the first word or two of the section or chapter. Some are well known, such as *Ad abolendam* and *Vergentis in senium*. Finally, a specific reference to the Friedberg edition, in terms of volume number and column number(s), has been given. For example, Clem. 5.11.2 *Saepe contingit*, in Friedberg, vol. 2, col. 1143; and C.24 q.3 c.31 *Qui in ecclesia*, in Friedberg, vol. 1, col. 998.

The abbreviations of legal citations used herein are as follows:

a.c.	*ante canon*, a dictum of Gratian preceding a chapter
C.	*Causa* (case), a division of part 2 in Gratian's *Decretum*
c.	*canon* or *capitulum*, chapter
Clem.	Clementines or the Constitutions of Pope Clement V (1305–1314)

D.	*Distinctio* (distinction), a division of part 1 of Gratian's *Decretum*
Dig.	*Digest* of Justinian
d. init.	*dictum initiale*, Gratian's case outline at the beginning of a *Causa*
Extrav. comm.	Frequently cited decretals, not in canon law, added by Jean Chappuis in 1500
Extrav. Jo.	Decretals of Pope John XXII (1316–1334)
Glos. ord.	Glossa ordinaria
p.c.	Dictum of Gratian following a chapter
q.	*Quaestio* (question), a subsection within a *causa* (case) in the *Decretum*
Sext.	The *Liber sextus* of Pope Boniface VIII (1294–1303)
VI	Alternative reference to the *Liber sextus* of Pope Boniface VIII
X	The *Liber extra* of the decretals of Pope Gregory IX (1227–1241)

Introduction

"THE PAST IS a foreign country: they do things differently there."[1] The observation cannot be stressed too much when dealing with a six-hundred-year-old topic. In 1967, the medievalist Howard Kaminsky wrote: "what the historian wants is not a careful demonstration that Hus should not have been burned, but a reasonable explanation—in a sense even a justification—of why he was."[2] This book provides that explanation. To achieve this, I have looked closely at the entire legal process involving Jan Hus and the Latin church from 1410 to 1415. The narrative does not aim at retelling the general story of Hus's ordeal and death but instead has two particular foci. The first is a legal assessment of the trial and the procedures that characterized the case of Hus against prevailing canonical legislation and procedural law in the later Middle Ages. Was his trial legal? In the modern world, there is an instinctive sympathy for a man burned alive for his convictions and the presumed conclusion that any court sanctioning such behavior must have been irregular. Second, I have undertaken an evaluation of the case against Hus from a theological point of view. Was Hus guilty of heresy? Were his doctrinal convictions contrary to established ideas espoused by the Latin church? Upon what basis does the trial verdict rest? From the time of his death to the present, he has been considered either a holy martyr or the worst heretic.[3] The only full-scale study of the Hus trial has been undertaken by the Czech medieval canon law specialist Jiří Kejř.[4] I find little disagreement

---

1. L. P. Hartley, *The Go-Between* (London: Hamish Hamilton, 1953), p. 9.

2. Kaminsky, HHR, p. 35.

3. This is reflected in the lecture title "*Sanctus martyr* or *pessimus haeresiarcha*? The Trial of Jan Hus at Constance," by Paweł Kras, Central European University, Budapest, 2011.

4. *Husův proces* (Prague: Vyšehrad, 2000).

with his work, and while I draw upon it and have been instructed by it, I have investigated the trial of Hus more broadly and in some places more deeply. I have learned much about medieval law and criminal procedure from James Brundage, Richard Helmholz, Tom Izbicki, Jiří Kejř, Henry Ansgar Kelly, Stephan Kuttner, Kenneth Pennington, Edward Peters, and Massimo Vallerani. I am not a lawyer, but I have read canon law and studied heresy trials and legal procedures in the Middle Ages, and I have taken the history of law into account in my university lectures and post-graduate supervisions during a fifteen-year period. I have consulted with canon law specialists, especially Jiří Kejř. I have read the works of medieval legal experts, chiefly but not limited to those whose names appear above. Moreover, I have had the misfortune of being involved in four separate judicial procedures as a named party. In one of those legal cases, spanning three and a half years, I worked full-time in the offices of the lead prosecuting attorney. This does not qualify me as a legal specialist by any means, but I attended numerous court hearings, legal briefings, and two dozen depositions. I wrote and organized the interrogatories for all but one of those deponents. All of these experiences enabled me to appreciate some of the finer points of legal procedure in the judicial case involving Jan Hus. Beyond this, my understanding of heresy was shaped to some extent by many stimulating conversations with Bob Scribner in his rooms at Clare College, Cambridge, more than two decades ago. His untimely death has always been a matter of considerable loss.

This is the third volume in a trilogy devoted to the medieval Czech priest and martyr Jan Hus. The first volume contained a schematic treatment of the trial suggesting my own convictions and understanding.[5] Later, I examined the role of Michael de Causis, one of Hus's main antagonists, in light of the legal process.[6] Even earlier, I explored basic questions concerning heresy and the trial.[7] None of these is adequate. A book-length study is mandatory in order not simply to state but to lay out the complex and complicated nature of the topic, subject it to a robust, critical analysis, and demonstrate the rationale and evidence behind the assumption. Nearly thirty years ago, my initial introduction to Hus was via the *Relatio*,

5. Fudge, *Jan Hus*, pp. 117–146.

6. Fudge, *Memory and Motivation*, chapter 5.

7. Thomas Fudge, "*Infoelix Hus*: The Rehabilitation of a Medieval Heretic," *Fides et Historia* 30, no. 1 (1998): 57–73.

one of the firsthand accounts of the latter stages of his trial, which I read while commuting on the C Train in Calgary, Canada. Not long thereafter, I discovered another (though utterly fraudulent) account of the Hus trial, which prompted my first research project on Hus encouraged by Professor Irv Brendlinger.[8] It seems fitting to come full circle after three decades and take up the trial of Hus as a comprehensive study, especially as the sexcentennial of its culmination looms before us.

The tragedy of the Jan Hus trial is that the defendant insisted on dying. Alternatively, one might argue that the glory or the triumph of the legal process is that Hus refused to live. My findings, arguments, and conclusions will be controversial. I have already been characterized as a right-wing Roman Catholic. The charge is amusing, but I cannot retreat from my findings concerning the Hus process. I must admit an attraction to dissenters and heresy. I am unwilling to regard those of different persuasions or religious convictions as automatic enemies of the faith. That all-too-frequent modern perspective has medieval antecedents. Such intolerance can be found throughout the Hus trial. It reflects the times. It makes the trial of Hus understandable. From a Christian perspective, I have been reluctant to have fewer brothers and sisters than God has sons and daughters. Only the intolerant should not be tolerated. While I recognize and understand (to some extent) the perspective of the prosecutors and judges in the case against Hus, this does not imply that I agree. However, it is without merit to interpret the past and its events in order to make it more acceptable to modern audiences who find it comforting to demonize whatever they find strange or disagreeable. The historian has no business neutering the past.

From the outset, we must disabuse ourselves of the assumption that the trial of Jan Hus was committed to matters of truth or justice. In that sense, it is rather like contemporary civil law cases. The court generally is not interested in such questions. Hus's trial was not a civil case. The modern criminal law courts are more concerned with such matters. The Hus trial was a heresy trial. By medieval legal definition, heresy was a crime, so in that sense, it was a criminal proceeding. That said, there was still no pressing preoccupation with truth and justice. If the judicial process that convened at the papal Curia and later at the Council of Constance was

---

8. *Hus the Heretic by Poggius the Papist: The Trial of Hus*, ed. Beda von Berchem (New York: Carl Granville, 1930). See Fudge, *Jan Hus*, pp. 223 and 314, n. 117, for a summary overview of this.

not concerned to any significant degree with truth or justice, we must wonder about the prevailing interest. Issues of power, authority, and control emerge. Did the court hearing the Hus case deliberately manipulate evidence? By comparison, do attorneys deliberately manipulate evidence in modern Western judiciaries? The answer must be yes. Lawyers have a duty to represent their clients.

This volume is the final result of a long research project that has already yielded my *Jan Hus: Religious Reform and Social Revolution in Bohemia* (2010) and *The Memory and Motivation of Jan Hus, Medieval Priest and Martyr* (2013). The general conventions adopted in those books on sources (excepting canon law), interpretation of Hus, and the rendering of Czech proper names have continued. My position on nomenclature, especially on controversial historiographical constructs such as "heresy" and "Hussites," continues with the full benefit of careful consideration. The same repositories and archives that have served me well since the 1980s, on both sides of the Atlantic, were utilized once again.

I would like to acknowledge the encouragement and stimulation from my students over the years in both the northern and southern hemispheres, individuals such as the late Bob Scribner, František Šmahel, the late Vilém Herold, Jiří Kejř, David Holeton, my father James Fudge, the late Jack Fergusson, Tom Izbicki, Norman Housley, Cary Nederman, Malcolm Lambert, Stephen Lahey, Paul Knoll, and my many colleagues from the biennial symposium "The Bohemian Reformation and Religious Practice." Sousou Cosette and Luboš Mlčoch helped with particular texts, while Marek Červený provided invaluable research assistance. I had extensive conversations with Jiří Kejř in Prague many times between 1991 and 2012 about the trial, legal procedure, canon law, and other aspects of the research undergirding this book. Thanks also to Kenneth Pennington for advice and direction and also to the anonymous readers for Oxford University Press and its executive editor Cynthia Read for their enthusiasm in bringing this study to publication. I am further grateful to Maureen Cirnitski and Wendy Keebler for the technical improvement of the text and to Jakoub Fudge for assistance with the index. I have lectured on aspects of the Hus trial in Portland, Vancouver, Prague, and Christchurch and remain grateful for audience response. Equally important has been the provision of space at Hewitt created by my friend of many years April Purtell, wherein I was able to write three volumes on Hus, which form the results of these years of research.

On account of the generosity of an American university that prefers not to be named, I have enjoyed a fully funded nine-year-long research project devoted to the study of Jan Hus. Being released from all normal academic responsibilities made it possible for me to spend these years working on Hus. This unexpected and magnanimous funding has provided all necessary resources for extensive international travel; attendance at conferences in places as far afield as New Zealand, Australia, Canada, the United States, Romania, Belgium, Poland, Slovakia, and the Czech Republic, where I spoke on Hussite topics; extensive work in archives, especially in Prague, Vienna, and Rome; and the concentrated research required to write three volumes on Hus. I regret being unable to write at greater length about my considerate benefactor. However, I am limited to these wholly inadequate remarks by the terms of this compelling arrangement. With the completion of this book, I now return full-time with great joy to the world of academe at the University of New England in Australia.

Finally, I remain grateful to Mary Tipton for a wonderful adventure in the summer of 2012, revisiting those places associated with the Hus trial in Europe, especially Prague and Constance; at Constance, we followed the footsteps of Hus from St. Paul Street to the stake. This book is dedicated to two of my Czech colleagues who have been an essential part of my interest in Jan Hus.

Thomas A. Fudge
Cistercian Abbey
Lafayette, Oregon

The Trial of Jan Hus

I

Jan Hus in History, Heresy, and Court

LATE IN THE year 1412, a condemned man appeared in south Bohemia. Many knew him. More than twenty years earlier, he had lived in the area but departed from the poor regions of the south for the fortunes of the capital city of Prague. One might say his ambitions had been fulfilled and his dreams had come true. During the Prague years, he climbed the ladder of success, attaining academic respect, an advanced degree, the pulpit of an influential ecclesiastical venue, the chancellorship of the university, and a reputation for honor at the royal court. In the two decades between his departure as a young man and his return, he had moved from the life of an unknown student to that of a national leader and perhaps the most famous priest in the realm. Now, after ten years of increasing renown, he was coming home stripped of his positions and prestige, an outcast, indeed, almost as one carrying an infectious disease. He had been judged unworthy of humanity and expelled from the Christian community. Should he die, he had no right to a proper religious burial; his corpse was considered fit only to be discarded. His arrival in the villages of south Bohemia meant that a dark cloud would hang over the environs, following him wherever he might go. This was the curse of interdict; wherever he might stop and rest, that community could be subjected to spiritual starvation, cut off from God, and exempted from the protections afforded by the most powerful institution of the day. Whoever might touch him, whoever dared speak to him or attempt to give him any assistance whatever ran the risk of criminal prosecution leading to a similar fate. He was cursed and without human remedy. The wanderer was a professor without students, a priest with no altar from which to minister, a preacher who had neither church nor congregation; he was bereft of protection and at the mercy of whoever happened upon him. The man was in exile and an outcast from the circles of influence and prestige he had once enjoyed. He had been condemned as a heretic and was awaiting the execution of his sentence, which in those days meant burning at the stake.[1] The man's real name was possibly Jan Michalóv of Husinec, but history remembers him as Jan Hus.[2] He was born on an indeterminate date, probably in the year 1371, in the southern part of Bohemia.[3] His story captivated the known world.

During his lifetime and in subsequent historiography, Jan Hus has consistently aroused deep emotion, much loyalty or loathing, and strong opinions. This centers mainly in his legal ordeal, which is regarded as either justice or judicial murder. Apologists on both sides have been unshakable. The raw image of a man burned alive has been sufficient to generate controversy and unrestrained reaction. Capital punishment frequently compels those responses. There were men at the Council of Constance, such as Michael de Causis, who believed steadfastly that Hus had to die, that his crimes were so heinous that nothing short of capital punishment could satisfy God and purge society. There were others, such as Jan Chlum, who were unashamed to extend public support to the condemned. Hus's story is not unlike that of many others in his time. What separates him from the rest was the manner of his dying. His story has been told elsewhere in some detail.[4] There are few, if any, biographical details still to emerge from surviving records. There are two questions that must detain us here. The first has to do with heresy, and the second relates to the legal process, which occupied a full five years. The court case involving Jan Hus was *the* heresy trial of the later Middle Ages.

---

1. Flajšhans, *Mistr Jan*, p. 311.

2. Flajšhans, *M. Jan Hus: Dle svých přednášek ve "Svazu osvětovém"* (Prague: Šimáček, 1915), p. 23. "Jan, son of Michael, from Husinec," since tradition names his father Michael; p. 19. This is based on a list of ordained priests in Prague in 1400 where "Johannes Michaelis de Hussynecz" is named. There is no consensus on this. See Novotný, *M. Jan Hus*, vol. 1, p. 2.

3. The best argument for 1371 has been advanced by František M. Bartoš, *Co víme o Husovi nového* (Prague: Pokrok, 1946), p. 24, and there is no compelling reason to object to it.

4. The standard biography is Novotný, *M. Jan Hus: Život a učení*. In Western languages, see also de Vooght; Spinka, *John Hus*; Ernst Werner, *Jan Hus: Welt und Umwelt eines Prager Frühreformators* (Weimar: Böhlaus, 1991); Hilsch, *Johannes Hus*; Fudge, *Jan Hus*; Thomas Krzenck, *Johannes Hus: Theologe, Kirchenreformer, Märtyrer* (Zürich: Muster-Schmidt, 2011); and Fudge, *Memory and Motivation*.

Heresy is a legal concept. Therefore, the law determines what counts as heresy in different times and places. This is remarkably easy to assert, but one must immediately inquire about the relevance of law. Legal statutes may exist, but are they practicable or enforceable? The measure cannot merely be that a proclaimed or written law is sufficient as a standard for practice. The application of law must be considered. In a sense, history is applied law. Laws that are enforced tend to have more meaning and influence in society. What does law enforcement mean in terms of heresy in the later Middle Ages? First, heresy law must exist. Second, the infraction or suspicion of noncompliance must be prosecuted. Third, a criminal prosecution generally follows a legal procedure leading to or including a court trial. Fourth, there must be conviction. Fifth, the court must return a verdict against the convicted felon in accordance with established sentencing guidelines. Sixth, the punishment must be serious. Seventh, the application of law and punishment must be carried out with equal sanction to those accused and those found guilty irrespective of social or political standing. Eighth, the enforcement of law against heresy must be a function of the courts and prosecutorial discretion. Ninth, the punitive consequences for offenders must be applied widely over time and space in order to inculcate a meaningful sense of the laws in question, the conduct they seek to control, and the understanding of their severity within the particular society. Thus considered, to affirm that heresy is a legal concept is more complex than it seems at first blush.[5]

There persists an enduring conviction that Jan Hus was unjustly accused, illegally tried, and thereafter murdered for his attempts to reform the church. The excuse used to justify these draconian measures has been the charge of heresy. Was Hus guilty of heresy? This remains one of the critical questions in assessing his life and forming an evaluation of his legal ordeal. To the modern mind, there is considerable feeling that even if Hus was guilty as charged by the judges and prosecutors during the various stages of his trial, his fate at the Council of Constance seems exceptionally cruel. The irony lies in the question that argues that he did not really deserve to be burned for not recognizing the primacy of the papacy, especially at a time when the largest council Christianity had ever known

---

5. Recent scholarship has begun to recognize this. Provvidente, pp. 103–106; and Sebastián Provvidente, *Política y eclesiología en el movimiento conciliar de los siglos XIV–XV: La causa Hus* (Buenos Aires: Editorial Hydra, 2013).

had just decided that not one but three popes were unworthy.[6] But was this the sole factor in determining a judicial verdict? A careful examination of the charges brought against the defendant helps to form an objective judgment.[7] Dissident men and women were routinely demonized at the end of the Middle Ages in the church's war on heresy, just as thoroughly as certain individuals and groups are demonized in the twenty-first century in America's war on terror. That process of marginalization is critical to formal condemnation and subsequent justification of that action. It is considerably easier to burn a man alive or cluster-bomb a community when it is believed that targets are less than human or, better yet, agents of Satan. There is, of course, a difference between the psychological distress caused theologically and conceptually by the heretic and the physical mayhem created by the modern terrorist, but the process of demonization is more or less the same. Terminology changes, but Jan Hus was advertised as posing a threat to the later medieval church on the same scale as certain governments today worry about presumed threats to national security. Ideas that are stated over and over through official or official-sounding media tend to become accepted in popular culture as facts. Even lies told with regularity tend to evolve into truths. Once those facts have been established and adequately disseminated, it becomes relatively easy to garner sufficient support for measures of repression, prosecution, and even extermination. The process in the late medieval world and those in the contemporary age are not as dissimilar as one might first assume. To continue the analogy, should the Irish Republican Army be considered a terrorist organization? Are groups such as Hamas, Hezbollah, and al-Qaeda properly termed terrorist? The answer depends, of course, on definition and perspective.

Was Jan Hus a heretic? Once more, the answer can be meaningful only after an evaluation of the word and an assessment of the perspective urging the term. First and foremost, the consolidation of conciliar power must be assessed.[8] Forty years after Hus's death, prominent Europeans considered the doctrines he promoted "treacherous insanity."[9] The Latin

---

6. De Vooght, p. 501.

7. I have undertaken this below, especially in chapters 4 and 7 and elsewhere in Fudge, "O Cursed Judas: Formal Heresy Accusations against Jan Hus," in *Political Uses of the Accusation of Heresy*, ed. Thomas M. Izbicki (forthcoming).

8. Provvidente, p. 108.

9. *Aeneae Silvii Historia Bohemica*, ed. Dana Martínková (Prague: Koniash Latin Press, 1998), chap. 35, p. 88.

church persisted in regarding Hus similarly for another century. He continued to be seen as "crooked as a snake and a slippery serpent."[10] Drawing upon motifs from classical and biblical sources, writers asserted that the "wicked Jan Hus" should be eternally punished, for he must be judged as worse than an infidel, a pagan, a Turk, a Tartar, and the Jews. He was worse than the most profligate men of Sodom, impure sisters, those who seize mothers, and even the Persians. He was worse than the frightful parricides such as Cain and Thyestes, the cannibal-istic tribe of the Laistrygones, and the renowned child killers Pharaoh and Herod. All of this may seem absurd, but heresy "is a monstrous crime" surpassing all other crimes for its unspeakable enormity, impi-ety, shamefulness, and impurity far exceeding all evil before God and must therefore be subjected to commensurate guilt and punishment.[11] The rhetoric was not only overwrought, but it also missed the main point about Hus. Demonizing him was fairly simple. Proving him guilty of heresy was somewhat more complex. Declaring him the "most steadfast champion of truth" was also a natural claim advanced in other quarters.[12] However, exonerating him from those serious charges, which bedeviled the last years of his life, is rather more difficult and complicated. The required nuances have not prevented scholars from advancing their opinions on Hus from the fifteenth century to the present. Before World War II, with few exceptions, Czech historians and scholars produced the most important work on the interpretation of Hus. Josef Kalousek, Václav Flajšhans, Václav Novotný, Jan Sedlák, Vlastimil Kybal, and Josef Pekař represent the earliest efforts, following Palacký, to recover the Hus of history.[13] The question of heresy was there and to some extent dealt with, but it remained in the shadows of other considerations, not least nationalistic concerns. Quite a number of the early scholars concluded that Hus was a minor figure in the religious history of medieval Europe and that his death catapulted him to a level of significance higher than

---

10. Johannes Cochlaeus, *Historia Hussitarum libri duodecim* (Mainz: Behem, 1549), p. 88.

11. Ibid., p. 98.

12. *Relatio*, p. 120.

13. Josef Kalousek, *O potřebě prohloubiti vědomosti o Husovi a jeho době*, 2 vols. (Prague: Nákladem a Tiskem Českoslovanské Akciové Tiskárny, 1915); Flajšhans, *Mistr Jan*; Václav Novotný and Vlastimil Kybal, *M. Jan Hus: Život a učení*, 2 vols. in 5 parts (Prague: Laichter, 1919–1931); Josef Pekař, *Jan Hus* (Prague: Bursik and Kohout, 1902). See Fudge, *Jan Hus*, pp. 209–225.

that merited by his life.[14] Others objected to that rather pedestrian point of view and advanced the argument that Hus was the greatest and most famous theologian of his time.[15] Again, either the matter of heresy is left aside, or a subjective judgment has been passed. In neither case has the matter been properly investigated. The question remains, "to what extent could Hus be accused of flagrant defiance of lawful authorities and in what points did he actually deviate from the Church doctrine?"[16] Commensurate with this question about Hus's alleged heresy is a consideration about what difference it makes. *Cui bono?* Who benefits from proving or disproving Hus's heresy? Of course, the question had life-or-death significance in 1415 and has been made to have ecumenical significance six hundred years later. But the question of heresy remains unavoidably central in evaluating the trial of Jan Hus.

Pierre of Versailles, the colleague of Jean Gerson who functioned as one of the chief prosecutors of Hus at Constance, commented a few months after Hus's execution that Hus would certainly not have been convicted had the court allowed him access to legal counsel.[17] How are we to understand that provocative comment? There seem to be three possibilities. First, should it be taken to mean that Hus was not really a heretic at all? Or does the comment imply that a shrewd lawyer might have gotten Hus off, irrespective of guilt? Or might it be assumed that in denying Hus proper representation, the trial committed a serious violation of the law, meaning that the defendant was denied his legal rights? This raises issues of both heresy and legal procedure. The Dominican Johannes Falkenberg said that Pierre of Versailles's comment itself should be dismissed as heretical in the strongest terms.[18] Ironically, Falkenberg was himself locked up at Constance on charges of heresy and later remanded to cautionary

---

14. Sedlák, ST, 3 vols., and *M. Jan Hus*; Rudolf Holinka, *Sektářství v Čechách před revolucí husitskou* (Bratislava: Filosofická Fakulta University Komenského, 1919); Augustin Neumann, *České sekty ve století XIV. a XV.* (Velehrad: Nákl. Cyrilometodějského Tiskového Spolku, 1920).

15. *Super IV Sententiarum*, in *Mag. Jo. Hus Opera omnia: Nach neuentdeckten Handschriften*, 3 vols., ed. Václav Flajšhans (Osnabrück: Biblio-Verlag, 1966), vol. 2, p. iv.

16. Otakar Odložilík, review essay in *American Historical Review* 67 (1962): 385; Odložilík, *Jan Hus* (Chicago: Nákl. Národní Jednoty Československých Protestantů ve Spojených Státech a Kanadě, 1953).

17. Finke, *Acta*, vol. 4, p. 352.

18. Ibid., pp. 352–354.

imprisonment.[19] Hus became a pawn in the historiography of the nine-teenth century. Czech nationalists proclaimed that Hus marked the begin-ning of a new period of religious history.[20] German rebuttals sometimes concluded that Hus was not simply a heretic but a common criminal who got what he deserved at the end of his trial.[21] I do not see any trace of serious effort in either perspective to adjudicate the matter of heresy. For uncritical followers of Palacký, the moniker of heretic was sheer propa-ganda aimed at destroying Hus. Those who accepted the Höfler thesis did so largely because it justified an a priori assumption. Scholars in the wake of these arguments tended to take one side or the other in modified form. Since Hus wished to establish a new church or an alternative form of religious expression apart from the official Latin church, he must be con-sidered heretical.[22] The judgment is one of perceived logical extension, as opposed to a conclusion reached after a careful analysis of Hus's doctrine compared with the medieval understanding of heresy. The man whom the Council of Constance condemned was an individual "reviled, loathed, prosecuted as a heretic, a revolutionary, the instigator of discord, and an impenitent demagogue."[23] We are still some distance from understanding properly the meaning of heresy in this context. Other scholars unambigu-ously conclude that the one thing without doubt during the latter stages of Hus's trial was the certainty of the heretical guilt of the defendant.[24]

If not guilty of heresy, Hus may be cast into the role of a subver-sive whose efforts at reform and defiance of established authority have been described as "insincere, undiscriminating, opportunistic, and demagogic."[25] These possibilities do not make one a heretic by any

---

19. Bernhard Bess, "Johannes Falkenberg, O.P. und der preußisch-polnische Streit vor dem Konstanzer Konzil," *Zeitschrift für Kirchengeschichte* 16, no. 3 (1896): 385–464.

20. František Palacký, *Dějiny narodu českého v Čechách a v Moravě* (Prague: Bursik & Kohout, 1893), vol. 3, pp. 1–120; Palacký, *Die Geschichte des Hussitenthums und Professor Constantin Höfler* (Prague: Tempsky, 1868), p. 160.

21. Konstantin von Höfler, *Magister Johannes Hus und der Abzug der deutschen Professoren und Studenten aus Prag, 1409* (Prague: Tempsky, 1864). I have elsewhere explored these issues in Thomas A. Fudge, "The State of Hussite Historiography" *Mediaevistik: Internationale Zeitschrift für Interdisziplinäre Mittelalterforschung* 7 (1994): 96–98; and Fudge, *Jan Hus*, pp. 214–216.

22. Pekař, *Jan Hus*, p. 20.

23. De Vooght, p. 510.

24. Brandmüller, pp. 235–236.

25. Kaminsky, HHR, p. 36.

medieval calibration. The Council of Constance did see Hus in this sense. The careful examination and doctrinal analysis of Hus's ideas flesh out points of theological controversy. One of the more thorough of these attempts isolated the root of Hus's eventual heresy when he adopted elements of John Wyclif's ecclesiology and developed an argument that concluded that the proper understanding of the church had to do with its essential composition as the body of the predestined.[26] Hus wrote an entire book delineating this conviction.[27] It is possible to see in this theological elaboration a significant contradiction in Hus's doctrine of the church wherein aspects of traditional Augustinian language have been joined, perhaps unequally, to Wyclifite constructs. If this is true, then Hus's unwillingness to see the problem and retract his position in the face of censure brought him into the dangerous orbit of heresy. From the conciliar point of view, Hus persisted in his errors and in doing so exposed himself to death. The Council could have chosen a form of punishment other than death, and there have always been voices lamenting the lack of mercy at the conclusion of the Hus trial.[28] The issue remained heresy. It was heresy or the suspicion thereof that brought Hus into a legal process before the papal courts and thereafter to final summary trial at the Council of Constance. Once the trial of Hus resumed there, the Council expanded the concept of heresy. The critical distinction was that heresy manifested itself in intellectual or cognitive terms and also in the human will, which could lead to contumacy.[29] At the time of Hus, heresy was handled as crime and sin.[30] The court hearing the case against Hus was concerned with both.

If there were those regarding Hus as heretic, other converse opinions were equally firmly voiced. Hus was a man filled with "piety, candor, simplicity, zeal, charity, constancy, and a greatness of soul worthy of the apostolical ages."[31] The work of Paul de Vooght illumines clearly that Hus

---

26. Paul de Vooght, *Hussiana* (Louvain: Publications Universitaires de Louvain, 1960), pp. 9–25.

27. Hus, *De ecclesia*.

28. Hefele and Leclercq, vol. 7, part 1, pp. 330–331. The observation is Leclercq's.

29. Brandmüller, p. 237.

30. Christine Caldwell Ames, "Does Inquisition Belong to Religious History?" *American Historical Review* 110, no. 1 (2005): 19.

31. Jacques Lenfant, *The History of the Council of Constance*, 2 vols. (London: Rivington, 1730), vol. 1, pp. 24–25.

was considerably more orthodox in certain matters of doctrine than has hitherto been recognized. Still, the argument that Hus was barely heretical is somewhat like saying that a woman is barely pregnant. At the end of his lengthy and careful study of Hus, de Vooght felt compelled to say, "I also agree Hus probably professed heresy."[32] De Vooght argues that the final thirty charges brought against Hus by the church, three years after his death, deserved the judgment and assessment that Pope Martin V used to describe them. From the perspective of late medieval ecclesiastical dogma, they were "heretical, false, reckless, seditious, offensive to pious ears, and they are in the work of Hus." It is true that the conclusions represent a caricature of his teaching, but they are neither entirely false nor ultimately completely misleading. In places, "Hus obviously deviated from church teaching."[33] Others disagree, finding essentially no real heresy whatever in Hus.[34] A careful consideration of the trial leads many to conclude that Hus's reluctance to acquiesce in the condemnation of Wyclif led to his own death. We have, then, a guilt-by-association verdict rather than a finding of error on Hus's part.[35] Those evaluating the issue of heresy are often content with a definition restricted to doctrinal deviation from the official teachings of the church. Thus, we find comments that Cardinal Colonna excommunicated Hus for nonappearance, not because of heresy, and that Cardinal Stephaneschi placed Hus under major excommunication not for heresy but on account of disobedience.[36] The same comments are made in major works.[37] Little attention is paid to canon law. Others conclude that any reference to Hus as a heretic can be understood only in the ironic sense.[38] Scholars in this camp are ever hopeful that the Roman Catholic Church will at some point annul the "unjust and harmful verdict" pronounced against Hus at Constance.[39]

---

32. De Vooght, p. 514.

33. "M. Štěpán z Pálče a Husův proces," in Kejř, *Počátků*, p. 122.

34. Joseph Rostislas Stejskal, *Le procès de Jean Huss: Étude historique et dogmatique* (Paris: Picart, 1923).

35. Lenfant, *The History of the Council of Constance*, vol. 1, pp. 444–445.

36. Matthew Spinka, "Hus' Trial at the Council of Constance," in *Czechoslovakia Past and Present*, ed. Miloslav Rechcigl (The Hague: Mouton, 1968), vol. 2, pp. 1211–1212.

37. Spinka, *Church*, pp. 103, 137; Spinka, *John Hus*, pp. 119–120, 161.

38. David R. Holeton, "The Celebration of Jan Hus in the Life of the Churches," *Studia Liturgica* 35 (2005): 58–59.

39. De Vooght, p. 517.

Others find it amazing that Hus agreed to go to the Council of Constance. He had been so critical of the corruption that he perceived as endemic in the church, yet he considered the opportunity to speak formally before the Council worthwhile. Some find it amazing that he even imagined he could possibly get a fair hearing.[40] Legal doctrine for at least one hundred years before Hus affirmed the principle of *item quilibet presumitur innocens nisi probetur nocens*, meaning that the defendant was presumed innocent until proven guilty. This was a later medieval judicial maxim. Often in practice, that ideal suffered from the ravages of bias and prejudice.

It is not difficult to form hostile opinions of the Council of Constance when looking at the trial of Jan Hus.[41] There are vivid and inflammatory reports on the public hearings in the Hus case, and even if a verdict of heresy was unwarranted, the conduct of the court has been described as one of disrepute. The Council has been judged from some perspectives as forced into an unsolvable situation, in which if it burned Hus, it would come under withering criticism for harshness, lack of mercy, and the application of a disproportionate punishment. On the other hand, had the Council been lenient, critics on the other side would have accused the court of softness, failure to uphold the law, and a lack of resolve in meeting the stated objectives of the synod. The judges and prosecutors opted to err on the side of applying a harsh sentence. The Council of Constance could ill afford to ignore canon law and simply let a heretic off with a perfunctory slap on the wrist. The sentence of death was a strategy aimed at bolstering its own reputation for orthodoxy. The conviction and verdict of capital punishment were intended to send a message that dissent would not be tolerated. The court intentionally announced that it was going to be tough on crime. This stance was prompted by the Council's awareness that not all in Western Christendom were convinced of the legitimacy of the Council itself.[42] Condemning Hus strengthened conciliar authority and aided the Council's effort to solve the papal schism and achieve the eradication of heresy within the church. Inasmuch as they had some responsibility for bringing into effect the decree that established the superiority of the Council, it is possible that men such as Jean Gerson and Pierre d'Ailly

---

40. Matthew Spinka, *John Hus and the Czech Reform* (Hamden, Conn.: Archon Books, 1966), p. 51.

41. See, for example, the introductory essay and comments throughout Spinka, *Constance*.

42. Hefele and Leclercq, vol. 7, part 1, pp. 330–331.

felt the need to reassure themselves about their own personal orthodoxy, as they must have been worried about their political vulnerability and the canonical risks they took at Constance. So they took hold of what may have seemed a providential opportunity to burn a heretic. Such hypotheses are neither absurd nor impossible.[43] They must, however, be tempered with the fact that the Council did not wish to burn Hus and went to great lengths to avoid it.[44] Nevertheless, the judicial settings at the Curia and at the Council of Constance cannot be characterized as kangaroo courts, nor was the latter convened to persuade Christian Europe that a general council was capable of dealing with internal threats to the Christian faith without specific papal guidelines. All of this said, the question of motivation on the part of the judges in the Hus trial remains controversial.[45]

Jan Hus is remembered more for his death than for his life. There is considerable drama. From the last hearings, we have glimpses of the courtroom and legal proceedings at Constance during his trial. We hear people shouting in loud voices all at once; we see a courtroom circled by "numerous city guards armed with swords, crossbows, axes and spears." We are privy to cardinals asking weighty questions; we witness confrontations and see evidence of exasperation. We listen as accusers take the floor. From time to time, there is much laughter, and we see witnesses imploring the court for permission to speak, only to be denied. We hear men crying out passionately, "reverend fathers, listen to me please." We see the most powerful secular ruler in all of Europe exploding in rage and threatening to burn the defendant personally. We find the judge "indignantly shaking his head and face and scowling," while a prosecutor urges a notary to record carefully certain points of procedure. We witness the defendant escorted to and from the court in manacles. At various times in the proceedings, we are told of "murmuring and tumult." There are objections made; some are sustained, others overruled. We are sometimes privy to private conversations going on in corners of the room. We hear prelates shouting for the king to be brought closer to the interrogation and orders for the defendant

---

43. De Vooght, pp. 507–508.

44. Jiří Kejř, "K Husovu procesu v Kostnici," *Acta Universitatis Carolinae—Historia Universitatis Carolinae Pragensis* 48, no. 1 (2008) : 15.

45. Karen Sullivan, *The Inner Lives of Medieval Inquisitors* (Chicago: University of Chicago Press, 2011), attempts to get inside the minds of heresy prosecutors. Her investigative goal is admirable, but I have some reservation about its achievement on account of its failure to deal properly with context. A text without a context is a pretext for a proof text.

to repeat previous statements. We read of instances in which legal statutes and specific laws are cited. We witness an inattentive king leaning out a window as the trial drags on. We see a "certain monk wearing a black cape on which something shiny black is draped," warning the court that the defendant is attempting to confuse the hearing. At other times, we find the responses of the prisoner openly mocked. There is pressure on the accused to recant. We hear piteous pleas from the defendant expressing fear of committing perjury. We are brought into sharp exchanges in which the king admonishes the prisoner to the effect that he is old enough to know better and can understand if he only wanted to, that he should do so, and "the sooner the better." We see an old, bald Polish bishop citing laws concerning heresy and a fat priest, "who looked like a Prussian," seated in a window wrapped in "an expensive tunic," shouting loudly that the court must not allow the defendant to revoke anything, for the accused is a liar. We observe another witness jumping to his feet, saying, "listen to me, I pray, just two words." We see judges looking at one another in stunned amazement as the case proceeds. We witness the unsolicited testimony of two men solemnly declaring to the judges that their role in prosecuting the accused was entirely honorable, without "malicious zeal or personal hatred." In the grimness of the proceedings, we observe the humane gesture of a brave man shaking the hand of the defendant and consoling him as the latter is led from the court chambers.

There is intrigue. We are brought into ex parte conversations, whose participants are unaware of being overheard by eavesdroppers lurking nearby, advising the court to shorten the proceedings, return a guilty verdict forthwith, and condemn the defendant to capital punishment. We read racy tales of attempted escapes. A man is discovered with a "flask of wine and a loaf of white bread," hiding in a wagon about to pull out of town. Another report tells of the prisoner leaping from a horse in an effort to disappear into a throng of some eighteen thousand people. In haste, all city gates are ordered closed. Once more, the narrative sources refer to guards armed with "swords, crossbows, and long axes," who attended every hearing. We catch a glimpse of a nameless monk hearing the confession of the condemned man in a prison cell and granting absolution. We observe the prisoner forbidden to enter the cathedral during the divine liturgy and made to wait in the company of an archbishop just outside the doors. We are able to hear a sung Mass celebrated by a Polish prelate, which ends with the words "beware of false prophets" who come in disguise. Immediately thereafter, the defendant is led into the cathedral. We learn that the accused was placed on an elevated chair for all to see, and we hear judges instructing guards to force the prisoner to maintain silence. The emperor sits in some splendor. A German military governor bears the imperial mace. A Bavarian prince holds the gold crown. A Hungarian knight wields the royal sword. We read of fervent prayers and details of the defendant crying out in despair of justice. There are accusations and arguments. We read of jeers from the men whom the prisoner forgives. We listen as an archbishop mounts the pulpit and delivers a bombastic sermon against the accused, insisting that the body of sin must be eradicated without delay. An old, bald auditor reads the official verdict. When the man who is about to die turns to look at the king, we are told that the embarrassed monarch "blushed deeply and turned red" but never uttered a word. We are brought closely into an emotionally charged scene wherein the defendant is defrocked in an elaborate ceremony of degradation. He holds a chalice, which is taken from his hands as he is cursed and given the moniker Judas. The stole is removed. Then the chasuble. Then the rest of the priestly vestments are stripped from the prisoner. As each item is removed, an appropriate curse is intoned. We find the man weeping, and there are disagreements over how best to obliterate his tonsure. The humiliation continues as the ex-priest is forced to accept an example of the *poenae confusibiles* and wear a paper miter adorned with demons and bearing letters indicating his crime, while formal maledictions are pronounced by seven bishops over the condemned man.

These glimpses are tense and moving and fraught with dramatic overtones. The scene shifts from the cathedral precincts. We are taken past a scene where books are thrown into a roaring fire in view of the public. We join a great throng; we come to a gate, cross a bridge, and follow a large procession to the place of execution among the gardens in a meadow between the city and an ancient fortress, between the moats, outside city gates in the Brüel Field. A priest wearing a "green garment with red silk lining," sitting on a horse, objects to the suggestion that the condemned be allowed a confessor. Under close guard, the convict is permitted to go among the bystanders. We hear him pleading with those present not to believe his guilt, insisting that he has been charged by mendacious witnesses. We hear the convicted felon asking to see his prison guards, and when those men come near, the man surprisingly thanks them for their humanity. There is disagreement over which direction the convict should face at the place of death. We witness the stripping of the prisoner. Wearing only a gown, he has his hands tied behind his back, his neck fastened to the stake with a "sooty chain," one foot shackled. He is made to stand on a stool so that wood can be placed under his feet and the gathered multitudes can better see a man dying in the fire. An eyewitness notes that the condemned man is still wearing his shoes as the executioner's assistants unload two wagons filled with wood and pile the faggots to his chin. Straw and some pitch are added, and the moment of truth arrives. Two men, one of them the imperial marshal, implore the convicted prisoner to reconsider his position. We note a final opportunity to save his life extended to the man about to die. We listen to his poignant refusal. Onlookers marvel at his pious words. We read of a futile attempt to deliver one last sermon from inside the woodpile. The marshal claps his hands, and the executioner takes the torch. Then come the flames, and the "worst stench arose that one could smell" on account of a mule's carcass recently buried beneath the pyre. As the inferno roars, we hear the convict break forth in screams and song: "Christ, son of the living God, have mercy on me." Death mercifully comes quickly. We are told of the careful desecration of his remains, the smashing of bones with clubs, the crushing of the skull, the roasting of the heart at the end of a sharpened stick held in the flames, the burning of all personal effects, including his shoes, and how the remaining ashes were meticulously loaded onto a cart and carefully dumped into the river, in hopes of erasing his memory forever.[46]

These are glimpses, emotionally charged moments, in the last appearances of Jan Hus before the court, on trial for his life, struggling with the enormity of the confrontation, engaged in the hopeless task of achieving a reconciliation of ethics and law. We know in graphic and disturbing detail how his trial ended. Few might defend every aspect of the legal process, and even fewer would be happy to say that all things were conducted decently and in order. From a strictly historical point of view, it is rather unhelpful to respond to the question "Why was Hus burned at the stake?" by answering "Because he was guilty of the crime of heresy."[47] This is

---

46. There are three main narrative sources written by men who can reliably be placed at Constance during the trial of Jan Hus. *Relatio*, pp. 72–120; Richental, *Chronik*, in Buck, pp. 60–66; *Passio etc secundum Iohannem Barbatum, rusticum quadratum*, FRB, vol. 8, pp. 14–24. There is a translation of this last source with commentary. Thomas A. Fudge, "Jan Hus at Calvary: The Text of an Early Fifteenth-Century *Passio*," *Journal of Moravian History* 11 (2011): 45–81. There are two other sources: a Czech translation of the *Relatio*, which adds to the original in places, and there are additional useful remarks in this so-called *Passio*, FRB, vol. 8, pp. 121–149; and a Czech *Acta* in the Freiburg Codex, FRB, vol. 8, pp. 247–318. The preceding summary draws on all five sources.

47. De Vooght, p. 508.

simplistic. The rejoinder is cliché. Why Hus was considered heretical, by whom, and according to which definition are the sorts of questions required. There are generally two schools of thought on the trial of Jan Hus. The first maintains that canon law and prevailing legal practice were more than sufficient to justify the condemnation and execution of Hus.[48] It is possible to argue that the Council acted both legally and lawfully in the case of Hus, especially as we shall see that the court did, in fact, discriminate on the varieties of charges lodged against the defendant and set aside those it adjudicated as spurious.[49] Other scholars conclude that the court acted properly in accordance with the law and agree that the process, though distasteful in aspects and morally repugnant in procedure and outcome, was nevertheless just and proper.[50] Looking closely at components of the Hus legal process, we find that the desecration of Hus followed traditional practice. There were variations but hardly the introduction of anything cruel or unusual.[51] Jean Gerson and Pierre d'Ailly were the two men at the court in Constance most responsible for the condemnation of Hus, but it would be overwrought to claim that they sent Hus to the stake. Theologically, their opinions were decisive and persuasive.[52] But the power of persuasion and the arguments of the prosecution technically were constrained by the rule of law, which for many scholars is the crucial point.

After Hus was sent to the stake, violence broke out in the "streets of Prague and the highways of Bohemia" with some ferocity. One side shouted, "Hus forever," while the other cried, "long live the pope."[53] The execution of Hus was a key factor in the outbreak of the Hussite wars and the protracted crusade preached against those aligning themselves

---

48. Hefele and Leclercq, vol. 7, part 1, pp. 330–331. The sentiment is Hefele's.

49. An example would be the work of Jan Sedlák, ST, 3 vols., and his *M. Jan Hus.*

50. In addition to Sedlák, we might note Ferdinand Seibt, "Die Zeit der Luxemburger und der hussitischen Revolution," in *Handbuch der Geschichte der böhmischen Länder,* 4 vols., ed. Karl Bosl (Stuttgart: Anton Hiersemann, 1966–1974), vol. 1, p. 505; Jaroslav Kadlec, "Johannes Hus in neuem Licht?" *Theologisch-Praktische Quartalschrift* 118 (1970): 166; Brandmüller, *Konzil,* vol. 1, p. 362; František Graus, "Der Ketzerprozeß gegen Magister Johannes Hus (1415)," in *Macht und Recht: Große Prozesse in der Geschiche,* ed. Alexander Demandt (Munich: Beck, 1990), p. 117.

51. Kejř, *Husův proces,* p. 177; Bernhard Schimmelpfenig, "Degradation von Klerikern im späten Mittelalter," *Zeitschrift für Religions und Geistesgeschichte* 34 (1982): 313–316.

52. Paul de Vooght, "Jean Huss et ses juges," in *Das Konzil von Konstanz,* ed. August Franzen and Wolfgang Müller (Freiburg: Herder, 1964), p. 166.

53. Lenfant, *The History of the Council of Constance,* vol. 2, p. 58.

with the executed priest.[54] All of the major studies on Hus deal with his trial in some detail, although the coverage and nature of investigation vary from case to case. The assessments run the gamut from adjudicating the court process as legal to arguing that it was illegal.[55] The second school of thought contends that the trial was invalid. There were questions about the trial from the time of the Council. Nicolas of Clamanges, a disciple of Gerson and a conciliar supporter, did not attend the Council of Constance but seems to have undertaken the task of warning members of the synod about certain irregularities. He collected evidence of the proceedings with respect to what happened during the Hus trial process. Nicolas says he often heard disturbing things indicating more "works of the flesh" operated at the Council than evidence of the spirit. These he enumerated as "contentions, jealousies, dissensions, sects, animosities, and additionally, shouts of derision which are not consistent with the burden of decorum," and these factors "abolish completely the spirit of peace in the Council and this ought not to have been."[56] Jiří Kejř has expressed the view that from a strictly legal perspective, there were a number of irregularities, including the matter of false witnesses, bribery, intrigue, procedures that ran counter to the rule of law, and so on.[57] More recent scholars argue that Hus did not go to Constance as a condemned heretic but as an invited guest of

---

54. On the subsequent history, see Kaminsky, HHR; František Šmahel, *Die Hussitische Revolution*, 3 vols. (Hannover: Hahnsche Buchhandlung, 2002); Frederick G. Heymann, *John Žižka and the Hussite Revolution* (New York: Russell & Russell, 1969); Franz Lützow, *The Hussite Wars* (London: Dent, 1914); Thomas A. Fudge, *The Crusade against Heretics in Bohemia, 1418–1437: Sources and Documents for the Hussite Crusades* (Aldershot, U.K.: Ashgate, 2002).

55. Coverage can be found scattered throughout Flajšhans, *Mistr Jan*, pp. 373–473; Franz Lützow, *The Life and Times of Master John Hus* (London: Dent, 1909), pp. 208–292; David S. Schaff, *John Huss: His Life, Teachings and Death after Five Hundred Years* (New York: Scribner's, 1915), pp. 85–259; Sedlák, pp. 133–141, 152–157, 165–170, 175–181, 203–211, 315–360; Novotný, *M. Jan Hus*, vol. 2, pp. 355–460; Bartoš, *Čechy*, pp. 320–449; de Vooght, pp. 110–126, 158–173, 272–454; de Vooght, *Hussiana*, pp. 211–230; Spinka, *John Hus*, pp. 86–164, 219–290; Spinka, *Church*, pp. 79–150, 329–382; Werner, *Jan Hus*, pp. 98–121, 183–215; Hilsch, *Johannes Hus*, pp. 116–146, 248–283; Kejř, *Husův proces*; Fudge, *Jan Hus*, pp. 117–146; Krzenck, *Johannes Hus*, pp. 146–183; Fudge, *Memory and Motivation*, chap. 5.

56. This is noted with references to the primary sources in de Vooght, p. 454. On Clamanges, see also Christopher M. Bellitto, *Nicolas de Clamanges: Spirituality, Personal Reform, and Pastoral Renewal on the Eve of the Reformations* (Washington, D.C.: Catholic University of America Press, 2001).

57. This is pointed out in his monograph *Husitský pravník: M. Jan z Jesenice* (Prague: ČSAV, 1965) and more extensively in his *Husův proces*, pp. 202–208. Provvidente, pp. 121–122, is not accurate in saying that Kejř ignored these anomalies.

the highest secular authority in Europe.[58] This is an observation requiring both context and nuance. Shortly after Hus arrived at Constance, a warrant for his arrest was issued, and he was detained and incarcerated. "The crime of the Fathers of the Council of Constance was especially heinous not only in its outcome, but in how the trial was conducted." The trial proceedings were "a mixture of stupidity and wickedness, carried to the extreme limit of ignominy."[59] Other perspectives conclude that there were various abuses of procedure.[60] One might be inclined to place the blame on certain members of the Council or on the indiscretions perpetrated by malevolent prosecutors such as Michael de Causis. But the portrayal of the men of the Council in some of the more fulsome accounts of the Hus trial in its final stages, where they appear as bitter and hateful men quite unconcerned with issues of truth and justice, is a portrait accepted by leading scholars as altogether accurate.[61] This means that Hus was condemned not by the worst men at Constance but by the best.[62] The picture is sobering.

There is, of course, plenty of evidence suggesting that Hus was prejudged by the Council before he ever set foot in Constance.[63] "He died tragically because in an excess of piety and not without a certain amount of holy innocence, he had come to engage with the Council."[64] This was not what the court at Constance was prepared to do. There are scholars who maintain that because Hus was not permitted to engage in a dialogue with the court, the procedures that followed were on that account hopelessly prejudiced, leading to a verdict that rendered Hus the victim of judicial murder.[65] This has been stated strongly in some publications

---

58. Phillip Nelson Haberkern, "The Presence of the Past: History, Memory, and the Making of St. Jan Hus," PhD dissertation, University of Virginia, 2009, p. 54.

59. De Vooght, pp. 506–507.

60. Henry A. Kelly, "Trial Procedures against Wyclif and Wycliffites in England and at the Council of Constance," *Huntington Library Quarterly* 61, no. 1 (1999): 1–28.

61. Howard Kaminsky, "The Hussite Movement in History," PhD dissertation, University of Chicago, 1952, p. 11.

62. Roland H. Bainton, *The Medieval Church* (New York: D. Van Nostrand, 1962), p. 72.

63. Kaminsky HHR, p. 35.

64. De Vooght, p. 515.

65. Among those representing this position are Wilhelm Berger, *Johannes Hus und König Sigismund* (Augsburg: Butsch, 1871); Gotthard Viktor Lechler, *Johannes Hus: Ein Lebensbild*

without reserve.[66] It has become somewhat routine to find uncritical references to the "murder" of Hus and claims that his judges were accomplices in a travesty of justice.[67] Others submit that this type of criticism of the Hus trial cannot be considered an example of judicial murder or political intrigue.[68] Still others draw attention to the numerous false accusations against Hus as a means of underscoring the questionable aspects of the trial itself. The verdict and sentence constituted malfeasance.[69] Certain analyses cannot avoid the conclusion that what happened to Hus at the culmination of his trial was an inexplicable crime.[70] More cynical positions have also assumed that when the Council was unable to prove Hus guilty of heresy on the basis of scripture and the teachings of the church fathers, the court abandoned reason and legality and resorted to force and an unjust process to achieve the same end, which was a verdict of guilt.[71] There is a fair amount of irony inasmuch as Hus was sentenced on account of his doctrine of the church by a council whose most influential members, such as Gerson and d'Ailly, professed similar views on the same doctrine and perhaps even more aggressively than Hus.[72] Some modern scholars condemn Hus for what is essentially a sound doctrine of the church as the *universitas praedestinorum* consistent with the Augustinian tradition.[73] Others are willing to conclude that Hus was theologically incorrect because Augustine's

---

aus der Vorgeschichte der Reformation (Halle: Vereins für Reformationsgeschichte, 1889), p. 78; Flajšhans, Mistr Jan, and in his foreword to the edition of Hus's works Spisy M. Jana Husi (Prague: Jaroslav Bursík, 1903), vol. 2, p. vi; Jiří Spěváček, Václav IV. 1361–1419 k předpokadům husitské revoluce (Prague: Svoboda, 1986), p. 461; Hilsch, Johannes Hus, p. 281.

66. Especially in Gotthard Viktor Lechler, Jan Hus, 2nd ed. (Pardubice: Hoblík, 1910), pp. 77–78.

67. Marcela K. Perett, "Vernacular Songs as 'Oral Pamphlets': The Hussites and Their Propaganda Campaign," Viator 42, no. 2 (2011): 374; Spinka, John Hus, pp. 248–249.

68. Seibt, "Die Zeit der Luxemburger," pp. 500–512.

69. Václav Flajšhans, "Husovo kacířství," in Národní Listy 187 (1904): 8.7. I owe the reference to Jiří Kotyk, Spor o revizi Husova procesu (Prague: Vyšehrad, 2001), p. 44.

70. De Vooght, pp. 482–491.

71. Stejskal, Le procès de Jean Huss, p. 131; Flajšhans, "Husovo kacířství," 8.7.

72. De Vooght, p. 515.

73. Brandmüller, Konzil, vol. 1, p. 331. This is taken up with more balance in de Vooght, pp. 443–456, and Hussiana, pp. 412–423. See also Vilém Herold, "Master Jan Hus and St. Augustine," in BRRP 8, pp. 42–51.

teaching on the doctrine of predestination was wrong.[74] This is a minority view.

Medieval heresy trials and inquisitorial method often prompt the assumption that "it is not far off the mark" to accept that these were conducted in secret against a defenseless suspect who was the target of unknown accusations and who was forced by torture and trickery to recant.[75] The premise is evidentially weak. Among some modern scholars, there is considerable indignation over what amounts to "illegal condemnation." A representative quotation makes the point: "Imputing illegality to Hus's trial is not an anachronism when it can be demonstrated that the trial at Constance did not follow the legal norms of the time. To have a judgment overturned because the trial itself did not follow the legal procedure of its own time is a matter of simple justice."[76] The observation is a sobering one. What the historian requires is not a declarative statement that the trial was irregular or illegal but hard evidence from law and legal procedure that such a claim can be made and supported. An examination of the Hus trial must establish questions of illegality and justice within the context of the later Middle Ages. One cannot merely state that something is anachronistic or adjudicate what is legal and illegal or pronounce judgments of justice and injustice without first establishing a proper basis upon which to make those judgments.[77] To do so is to engage in the very

---

74. Karel Skalický, "Predestinace jako tajemství spásy v teologii Vladimíra Boublíka," in *Česko-římský teolog Vladimír Boublík: Symposium (Teologické fakulty Jihočeské univerzity) k jeho nedožitým 70. narozeninám,* ed. Karel Skalický and Monica Schreier (České Budějovice: Jihočeská Univerzita Teologická Fakulta, 1999), pp. 26–27.

75. Frank R. Herrmann and Brownlow M. Speer, "Facing the Accuser: Ancient and Medieval Precursors of the Confrontation Clause," *Virginia Journal of International Law* 34, no. 3 (1994): 522.

76. Holeton, "The Celebration of Jan Hus," p. 58.

77. This is the burden of this study. Holeton appeals to the work of Jiří Kejř, *Odvolání* and *Husův proces,* pp. 200–212. The problem is that while Holeton points out correctly the findings from Kejř's research that demonstrate irregularities in the court procedures, nowhere does Kejř assert that the trial at Constance was illegal or failed to follow established procedures, nor does he suggest that the verdict be overturned. As a matter of fact, Kejř argues precisely the opposite conclusions. Kejř, "Jan Hus sám o sobě," in *Počátků,* p. 31. Those who call upon Kejř to support assumptions about the trial at Constance may wish to take note of his considered opinion based on the full spectrum of his findings, which I provide here in his own words: "So far as the procedural part is concerned, no mistake of the court has been found.…[T]hings that today seem to us cruel and unjust were performed according to the accurate rules of canon law. Hus's cruel imprisonment, denial of legal assistance, the form of defrocking—all of this was in accordance with the rules of legal procedure." Moreover, it

unhelpful exercise of retroactive rule making. Another possibility when evaluating the trial of Jan Hus must take into account the nature of the Council of Constance and determine if this synod was lawfully convened. There is opinion concluding that the Council was not legitimately convened until July 14, 1415, that is to say, eight days after Hus was burned.[78] There are, of course, counterarguments that develop the idea that the decree *Haec sancta* is valid as a statement limiting papal power and was the result of a long tradition within the church seeking to moderate the authority of popes and Curia. Martin V ratified Constance as an ecumenical council. No one at the Council thought a formal papal pronouncement was necessary to legitimate Constance.[79] It is, of course, possible to question the nature of the trial and to raise queries about whether the sentence was just and to speculate about whether Hus was truly heretical. Are there legal solutions to these questions? Paul de Vooght did not think so. He pointed out that even today, those on both sides of the questions continue calmly to maintain their positions. What some scholars perceive as procedural violations, others interpret as normal. When Hus refused to appear at the Curia when ordered by the court, a suspicion of heresy became a presumption of guilt. The trial judges thereafter made certain procedural decisions that might be regarded as falling within the jurisdictional purview of the court, rather like interlocutory rulings.[80] The real conflict lies in a deep dispute over law and legal procedure.[81] It is only in the investigation of these matters that supportable conclusions can be located. Unfortunately, too many historians have been relatively uninterested in legal procedure.

---

was Hus himself, Kejř argues, who "brought himself into a hopeless situation by violating the rules of process by appealing to Christ and brought his tragedy to completion by not understanding that he was going to Constance to a court and not to a scholastic disputation." Kejř, *Husův proces*, p. 211. Of course, Kejř might be wrong about all of this. Such claims must be determined by means of a careful evaluation of law and medieval legal procedure. This book has established an independent judgment. Regardless, Kejř cannot be used to support an argument that the trial was illegal or unjust.

78. Ferdinand Seibt, "'Neodvolám!' Jan Hus před koncilem kostnickým," in *Velké procesy: Právo a spravedlnost v dějinách*, ed. Uwe Schultz (Prague: Brána, 1997), p. 91.

79. Paul de Vooght, *Les pouvoirs du concile et l'autorité du pape au concile de Constance: Le décret "Haec Sancta Synodus" du 6. avril 1415* (Paris: Édition du Cerf, 1965), defends this perspective.

80. Kelly, "Trial Procedures against Wyclif and Wycliffites," sees abuses. He is opposed by Kejř, *Husův proces*.

81. De Vooght, p. 271.

Assessing the trial of Jan Hus means first coming to terms with the problem of sources. The various writings of Hus are essential. Here we find clues about the legal process not available elsewhere. Among the most useful are the many letters written by Hus while imprisoned awaiting trial.[82] There are legal records such as Hus's appeal to the popes and the excommunication citations.[83] There are more than a dozen cycles of accusations and criminal charges lodged against Hus, which form the basis for the complaint.[84] We have eyewitness reports of the last stages of the court case from several perspectives, especially accounts of the unprecedented public hearings.[85] There are polemical writings that are useful for establishing various points of doctrinal controversy.[86] "It is always the doctrine, the great intellectual and spiritual adventure of Jan Hus, which has remained at the center of interest."[87] The trial of Hus was an inquisitorial procedure into allegations of heresy. The process against Jerome of Prague in 1415 and 1416 was considered inquisitorial. Inasmuch as that court procedure appears to parallel that of Hus, was conducted in the same venue, and featured many of the same dramatis personae, we may identify the Hus trial as an inquisitorial process.[88] Although there were many parallels, secular and ecclesiastical procedures were not identical, but heresy trials followed the same legal rules as all other court cases.[89] At Constance, the inquisitorial procedure was applied in matters of faith, and this approach allowed the Council to consolidate and

---

82. Novotný, *Correspondence.*

83. Many of these have been collected in *Documenta.*

84. These are outlined in some detail in chapters 4, 7, and 8 herein and are drawn mainly from the collections in the *Documenta.*

85. *Relatio*, pp. 72–120 (written immediately after the execution); the Czech *Passio*, FRB, vol. 8, pp. 121–149 (written between 1417 and 1420); Richental, *Chronik*, in Buck, pp. 60–66 (written between 1423 and 1433); and the *Passio etc secundum Iohannem Barbatum, rusticum quadratum*, FRB, vol. 8, pp. 14–24 (written between 1415 and 1418). There is also the anonymous *Relatio de concilio constantiensi*, FRB, vol. 8, pp. 11–13 (written in 1415 or 1416), and the Czech *Acta* in the Freiburg Codex, FRB, vol. 8, pp. 247–318 (prepared around 1450). There is unique information in each.

86. Of numerous examples: Štěpán Páleč, *Antihus*, in Sedlák, *Miscellanea*, pp. 366–507.

87. De Vooght, p. xvii.

88. Hardt, vol. 4, col. 766, and stated in the sentencing of Jerome. Vallerani, pp. 79–81.

89. R. H. Helmholz, "The Early History of the Grand Jury and the Canon Law," *University of Chicago Law Review* 50 (1983): 613–627, especially p. 625.

establish its superiority.[90] Theology is a critical component of the legal proceedings, for heresy trials demand a specific faith value. The work of Jan Hus the theologian and Jan Jesenice the lawyer are crucial sources. There were numerous documents presented to the court, and many of these have been incorporated into other records, the best example being the collections included in the narrative prepared by Petr Mladoňovice.[91] The *Relatio* of Mladoňovice is neither a chronicle nor a history of events. Indeed, only about one-fifth of the *Relatio* is narrative or commentary by Petr Mladoňovice, but some experts consider it the most significant of sources we have about Hus.[92] To these we might add synodal records kept by the Prague consistory.[93] These are ancillary to the trial itself, but the background is useful, especially in terms of decisions on controversial issues such as the widely debated and eventually condemned "forty-five articles" of John Wyclif. Elsewhere we find reference to records in the apostolic see and the Curial court.[94] The *Acta* of the Council of Constance remains something of an unsolved mystery. Two decades after its sessions, we learn that the records were never included in the Vatican archives, but one manuscript belonging to Guillaume Fillastre, cardinal-priest of St. Mark's, was brought to the Council of Basel, where it was used.[95] This was first published at Hagenau in 1500. There are useful documents and sources in several multivolume collections.[96] To this we might add the sermons preached during the Council, some of which address the Hus case.[97] There are also diaries of Council participants,

---

90. Provvidente, p. 138.

91. Especially in the earlier portions of the *Relatio*, pp. 25–110.

92. Novotný's introductory comments in FRB, vol. 8, p. xxi.

93. Kadlec, *Synods*, pp. 227–293.

94. *Documenta*, p. 197.

95. Juan of Segovia, *Historia gestorum generalis synodi basiliensis*, in *Monumenta conciliorum*, ed. Ernest Birk (Vienna: Typis C.R. Officinae Typographicae Aulae et Status, 1873), vol. 2, pp. 75–76.

96. Especially Hardt; Mansi, vols. 27–28; Finke, *Acta*. On the acts of the Council, see especially C. M. D. Crowder, "Le concile de Constance et l'édition de von der Hardt," *Revue d'Histoire Ecclésiastique* 57 (1962): 409–445; Phillip Stump, "The Official Acts of the Council of Constance in the Edition of Mansi," in *The Two Laws: Studies in Medieval Legal History Dedicated to Stephan Kuttner*, ed. Laurent Mayali and Stephanie A. Tibbetts (Washington, D.C.: Catholic University of America Press, 1990), pp. 221–239.

97. A good place to start for sermons is Chris Nighman and Phillip Stump, "A Bibliographical Register of the Sermons and Other Orations Delivered at the Council of Constance (1414–1418)," http://www.bibsocamer.org/BibSite/Nighman-Stump/index.html.

although these do not yield much on the trial itself.[98] Around the middle of the fifteenth century, a Czech translation of documents from the Council of Constance, as they relate to Hus and his colleague Jerome of Prague, appeared. This is the so-called Freiburg Codex.[99] These "acts of the Council" include Hus's letters from prison, the last part of the *Relatio*, letters of Czech nobles supporting Hus, a number of documents about Jerome, and later Hussite history. Notably, we find in these *Acta* details that do not appear in the *Relatio*, especially pertaining to the final court session of July 6, 1415. In addition, we find quite a number of comments in the polemical literature written by Hus referring to the court case.[100] Of importance also in this regard is his Czech *Postil*.[101] In these works, we find allegations of false accusations, judicial bias, improper hearings, malevolence of witnesses, and considerable frustration at the failure to obtain an acceptable hearing (*cognitio*), and Hus tells us why he ignored legal process at various junctures in the court proceedings. Of course, comments criticizing the legal system must be taken with some caution. Plaintiffs and defendants seldom are satisfied with a court hearing or trial unless the returned verdict is accepted as the right one. If the verdict is satisfactory, the process is hardly considered and never criticized. On the other hand, when an unexpected or undesired verdict is returned, the plaintiff or defendant immediately seeks to expose flaws in the system and denounces the process as unjust, the result an injustice and a travesty to all that is right and proper. "Evidence" is advanced to support the grievance. The trial of Hus is no different in this regard from formal civil or criminal proceedings in the modern world, especially in highly litigious societies such as the United States.

Regrettably, the official court *Acta* appears lost. Jiří Kejř suggests that these records were kept at Constance, but once the trial ended and, more

---

98. For example, Cardinal Guillaume Fillastre's diary, in Finke, *Acta*, vol. 2, pp. 13–170; and the *Liber gestorum* of the papal notary Giacomo Cerretano, in Finke, *Acta*, vol. 2, pp. 171–348.

99. FRB, vol. 8, pp. 247–318.

100. There are various comments in several books written against John Stokes, Štěpán Páleč, Stanislav of Znojmo, and a number of unnamed opponents. These have been collected in Hus, *Opera omnia*, vol. 22. One crucial document of the same genre is Hus's polemic against an anonymous priest working in an estate kitchen. *Knížky proti knězi kuchmistrovi* [Books against the Priest-Cookmaster], in Hus, *Opera omnia*, vol. 4, pp. 312–323. I have discussed this writing in some detail in Fudge, *Memory and Motivation*, chapter 4.

101. Hus, *Opera omnia*, vol. 2.

important, once the Council concluded, these records were left behind and over time were lost.[102] Kejř does not think it possible that detailed records of the trial proceedings were not kept, because meticulous documentation was expected and was a standard feature of late medieval courts. Procedurally, it was required that such *Acta* be maintained.[103] There is no reason to assume that this principle was not practiced during the Hus trial. There is some possibility that the *Acta* were removed to the papal Curia by the new administration of Pope Martin V, but no trace of these records has been found by scholars who have worked in the several Vatican repositories, although there are many briefs on the subsequent Hussite problem.[104] There is no compelling argument to assume that the Curia of Martin V removed the *Acta*, and it is more likely that those records were left behind in Constance, possibly in the library of the bishop.[105] Martin was interested in other things, not in a trial predating his coronation and irrelevant to the tasks at hand that Martin made the priorities of his papacy. There is evidence that the *Acta* did exist. Hus's lawyer noted that the activity at the papal court with respect to the defendant was conducted with references to "acts and registers" during certain legal proceedings.[106]

We find reference to court officials reviewing legal records pertaining to the trial.[107] After the legal proceeding shifted its venue to Constance, newly appointed judges in the case had specific records turned over to them that were specified as "a register of the process and case made by the commissioners against Jan Hus."[108] During the hearings at Constance, notaries were involved at various stages. When Hus provided responses to one series of charges, he did so in the presence of a notary.[109] On May

---

102. Kejř, *Husův proces*, p. 17.

103. Ibid., pp. 17–18.

104. More than five hundred have been noted in Karl August Fink, "Die politische Korrespondenz Martins V. nach den Brevenregistern," *Quellen und Forschungen aus Italienischen Archiven und Bibliotheken* 26 (1935–1936): 172–244.

105. The Diocese of Constance dates to the late sixth century. The prince-bishopric was dissolved in 1803 and became part of the Margraviate of Baden. The diocese itself was dissolved in 1821. Parts of it thereafter were incorporated into the Archdiocese of Freiburg. Otto III of Hachberg was Bishop of Constance during the Hus trial from 1410 until 1434, when he was deposed.

106. Jesenice, *Repetitio*, in HM, vol. 1, p. 416.

107. *Ordo procedendi*, p. 229.

108. Hardt, vol. 4, p. 100.

109. *Documenta*, p. 221.

18, 1415, we find reference to discussions between members of the Czech nobility and Council delegates in which the acts of the case at the papal court were discussed.[110] On two separate occasions, Cardinal Zabarella specifically instructed one of the court notaries to take special care in recording particular testimony.[111] During the final session in the trial of Hus, the defendant made reference "to the acts of the trial," arguing that important things had been more fully recorded.[112] All of this suggests that there can be no convincing argument that specific records and court *Acta* were not kept. Unfortunately, these documents have been lost to the enormous depreciation of our knowledge and understanding of precisely how the hearings proceeded and the salient issues that governed the trial from an official or prosecutorial point of view. Given the unavailability of the official *Acta*, there are gaps in the sources. These gaps cannot be adequately bridged, and particularly when dealing with legal records, it is perilous to construct theories and hypotheses, especially to the extent of assuming that something must have happened in a certain order and by a specific means. We know from surviving documents that certain court papers existed and particular legal documents were drawn up. But we have no way of knowing precisely what they said and, just as important, how they were framed. These challenges mitigate against assuming too much on too little and drawing conclusions on technical matters of law and procedure. Arguments from silence must be treated with considerable reserve. We must then rely on those sources that are extant, and even these must be treated with caution. Too many of our sources are suspect in one sense or another. They are predicated upon memory, and some of those memories are fraught with anxiety or particular prejudice or are tortured memories. We are confronted with hearsay and rumor. At many turns in the legal process, we encounter evidence based on what someone heard or thought he or she heard or what was stated about what someone knew. We are forced to make decisions about which witnesses are reliable and try to determine what makes the testimony of certain observers more trustworthy than that of others. There is, further, the almost hopeless task of verifying critical points from more than one record or deciding to accept at face value what cannot be verified. How safe is it to assume uncritically

---

110. *Relatio*, p. 50.

111. Ibid., pp. 82, 92.

112. Ibid., p. 115. I have followed the outline of this evidence as summarized in Kejř, *Husův proces*, pp. 17–18.

that everything Hus said or wrote, a man on trial for his life and badgered by hostile prosecutors, judges, and witnesses, during his several interrogations, is accurate? These are fundamental sources, but handling them is not as simple as one might assume.[113]

One of the great misunderstandings about the trial of Jan Hus is that it occurred at the Council of Constance in 1415. This assumption is both true and false. All scholars working on the subject note legal events between 1410 and 1414 but mostly in the general sense that all of this was prefatory for the trial, when in reality, the legal process began in 1410 and only culminated in 1415.[114] The procedures before the papal court between 1410 and 1412 cannot be detached from events at Constance.[115] Efforts to understand the course of events that transpired at Constance can only be evaluated properly in light of the legal process that preceded the Council. What many scholars dealing with the trial of Hus have failed to appreciate is that the appearance of Hus at Constance was a continuation of a legal process. It was a trial. It was nothing less than a court appearance. It may be too strong to say that Hus was subpoenaed to appear before the ecclesiastical court in Constance, but it is not possible to characterize him as anything less than a defendant in a criminal proceeding who had been censured by a papal court and whose case remained on the court's docket as pending. What was Hus doing at Constance? It was not an invitation to a conversation. It was an examination. It was not a university debate. It was a formal inquisition.[116] Therefore, it is specious to suggest that the court convened at the Council of Constance should have treated Hus differently.[117] All of the significant studies of Hus take into account the legal proceedings. There are important insights offered by most of them.[118] Particular investigations offer detailed commentary on the trial

---

113. There are useful observations on trial records in Alain Demurger, *The Last Templar: The Tragedy of Jacques de Molay Last Grand Master of the Temple*, trans. Antonia Nevill (London: Profile Books, 2004), pp. xv–xvi.

114. Hilsch, *Johannes Hus*, and Kejř, *Husův proces*, are two scholars who have properly dealt with the trial over the full course of its five-year process.

115. Hilsch, *Johannes Hus*, pp. 116–146; Kejř, *Husův proces*, pp. 52–136.

116. I subscribe to the understanding proposed by Richard Kieckhefer, "The Office of the Inquisition and Medieval Heresy: The Transition from Personal to Institutional Jurisdiction," *Journal of Ecclesiastical History* 46, no. 1 (1995): 36–61.

117. De Vooght, pp. 393–398, 501–508.

118. Among these are Sedlák, *M. Jan Hus*; Novotný, *M. Jan Hus*; Bartoš, *Čechy*; de Vooght; Werner, *Jan Hus: Welt und Umwelt*; Hilsch, *Johannes Hus*.

and attempt to understand it in both a theological and a historical context.[119] Most analyses do not devote any special attention to canon law or
legal procedure per se. Many focus instead on the court case and deal
principally with the theology of Hus compared with that of his opponents,
especially the leading members of the Council such as Jean Gerson and
Pierre d'Ailly.[120] We are fortunate to have a detailed study of Hus's main
attorney, who played a considerable role in the case before the papal court
and in advising Hus before the commencement of the Constance phase
of the trial.[121] Confessional perspectives tend to shape the treatment of the
topic, but there is excellent scholarship from both Catholic and Protestant
points of view.[122] The strident and historically anti-Hus perspective that
characterized so much of German scholarship before World War II is
ameliorated by some very solid work of German scholars, although this
does not mean that the views or conclusions are sympathetic.[123] The trial
of Hus has provided considerable fodder for popular audiences, and many
of those works lack the balance and perspective of serious scholarship.
There are exceptions to that general observation.[124] The most recent work
on the trial has turned attention once more to the question of whether
Hus was heretical and if the court that tried him did, in fact, represent the
universal church.[125] The essential analysis of medieval law and a careful
investigation of legal procedure and relevant canon law, especially as it
relates to heresy and inquisitorial process, have now made an impact on

---

119. This is especially true of Spinka's books, *Church* and *John Hus*.

120. The subtitle of Stejskal, *Le procès de Jean Huss: Étude historique et dogmatique*, is
revealing.

121. Kejř, *Jesenice*.

122. On the Catholic side, the work of Jan Sedlák is representative. See his "Proces kostnický," ST 2, no. 1 (1915), pp. 1–34, and *M. Jan Hus*, while the Protestant Spinka considers Hus
from that point of view. The introductory essay and notes in his *Constance* are examples.

123. In addition to Hilsch and Werner, noted previously, see especially the collected essays of
Ferdinand Seibt, *Hussitenstudien: Personen, Ereignisse, Ideen einer frühen Revolution* (Munich:
Oldenbourg, 1987), pp. 153–173, 229–240; Rudolf Hoke, "Der Prozeß des Jan Hus und das
Geleit König Sigmunds: Ein Veitrage zur Frage nach der Kläger—und Angeklagtenrolle im
Konstanzer Proceß von 1414/1415," AHC 15 (1883): 172–193.

124. František Šmahel, "Husův proces v Kostnici," *Slovo k Historii* 18 (1988): 1–40, lacking references but lavishly illustrated and exhibiting penetrating observations by one of the
most important interpreters of Hussite history. See also his *Hranice pravdy* (Prague: Naše
Vojsko 1969), *Mistr Jan Hus* (Prague: Svoboda, 1985), and "Jan Hus—Heretic or Patriot?"
History Today 40 (April 1990): 27–33.

125. Provvidente, pp. 103–138.

the study of the Jan Hus trial.[126] Apart from large monographs, a variety of shorter studies contribute to our understanding of the trial.[127]

It is evidentially manifest that no one connected to the Hus case could possibly see the implications or consequences of the Hus trial. No one seems to have imagined that it would extend well beyond the summer of 1415. "The Hus process cannot be understood as the trial of one heretic isolated from other events in the Czech and ecclesiastical scene of politics and ideology."[128] There has been much research undertaken on Jan Hus, and the international historiography is vast. Numerous scholars from many different persuasions and perspectives have contributed to our knowledge about virtually every aspect of his life. Much has been clarified. In terms of the trial, the only significant legal analysis has been undertaken by Kejř, and his work has been done in the Czech language. There is nothing comparable in any major Western language.[129] In English, prior to this study, nothing has been attempted on the scale and to the standard set by Kejř. Questions linger about whether the legal proceedings were in accordance with established law. Were the procedures of the various courts legal and defensible or a breach of due process? An investigation of all of the legal factors enables the scholar to determine more accurately whether political pressure or systemic prejudice led to the commission of wrongful acts, that is, specifically to judicial malfeasance. Numerous and sundry opinions have been expressed, but until Kejř undertook his research, no one seems to have thought to look at the Hus trial through the lens of canon law and legal procedure and to do this in terms of the entire five-year legal process. Were the actions undertaken in the various courts legally sound or judicially inappropriate and leading to misfeasance? Surprisingly, many scholars voicing opinions on these concerns have not scrutinized canon law, legal procedure, and the established process that was employed in

---

126. Sebastián Provvidente, "Inquisitorial Process and *plenitudo potestatis* at the Council of Constance (1414–1418)," in BRRP 8 (2011), pp. 98–114; Fudge, *Jan Hus*, pp. 117–146; but above all, Kejř, *Husův proces*.

127. Graus, "Der Ketzerprozeß," pp. 103–118; de Vooght, "Jean Huss et ses juges," pp. 152–173; Brandmüller, pp. 235–242.

128. Kejř, *Husův proces*, p. 15.

129. Kejř's major study, *Husův proces*, has been translated into German by Walter Annuß as *Die Causa Johannes Hus und der Prozessrecht der Kirch* (Regensburg: Pustet, 2005). The forthcoming work of Sebastián Provvidente in Spanish and this author's in English are the sole supplements.

criminal courts when dealing with charges of heresy. At times, there was no action or response whatever at various junctures in the Hus case. The investigation of legal traditions helps to address the matter of nonfeasance. A careful consideration of the surviving records helps shed light on issues such as bribery and suggestions that the legal process applied in the courts hearing the case against Hus was flawed or contrary to the *ordo iudiciarius* of standard procedure and due process. The same analysis also helps to determine if Hus, initially as plaintiff and subsequently as defendant, acted lawfully or if he inadvertently or deliberately violated rules governing legal cases such as his. One cannot either assume innocence with respect to legal procedure on Hus's part or presume that he would only follow established protocol. All possibilities must be allowed. Ultimately, a strictly and focused analysis of canon law and legal procedure enables the scholar to determine how and why Hus was condemned, and it also provides a basis for concluding what role, if any, Hus played in the verdict handed down at the end of the trial.[130]

The massive differences of interpretation of the Hus trial can be attributed largely, though not exclusively, to the application of subjective value judgments applied to the documentary evidence and to an unwillingness or inability to undertake the sort of thorough legal analysis required in order to place the Hus trial in a context where conclusions may be established upon a sound basis. It is not necessary to agree that late medieval canon law and criminal procedure on the scale that applied to the Hus case were salutary, but it is essential to understand them. Without the firm foundation of law and the prevailing *ordo iudiciarius*, interpretations of this tragic episode in late medieval history are little more than emotional responses, anachronistic assumptions, and confessional or philosophical opinions. Those interested in truth and justice as understood in the fifteenth century must divorce themselves from modern ideas of tolerance, diversity, democratic ideals, and subjective notions of fairness. Modern constructs of "cruel and unusual" procedures and punishments cannot be uncritically applied to the trial of Hus if the intention is to understand what happened and why. What is unethical is not necessarily illegal. What may be judged immoral may not be contrary to law. What seems offensive may not, in fact, contravene due process. What can be judged unfair on one hand may not be considered criminal on the other hand. What might be condemned as unjust is not the same thing as finding it to be against

---

130. Kejř, *Husův proces*, p. 15.

the law. In short, elements of the Hus trial may be adjudicated as irregular, but this is not the same thing as concluding that the process was invalid. Before turning to the particulars of the trial, we look first at the nature of heresy in the Middle Ages and then at the relevant laws, court practices, and legal procedures that were established and normative in late medieval Europe at the time the case of Jan Hus was heard by the courts.

2

Inventing Medieval Heresy

In terms of procedural order, it must be observed the method of procedure is dictated by its outcome. The objective of the inquisition is the destruction of heresy. Heresy cannot be destroyed unless heretics are destroyed. Moreover, heretics cannot be destroyed unless their receivers, fautors and defenders are destroyed.... Heretics are destroyed in two ways; either when they are converted from heresy to the true Catholic faith ... or when they are abandoned to the secular arm to be physically burned.[1]

WHILE THERE HAS always been a modicum of unity within the Christian religion, a great deal of diversity can also be observed from its inception. It is possible to argue that important differences—the religious and social phenomena of heresy—have existed alongside orthodoxy from earliest times. One might even find competition for the definition of orthodoxy.[2] Even in the mid-first-century Saint Paul declared, "oportet et hereses esse"—there must be heresies.[3] The nominated founder of Christianity suggested that in his father's house were many rooms. That ideal of tolerance and diversity was soon vitiated when his disciples began insisting that the faithful should all live in the same room.[4] There were always some Christians who

1. Gui, *Practica*, pp. 217–218. Parts of this source are translated in Janet Shirley, ed., *The Inquisitor's Guide: A Medieval Manual on Heretics* (Welwyn Garden City, U.K.: Ravenhall Books, 2006).

2. Walter Bauer, *Orthodoxy and Heresy in Earliest Christianity* (London: SCM Press, 1972).

3. I Corinthians 11:19 (Latin Vulgate). Its exegetical history has been explored in Herbert Grundmann, "Oportet et haereses esse: Das Problem der Ketzerei im Spiegel der mittelalterlichen Bibelexegese," in *Herbert Grundmann: Augewählte Aufsätze*, 3 vols. (Stuttgart: Hiersemann, 1978), vol. 1, pp. 328–363.

4. Robert I. Moore, *The Origins of European Dissent* (London: Penguin, 1977), p. 1.

disagreed with that one-room policy. This resulted in dissent, often called heresy, becoming an integral part of the Christian heritage in the patristic age, surviving the urge to purge differences that characterized the Nicene period, and later persisting along the margins of medieval Christendom as it shaped European civilization. A millennium after Nicaea, heresy was endemic in late medieval society. Heresy did not arise from religious indifference. The phenomena of heresy instead, both East and West, were in many instances the natural outcome of religious zeal. The records of heresy hunting and writings of accused heretics suggest that these heretical men and women did not die for ideas and practices they considered irrelevant with little or no meaning for their lives and faith. Whatever caused men and women to yield to the heretical inclination was mainly a voluntary response and a consequence of personal conviction. As Saint Augustine noted in the fifth century, "one should not assume heresies could be produced by little souls. No one except great men [and women] have been the authors of heresy."[5] As we examine the heretics of the later Middle Ages, the Augustinian observation is proven. Jan Hus was a great man. The medieval church determined that he was guilty of intellectual mistakes (*error intellectus*) and voluntary stubbornness (*pertinacia voluntatis*), the two predominant features of heresy. That finding does not negate his stature.

The Process of Defining Heresy

Various records provide indication that by the eleventh century, heresy was noticeable in western Europe. In the course of the high Middle Ages, the phenomenon had spread across the continent. Part of that stream of expansion came through the Balkans, although I do not believe that heresy can be regarded solely as a foreign influence introduced into Western Christendom.[6] Further, I cannot conclude from the surviving sources that heresy was a hegemonic imposition upon medieval society. My reading of the documentary histories of medieval heresy have obligated me to argue

---

5. Enarr. in Ps. cxxiv, 5, in CCL, vol. 40, p. 1839.

6. There is still scholarly opinion supporting the entrance of heresy into the West via the Balkans and also Bogomil influence on Western heretical movements in the eleventh century. Bernard Hamilton, "Wisdom from the East: The Reception by the Cathars of Eastern Dualist texts," in *Heresy and Literacy, 1000–1530*, ed. Peter Biller and Anne Hudson (Cambridge, U.K.: Cambridge University Press, 1994), pp. 38–60.

that heresy and the heretical inclination constitute an essential aspect of the later medieval European identity. Doubt is an integral aspect of faith. Difference, diversity, and dissent have always characterized the Christian faith. In this sense, heresy belongs quite firmly to the intellectual history of Europe. The essential key to understanding heresy lies in the particular context of whichever manifestation of heresy is under consideration. This suggests rather naturally the inherent problem in defining both orthodoxy and heresy. These definitions were never absolute. In the case of the former, the fifth-century Vincentian canon of true Christian belief promoted the principle that orthodoxy was "that which has been believed everywhere, always and by everyone."[7] That was the ideal but hardly the reality. This perceived monolithic orthodox wholeness was never fully realized, but it was successfully marshaled as a bulwark against the equally perceived onslaught of deviance and theological mischief.

Early in the Middle Ages, heresy and heretics were viewed somewhat vaguely in terms of specific identification, although common characteristics were soon attached to these largely unnamed and unknown phantoms of the religious world. As early as the seventh century, Isidore of Seville, following an even older idea, linked heresy to human choice. The Greek root of the word *haeresis* implies choice. Choices made by human reason, Isidore argued, result in perverse dogmas, and by natural consequence departure from the church occurs. Heresy is derived from this perversity of choice wherein each heretic decides according to his or her will what he or she believes. The fundamental problem for Isidore is that it is not possible to believe whatever one wishes on the basis of human will. Furthermore, it is reprehensible to imagine that one might choose to believe what someone else had formulated on the basis of human choice. Religious authority for Isidore is based on apostolic authority, which in turn has its foundation in something other than the human will and choices of the apostles. Isidore concludes that the apostles transmitted to all the world what they received from Christ. In other words, even if divine angels appeared with other ideas, they should be rejected.[8] Many of these formulations would be taken up in later medieval history.

---

7. Vincent of Lérins (d. ca. 450), *Commonitorium*, chapter 2, part 6, in PL, vol. 1, col. 639.

8. W. M. Lindsay, ed., *Isidori Hispalensis Episcopi Etymologiarvm sive Originvm Libri XX* (Oxford: Clarendon Press, 1911), bk. 8, pt. 3 ("De haeresi et schismate"). This echoes the Pauline injunction "even if we, or an angel from heaven, should preach to you a gospel contrary to that which we preached to you, let him be accursed." Galatians 1: 9–10.

The twelfth century witnessed an upswing in heretical activity, along with stronger efforts on the part of the official church to define the problem and defend against it. The third Lateran Council in 1179 denounced heretics and provided means for censuring them.[9] Prior to this, on November 4, 1184, Pope Lucius III issued the decretal *Ad abolendam* wherein heresy was given more specific definition. Any person denying ecclesiastical doctrine related to the Eucharist, baptism, the remission of sins, or marriage was considered heretical. Any individual protecting or defending such persons was considered anathema.[10] This papal pronouncement has been read as an inquisitorial charter for the repression of heresy. It does differ from previous bulls insofar as it manifests a sort of international character.[11] When Raymond of Peñafort drew up guidelines in 1242 for the archbishop of Tarragona, who thought it prudent to better identify the "fact of heresy," Peñafort developed seven categories of identification. These were practicing heretics, those clearly adhering to them, those suspected of holding the heresy, those refusing to disclose information concerning heretics, those agreeing not to provide evidence, those who welcomed or were friendly to heretics, and those defending heretics.[12] Already, the official church had declared itself apostolic, thus specifically defining itself as the guardian of normative religious truth and practice.[13] Innocent III in his struggle against heresy asserted the absolute necessity of defining heretics as persons preaching or otherwise publicly proclaiming and defending ideas contrary to the teachings of the official church.[14] On March 25, 1199, Innocent issued a stern decretal against heretics. That decree, *Vergentis in senium*, condemned heresy and linked it with treason. For the first time, heresy was juxtaposed with lèse-majesté. Innocent deliberately attached ecclesiastical disobedience with crime. Heresy was high treason

---

9. 3 Lat c.27 *Sicut ait beatus Leo*, in Tanner, DEC, vol. 1, p. 224–225.

10. Mansi, vol. 22, cols. 476–478; and PL, vol. 201, cols. 1297–1300. The document identified several groups of heretics, including Cathars, Humiliati, Patarines, Waldensians ("Poor Men of Lyons"), Passagians, Josephini, and Arnoldists. Later incorporated into canon law. X 5.7.9 in Friedberg, vol. 2, cols. 780–782.

11. Malcolm Lambert, *The Cathars* (Oxford: Blackwell Publishers, 1998), p. 83.

12. José Rius Serra, ed., *Sancti Raymundi de Penyafort opera omnia* (Barcelona: Universidad de Barcelona, 1954), vol. 3, pp. 74–82.

13. Pope Gregory VII, for example, regarded the words *apostolic* and *papal* as virtual synonyms. Grundmann, pp. 220–221.

14. Note his letters in PL, vol. 215, col. 71, and vol. 215, col. 915.

against God.[15] Thereafter, official documents frequently describe heresy as a crime.[16] In this sense, more than two hundred years later, Jan Hus could be considered a criminal. The policies of Innocent III were an important stage in the legal definition of heresy. Incorporating the formulations of Augustine, Thomas Aquinas defined heresy as a corruption of Christian faith and concluded that in this sense, heresy constituted sin.[17] Thus, Hus was characterized as a sinner.

The formulation of heresy in canon law played no small role in the later prosecution of religious dissent. In the fifth century, Jerome defined heresy as choice, in deciding which teaching to follow.[18] Accordingly, all persons understanding scripture other than that proscribed by the official church were by virtue of that fact heretics. Those who refused to accept the teaching of the church, as defined by papal or episcopal authority, were thus outside the communion of the faithful.[19] Canon law declared such persons schismatic.[20] Theologically, this applied to Jan Hus. Augustine's idea concerning stubborn opinion and resistant adherence in the face of ecclesiastical correction as heresy likewise became codified in the legislature of canon law.[21] Peter Damian's decision that heretics are those failing to agree with the official church is entirely consistent with ecclesiastical law as it developed by the eleventh century.[22] The fourteenth-century canonist Guido de Baysio argued that there were two essential characteristics of heresy: error in reason and pertinacity in will.[23] The legal meaning of

---

15. Decretal in PL, vol. 214, cols. 537–539, and in canon law as X 5.7.10 in Friedberg, vol. 2, cols. 782–783.

16. For example, the 1298 decree of Boniface VIII, which appears as Sext. 5.2.8 *Ut inquisitionis*, in Friedberg, vol. 2, cols. 1076–1077.

17. *Summa theologiae*, 4, p. 88, where Thomas makes it clear, in 2a, 2ae, q. 11, art. 2, "Dicendum quod de haeresi nunc loquimur secundum quod importat corruptionem fidei Christianae."

18. PL, vol. 26, col. 445.

19. Both dictums appear in canon law as C.24 q.3 c.27 and C.24 q.1 c.20 and c.25, in Friedberg, vol. 1, cols. 973, 975–976, and 997–998.

20. Gloss by Johannes Teutonicus on C.24 q.1, in Friedberg, vol. 1, cols. 966–984.

21. C.24 q.3 c.31 *Qui in ecclesia*, in Friedberg, vol. 1, col. 998.

22. "Eos sacri canones hereticos notant qui cum Romana ecclesia non concordant." Noted in a letter to Cadalus, bishop of Parma, bk. 1, letter 20, in PL, vol. 144, cols. 237–247, at col. 241.

23. Jesse D. Mann, "William of Ockham, Juan de Segovia, and Heretical Pertinacity," *Mediaeval Studies* 56 (1994): 69. The entire article is instructive.

heresy, then, can be read as persistence in error and contempt for ecclesiastical authority. Persistence in matters declared schismatic by ecclesiastical authorities yielded heresy.[24] The arguments were relevant to the trial of Jan Hus. Canon law defined heresy as espousing views chosen by human perception, contrary to holy scripture, publicly declared and stubbornly defended.[25] These elements of heresy can apply equally to doctrine (ideas) or practices (behavior). As the history of heresy demonstrates, the notion expressed by the sixteenth-century Spanish jurist Iacobo de Simancas that "a heretic is not one who lives badly, but one who believes badly" is untenable.[26] Medieval heresy and its social implications were simultaneously ideological and practical. According to canon lawyers of the twelfth and thirteenth centuries, it is possible to identify at least eleven definitions of heresy.[27] Moreover, a legal distinction was drawn between heretics and their deeds.[28]

In the Latin church generally, both orthodoxy and heresy came to be linked to papal decree. Orthodoxy has been defined as the position of the pope at any given moment.[29] Heresy, on the other hand, came to be whatever the papacy implicitly or explicitly condemned.[30] This definition, while generally true, lacks the necessary specificity of the varieties and patterns of medieval heretical inclination and potentially ignores the fundamental

---

24. See glosses on C.7 q.1 c.9 *Dicimus omnino* and C.24 q.1 c.31 *Denique quam sit*, in Friedberg, vol. 1, cols. 977–978 and 569–570. Fifteenth-century conciliarists such as Simon de Cramaud cited these aspects of canon law in arguments for deposing popes and advocating the authority of general councils. For example, Simon de Cramaud, *De substraccione obediencie*, ed. Howard Kaminsky (Cambridge, Mass.: Medieval Academy of America, 1984), pp. 108–109.

25. C.24 q.3 c.27–c.31, in Friedberg, vol. 1, cols. 997–998.

26. "Non est hereticus, qui male vivit, sed qui male credit." Iacobo de Simancas, *De Catholicis Institutionibus liber, ad praecavendas et extirpandas haereses admodum necessarius* (Rome: In Aedibus Populi Romani, 1575), pp. 119, 228.

27. Othmar Hageneder, "Der Haeresiebegriff bei den Juristen des 12. und 13. Jahrhunderts," in *The Concept of Heresy in the Middle Ages*, ed. W. Lourdaux and D. Verhelst (Leuven: Leuven University Press, 1976), pp. 42–103. See also Edward Peters, "*Crimen exceptum*: The History of an Idea," in *Proceedings of the Tenth International Congress on Medieval Canon Law*, ed. Kenneth Pennington, Stanley Chodorow, and Keith H. Kendall (Vatican City: Bibliotheca Apostolica Vaticana, 2001), p. 161, n. 57.

28. *Glos. ord.* to C.23 q.4 c.5.

29. Jeffrey Burton Russell, *Dissent and Reform in the Early Middle Ages* (Berkeley: University of California Press, 1965), p. 3.

30. This is the definition offered by Lambert, *Medieval Heresy*, p. 8.

character of heresy itself. Heresy may also be defined further as those doctrines, groups, tendencies, and movements aimed at Christian renewal that are detached from, or excluded by, the established Christian community and official forms of religion. Clearly, heresy must be related in some way to doctrinal or dogmatic deviance along with continued disobedience. The latter is as germane as the former and comes into vivid focus in the trial of Jan Hus. As Christine Thouzellier puts it, "one is a heretic who criticizes or refuses to accept Christian dogmas and rejects the teaching authority of the Roman Church, which one had recognized before."[31]

Making the papacy the arbiter of orthodoxy and heresy also forced canonists to define papal power. There are allusions in canon law that can be read to suggest that popes are beyond human judgment.[32] Some jurists argued for exceptions to that rule. However, the sole exception in the body of canonical legislation is on the grounds of heresy.[33] When Western Christendom became mired in the fifteenth-century papal schism, it was to this provision that conciliarists at the Council of Pisa turned in 1409. The Council deposed the feuding popes Benedict XIII and Gregory XII on charges that they were "criminals, schismatics, promoters of schism, notorious heretics, contumacious and stubborn" in their heresy. The language of canon law appears in their formal depositions on June 5, 1409.[34] The problem of the papal schism is a matter too complex and, for our purposes here, too digressive to investigate further. It is sufficient to acknowledge that accusation and conviction of heresy are tools of considerable power. One can legitimately argue that heresy is a political matter because its explication is closely related to the definition of roles with the power structure of church politics.[35]

---

31. Quoted in Edward Peters, ed., *Heresy and Authority in Medieval Europe* (Philadelphia: University of Pennsylvania Press, 1980), p. 4.

32. See Brian Tierney, *Foundations of the Conciliar Theory: The Contribution of the Medieval Canonists from Gratian to the Great Schism* (Leiden: Brill, 1998), pp. 43–61, for an outline of this theory with references to canon law.

33. Walter Ullmann, *Medieval Papalism: The Political Theories of the Medieval Canonists* (London: Methuen, 1949), p. 156, with references. (D.40 c.6 *Si papa*, in Friedberg, vol. 1, col. 146.) On this problem, see Jeffrey A. Mirus, "On the Deposition of the Pope for Heresy," *Archivum Historiae Pontificiae* 13 (1975): 231–248.

34. The document can be found in Martène and Durand, vol. 7, cols. 1095–1098.

35. Sebastián Provvidente, "Inquisitorial Process and *Plenitudo Potestatis* at the Council of Constance (1414–1418)," in BRRP 8, p. 101.

Canonical legislation determined the presence of heresy when a person refused to accept the judgment of an authorized body or individual that his or her expressed views were incorrect or at variance with the accepted teachings of the church. In other words, heresy can exist only in relation to orthodoxy. The legal proceedings against Jan Hus bear this out in exacting detail. Non-Christians or infidels such as Jews and Muslims are necessarily excluded from consideration under the strict, technical, and legal interpretation of heresy. The existence of formal heresy must be predicated upon a declaration of its existence. The modern construct of the freedom to think independently was in no sense, however qualified, part of the medieval ecclesiastical or legal mind, in either the Latin or the Greek church. One was not permitted to believe whatever one wished.[36] The accusation of heresy evolved into a powerful ecclesiastical and political weapon. In the course of the later Middle Ages, heresy became an instrument of power created by the church to safeguard its own interests and authority. In this purely arbitrary invention, the church provided the context for the rise of heresy, which gave birth to even further, perhaps unintended, social consequences. For legal scholars and specialists on the subject of medieval heresy, the assertion that heresy was the purely arbitrary invention of the medieval church may seem injudicious, erroneous, or purely arbitrary itself.[37] There are reasons for assuming otherwise. By defining what was orthodox, everything at that time or thereafter that lay outside the line drawn in the theological sand of the Middle Ages was ipso facto heresy or potential heresy. Popes, canon lawyers, and theologians did not necessarily set out either to create heresy or to label all heresies. Their deliberate and protracted doctrinal formulations, however, had certain unintended consequences. One of those results was the purely arbitrary definition of heresy and heretics for all ideas and persons falling outside the predetermined categories of correct teaching and religious practice.

The politics and subjective factors that often figured into the naming of heresy and heretics sometimes meant that the separation between the heretic and the saint became blurred. For example, Valdes (the originator of the Waldensians) and Francis of Assisi were practically identical in

---

36. This idea was articulated explicitly by Isidore of Seville (d. 636) and adopted widely as an appropriate ecclesiastical stance in dealing with dissent and heresy. See his *Etymologiarvm*, bk. 8, pt. 3.

37. I answered the objections of Malcolm Lambert on this point in some detail during a spirited debate at Queens' College, Cambridge, in July 1992.

their teachings. If this is true, how can one account for the condemnation of Valdes and the canonization of Francis? This indicates that a very fine line existed between the safety of orthodoxy and the peril of heresy. It also suggests that no special skill or qualification was required to wander back and forth across that invisible thread without being fully aware of it. In many respects, theological boundaries within the medieval church were often left without proper guards in the same manner as medieval political borders. It was rare in the Middle Ages for one to be a reformer without simultaneously being a suspected or de facto heretic. Without minimizing the real legal and ecclesiastical complications, it must be pointed out that in many instances, reform and heresy were twins, or two sides of the same coin. This is especially true when we examine the contours of movements such as the Waldensians, the Lollards, and the Hussites. It remains a puzzling observation that in the multiple worlds of the Middle Ages, popular preachers often became monks, entered cloisters, and withdrew from the world, while others who insisted on remaining in the world to engage deliberately in models of *imitatio Christi* frequently evolved into heretics.[38] As a historical phenomenon (distinct from heretical ideas), heresy can be described as possessing several necessary elements within its constellation. It must be recognized and denounced by an authoritative body in order to exist. It must be deliberate and persistent dissent. Further, heresy exists as an act of faith or conscience. These acts possess theological, social, and political implications. The manifestations of heresy exist outside the scope of approved teaching and persist in many cases beyond the parameters of acceptable behavior. Finally, heresy in its myriad forms must be publicly asserted, consistently defended, and actively maintained. When these constituent parts are brought together, the result is a challenge to the church and its authority, in terms of both belief and practice. The perceived challenge of heresy constituted a fundamental threat to the social and religious order of the later Middle Ages. In other words, heretics were the medieval equivalent of terrorists, in the sense of threatening the stability and tranquillity of Christianity as determined by the Latin church. On account of persistent heresy and in an effort to prevent religious dissent from spiraling out of control, the Council of Toulouse in 1229 required auricular confession thrice annually.[39]

---

38. Christopher N. L. Brooke, "Heresy and Religious Sentiment: 1000–1250," *Bulletin of the Institute of Historical Research* 41 (November 1968): 121.

39. Mansi, vol. 23, col. 197.

The crucial issue in the rise and definition of heresy is the properly defined and recognized ecclesiastical authority.[40] Heresy is rarely passive. Instead, it becomes public and social. It is only in this sense that it becomes detectable, observable, and problematic. It is deliberate and intentional denial of orthodoxy and, beyond this, a persistence in that denial. The existence of heresy requires the minimal presence of two figures: (1) the representative of orthodoxy, a body or individual recognized and empowered as authoritative within the Christian community, and (2) the perpetrator of deliberate and persistent error coupled with disobedience.[41] From a theological perspective, heresy is simply doctrinal error held in defiance of authority, although that same defiance may also find primary expression in social and political matters.[42] As previously noted, heresy as a historical phenomenon is distinct from heretical ideas.

It is demonstrable that there exists a progression in heretical inclination, and thus the various cognates sometimes denoted as synonyms for heresy are not the same thing as heresy itself but rather are indicators of the passage from orthodoxy to outright heresy. There is some precedent in ecclesiastical history for this distinction. In the fourth century, Basil the Great clearly separated heresy, schism, and "unlawful congregations," the first being by far the most serious. By the thirteenth century, Thomas Aquinas likewise separated heresy and schism, insisting that while schism disrupted ecclesiastical unity, heresy actively opposed the faith. Figure 2.1 is a diagram illustrating a scale of typologies between firm adherence to official dictates and stages of deviance leading to heresy.

The limitations of this diagram are obvious. There is more to the complex historical phenomenon of heresy, which cannot be shown in two-dimensional space. For example, one must consider the coercive measures—denunciations, disqualifications, and force—used against heresy, the negotiation of power and authority, particular social factors, the specificity of individual heresies, and a host of other intangibles. What the diagram does show, moving from left to right, is a progression of thought and

---

40. Gordon Leff, *Heresy in the Middle Ages: The Relation of Heterodoxy to Dissent c.1250–c.1450*, 2 vols. (Manchester, U.K.: Manchester University Press, 1967), vol. 1, p. 1.

41. Lambert, *Medieval Heresy*, p. 5.

42. Wakefield, *Heresies*, p. 2.

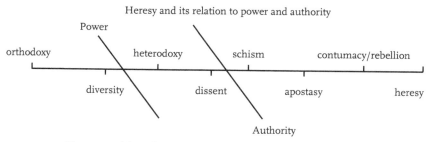

FIGURE 2.1 Heresy and its relation to power and authority

practice from orthodoxy to heresy and contumacy or outright rebellion. Armed conflict or open rebellion (social, political, and ecclesiastical) were sometimes historical and social manifestations of heresy. The crusade against the Cathars and the wars of religion in Bohemia (the Hussite crusade) are two examples. Hence, *dissent, schism,* and *heresy* are not synonymous.[43] The horizontal scale is fixed, while the vertical scales can move laterally back and forth across the full scope of the continuum. Of course, there may be some negotiation regarding the order of stages as one moves from left to right. Since heresy, as full secession from the church, is our concern here, it will suffice to leave the other terms representing various stages of relation to ecclesiastical obedience. Power and authority are likewise not identical. In most cases, authority in matters pertaining to heresy, in late medieval Europe, rested in the church. However, the church or the local representatives of orthodoxy did not always possess sufficient power to assert the church's authority. For example, Archbishop Zbyněk ultimately was unable to control the influence exerted by Jan Hus in the Bohemian province. In Cathar Languedoc, power lay with heretics and their protectors for some time. In the case of Hussite Bohemia, both power and authority eventually came to reside with the heretics. At Tábor, for example, both ecclesiastical and civil authority were controlled by the Hussites. Since authority was in the hands of the heretics and the early community was entirely Hussite, obviously power existed de facto in the realm of heresy and not in the sanctuary of the official church. With this convergence of power, authority, and heresy, the heretical inclination was institutionalized. On this basis, the Hussite movement may be considered

---

43. I maintain this despite arguments that schism is formal heresy. See Howard Kaminsky, *Simon de Cramaud and the Great Schism* (New Brunswick, N.J.: Rutgers University Press, 1983), pp. 171–176. See C.24 q.3 c.26 *Inter heresim,* in Friedberg, vol. 1, col. 997.

the medieval heresy par excellence. There is no monogenesis model for the Hussite heresy, but the person of Jan Hus plays a crucial role. As for the apparent neatness of this theoretical heretical inclination, it must be qualified in terms of the model being useful only for distinguishing and understanding the various types of nonorthodox beliefs, positions, and practices and above all for underscoring the complex nature of heresy itself.

In the later medieval church, heresy had evolved into a complex dilemma. Sources overwhelmingly refer to its varied manifestations by the term *heretica pravitas*. Papal correspondence, inquisitorial records, and literature on these deviants make repeated reference to this "heretical sin or wickedness." One should be wary of assuming too much unanimity in these injunctions, but it seems apparent that the category of heresy had become a useful construct for the Latin church. In the period roughly between 1100 and 1500, *heresy* was consistently a pejorative term indicating choice in error, deviation from the true faith, and rejection of ecclesiastical authority. There was nothing positive about heresy in the minds of either church or civil authority.[44] Then and now, it signified a single construct with many facets but linked by common themes. The third canon pronounced by the fourth Lateran Council in 1215 famously put it thus: "We excommunicate and anathematize every heresy.... We condemn all heretics, whatever names they go under. They have different faces indeed, but their tails are tied together inasmuch as they are alike."[45] The theme was commonplace. Heretics were little foxes that ruined vines. Peter Damian drew the analogy between the proverbial foxes spoiling the vines and the foxes captured by Samson in the Hebrew Bible narratives, who tied their tails together with burning torches and drove them into the

44. Howard Kaminsky, "The Problematics of Later-Medieval 'Heresy,'" in *Husitství—Reformace—Renesance: Sborník k 60. narozeninám Františka Šmahela*, 3 vols., ed. Jaroslav Pánek, Miloslav Polívka, and Noemi Rejchrtová (Prague: Historický ústav, 1994), vol. 1, pp. 133–134.

45. 4 Lat c.3 *De haereticus*, in Tanner, DEC, vol. 1, p. 233. In 1231, Gregory IX used the same imagery of different appearances and common tails in a decretal that was later part of canon law. X 5.7.13 *Excommunicamus*, in Friedberg, vol. 2, cols. 787–789. The concept was used by Innocent III in April 1198, when he wrote that heresies in Languedoc were like little foxes with different faces but tied together by their tails in a common source of infamy. Othmar Hageneder and Anton Haidacher, eds., *Die register Innocenz' III* (Vienna: Verlag der Österreichischen Akademie der Wissenschaften, 1964), vol. 1, p. 94; and also in X 5.7.10 *Vergentis in senium*, in Friedberg, vol. 2, col. 782.

fields of his enemies.[46] We find an interesting example of this in the "book of the generations" of heretics within a parody of the Mass:

> The book of the generations of all the accursed sons of the heretic: Wyclif, the son of the devil...Stanislav of Znojmo begat Jan Hus, Hus begat Marek of Hradec, Marek begat Zdeněk of Labouň, Zdeněk begat Šimon of Tišnov, Šimon begat Petr of Koněprusy...[Matěj] Knín begat Jerome [of Prague], the athlete of Antichrist, Jerome begat Jan Jesenice before the migration of the three nations [1409] and after the migration Jesenice begat Zdislav the Leper.[47]

Linking one heresy to another and to historical antecedents meant that condemnation was guaranteed. The canon law definition of the heretic proved compelling, and the prosecutors of heretical pravity routinely reflected its conviction.[48] In some cases, particular regions in Europe were connected with certain heretics: Italy with Arius, German territories with Wyclif, Meißen with Luther, and Bohemia with Hus.[49] The progenitors of Hus were all the heretics of the church from Arius to Wyclif. The impulses and patterns of heresy were many and varied, as were their emphases. However, the Lateran fathers were correct in perceiving a common element among the heretics. That lowest common denominator involved deviation from obedience and from submission to ecclesiastical authority. That concern formed part of the case in the trial of Hus. The reality of the Middle Ages made the appearance of heresy a natural and not unexpected consequence of Christianity. As the heresy literature of medieval Europe makes clear, the social implications of heresy were legion, and the masks of the heretics, though sometimes ill fitting, were widely worn.

---

46. The fox motif is from the Song of Solomon 2:15. See its use by Honorius of Autun in PL, vol. 172, col. 503. The tale of Samson is in Judges 15:4–5, and Peter Damian's allusion is in PL, vol. 145, col. 419.

47. Missa Wiklefistarum, Vienna, ÖNB MS 4941, fols. 262ʳ–263ᵛ.

48. C.24 q.1 a.c. 1 asserts that every heretic follows a previously condemned heresy. Friedberg, vol. 1, col. 966.

49. These associations are drawn in a sixteenth-century inscription. Brno, Moravian Regional Library, MS 109, fol. 137ʳ. I owe the reference to Michael van Dussen, *From England to Bohemia: Heresy and Communication in the Later Middle Ages* (Cambridge, U.K.: Cambridge University Press, 2012), p. 186.

The medieval sources on heresy tend to present its implications in several different but concrete ways. It may be useful to think of heresy from the point of view of the later medieval church as a haunted house in which the heretics dwell together. In this house of horror, there are nine windows. Each portal provides a different perspective on the deviants and additional understanding of their behavior. By peering through these nine windows, it is possible to construct a profile of the medieval heretic as conceived and advertised by the Latin church. Each window illuminates an even more serious dimension of the ideas surrounding those men and women known in the historical records as heretics.

Heresy as Intellectual Deviance

Heresy frequently finds its place of origin in the realm of ideas.[50] This is the first window. Medieval universities were principally places where scholars congregated, studied, worked, thought, debated, and tested ideas. Pushing out the boundaries of conventional wisdom in pursuit of deeper understanding sometimes brought these scholars to the brink of acceptable teachings. It was popularly said at Paris there were as many errors as teachers.[51] According to some, it was better not to engage in research or active questioning. The result could lead to heresy.[52] In some places, the word *scholar* was accepted as a synonym for *heretic*.[53] Heresy of the mind revolved around philosophical and theological concepts and was, as long as it stayed in that context, a purely theoretical or academic form of deviance. The final and definitive sentence of the Council of Constance against Jan Hus declared his books and ideas "erroneous, scandalous, offensive, rash, seditious and notoriously

---

50. Gerard Verbeke, "Philosophy and Heresy: Some Conflicts between Reason and Faith," in *The Concept of Heresy in the Middle Ages*, ed. W. Lourdaux and D. Verhelst (Leuven: Leuven University Press, 1976), pp. 172–197.

51. According to the *Chartularium Universitatis Parisensis*. For references, see Heinrich Fichtenau, *Heretics and Scholars in the Middle Ages 1000–1200*, trans. Denise A. Kaiser (University Park: Pennsylvania State University Press, 1998), p. 314.

52. So said the preacher Radulfus Ardens, whose master Gilbert of Poitiers had been charged with heresy. PL, vol. 155, col. 1947. I owe the reference to Fichtenau, *Heretics and Scholars*, p. 1.

53. According to Berthold of Regensburg, in Anton Emil Schönbach, *Studien zur Geschichte der altdeutschen Predigt*, 3: *Das Wirken Bertholds von Regensburg gegen die Ketzer* (Vienna: Sohn, 1904), p. 45.

heretical."[54] Heresy of this nature can be traced easily through the centuries of Christianity back to its beginnings. Some of the great thinkers of the Middle Ages were either suspected of or condemned for heresy. Perhaps the most famous was Peter Abelard.[55]

Twice tried for heresy, Peter Abelard was regarded in his own lifetime as possessing one of the keenest minds in all of Latin Christendom. His main opponent was the Cistercian Bernard of Clairvaux, who described him as a clear and present danger to the faith. "Peter Abelard has demonstrated through his life and behavior and also through his books, which are now exposed by the light of day, that he is an assailant of the Catholic faith and an enemy of the cross of Christ. On the outside he appears to be a monk, but on the inside he is a heretic."[56] Abelard was enormously successful and popular as a teacher, and therein lay his real threat to the official church. His heretical ideas were broadcast to eager listeners. Three hundred years later, a similar charge was laid against Jan Hus. The cleverness of Abelard's words and his relentless defense of his ideas were characteristics of his heresy.[57] Even Abelard admitted the duplicity of words. Quite frequently, Abelard observed, the same words have very diverse meanings and can mean multiple things to different people, who may likewise understand various meanings and significance in them.[58] This worried his opponents. Abelard was altogether too clever. Independence of thought and judgment, so obvious in Abelard, were considered general attributes of medieval heretics. Had he not been taught by another heretic, Roscelin? His ruminations on the Trinity and other holy matters were potentially deceitful and capable of leading others astray.[59] At Soissons, Abelard was condemned as a

---

54. The sentence is in FRB, vol. 8, pp. 501–503.

55. The best treatments of Abelard in English include M. T. Clanchy, *Abelard: A Medieval Life* (Oxford: Blackwell, 1997); Constant J. Mews, *Abelard and Heloise* (New York: Oxford University Press, 2005); and Constant J. Mews, *Abelard and His Legacy* (Aldershot, U.K.: Ashgate-Variorum, 2001).

56. Jean Leclercq, C. H. Talbot, and H. Rochais, eds., *Sancti Bernardi Opera*, 8 vols. (Rome: Editiones Cistercienses, 1957–1977), vol. 8, p. 269.

57. Ibid., p. 45.

58. Peter Abelard, *Sic et Non: A Critical Edition*, ed. Blanche B. Boyer and Richard McKeon (Chicago: University of Chicago Press, 1976), p. 89.

59. Constant J. Mews, "The Lists of Heresies Imputed to Peter Abelard," *Revue Bénédictine* 95 (1985): 73–110.

Sabellian heretic.[60] Of all his detractors, Bernard of Clairvaux thought he saw Abelard's heresy clearest. At the second heresy trial, convened at Sens in June 1140, Bernard compared the heretic to the seven-headed beast of the Apocalypse: "[he had] one head, one of his heresies was cut off at Soissons, but seven greater heresies have grown to take its place."[61] Bernard attached as many ancient heresies as he could to Abelard: "When he talks about the Trinity, it sounds like Arius. When he speaks of grace it resembles Pelagius. When he discusses the person of Christ it is reminiscent of Nestorius."[62] Anselm of Canterbury operated on the premise *credo ut intelligam*: "I believe in order to understand."[63] Abelard championed the philosophy *intelligio ut credam*: "I understand in order to believe." For Abelard, faith was an opinion. To Bernard of Clairvaux, faith was absolute truth.[64] The collision of ideas was inevitable. Even the shrewd philosopher of Notre Dame could not forever remain immune to the inventing of heresy. The trial at Sens yielded the result that on July 16, Pope Innocent II condemned Abelard as a heretic.[65]

Abelard's heretical ideas certainly had social implications when applied. The same can be said all the more for the political philosopher Marsiglio of Padua, who likewise came to represent the face of medieval heresy. Although today it is often referred to and seldom read, his famous and somewhat influential book *Defensor pacis* (1324) caused resounding reverberations throughout late medieval Europe. The social implications of Marsiglio's heresy were clear; the official church would revert to its original historical position as subservient to, and existing under, the jurisdiction of secular power. Reformers and heretics later seeking to alter social order were routinely condemned by ecclesiastical authorities as being under the influence of the "accursed Marsiglio."[66] Such ideas

---

60. "*Sabellianus haereticus.*" Otto of Freising, *The Deeds of Frederick Barbarossa*, trans. Charles Christopher Mierow (New York: W. W. Norton, 1966), p. 84.

61. *Sancti Bernardi Opera*, vol. 8, p. 269.

62. Ibid., p. 44 (letter 192).

63. *Proslogium*, ch. 1 in PL, vol. 158, col. 227.

64. *Sancti Bernardi Opera*, vol. 8, p. 27 (letter 190, c.9).

65. PL, vol. 79, cols. 515–517.

66. On Marsiglio, see Cary J. Nederman, *Community and Consent: The Secular Political Theory of Marsiglio of Padua's* Defensor pacis (Lanham, Md.: Rowman and Littlefield, 1995).

were considered plain and manifest heresy. Similar allegations were leveled against Jan Hus.

Another thinker advancing similar ideas and falling into the same category as Marsiglio was William of Ockham. The two thinkers were not
identical in either content or approach and should not be linked. William
claimed that the official church did not possess legitimate authority to
administer and control civil law and its jurisdiction and proposed a different scheme of authority, which included scripture, noncanonical apostolic
literature, historical chronicles, inferences from the above, and, finally,
special revelation.[67] Conspicuously absent are canon law and papal decretals. According to William, popes were obliged to adhere to the law of God.
If ecclesiastical power persisted in issuing demands contrary to the law of
God, Christians were simply to disobey. He railed against the papacy, and
there is fierce polemic in some of his antipapal tracts when he charged
John XXII with heresy.[68] In a similar vein to Marsiglio, William concluded
that ecclesiastical authority must be submissive to civil power in temporal
matters. Conversely, the opposite was also true, although William comes
close to affirming a policy of popular sovereignty. In 1323, fifty-six articles extracted from his works were submitted to the papal see at Avignon
on suspicion of heresy. In 1325, fifty-one of those articles were declared
"open to censure" but not formally condemned. Notwithstanding this,
William of Ockham eventually was excommunicated and expelled from
the Franciscan order.

In a final example, heresy as doctrinal deviance can be seen plainly in
the career and thought of the archheretic of late medieval history, John
Wyclif. In his later career, Wyclif taught that all things ought to be held in
common among all people, that secular power should be in the hands of
civil authorities, while under certain conditions secular authorities could
seize ecclesiastical property. He developed an alternative locus of authority

---

67. *An princeps*, in H. S. Offler, ed., *Opera politica*, 3 vols. (Manchester, U.K.: Manchester
University Press, 1940–1963), vol. 1, pp. 238, 242. *Dialogus*, pt. I, bk. 2, ch. 5, *William of
Ockham, Dialogus: Latin Text and English Translation*, ed. and trans. John Kilcullen, George
Kynch, Volker Leppin, John Scott, and Jan Ballweg, at www.britac.ac.uk/pubs/dialogus/ock-
dial.html.

68. William of Ockham's view of the popes is in *De imperatorum et pontificum potestate*, in
Opera politica, vol. 4, pp. 263–355; and his *Tractatus contra Joannem*, in *Opera politica*, vol.
3, pp. 19–156. His *Breviloquium* must be numbered among the most vitriolic of his tracts.
Richard Scholz, *Wilhelm von Ockham als politischer Denker: Und sein Breviloquium de princi-
patu tyrannico* (Stuttgart: Hiersemann, 1952).

based in scripture and ultimately rejected the papal office, referring to one pope as the *"horrendus diabolus."*[69] He rejected the idea that the church consisted in its essence of bishops and princes and instead postulated that the church be identified with all persons confessing the faith. Since the clergy had forfeited their right to authority on the basis of continual sin, Wyclif suggested that the laity need no longer be compelled to submit their tithes to the church coffers. There are clearly anarchical implications in Wyclif's ecclesiology. Most serious of all, Wyclif went the full distance in rejecting the central tenet of the heart of late medieval piety in his denunciation of the doctrine of transubstantiation.[70] For this, he was severely criticized by ecclesiastical authorities. He also called for eliminating indulgences, the veneration of images, private religion (that is to say, anything apart from the community of believers), endowments of the church, and religious orders. By the time of Jan Hus, Wyclif was by reputation alone persona non grata.

Not all of this, of course, can be made out to be heresy, and indeed that is not the intention, but many of Wyclif's ideas yielded serious consequences for the official church of later medieval England. Wyclif, Abelard, and others demonstrate conclusively that heresy as intellectual deviance was both contemptuous and deliberate. Contempt for ecclesiastical teaching was an essential component of heresy. More than that, heresy was not accidental. In the end, as Peter the Venerable concluded, all heresy was deliberate. The official church was cognizant of the dangers of unlettered simple laypeople having access to scripture in the vernacular. The endless possibilities of interpretation, application, and practice would almost certainly produce deviation from the well-worn and time-proven paths laid out exactingly by the official church and ecclesiastical tradition. Innocent III made clear that the faith (i.e., holy scripture) ought not to be explained by those who are unqualified. The guardian of biblical interpretation was

---

69. *Tractatus de civili dominio*, bk. 1, in JWLW, vol. 2, pt. 1, p. 96; *Tractatus de Blasphemia*, in JWLW, vol. 13, p. 190; *Determinatio, De dominio divino*, in JWLW, vol. 10, and *Tractatus de civili dominio*; *De veritate sacrae scripturae*, in JWLW, vol. 18. Wyclif does emphasize a literalness in the interpretation of scripture. He neither successfully nor satisfactorily resolves the problem of tradition as a component in biblical exegesis. See also his references to and use of the Bible in his *Postilla, Trialogus,* and *Sermones Quadraginta*, in JWLW, vol. 7, pts. 1–4; *De potestate papae*, in JWLW, vol. 19. See also *De ecclesia*, in JWLW, vol. 4, pp. 5, 28–35, 88, 89, 355, 358.

70. On the church, see his *De ecclesia*, and on the Eucharist, his *De eucharistia*, in JWLW, vol. 12.

the traditional role of the church.[71] If the house of heresy revealed diversity of opinion, many of those within that prefabricated dwelling considered themselves faithful Christians laboring for the good of the faith. Jan Hus certainly perceived himself in this sense. Nevertheless, medieval heretics claimed a distorted faith. This is the first window.

Heresy as Religious Formation and Reform

As a general rule, medieval heretics did not perceive themselves as heretics. They regarded themselves as good and faithful Christians interested in the improvement of religion.[72] This is the second window. Movements of reform and reformation were almost always in their early stages related to dissent and not infrequently to heresy. The presence of heretics may be seen as evidence of intense spiritual questing.[73] The desire to see ideals of the primitive church revived was sufficient impetus for movements of reform within the official church. The motivation of apostolic poverty was a common and powerful impulse in the eleventh and twelfth centuries. Movements of this genre possessed an internal heretical coherence. That unanimity was not dogma but the *vita apostolica*, the pursuit of the apostolic life. This led heretics to attack the official church in all areas where the institution departed from the apostolic model. Protest surrounding numerous abuses became fuel for dissent, reform, and later heresy. Moral failings of the clergy were labeled heresy by the so-called heretics, and the label functioned as a term of abuse.[74] Jan Hus considered many of his colleagues in the Prague priesthood in this sense. Concubinage, simony, nepotism, absenteeism, abuses of the confessional, immorality, charging fees for religious services, luxury, drunkenness, and overt worldliness were frequent complaints made by accused heretics against the official church. If the evidence for those complaints was restricted to the realm of heretical polemic, it might be discounted and dismissed. Some of these complaints

---

71. PL, vol. 214, cols. 695–699. It is important that nowhere in this context does Innocent forbid absolutely translations of the Bible.

72. Herbert Grundmann, *Ketzergeschichte des Mittelalters*, vol. 2, in *Die Kirche in ihrer Geschichte: Ein Handbuch*, ed. Kurt Dietrich Schmidt and Ernest Wolf (Göttingen: Vandenhoeck & Ruprecht, 1963), p. 2.

73. See the comment in Walter L. Wakefield, *Heresy, Crusade and Inquisition in Southern France 1100–1250* (London: George Allen & Unwin, 1974), p. 77.

74. See Jean Leclercq, "Simoniaca haeresis," *Studi Gregoriani* 1 (1947): 523–530.

clearly were unwarranted, unfounded, and hyperbolic. That said, visitation records, parish registers, and other official documents demonstrate the presence of these and others factors within the life of the official church, and this is certainly true for the Bohemian province. Strigolniki in western Russia protested against simony, Hussites condemned worldliness and immorality, Waldensians abhorred ecclesiastical wealth, other sects emphasized simplicity of life, and in each case, such protests were aimed at the hierarchy of the church from parish priests on up. Those who sought to correct abuses (such as Jan Hus) had no desire to separate from the one holy church. Their objective was to cleanse the church of its shortcomings and return it to its original holy state. These people became heretics, reluctantly, when their reform program was pushed too far, too zealously, too persistently. When this occurred, heretics refused to recognize the order of the official church. Reform can threaten order and stability, and when it does, it becomes transmuted into something evil, and the invention of heresy ensues. The heretic was a failed reformer. This is the second window.

Heresy as Contumacy

Heresy is only committed when one obstinately refuses to acquiesce in proper ecclesiastical dogma.[75] This is the third window. Inquisitors made much of this point. Following Thomas Aquinas, the fourteenth-century Nicholas Eymeric described heresy as doubting official dogma and persistently maintaining that doubt.[76] That opinion was consistent with canon law. Contumacy was a legal category and could be incurred for a number of reasons, all of which were deemed aspects of persistent and active disobedience to established authority.[77] The issue could easily be characterized as contempt of court, but more specifically in the context of heresy inquiries, it was contempt of ecclesiastical authority. Canon law closely connected contumacy with heresy.[78] Moreover, the penalty for contumacy was formal excommunication.[79] Contumacy was judged a serious matter in the

75. Peter the Venerable, *Contra Petrobrusianos*, in *Corpus Christianorum Continuatio Mediaevalis*, vol. 10, ed. J. V. Fearns (Turnhout, Belgium: Brepols, 1968), p. 146.

76. Eymeric, *Directorium*, pp. 230–232.

77. C.11 q.3 c.43 *Certum est*, in Friedberg, vol. 1, col. 656.

78. X 5.37.13 *Graven dilectorum*, in Friedberg, vol. 2, col. 884. Vallerani, p. 19.

79. C.11 q.3 c.41–c.64, in Friedberg, vol. 1, cols. 655–661.

canonical understanding of heresy. Those in the church of Christ whose thinking was diseased and perverted and who were offered instruction but refused this contumaciously were heretical.[80] Stubborn disobedience was the same thing as heresy; indeed, contumacy was heresy.[81] In the conciliar age, *pertinacia* and *contumacia* were essential categories in understanding heresy. Jean Gerson took the position that contumacy occurred when an individual notoriously refused to listen to the church. When this situation became obvious and was judged irreversible, the offender should be excommunicated as a heretic.[82] The canon lawyer Francesco Zabarella and Cardinal Pierre d'Ailly concurred. All three took active roles in the trial of Jan Hus. Heresy was not simply intellectual deviance or a sort of cognitive disagreement with church teachings; indeed, it included a volitional component, which Augustine, Thomas Aquinas, and the canonists noted. On one hand, there were heretics who erred in matters of faith and contradicted the church but, following correction, might turn back to the truth. On the other hand were heretics who refused instruction, persisted in their own opinions, and were completely aware of the situation. It was in response to this second group that the provisions of canon law were developed.[83] Beliefs might be deemed erroneous, but the condemnation came as a result of refusal to follow the correction of the authoritative body.[84] By the later Middle Ages, the Latin church had firmly equated contumacy with heresy.[85]

There are examples of heresy cases in which contumacy is a prominent component. The Council of Pisa deposed and excommunicated Popes Gregory XII and Benedict XIII in 1409, denouncing them as notorious and contumacious.[86] The definitive sentence against Jan Hus described him as "excessively stubborn...obstinate and incorrigible." The court ruled there was nothing further the church could do with Hus because

---

80. C.24 q.3 c.26–c.31 *Inter heresim*, in Friedberg, vol. 1, cols. 997–998.

81. Johannes Teutonicus, gloss on D.40 c.6.

82. *De potestate ecclesiastica et de origine iuris et legum*, in Glorieux, vol. 6, p. 218.

83. Brandmüller, pp. 235–242.

84. Hus, *Super IV Sententiarum*, in *Mag. Jo. Hus Opera omnia: Nach neuentdeckten Handschriften*, 3 vols., ed. Václav Flajšhans (Osnabrück: Biblio-Verlag, 1966), vol. 2, p. 612.

85. Kaminsky, "The Problematics," pp. 133–154.

86. Martène and Durand, vol. 7, cols. 1095–1098.

he was contumacious.[87] Jerome of Prague was arrested on the orders of the Council of Constance in the spring of 1415, and contumacy proceedings against him were initiated by an ecclesiastical court.[88] Church dogma requires obedience. Jan Hus was counseled at Constance to submit to the wisdom of the fathers and "hold nothing obstinately."[89] As we have seen, the *Glossa Ordinaria* allowed canon law to equate contumacy with heresy. Sin became crime. The heresy lay in stubborn persistence, not necessarily in actual theological deviance. Thus, we find the judgment against Waldensians early on to be less about doctrine and more about contumacious resistance in obeying ecclesiastical instruction.[90] This persistent public denial causes heresy to function as a historical and social phenomenon. In this sense, heresy goes well beyond heretical ideas. Heretics stubbornly opposed proper authority. This is the third window.

Heresy as Challenge to Social Order

The view from the fourth window reveals that medieval social order considered itself ordained by God. In practice, this meant that the church, the government, the law, the judicial system, the social estates, the place of each individual in his or her respective station of life, and the relationships among these categories of existence were all approved by God. Once heretics began challenging the authority and structure of the medieval church, these men and women sometimes moved into the role of actively challenging social order. Hus's disciple Jakoubek Stříbro and Czech heretics at Tábor in the 1420s, following Wyclif, regarded the papacy as Antichrist.[91] It was a short step to declaring kings and rulers who were loyal to popes

---

87. FRB, vol. 8, pp. 501–503.

88. Hardt, vol. 4, col. 760 and p. 142.

89. As recorded by the eyewitness Petr Mladoňovice in his *Relatio*, p. 103.

90. Christine Thouzellier, *Catharisme et valdéisme en Languedoc à la fin du xii* et au début du xiii* siècle*, 2nd ed. (Louvain: Nauwelaerts, 1969), p. 46. This is consistent with medieval trends vis-à-vis heresy.

91. See Jakoubek's sermon *Ecce mulier* of ca. 1410, in ST 2, pp. 462–477; and his 1412 *Utrum sicut ex scriptura plane constat Christum in plenitudine temporis personaliter advenisse, ita evidenter sit deducibile ex eadem antichristum in complemento seculi propria venire in persona*, published in Vlastimil Kybal, "M. Matěj z Janova a M. Jakoubek ze Stříbra," *Český Časopis Historický* 11 (1905): 22–37; and Mikuláš of Pelhřimov, "Commentary on the Apocalypse," Vienna, ÖNB MS 4520 fol. 293ʳ and passim.

also as Antichrist.[92] Within Hussite Bohemia, we find a vivid tradition of antipapalism and condemnation of secular authorities loyal to Rome.[93] Many individuals who became part of heretical sects of this type were already socially disadvantaged and saw in the heretics the opportunity to improve their lot in life. There were exceptions to this rule, but the bulk of evidence weighs heavily in this direction. Heresies in different regions of Europe, at different times, made concerted efforts to overthrow the constructs of social order: Hussites at Tábor and, in more subtle, less visible ways, Waldensians in the Alps and Cathars in Languedoc. Because of representation at all levels of society in Cathar and Hussite communities, it is not possible to argue that Catharism or Hussitism was a fundamental class struggle. In general, heresy was not a social struggle. Its proliferation across the full spectrum of social strata prevents such a conclusion. When speaking of medieval heretical movements in general, one discovers in the sources aristocrats and clergy (higher and lower), townspeople, craftsmen, artisans, peasants, intellectuals, unlettered, men, women, children, wealthy, impoverished, royal courts, palaces of archbishops, rural villages, cities, country hills, and universities all represented. This precludes identifying heresy strictly in political, social, economic, or geographical terms. In areas of wealth, affluence, and growth, heresy can be found just as it was present in regions of poverty, degradation, and recession.

One might be tempted to define heresy as a type of social evolution, especially in relation to experiments such as Hussite Tábor, but this would require metahistorical judgments and subjective interpretation and thus is best left aside. To interpret the Hussite heresy, at least in its radical forms, as essentially an economic and social critique demands an oversimplified determinism along economic lines. To follow such an argument almost entirely eliminates external influences and other noneconomic factors to the point where conclusions are indefensible when submitted to the bar

---

92. In the Hussite context, "The verse accusation of the Czech Crown" and "the prophet of the Czech Crown to the Czech lords on the coronation of the Hungarian king" are examples of the vilification and denunciation of a ruler (in this case, Sigismund) on the grounds of heresy, blasphemy, and illegitimacy. The best edition is Jiří Daňhelka, ed., *Husitské skladby budyšínského rukopisu* (Prague: Orbis, 1952). A useful essay is Karel Brušák, "Reflections of Heresy in Czech Fourteenth- and Fifteenth-Century Rhymed Compositions," *Slavonic and East European Review* 76, no. 2 (1998): 241–265.

93. For example, *De antichristo & membrorum ejus anatomia*, in HM, vol. 1, fols. 336b–368a, especially fols. 352a–353a and 363a–366a. The tract has often but erroneously been attributed to Hus. A recent study is Lawrence P. Buck, "*Anatomia Antichristi*: Form and Content of the Papal Antichrist," *Sixteenth Century Journal* 42, no. 2 (2011): 349–368.

of wider, critical examination. The results are facile. To persist only reveals a greater propensity and interest in ideologies and in factors of determinism than in history or heresy itself. Clearly, heresy as challenge to social order in most cases constitutes a revolt against social injustice, real and perceived.[94] There are representative cases that demonstrate the close relation between civil and ecclesiastical power and how challenge to the state came to be viewed as heresy.[95] These revolts (some of which became revolutions) further extend the social implications of heresy. Within the house of heresy, we find men and women actively challenging medieval social order. This is the fourth window.

Heresy as Civil Disorder

From time to time in the history of medieval heresy, popular movements of religious reform and dissent manifested themselves visibly and socially in different forms of active civil disobedience. This is the fifth window. As early as the twelfth century, heresy was regarded as an attack on peace and civil order.[96] The papal legate Milo described his mission in Provence in 1209 as combating heresy in order to secure the peace and stability of the region.[97] Heresy as disorder is readily apparent in a context where religion prevails as the single most important pervasive and persuasive social force. Late medieval Europe knew little of political ideas mandating separation of church and state. The prince-bishops in the German lands exemplify this point very well. Bishops might celebrate the divine mysteries of the Mass at the cathedral altar, clad in chasuble, then hurry from the

---

94. See the interpretations of Martin Erbströsser and Ernst Werner, *Ideologische Probleme des mittelalterlichen Plebejertums: Die freigeistige Haeresie und ihre sozialen Wurzeln* (Berlin: Akademie-Verlag, 1960); Gottfried Koch, *Frauenfrage und Ketzertum im Mittelalter: Die Frauenbewegung im Rahmen des Katharismus und des Waldensertums und ihre sozialen Wurzeln (XII–XIV Jahrhundert)* (Berlin: Akademie-Verlag, 1962); Antonino de Stefano, *Riformatori ed eretici del medio evo* (Palermo: Società Siciliana per la Storia Patria, 1990); Ernst Werner, *Pauperes Christi: Studien zu sozial-religiösen Bewegungen im Zeitalter des Reformspapsttums* (Leipzig: Köhler and Amelang, 1956); and Luigi Zanoni, *Gli Umiliati nei loro rapporti con l'eresia, l'industria della lana ed i comuni nei secoli XII e XIII* (Rome: Multigrafica, 1970).

95. For example, Stefano Brufani, *Eresia di un ribelle al tempo di Giovanni XXII: Il caso di Muzio di Francesco d'Assisi* (Florence: La Nuova Italia Editrice, 1989), containing the fourteenth-century trial records, illustrates the point.

96. For example, the decretal of Innocent III, later in canon law, X 5.7.10 *Vergentis in senium*, in Friedberg, vol. 2, cols. 782–783.

97. He characterized his work as a mission "contra hereticos et pro pace ac quiete Provinciae stabilitum" in a letter to Pope Innocent III. PL, vol. 216, cols. 124–126.

sanctuary and change into a coat of mail, swing into the saddle of a waiting stallion, and ride off to put down an uprising in the hills. The disturbances caused by heresy might have begun innocently enough in a theological or religious sphere, but the social implications of heresy can neither be confined to the academy nor suppressed for long. To engage in heretical behavior and put into practice the principles of heresy sometimes led to civil disorder. To protest against civil authorities usually meant confronting the official church. To demonstrate against the ecclesiastical establishment often also meant having to deal with civic officials. In the case of Jan Hus, both church and civil authorities were invested.

Despite the conviction that a heretic in the first instance was a sinner needing salvation and conversion before that individual was a criminal requiring punishment, it was impossible to prevent civil authorities from becoming involved in the civil disorder and subsequent prosecution of heretics. Heretics were, in fact, criminals. They were guilty of breaking the law of God. They were also sinners. Heretical offenses occurred simultaneously on these two levels. The heretical offender was both sinner and criminal. For a sinner, repentance and penitential acts were required in order for divine forgiveness to be effective. For a criminal, satisfaction and restitution had to be made to the community in order for full justice and rehabilitation to transpire. The definition of heresy codified in canon law spoke of heresy as an offense against the community.[98] With heresy functioning simultaneously on these two levels, both ecclesiastical and civil officials were involved when heresy became civil disorder. If these two bodies of power and authority were united in the same individual, that did not alter any of the foregoing. A single individual might be tried separately but simultaneously in both civil and ecclesiastical courts.[99]

Civil disorder disrupted the patterns of religious and social order in many ways. Bogomils in southeastern Europe refused to pay taxes, obey their lords, or submit themselves for military service.[100] Henry of Clairvaux reported that heretics in Toulouse openly mocked papal

---

98. See Edward M. Peters, "Transgressing the Limits Set by the Fathers: Authority and Impious Exegesis in Medieval Thought," in *Christendom and Its Discontents: Exclusion, Persecution, and Rebellion, 1000–1500*, ed. Scott L. Waugh and Peter D. Diehl (Cambridge, U.K.: Cambridge University Press, 1996), p. 338.

99. This was true of Gilles Rais in 1440. Georges Bataille, *Le procès de Gilles de Rais* (Paris: Société Nouvelle des Editions Pauvert, 1997).

100. John V. A. Fine, Jr., *The Bosnian Church: A New Interpretation* (Boulder, Colo.: East European Quarterly, 1975), p. 116.

legates in the streets, made obscene gestures, and called churchmen bad names.[101] In 1145, a preacher of the official church attempted to speak out of doors in the town of Verfeil, east of Toulouse, but was prevented by the din created by knights who deliberately drowned out the preacher's words with the clanging of their armor.[102] On account of heresy, Verfeil was regarded as "the seat of the Devil."[103] There were other forms of disorder. The Cathar heretic Hugo Faber of Toulouse went into a church, defecated beside the altar, and wiped his posterior with the altar cloth. In 1209, other heretics in Béziers seized a priest, violently took his chalice, stripped him of clothing, and then urinated on him.[104] Certain accounts of the crusaders approaching Béziers in that same year allege that heretics took Bibles, urinated on them, and threw the books from the walls onto the heads of the besieging soldiers with cries of mockery and ridicule.[105] Hussites in fifteenth-century Bohemia engaged in violent acts of iconoclasm, cutting off noses, gouging out eyes, hacking off hands and feet, and chopping off heads of numerous statues. On March 31, 1414, a Hussite heretic entered the Church of St. James in Prague and in front of pious worshipers smeared the crucifix with excrement.[106] In 1395, the "Twelve Conclusions of the Lollards" were attached to the doors of St. Paul's Cathedral and Westminster Abbey in London, outlining the main tenets of the Lollard faith. The Peasants' Revolt of 1381 and the Lollard uprising of 1414 under the direction of Sir John Oldcastle may be seen as more drastic expressions of heretically inspired civil disorder.[107] Civil disorder also manifested itself in blatant disregard for religious propriety

---

101. Henry's mission against heresy in Languedoc is described in PL, vol. 204, cols. 235–240.

102. See the comment in Lambert, *The Cathars*, p. 40.

103. Saint Bernard of Clairvaux, *Vita prima*, in PL, vol. 185, cols. 410–416.

104. The incidents are told in Peter of les-Vaux-de-Cernay, *Historia Albigensis*. Critical edition in *The History of the Albigensian Crusade*, trans. W. A. Sibley and M. D. Sibley (Woodbridge, U.K.: Boydell Press, 1998), pp. 24, 49.

105. Tale related by Caesarius of Heisterbach, *Dialogus miraculorum*, ed. Joseph Strange (Cologne: Heberle, 1851), vol. 2, pp. 300–303.

106. Hardt, vol. 4, cols. 674–675.

107. Relevant documents are in A. R. Myers, ed., *English Historical Documents*, vol. 4, 1327–1485 (London: Eyre & Spottiswoode, 1969); the conclusions, pp. 848–850; revolt of 1381, pp. 127–144; Oldcastle's first trial (1413), pp. 859–862; the rebellion of 1414, pp. 862–863; the execution of Oldcastle (1417), pp. 863–864.

and social order. There are numerous examples of clerics being mistreated in the performance of their duties or being subjected to indecent exposure by brazen heretics. In 1452, the renegade heretic Stefan Vukčić of Hercegovina engaged in protracted campaigns of violence and iconoclasm in Dubrovnik, Konavli, and elsewhere in that region. Stefan and his men destroyed churches, wrecked villages, cut down trees, desecrated religious houses, defaced other churches, threw crucifixes and other sacred objects into the streets, abused priests celebrating Mass, and left in their wake a trail of disrupted communities.[108] Civil disorder perpetrated by heretics in fourteenth-century Ireland precipitated a request to Pope John XXII to call a crusade against Irish heretics.[109]

Apart from these representative instances, the general cases of many heretical movements provide examples of heresy threatening civil order and displaying signs of clear subversive tendencies with potential drastic social implications. Heresy was a crime; heretical activities in their social dimensions constituted criminal behavior. From the twelfth century, heresy was regarded as lèse majesté. Bishops and princes were called to mediate, judge, prosecute, and eliminate the sources of disorder and preserve the natural and divinely ordained patterns of medieval life. Heretics were threats to social order. This is the fifth window.

Heresy as Madness

Peering through the sixth window into the house of heresy, we find even more disturbing characters whom the church considered threatening. In a substantial number of sources, the idea of lunacy was attributed in cases of heresy. Raoul Glaber wrote about heretics in the eleventh century and frequently used the idea of insanity to describe them.[110] From

---

108. Several letters outline what Stefan ostensibly did in his heretical rage. See Fine, *The Bosnian Church*, p. 316, with references. On Stefan more generally, see John V. A. Fine, Jr., *The Late Medieval Balkans: A Critical Survey from the Late Twelfth Century to the Ottoman Conquest* (Ann Arbor: University of Michigan Press, 1987); see the index for the numerous relevant pages.

109. The letter of ca. 1331 seems to have originated in the Cathedral Chapter of St. Patrick's in Dublin. Rome, Vatican Library MS Vat. Barberini Lat. 2126, fol. 125ʳ. Translation in *The Sorcery Trial of Alice Kyteler*, ed. L. S. Davidson and J. O. Ward (Binghamton, N.Y.: Medieval & Renaissance Texts and Studies, 1993), pp. 87–89.

110. *Raoul Glaber: Les cinq livres de ses histoires (900–1044)*, ed. Maurice Prou (Paris: Picard, 1886).

this perspective, "heresy was a form of contagious madness."[111] Men and women rejecting the authority of the official church and following pathways of heresy were quite clearly mad. How else could authorities explain the departures of these people from the ark of safety? The Middle Ages did not distinguish precisely between fools and lunatics. Fools were tolerated and in certain contexts played important social roles. Lunacy or mental derangement was another matter. Authorities used the term *madness* indiscriminately when referring to foolishness and lunacy. In the context of heresy, it was most often used to signify the various forms of disbelief in the heretics themselves. Sources sympathetic to the official church expressed their consternation at iconoclasm and other acts of barbarity against sacred space. The abuse of priests and other religious was often termed "madness."[112] The teachings of heretics frequently bore the label of "insane" ideas.[113] Thirteenth-century Cathar heresy was described as "lunacy," "insane belief," "crazy," amounting to "mad ideas."[114] Clearly, the notion of madness in these instances cannot be related to concepts of insanity. Another example of the concept of madness has to do with the inability of authorities to comprehend the motivation behind the protection of heretics. Innocent III could not fathom why Count Raymond VI of Toulouse did not exterminate heresy from his realm. Innocent writes to Raymond and asks, "What madness has caused you to persist in this fashion?"[115] Once again, the madness in question is not connected to any modern or clinical idea of actual lunacy.

Insanity, however, cannot be ruled out in some cases of religious dissent and deviant behavior and teaching. For example, while resisting the temptation to psychoanalyze, one thinks of the story of Leutard, a peasant

---

111. Lambert, *The Cathars*, p. 6.

112. For examples, see *Historia Albigensis*, pp. 106, 158, 169.

113. In its condemnation of Jan Hus, the Council of Constance declared Wyclif's ideas "insane." See FRB, vol. 8, pp. 501–503. Cathar heretical ideas at Cologne in the twelfth century were also regarded as examples of madness. Documents using this language have been translated in Peter Allix and Samuel Roffey Maitland, *Facts and Documents Illustrative of the History, Doctrine, and Rites of the Ancient Albigenses and Waldenses* (London: Rivington, 1832), pp. 350–362.

114. These terms occur in the *Chanson de la croisade albigeoise* by Guillaume de Tudèle. See Janet Shirley, ed. and trans., *The Song of the Cathar Wars: A History of the Albigensian Crusade* (Aldershot, U.K.: Scolar Press, 1996), pp. 12, 24, 33, 55.

115. This language appears in the papal correspondence of May 29, 1207, in PL, vol. 215, cols. 1166–1168.

in early-eleventh-century Gaul whose body ostensibly was invaded by a great swarm of bees that gave him instruction about things he was to do. Thereafter, he committed acts of iconoclasm. Bishop Gebuin, upon examination, declared the "lunatic [Leutard] had become a heretic." The bishop rescued the followers of Leutard from this insanity through persuasion and catechism. The madman proved irredeemable and committed suicide by throwing himself into a well.[116] Robert of Arbrissel in Brittany and Anjou at the end of the eleventh century bore all the characteristics of a lunatic: wild eyes, matted beard, unkempt hair on end, disheveled appearance, bare feet, animal skins for clothing. His followers were said to be whores and thieves who roamed the hinterlands with their prophet and preacher.[117]

Between the years 1112 and 1114, Tanchelm of Antwerp sought to reform the church in the Lowlands. He was regarded as utterly deranged. Tanchelm declared himself God and publicly married a statue of the Blessed Virgin Mary. He went about the town preaching, clothed in luxurious dress, his hair tied up with ribbons, followed by a great multitude, which we are told included, somewhat incredibly, three thousand armed men. His loyal followers were alleged to worship the heretic with such devotion that they drank the water in which he bathed.[118] Eudo of Brittany in the mid-twelfth century advanced similar claims and likewise was considered mad, indeed, "deranged by the delusions of demons." Eudo claimed he was the son of God, engaged in the desecration of churches, and gathered a following.[119]

Finally, the tale of Gherardo Segarelli, a thirteenth-century enthusiast in Parma, is also instructive. Segarelli applied for entrance into the Franciscan order but was rejected, whereupon he set himself the task of outdoing Saint Francis in the imitation of Christ. Segarelli had himself

---

116. *Raoul Glaber: Les cinq livres*, pp. 49–50. It is possible that Leutard suffered from St. Anthony's fire, which recurred with some frequency in Europe between the ninth and twelfth centuries. The ergot fungus contained numerous toxins, including the hallucinogen LSD. The symptoms are consistent with cases of ergotism. Moreover, insanity was one of the supposed consequences of St. Anthony's fire. Herbert Grundmann concluded that Leutard was insane in his *Ketzergeschichte des Mittelalters*. The assessment is compelling.

117. According to Marbod, bishop of Rennes. PL, vol. 171, cols. 1483–1484.

118. Documents on Tanchelm have been translated in Wakefield, *Heresies*, pp. 96–101. Exaggeration and propaganda are rife in these reports.

119. Documents in ibid., pp. 141–146. Robert Moore says he read the documents about Eudo to a group of psychiatrists who concluded that "they describe a textbook case of paranoid schizophrenia." R. I. Moore, *The Birth of Popular Heresy* (London: Arnold, 1975), p. 63.

circumcised, wrapped in swaddling clothes, and suckled by a woman. After this initial process of initiation into the life of Christ, he stalked through the streets of the town, calling all people to repentance. Ostensibly, he gained a substantial following in Parma, in other parts of Italy, and even as far afield as Germany. With these developments, the religious authorities moved against him. His followers were persecuted, the movement suppressed, and Segarelli executed, albeit not by crucifixion, at Parma in 1300.[120] Some heretics were thought to be simply and utterly deranged. For example, Innocent III attributed the errors of Amoury de Bébe more to insanity than heresy, ostensibly convinced that the poor man truly was mad.[121] Others were regarded as possessed by mad foolishness. A German female heretic alleged that she had, in fact, suckled Jesus. When asked about reproving her heresy, Albert the Great declared that her assumptions were not heresy, which ought to be theologically disproven, but insanity, which deserved a good thrashing.[122] Even legal texts sometimes described heretics as insane.[123] Madness and mayhem. This is the sixth window.

Heresy as Disease

If the specter of madness among heretics cast a pall over the church, an even more dire observation could be made within the house of heresy. This is the seventh window. The inhabitants of the depraved dwelling were also associated with disease, illness, and infection. The genre of medieval Last Judgments often portrayed sinners and heretics as diseased persons. The most striking example, among many, is the enormous late-fifteenth-century Last Judgment fresco in the Cathedral of St. Cécile in Albi.[124] Here the damned being cast into the tortures and horrors of hell are ill, deformed, and diseased individuals. This was the alleged outcome of persistent disobedience and exposure to the infection of heresy.

---

120. *Cronica fratris Salimbene de Adam ordinis minorum*, in MGH, *Scriptores*, vol. 32, pp. 255–293.

121. Mansi, vol. 22, col. 986.

122. Cited in Grundmann, p. 176.

123. Sext. 5.2.3 *Filii vel heredes*, in Friedberg, vol. 2, col. 1007.

124. Thomas A. Fudge, "To Hell with the Theologians: Sex, Sodomy and Punishment in the Medieval Last Judgment," Texas Medieval Association Conference, Southern Methodist University, Dallas, September 26, 2010.

The motifs of sin and disease were related frequently in the Middle Ages. *Leprosy* sometimes was used interchangeably with *sin*.[125] As early as the Carolingian period, heresy and leprosy were synonymous afflictions. "Leprosy is the false teaching of heretics, and lepers are heretics."[126] Literature from the medieval period often uses a variety of epidemiological nomenclature when speaking of heresy. Frequent terms include "infection," "virus," "contaminate," "poison," "cancer," "plague," and "leprosy." Heresy was perceived as a chronic and fatal disease requiring excision from the body of Christ before it corrupted the entire church. Canon law insisted that people could be contaminated by a single sinner just as one diseased sheep might infect an entire flock.[127] Radical solutions were demanded. An epidemiology of heresy began. Heresy constituted an infectious, aggressive disease, which required immediate containment. The Council of Vienne characterized it as a contagion of unusual proportions, "a monstrous infection."[128] Heresy was the AIDS of the Middle Ages. Heretics were already—unwittingly, perhaps—infected and were contagious. Eudo of Brittany was described as a carrier of plague.[129] The plague of heresy only spread filth, causing further contamination; in many cases, the poison of heresy infected entire towns.[130] Wandering heretics visiting towns and communities were thought to be infecting people with the poison of their wicked heresies.[131] The social implications of this association were clear: the disease of heresy could infect entire communities, and the poison of the heretical plague was deadly. The diocese of Albi was considered "a damnable region tainted with heresy which flows through it like a great sewer."[132] The heresy perpetrated by

---

125. See Beryl Smalley, *The Becket Conflict and the Schools: A Study of Intellectuals in Politics* (Oxford: Basil Blackwell, 1973), p. 132; and R. I. Moore, *The Formation of a Persecuting Society: Power and Deviance in Western Europe, 950–1250* (Oxford: Basil Blackwell, 1987), pp. 62–65.

126. Rhabaus Maurus, *De universo*, quoted in Moore, *The Birth of Popular Heresy*, p. 5.

127. D. 45 c.17 *Sed illud*, in Friedberg, vol. 1, col. 166.

128. In canon law as Clem. 5.3.1 *Multorum querela*, in Friedberg, vol. 2, cols. 1181–1182.

129. From William of Newburgh's account of Eudo in Wakefield, *Heresies*, p. 144.

130. *Historia Albigensis*, pp. 8, 48, 181–182, 189. Heresy was a poison with a high degree of infectiousness. Ibid., p. 267.

131. Rudolf Glaber, *Rodulfi Glabri Historiarum Libri Quinque*, ed. and trans. John France (Oxford: Clarendon Press, 1989), pp. 138–139. This eleventh-century source refers to the rise of heresy at Orléans, culminating in the trial and execution by fire of a number of heretics.

132. Henry of Clairvaux's impression of the town in 1178. PL, vol. 204, col. 240.

Peter Abelard was regarded as contagious, and this conviction justified his swift prosecution, condemnation, imposed silence, and exile.[133] The Council of Constance concluded that John Wyclif was a "root of poison," while his ideas bore death. The Council declared that unless the "knife of ecclesiastical authority" was used, the "cancer" would wreak havoc.[134] In 1431, Joan of Arc was condemned as an incorrigible heretic and rejected from the communion of the Church as "infected with the leprosy of heresy."[135] Immediate containment was essential. Disasters that struck late medieval communities were sometimes linked to the inhabitants of the medieval underworld such as criminals, prostitutes, Turks, lepers, Jews, and heretics. These were sinners, their sin was infectious, the infection brought disease, and disease when it had run its course brought death. There were consequences of divine judgment for those who tolerated heresy and sin. The great earthquake of 1222 in Lombardy and other natural disasters were considered divine judgment on account of heresy.[136] The perceived consequences of allowing sinners (or heretics) to go unpunished were too great and the social implications too profound. Societies require scapegoats to explain catastrophe, and the fires that consumed witches and heretics were rituals of purification aimed at cleansing society and pacifying the anger of God. Church authorities in the Czech province reflected this concern.

The disease of heresy, with its putrefying and contaminating potential, was one such malady requiring excision. In the twelfth century, William the Monk told Henry of Lausanne, "you too are a leper, scarred by heresy, excluded from communion by the judgement of the priest, according to the law, bare-headed, with ragged clothing, your body covered by an infected and filthy garment; it befits you to shout unceasingly that you are a leper, a heretic and unclean, and must live alone, outside the camp, that is to say outside the Church."[137] Heresy was dreaded as a contagion

---

133. Archbishop Henry of Sens in 1121 wrote to Pope Innocent II declaring that Abelard's heresy had infected many people already and that its contagious nature was epidemic. Quoted in Clanchy, *Abelard*, p. 309.

134. FRB, vol. 8, pp. 501–503.

135. According to the definitive sentence handed down on May 30. Pierre Tisset, ed., *Procès de condamnation de Jeanne d'Arc* (Paris: Klincksieck, 1960), vol. 1, p. 414.

136. See *Cronica fratris Salimbene de Adam ordinis minorum*, in MGH, *Scriptores*, vol. 32, p. 34.

137. The statement comes from the debate between Henry and William in the mid-1130s. Translated in Moore, *The Birth of Popular Heresy*, p. 57. Essentially, all sources on Henry appear in Moore, pp. 33–60.

that spread secretly and mysteriously, crawling through communities like snakes, its poison dispensed slowly, the heretical virus. The Cathar heresy was described in the twelfth century as a creeping menace, like a crab, a poison flowing near and far, leprosy infecting the body of Christ everywhere.[138] This realization of danger was not isolated. Raymond V, count of Toulouse, wrote to the General Chapter of the Cistercians in 1177 about the infection of heresy: "This rotten plague of heresy spreads to such an extent" that its consequences are terrible.[139]

Religious epidemiologists were fairly quick to diagnose the situation. The canons of Liège in 1145 begged the pope to do something about the poison of heresy which had spread throughout their lands.[140] In 1163, the Council of Toulouse, in its running battle against Waldensians and Cathars, identified the spread of heresy as cancer threatening the health of everyone and everything it came in contact with.[141] In the same year, the fourth canon of the Council of Tours likewise described heresy as a cancer.[142] Lucius III's decretal of 1184 pronounced heresy pestilential.[143] In a letter to the archbishop of Auch, Pope Innocent III used similar terminology.[144] These heretics have overrun the land, and their awful poison threatens the church. Their cancerous venom attacks every bastion of truth and, like leprosy, infects everything.[145] Political rulers were warned that their regions were infected with the horrible disease of heresy, or the poison of depravity, and the evil contamination of heretical tendencies.[146] Innocent declared that Provence had been infected with "a plague of heretical depravity," which had grown like "cancer," striking the entire region.[147] Guibert of Nogent noted that the execution of heretics prevented

---

138. Eckbert of Schönau, sermon against Cathars, in PL, vol. 195, cols. 13–21. Eckbert preached thirteen anti-Cathar sermons. See PL, vol. 195, cols. 11–102.

139. "Putrida haeresis tabes praevaluit." The letter appears in Gervase of Canterbury, *Chronica*, in *The Historical Works of Gervase of Canterbury*, ed. William Stubbs (London: Longmans, 1879), p. 270.

140. PL, vol.179, cols. 937–938.

141. Mansi, vol. 21, col. 1177.

142. Ibid., cols. 1177–1178.

143. Ibid., vol. 22, cols. 476–478.

144. "Velut cancer irrepit." PL, vol. 214, col. 71.

145. Eckbert of Schonau, *Sermones contra Catharos*, in PL, vol. 195, col. 13.

146. Examples of such warnings are Innocent III to Raymond of Toulouse, PL, vol. 215, cols., 1166–1168; and Innocent to Bishop Hugh of Riez, PL, vol. 216, col. 173.

147. Letter 136, autumn 1204, in PL, vol. 215, cols. 426–427.

the spread of heretical cancer.[148] Innocent III regarded heresy as a cancer that moved like a snake.[149] Jean Gerson used the same terminology at the Council of Constance.[150] The word *pestis* became a favored term describing heresy from the fourteenth century on. Heresy was as deadly a plague as the Black Death. The latter brought physical, temporal death, the former spiritual and eternal death.[151] Instances in which authorities did legitimately associate heretics with diseased persons or communities only further strengthened this assumption of heresy as disease. Inquisitorial records indicate that Cathars sometimes took refuge or actually lived in leper houses.[152] Elsewhere, the transmission of heresy was viewed as occurring, like many diseases, through personal contact. As late as 1551, the physician Guglielmo Gratarolo was described as a plague upon true faith everywhere he went. The physician, being infected, contaminates all of his patients, and rather than containing the virus, such perverse medical treatment only hastens its spread. The transmission of the heretical virus also occurred through books. Roberto Bellarmino in 1614 echoed a common medieval conviction that heresy is spread through books, and the profusion of books after the mid-fifteenth century was described by Bellarmino as a virtual plague.[153] The plague was one of dire unfaithfulness.[154] The disease of heresy frequently was terminal. Some of the main prosecutors of Jan Hus, such as Michael de Causis, warned that his teachings were pestilential. This is the seventh window.

Heresy as Perversion

If all of this was not sufficiently ominous, it must be said that in the minds of many ecclesiastical and civil authorities, heresy was perversion and

---

148. Guibert of Nogent, *Monodiae*, bk. 3, ch. 17, in *A Monk's Confession: The Memoirs of Guibert of Nogent*, ed. Paul J. Archambault (University Park: Pennsylvania State University Press, 1996), p. 198.

149. Letter 138, January 1211, PL, vol. 216, col. 502.

150. This was in a sermon before the conciliar gathering. In du Pin, vol. 2, p. 207.

151. Heresy is called a plague in numerous texts. See, for example, the *Historia Albigensis*, pp. 9, 10, 181–182, 189.

152. Malcolm Barber, "Lepers, Jews and Moslems: The plot to Overthrow Christendom in 1321," *History* 66 (1981): 14.

153. See Richard Palmer, "Physicians and the Inquisition in Sixteenth-Century Venice," in *Medicine and the Reformation*, ed. Ole Peter Grell and Andrew Cunningham (London: Routledge, 1993), p. 118.

154. *Historia Albigensis*, p. 8.

vice.[155] In short, looking through the eighth window revealed the house of heresy filled with various and sundry perverts. This condition was wrought by the devil. Theoretically, no heretic was exempt.[156] The perversion of heretics occurred on a variety of levels, from teaching to lifestyles. The most baleful form of this heresy was the perversion of sexual deviance. Sex, sexual perversion, and heresy were not infrequently related in conceptions of religious deviance in later medieval Europe. For example, the term *ketzerei* in southern Germany could mean either heresy or sodomy.[157] The laws against sodomy, while lacking a unanimous definition of the term or practice itself, were at times severe. Heretics were sodomites in the broad and general sense and social perverts posing a threat to law, order, and godliness. The equally opprobrious terms *bugger* and *buggery* originate in the Middle Ages. Both terms are associated with the origins of heresy in the West and underscoring a certain preoccupation with sexual immorality. The appearance or entrance of heresy in western Europe was sometimes regarded as occurring through the Balkans and particularly related to the Bulgarians. The name *Bulgarian* became associated with heresy itself. *Heretic* meant *Bulgarian*, and conversely *Bulgarian* implied *heretic*. Latin and Old French sources provide evidence of this association. For example, *Bulgari, Bulgri, Bugari, Burgari, Bugares, Bugri, Bogri, Bougres, Boulgres, Bogres*, and *Bulgarorum* are terms found related to heresy and heretical activities. Heretics in southern France were called Cathars as early as 1163, but by 1201, they were sometimes identified as "Bulgari."[158] The pejorative sexual connotation can be traced from the early thirteenth century.[159]

Modern languages have retained variations of the word *bugger* with different meanings. It is frequently used as a synonym for something

155. Among a plethora of evidence in the sources, Pope Honorius III in September 1220 called heresy a vice. MGH, *Epistolae*, vol. 1, p. 101.

156. The *Historia Albigensis* regards the heretic Bernard of Cazenac and his wife, Hélis of Monfort, as perverted by the devil. A litany of their alleged savagery of nonheretics, including iconoclasm and bodily mutilation, is included. See pp. 237–238.

157. Eduard Osenbrüggen, *Das alamannische Strafrecht im Deutschen Mittelalter* (Schaffhausen: Hurter, 1860), pp. 289–290, 375–376.

158. The first occurrence of the term *Cathar*, as far as I know, is Eckbert of Schönau in PL, vol. 193, col. 13. The texts in a manuscript collection of Saint Vaast dating from ca. 1200 use "Bougres" as heresy. Translation in Bernard Delmaire, "Un sermon arrageois inédit sur les 'Bougres' du nord de la France," *Heresis* 17 (1991): 1–15.

159. See Mark D. Jordan, *The Invention of Sodomy in Christian Theology* (Chicago: University of Chicago Press, 1997); and Helmut Puff, *Sodomy in Reformation Germany and Switzerland, 1400–1600* (Chicago: University of Chicago Press, 2003).

terrible, filthy, lewd, perverted, or otherwise disgusting. The association is
not accidental and can be explained. The official church, in its repression
and hatred of heretics and heresies, demonized these people by ascribing to them all forms of human depravity, wickedness, sin, and perversion. Other Western languages contain words of the same origin, some of
which have an objectionable meaning. The old Venetian *buzzerone*, like the
German *ketzerei*, can mean either heretic or sodomite. The Italian *gazari*
and *gazzerare* have similar derogatory meanings. In English, the word
bugger can mean a foul person or, more specifically, a sodomite. *Bugger*
and *buggery* can be traced to the medieval *Bulgarus*, which was widely
understood to refer to a heretic from Bulgaria, a perverted and depraved
individual supposed capable of any perversion or crime.[160] This was the
reputation of the medieval heretic. This was a common assumption about
those dwelling in the house of heresy at the end of the Middle Ages.

Heresy and its several manifestations found absolute links both to
the devil and to sexual activity and perversion. The defenders of social
order and the guardians of revealed truth worked hard at demonizing
heretics by engaging in propaganda campaigns aimed at scandalizing
the community.[161] Making connections, however tenuous and strained,
between heretics and the demonic proved effective. A fourteenth-century
chronicle concluded that the destruction of the biblical cities of Sodom
and Gomorrah was divine punishment for heresy.[162] Even Abelard had
been cast into the mold of popular magic with all its suspiciousness.[163]
As early as the eleventh century, heretics were characterized as sexual
perverts. Heretics in Aquitaine enjoyed fleshly pleasure even though they
pretended to be celibate.[164] In the twelfth century, Tanchelm of Antwerp
ostensibly had intercourse with young girls in the presence of their

---

160. See Borislav Primov, "Medieval Bulgaria and the Dualistic Heresies in Western
Europe," *Etudes Historiques* 1 (1960): 100. Also see Jean Duvernoy, *Le Catharisme: La Religion
des Cathares* (Toulouse: Éduard Privat, 1976), pp. 309–311.

161. See especially Norman Cohn, *Europe's Inner Demons: The Demonization of Christians in
Medieval Christendom*, rev. ed. (Chicago: University of Chicago Press, 1993), pp. 35–78.

162. Jacob Twinger von Königshofen, *Chronik*, cited in Robert E. Lerner, *The Heresy of the
Free Spirit in the Later Middle Ages*, rept. ed. (Notre Dame, Ind.: University of Notre Dame
Press, 1991), p. 4.

163. *Sancti Bernardi Opera*, vol. 8, p. 26.

164. According to the chronicle of Adhémar of Chabannes, *Historia pontificum et comitum
Engolismensium*, in MGH, *Scriptores*, vol. 4, p. 138.

mothers and with married women in front of their husbands. The heretic claimed that these acts were spiritual. Around 1113, the canons of Utrecht alleged that Manasses, a local blacksmith, formed a heretical brotherhood made up of twelve men and one woman representing the twelve apostles and the Blessed Virgin Mary. To confirm their brotherhood, these apostles had sex with the woman, and to confirm her virginity, she "had carnal intercourse with each one in the vilest manner."[165] Around the same time, Henry of Lausanne was denounced on similar grounds. It was alleged that he allowed both boys and girls to fondle his genitals and buttocks publicly to the point of mutual arousal.[166] Accusations and stories like these in an age obsessed with order yielded results that were often drastic and destructive.

Among those regularly thought to be sexual perverts were the so-called Free Spirit heretics.[167] These people were accused of committing rape and adultery and other acts of sensuality. There were claims (possibly coerced) that these heretics had discovered the way in which Adam and Eve had made love. The notion ostensibly was applied in practice that any woman engaging in sexual intercourse with a member of the heretical inner circle would automatically regain her virginity.[168] These same heretics confessed in 1339 at Constance that if a couple had sexual intercourse on an altar at the same time as the Eucharist was being consecrated, both acts (sexual and sacral) would have equal worth. The centrality of the Eucharist in later medieval piety and in popular consciousness made heresies connected to it all the more outrageous.[169] Further confession of Free Spirit heretics at the same trial revealed other acts of indecency and a strange mingling of theology and sexual perversion. For example, one of the heretics was asked by three women to explain the doctrine of the Trinity. He enjoined them

---

165. Wakefield, *Heresies*, pp. 99–101, for documents.

166. This apparently happened at Le Mans around 1116. The record is translated in Moore, *The Birth of Popular Heresy*, p. 34.

167. There is no prima facie evidence for the existence of a Free Spirit heresy. The best sources are Lerner, *The Heresy of the Free Spirit*, and Grundmann, pp. 153–186.

168. Lerner, *The Heresy of the Free Spirit*, p. 137.

169. According to Johannes of Winterthur in the 1330s, the Eucharist was the sacrament or object of religious devotion most relied on by Christians in the fourteenth century. *Die Chronik Johanns von Winterthur*, ed. Friedrich Baethgen, in MGH, *Scriptores*, vol. 3, p. 64. On the importance of the Eucharist in later medieval history, see Miri Rubin, *Corpus Christi: The Eucharist in Late Medieval Culture* (Cambridge, U.K.: Cambridge University Press, 1991); and John Bossy, "The Mass as a Social Institution," *Past and Present* 100 (1983): 29–61.

to remove all of their clothing and lie down. The women complied. The heretic tied their legs together, so the record states, and then proceeded to have sex with each of them "in the most scandalous manner." Then, the trial deposition states, the heretic, "leering at the naked shame of the women with his lecherous eyes," concluded his theological explanation of the Godhead by declaring, "here is the Holy Trinity."[170] The shock value of these testimonies and convictions, obviously repeated, told, retold, and embellished, within a religiously orthodox community requires no further commentary except to suggest that medieval societies could not perceive such behavior other than as a serious and sobering threat to both religious and social order. Such actions were all the more insidious on account of the conviction that heresy could be spread through a virus in semen.[171] Thus, every heretical ejaculation spread further the disease, madness, and perversion of opposition to the official church.

There are many stories from the sources on heresy in the later Middle Ages that provide the context for references in those same accounts to "committing heresy with one's body."[172] On this basis, serious doubt must be thrown on the conclusion drawn earlier by the Spanish canonist Simancas that a heretic is not one who lives badly. Pope John XXIII was declared heretical and deposed by the Council of Constance in 1415 on numerous charges of scandalous and heretical tendencies.[173] Immoral, perverted conduct and lifestyles did incur the wrath of ecclesiastical authorities and also brought the harsh penalty and consequences of the condemnation of heresy. Where such conduct was not immediately discernible, the process of prosecuting and punishing heretics frequently produced it. Heretics were routinely made to confess that they had willingly embraced perversions and sexual licentiousness as something intrinsically godly. Even austere Waldensians were regarded as sexual deviants who satisfied their lusts of the flesh indiscriminately.[174]

---

170. The account is told by the fourteenth-century chronicler Johannes of Winterthur. See MGH, *Scriptores*, vol. 3, pp. 148–150.

171. For several allusions, see Moore, *The Origins of European Dissent*, p. 248.

172. See the reference to a fourteenth-century condemnation in E. William Monter, *Frontiers of Heresy: The Spanish Inquisition from the Basque Lands to Sicily* (Cambridge, U.K.: Cambridge University Press, 1990), p. 280.

173. John XXIII was cited as a heretic, a schismatic, a simoniac, immoral, and incorrigible. Finke, *Acta*, vol. 3, pp. 156–209.

174. Gui, *Practica*, with a substantial excerpt translated in Jeffrey Burton Russell, ed., *Religious Dissent in the Middle Ages* (New York: John Wiley, 1971), pp. 42–52. The note about

Cathar heretics were alleged to believe that it was impossible to commit sin below the waist.[175] Cathars were depicted in art forms as sexually promiscuous.[176] This association of heresy with sexual licentiousness, though widespread on the Continent, is oddly almost entirely absent in England.[177]

Heretics were likewise accused of same-gender sexual behavior perhaps as early as the twelfth century. Orgies, possibly homosexual in nature, were said to have occurred among heretics in the town of Bucy-le-Long near Soissons.[178] The accusations became standard in the demonizing of heretics, and variations of the theme "vir cum viris" (men with men) and "femina cum feminis" (women with women) frequently occur in the sources in conjunction with sexual perversion and nocturnal heretical orgies.[179] Austrian heretics likewise engaged in sexual orgies, with women having sex with women and men with men.[180] Free Spirit, Cathar, and Templar heretics were stereotypically cast into these roles. Increasingly, "homosexuality," or same-gender sexual contact, became applied to heresy.[181] Albigensian heretics were reported to meet secretly in caves. During their rituals, the leader of the sect bared his buttocks before his followers, inserted a silver spoon into his anus, and deposited an offering on it. The heretics then kissed their leader's buttocks before extinguishing the lights and engaging in a sexual frenzy, once again featuring "men with men and women with women."[182]

---

sex is on p. 46. The allegation was repeated by the fourteenth-century inquisitor Eymeric, *Directorium*, p. 279.

175. *Historia Albigensis*, p. 14. The same assumption ostensibly was ascribed to Free Spirit heretics. Lerner, *The Heresy of the Free Spirit*, pp. 17–18.

176. See the illumination in Oxford, Bodleian Library, MS Bodley 270b, fol. 123ᵛ.

177. Lambert, *Medieval Heresy*, p. 303.

178. Guibert of Nogent, *Monodiae*, bk. 3, ch. 17, pp. 195–197.

179. Jeffrey Burton Russell, *Witchcraft in the Middle Ages* (Ithaca, N.Y.: Cornell University Press, 1972), pp. 126–127. Russell dates this initial occurrence to 1114. See also Gábor Klaniczay, "Orgy Accusations in the Middle Ages," in *Eros in Folklore*, ed. Mihály Hoppál and Eszter Csonka-Takács (Budapest: Akadémiai Kiadó, 2002), pp. 38–55.

180. According to the Franciscan Johannes of Winterthur in 1338. *Die Chronik Johanns von Winterthur*, MGH, *Scriptores*, vol. 3, pp. 144–145.

181. James A. Brundage, *Law, Sex, and Christian Society in Medieval Europe* (Chicago: University of Chicago Press, 1987), p. 473; and John Boswell, *Christianity, Social Tolerance, and Homosexuality: Gay People in Western Europe from the Beginning of the Christian Era to the Fourteenth Century* (Chicago: University of Chicago Press, 1980), pp. 283–286.

182. Testimony of a heretic describing such events can be found in *Beiträge zur Sektengeschichte des Mittelalters*, ed. Johann von Döllinger (New York: Burt Franklin, 1970), vol. 2, pp. 369–373.

Modern concepts of homosexuality aside, these same sources relate scenes of heretical debauchery, orgiastic lust, and kinky sex. Exhibitionism and masturbation foreshadow events to come. Promiscuous women are offered to all—men and women—for whatever pleasure is desired.[183] The veracity of these stories can be challenged successfully by modern scholars, but to the late medieval mind, they were hideous and appalling facts. Thirteenth-century opinion reflected the conviction that the licentiousness of heretics made Sodom and Gomorrah appear stainless.[184] Propaganda campaigns of this nature help to explain the urge to purge the world of heresy that characterizes ecclesiastical policy in the later Middle Ages. The heretic was depraved. This is the eighth window.

Heresy as Diabolism

The last perspective in the house of heresy reveals one further dimension of the assumptions concerning the nature of men and women who found themselves excluded from the household of faith. Late medieval authorities perceived heresy as intellectual deviance, reform, contumacy, challenge to social order, civil disorder, madness, disease, and perversion. Heresy was all of these things, but it was chiefly the work of the devil. This is the ninth window. Heretics were among the primary citizens in the city of Satan.[185] This *civitas diaboli* was the antithesis of the city of God. The words of heretics were often described as though legions of demons were speaking through their mouths.[186] Medieval heresy rarely lacks a demonological overtone. According to Jerome, heresy was worse than sin.[187] The demonic element was the basis for fear, and the fear-inspired repression created a stereotype that can be found with some regularity in the antiheresy records of later medieval Europe. This stereotype characterized the heretic as proud, unlettered, diseased, incorrigibly bent toward

---

183. Among many, Guibert of Nogent, *Monodiae*, p. 196; Cohn, *Europe's Inner Demons*, p. 147.

184. Bishop Lucas of Túy, *De altera vita*, bk. 3, ch. 15, in *Magna bibliotheca vetervm patrvm et antiquorum scriptorvm ecclesiasticorum*, ed. Marguerin de La Bigne (Cologne: Hierat, 1618), vol. 13, p. 283.

185. Lambert, *The Cathars*, p. 10.

186. For example, Henry of Lausanne was thus characterized at Le Mans around 1116. The document is in Moore, *The Birth of Popular Heresy*, p. 35.

187. "Against the Pelagians," in PL, vol. 23, cols. 544–548.

wickedness, and subversive. Its eventual association with medieval forms of witchcraft was inevitable. Waldensians were featured as worshiping the devil in the form of a goat, men and women taking turns kissing the devil's rear end, while in the skies above them, witches flew on broomsticks, and horned, winged demons rode on men and women.[188] Heresy as witchcraft was perhaps the greatest form and the highest creation in the inventing of heresy. Ecclesiastical authorities increasingly saw witchcraft as a form of heresy.[189] Throughout the Middle Ages, beliefs in witches, folklore, spells, the spirit world, and magic were fairly universal in Europe. In the course of the later Middle Ages, these ideas evolved into an organized, systematic demonology, which between the fifteenth and eighteenth centuries produced horrific chapters in the history of Europe. The topic is too large, too complicated, and too complex for discussion here and is, in any event, part of the harvest of the Middle Ages as opposed to a specific medieval topic.[190] A single point must suffice. The literature, or heresy-as-witchcraft handbooks, codified and publicized alleged diabolical deeds taking place throughout Europe.[191] The greatest *ketzerei* (heresy) was *hexerei* (witchcraft). When the *Malleus Maleficarum* was first published, it carried a bold statement on its title page: "to not believe in witchcraft is the greatest heresy." The wheel of demonization had come full circle since the early Middle Ages. Appended to the book was a papal bull from Innocent VIII. It is possible to overrate the significance of the bull, but the dual publication of book and bull should not be regarded as insignificant.[192] For late medieval

---

188. Frontispiece to the French version of the fifteenth-century work by Johannes Tinctoris, *Tractatus Contra Sectum Valdensium*, Paris, Bibliothèque Nationale, cabinet des manuscripts, fonds, français 961.

189. See the documents in Alan C. Kors and Edward Peters, eds., *Witchcraft in Europe 400–1700: A Documentary History* (Philadelphia: University of Pennsylvania Press, 2001), pp. 58–229.

190. Thomas A. Fudge, "Traditions and Trajectories in the Historiography of European Witch Hunting," *History Compass* 4, no. 3 (2006): 488–527.

191. Three representative handbooks are Nicholas Eymeric, *Directorium Inquisitorium*, 1376; Johannes Nider, *Formicarius*, 1437; and Heinrich Krämer and Jacob Sprenger, *Malleus Maleficarum*, 1486. All three are excerpted in Kors and Peters, *Witchcraft in Europe*, while the entire third text is available in Christopher Mackay, ed. and trans., *Malleus Maleficarum*, 2 vols. (Cambridge, U.K.: Cambridge University Press, 2006).

192. A warning against ascribing too much to the bull is argued in Eric Wilson, "Institoris at Innsbruck: Heinrich Institoris, the *Summa Desiderantes* and the Brixen Witch-Trial of 1485," in *Popular Religion in Germany and Central Europe, 1400–1800*, ed. Bob Scribner and Trevor Johnson (London: MacMillan, 1996), pp. 87–100.

Europeans, heresy had become endemic in many areas, where it maintained an essential, though diabolic, relation to social life. As early as 1324, trials treated the accused as members of an organized sect of heretics bent on the subversion and destruction of Christendom, and individuals were put to death on charges of heresy derived from witchcraft.[193] Condoning heresy in an age of anxiety was regarded as tantamount to tolerating the devil and, by extension, inviting an outpouring of divine wrath. In the same manner, general accusations were easily transmuted into heresy.[194] Heretics were the sons and daughters of Satan. This is the ninth window.

Canon law promoted ideas that heretics were wolves among sheep, foxes in the vineyard, and mute dogs unable to bark.[195] Plenty of antiheresy propaganda submitted that the deviants publicly appeared virtuous but privately were engaged in all manner of vice. The *causae haereticorum* in canon law was a matter of considerable concern and was dealt with in some detail. Those dwelling within the house of heresy and seen through the prism of these nine windows were presented as an appalling image that rendered the medieval heretic as an intellectual deviant, a would-be reformer hopelessly misguided, an incorrigible contumax, a threat to social order, a cause of civil unrest, a person deluded and unbalanced, someone infected with a terminal contagious disease, a degenerate given to unspeakable debauchery, and a person controlled by the devil. That profile characterizes widespread ecclesiastical opinion in the immediate context of the Jan Hus trial. This is the broadly conceived stereotype into which Hus was thrust during his legal ordeal. This disturbing composite portrait cannot be excluded from the concurrent rise and development of antiheresy legislation, legal procedure, and policies of repression aimed at controlling and eliminating the perceived threat. It is to this important consideration that we now turn.

---

193. See the procedural record in Davidson and Ward, *The Sorcery Trial of Alice Kyteler.*

194. Anne Gilmour-Bryson, "L'eresia e i Templari: 'Oportet et haereses esse,'" *Ricerche di Storia Sociale e Religiosa* 24 (1983) : 101–114.

195. X 5.7.10 *Vergentis in senium,* in Friedberg, vol. 2, col. 782. See Keith H. Kendall, "'Mute Dogs, Unable to Bark': Innocent III's Call to Combat Heresy," in *Medieval Church Law and the Origins of the Western Legal Tradition: A Tribute to Kenneth Pennington,* ed. Wolfgang P. Mueller and Mary E. Sommar (Washington, D.C.: Catholic University Press, 2006), pp. 170–178.

3

Law, Procedure, and Practice in Medieval Heresy Trials

> *Those who come up with morbid and improper teachings in the Church of Christ, and when corrected in order to adhere to sound healthy doctrines, resist contumaciously and refuse to change their poisonous and deadly doctrines but persist in defending them, are to be considered heretics.[1]*

FROM ITS ORGANIZATION in the twelfth century, canon law gradually but steadily eroded the protections of men and women accused of heresy while simultaneously making penalties ever more severe. The existence or perception of heresy in the high Middle Ages led to the formation of legislation, legal procedure, and a specific practice and implementation of those laws in order to protect the church and Christian communities from the various "poisonous and deadly" teachings that the medieval church thought resulted only in "morbid" and depraved practices. Heresy was applied criminology.[2] The two concepts became integrally related. In the 253 canons that make up *Causae* 23 and 24 of medieval canon law, Gratian set forth the case for the nontoleration of crime, sin, and offense (including heresy) and outlined a brief and justification for the use of force in combatting such dangers.[3] The trial of Jan Hus was a formal legal process defined within the scope and context of medieval canon law. Being accused of theological irregularity and suspected of heresy, Hus appealed against

---

1. C.24 q.3 c.31 *Qui in ecclesia*, in Friedberg, vol. 1, col. 998.

2. Thomas A. Fudge, "Obrana 'Kacířství: Teoretické pojednámí," *Medievalia Historica Bohemica* 9 (2003): 313.

3. Friedberg, vol. 1, cols. 889–1260.

decisions made by his ordinary, Archbishop Zbyněk of Prague. This set in motion a formal court case. Hus started what became his legal ordeal. It is evident that he had legal counsel, ultimately provided by the Czech attorney Jan Jesenice. Between 1410 and 1412, the relationship between Hus and Jesenice was crucial. Hus was a priest, a reformer, and a theologian. He is rightly characterized as an expert in theology. Jesenice was an expert in canon law and legal procedure. He knew the law. Together, the theologian and the attorney navigated the perilous course of a formal judicial process.[4]

In order to grasp the nature of canon law, criminal procedure, and legal practice in the context of medieval heresy trials, it may be useful to consider criminal procedure in modern, Western judicial systems. A basis of comparison can then be established. While there are variations, a basic outline of criminal procedure can be constructed. It is essential to note that the rules of procedure for heresy trials were the same theoretically as for all other court proceedings. In modern, Western societies, criminal procedure begins with the commission of a crime, that is to say, an act that violates some aspect of prevailing law. An investigation ensues. The identification of a suspect generally follows. The office of the district attorney (or its equivalent) decides whether there is sufficient evidence to file charges. If so, the perpetrator is arrested and remanded to custody. Attorneys are brought into the process. Cases for the defense and for the prosecution are undertaken. At the arraignment, the defendant is presented with charges, and a plea in response is entered. There follows a preliminary hearing, which may be waived, and if so, the process goes to trial. Concurrent with these developments, there are pretrial hearings; a variety of motions; discovery, which involves the gathering of evidence; depositions or sworn statements taken from potential witnesses; court rulings; interlocutory orders; the scrutiny of existing law to determine the nature of the charges; and evidence issues handled by means of *in limine* motions. Judges and attorneys are appointed. A formal trial, either by judge or jury, is scheduled. If the case will be decided by a jury, selection is determined by means of voir dire, which is a question-and-answer process. At trial, an argument is presented by the prosecutor in an opening

---

4. It is also possible to argue that Hus was well versed in law and cited canon law more often than any other source except scripture. Jiří Kejř, "Jan Hus jako právní myslitel," in *Jan Hus mezi epochami, národy a konfesemi*, ed. Jan B. Lášek (Prague: Česká Křesťanská Akademie: Husitská Teologická Fakulta Univerzity Karlovy, 1995), p. 197.

statement. This is normally followed by the defense attorney offering an opening statement to the court. The prosecution then examines evidence and witnesses. The defense may choose to cross-examine the same evidence and witnesses. There is opportunity for the prosecution to engage in redirect, which may be a reexamination of the said evidence or witnesses. The process is repeated by the counsel for the defense examining evidence and witnesses, cross-examination by the prosecutor, redirect, and finally, closing arguments by both sides. Thereafter, instructions are given to the jury, which retires to deliberate the foregoing. Eventually, a verdict is reached. If the decision supports the prosecution, sentencing of the convict follows. This may take place immediately or be scheduled for a later hearing. The sentence of the court is carried out. There is normally opportunity for the defense to file an appeal. At every stage, the accused is considered innocent until guilt has been established.

By the time Jan Hus was accused of theological irregularities, both heresy and antiheresy legislation were well defined. In terms of origins, the guiding procedural practices for ecclesiastical processes concerning heretics go back to Pope Innocent III, who issued two decretals—*Nichil est pene* and *Licet Heli*—in 1199 authorizing action *per inquisitionem.*[5] That process is described more fully in the decretal *Qualiter et quando* of 1206.[6] In 1215, the eighth canon of the fourth Lateran Council established the process as a regular form of criminal procedure. This act became incorporated into medieval canon law.[7] It is quite wrong to assume that inquisitorial procedure ordinarily used torture, forbade all legal representation, and routinely prevented the defendant from initiating an appellate process. One should regard Innocent as perhaps the organizer of legal procedure rather than the originator of it. Parallels with modern criminal proceedings can be drawn. The procedure included provisions that properly formulated charges should precede accusations, a warning should precede the denunciation, publication of the charges should come before the inquest, and the sentence should adhere to the rules governing legal procedure. The

---

5. Othmar Hageneder, ed., *Die register Innocenz' III. 2* (Vienna: Verlag der Österreichischen Akademie der Wissenschaften, 1979), vol. 2, pp. 434–436, 477–480. The latter text is X 5.3.31, in Friedberg, vol. 2, cols. 760–761. See also X 5.34.10 *Inter sollicitudines*, in Friedberg, vol. 2, cols. 872–874; and X 3.12.1 *Ut nostrum*, in Friedberg, vol. 2, cols. 509–512.

6. X 5.1.17, in Friedberg, vol. 2, cols. 738–739, 745–747.

7. 4 Lat c.8, Tanner DEC, vol. 1, pp. 237–239, incorporated into X 5.1.24 *Qualiter et quando*, in Friedberg, vol. 2, cols. 745–747.

arraignment and preliminary hearing in modern times may be advanced as the equivalent in medieval cases. However, this order need not apply in cases relating to ordinary priests, who can be removed from office by their ordinary. Canon three of the Lateran Council provided a broad foundation for seeing heresy as criminal activity and establishing the consequences for such criminality. Lateran IV anathematized every heresy and condemned every heretic. The convicts were handed over to secular authorities, although if these were priests, they first had to be degraded from holy orders according to a specified protocol. Those persisting in excommunication for more than one year were automatically condemned as heretics. Jan Hus would have been advised to this effect by his lawyer, Jan Jesenice. A number of social implications followed heresy convictions. The issue of contumacy was implied.[8] Excommunication for contumacy was legally codified, and if this produced no purgation, that is, if the defendant swore under oath his or her innocence, with corroborating witnesses, then anathema was applied on the grounds of increasing contumacy (*contumacia crescente*).[9] During the increase in criminal proceedings against suspected heretics in the thirteenth to fifteenth centuries, the inquisitorial procedure quickly replaced the older accusatory and denunciation models, and this new process clearly originated in the context of Romano-canonical law in the Middle Ages.[10] It is perhaps more accurate to say that inquisitorial procedure and the accusatory model worked together addressing different legal needs in the Middle Ages.[11] Being wary of anachronism, it can be stated that the rule of law, an evolving form of due process, and a more complex model of legal procedure emerged.[12] These were in place before the trial of Jan Hus convened. A cautionary note should be applied.

---

8. 4 Lat c.3 *De haereticis*, Tanner, DEC, vol. 1, pp. 233–235.

9. X 2.1.10 *Quum non*, in Friedberg, vol. 2, col. 242.

10. Maisonneuve is a study at once instructive and indispensable on legal procedure. More recent are Thomas Wetzstein, *Heilige vor Gericht: Das Kanonisationverfahren im europäischen Spätmittelalter* (Cologne: Böhlau Verlag, 2004); and Henry Ansgar Kelly, *Inquisitions and Other Trial Procedures in the Medieval West* (Aldershot, U.K.: Ashgate-Variorum, 2001). Winfried Trusen, "Der Inquisitionsprozeß: Seine historischen Grundlagen und frühen Formen" ZRG KA 74 (1988): 168–230, is not always reliable on the origins of inquisitorial procedure. For the accusatory system, see Vallerani, pp. 114–173.

11. Lotte Kéry, "Inquisitio—denunciation—exceptio: Möglichkeiten der Verfahrenseinleitung im Dekretalenrecht," ZRG KA 87 (2001): 226–268, but see especially Vallerani.

12. Kenneth Pennington, *The Prince and the Law, 1200–1600: Sovereignty and Rights in the Western Legal Tradition* (Berkeley: University of California Press, 1993), pp. 5–6.

Scholars examining medieval legal procedure must be careful to evaluate the subject without undue influence from modern concepts of procedural safeguards which may distort rather than illuminate and may obfuscate the range and role of the interpretation of law and due process in particular political and ecclesiastical contexts.[13] It is unwise to assume that canon law and inquisitorial procedure achieved an absolutely rigid form or that court structures were uniform in the European later Middle Ages. In practice, there was some latitude in the application of law, and court procedures varied from place to place according to a plethora of influences. Massimo Vallerani concludes, "it is difficult... to think of a unique homogenized antiheretical procedure."[14] By comparison, one can identify variations in practice and judicial process from one jurisdiction to another in places such as the modern United States. Basic to procedural law in matters of heresy are the processes described in *Licet Heli* and *Qualiter et quando*, the manner in which the church dealt with heretics as outlined in *Vergentis in senium*, and the handing over of criminally convicted priests to the secular authorities as provided for in *Novimus*.[15] In other words, *Vergentis in senium*, which considered heresy both criminal and treasonous, was the guiding legal principle in such matters at the time of the Jan Hus trial.[16] Jan Jesenice would have been *au fait* with this legal maxim.

The prosecutors of heresy were sometimes called "doctors of souls."[17] They adopted existing process. It is not true that accused heretics were regarded as guilty until proven innocent.[18] As we shall see, quite the opposite legal doctrine was advocated by canonists more than a century before Hus. The standard procedure—the *ordo iudiciarius*—consisted of several

---

13. Provvidente, p. 122; and Jacques Chiffoleau, "Le crime de majesté, la politique et l'extraordinaire: Note sur les collections érudites de procès de lèse majesté du XVIIᵉ siècle et leurs exemples médiévaux," in *Les procès politiques (XIVᵉ–XVIIᵉ siècles)*, ed. Yves-Marie Bercé (Rome: Collection de l'Ecole Française de Rome, 2007), pp. 577–662.

14. Vallerani, p. 42; Daniel Hobbins, *The Trial of Joan of Arc* (Cambridge, Mass.: Harvard University Press, 2005), p. 17; and Willibald M. Plöchl, *Geschichte des Kirchenrecht*, 5 vols. (Vienna: Verlag Herold, 1953–1969), vol. 2, p. 309, for a detailed description of canon law courts.

15. X 5.40.27 *Novimus expedire*, in Friedberg, vol. 2, col. 924.

16. Kenneth Pennington, "*Pro Peccatis Patrum Puniri*: A Moral and Legal Problem of the Inquisition," *Church History* 47, no. 2 (1978): 137.

17. Gui, *Practica*, pp. 236–237.

18. Walter Ullmann, "The Defense of the Accused in the Medieval Inquisition," *Irish Ecclesiastical Record* 73 (1950): 486.

steps according to the inquisitorial process, ranging from oaths, testimony of witnesses, the determination of a crime, the status of the accused, *indicia* (indications of criminal offense), *facti evidentia* (factual evidence), and so on.[19] This Romano-canonical legal process replaced older models and became standard procedure in Europe. It centralized judicial authority and placed legal procedure in the purview of the ecclesiastical prince. The formal petition initiating a legal process before a canonical judge was called a *libellus*. This was a writ or a valid formal accusation containing the relevant facts in the case, providing the judge with an adequate basis on which eventually to render a verdict. The *libellus* included details such as time, place, description of circumstances, and other relevant factors in the alleged crime. If anything was omitted, the case technically could be thrown out of the court as null and void. Once again, useful parallels with modern legal processes can be made.

Once a legal process began, a proper summons was issued by a judge who had jurisdiction over the accused. The judge was required to provide to the defendant, in writing, details of the charges along with an explanation of the accusations. Further, the names and testimony of the witnesses had to be supplied, and the judge was obligated to allow for objections by the deponent.[20] Legal citations were not standardized, but basic elements might appear. For example, some protocols required the name of the judge to appear in the writ; the date on which the accused was summoned, the name of the accused, and the place where the offense was committed might be noted. The summons to court, or the *citatio*, was personally delivered to the accused or attached to his or her dwelling in the presence of two witnesses. If neither delivery option was possible, the defendant might be cited orally, and in either case, there would be a specified period for response. Additional time frames might be established for making a formal defense or preparing a brief setting forth arguments for why the accused should not be condemned. Formal citations were essential in order to preclude a subsequent legal defense that the defendant had been unaware of legal proceedings.[21] That Hus retained legal counsel in 1410

19. For a comprehensive overview of the rules of procedure governing the medieval *ordo iudiciarius* between the eleventh century and 1234, see Wiesław Litewski, *Der römisch-kanonische Zivilprozeß nach den älteren ordines iudiciari*, 2 vols. (Kraków: Jagiełłion University Press, 1999).

20. X 5.1.24 *Qualiter et quando*, in Friedberg, vol. 2, cols. 745–747.

21. Carraway, pp. 105–106.

excludes suggestions that he was not conversant with legal procedure. We learn from Bernard Gui that aspects of canon law were followed properly in such matters. Once the citation had been sent out, should the *suspectus* not respond as cited, failure to appear prompted a provisional excommunication. The modern equivalent of an arrest warrant might be issued. If nonappearance persisted for more than one year, the censure became a definitive excommunication. The implications of this step extended to all persons, for no one was permitted to associate with the suspect, and all were under obligation to turn the accused over to the authorities. The initial citation could be repeated.[22]

The application of canon law with respect to heresy cases meant that secular authorities were obligated to assist in the apprehension of these ecclesiastical outlaws.[23] Failure to aid the church carried with it the burden of excommunication, interdict, and the suspicion of heresy itself.[24] It is necessary to draw attention to the fact that from the fourteenth century on, the presumption of innocence prevailed. The French canonist Jean LeMoine (ca. 1250–1313), better known as Johannes Monachus, was the first to argue that every defendant is "item quilibet presumitur innocens nisi probetur nocens" (innocent until proven guilty). The formulation is justified on the basis of a prior decretal handed down by Innocent III. The commentary on *Rem non novam* by Johannes Monachus eventually became the *glossa ordinaria* of the *Extravagantes communes* and thus was widely circulated, helping to establish crucial legal doctrine.[25] In practice, the accused could not legally be regarded as guilty or considered convicted until a verdict had been reached and judgment rendered.[26] According to legal procedure, after the preliminary

---

22. Gui, *Practica*, pp. 3–12.

23. Ibid., p. 214.

24. For the requirement, see C.23 q.3 p.c. 10 *Ecce*, in Friedberg, vol. 1, col. 775; C.23 q.5 a.c 26 *Querimonias*, in Friedberg, vol. 1, col. 810; *Glos. ord.* to C.23 q.3 c.10 (excommunication), X 5.7.9 *Ad abolendam*, in Friedberg, vol. 2, cols. 751–752 (interdict); Sext. 5.2.18 *Ut inquisitionis*, in Friedberg, vol. 2, cols. 1012–1013; and Sext. 5.2.6 *Praesidentes regimini*, in Friedberg, vol. 2, cols. 1007–1008 (heresy).

25. The decretal is Innocent III, X 2.23.16 *Dudum*, in Friedberg, vol. 2, cols. 358–359. The commentary by Johannes Monachus on *Extrav. comm.* 2.3.1 (*Rem non novam*) exists in London, British Library, MS Royal 10. E. I, fol. 214ʳ, and London, Lambeth Palace, MS 13, fols. 363ᵛ–364ʳ. I follow Kenneth Pennington, "Innocent until Proven Guilty: The Origins of a Legal Maxim," *Jurist* 63, no. 1 (2003): 104–124.

26. C.15 q.8 c.5 *Sciscitantibus vobis*, in Friedberg, vol. 1, cols. 760–761.

step of a formal citation procedure had been undertaken, the defendant was asked to take an oath. This corresponds to entering a plea during arraignment. Refusal to take an oath constituted presumption of guilt. Generally, oaths were taken, and the defendant either confessed to the veracity of the charges laid against him or her, or the defendant denied the charges. In the event of denial, the judge had to attempt to prove the charges by means of documentary evidence or on the basis of witness testimony. If there was insufficient evidence to sustain actual guilt on the charges but the witness testimony was deemed sufficient to establish *fama publica* (rumor), then purgation might be ordered. A finding of *fama publica* had to be predicated on the testimony of at least two reputable witnesses who presented their conviction and belief that the defendant was guilty of the charges. In cases of heresy, canon law permitted a wider latitude for determining "reputable witnesses."[27] While jurists such as Irnerius believed that every heretic should automatically be considered *infamia*, judges were required to establish *fama publica*.[28] This was a preliminary inquest (*inquisitio generalis*) into the reputation of the suspect or the accused, which was normally undertaken before a trial or hearing (*inquisitio specialis*) by an independent body, so that at the subsequent trial or hearing (*cognitio*), those findings might be taken under advisement for evaluation.[29] Commenting on the *Liber extra*, the thirteenth-century canon lawyer Hostiensis noted that the establishing of notoriety or bad reputation (*mala fama*) was crucial to the integrity of an inquisitorial trial. While the defendant had to swear his or her innocence concerning the charges lodged, the defendant was not obliged to swear to anything more than that. The defendant had the right to silence (a medieval Miranda protection) and, indeed, was under no obligation to respond to questions prior to formal charges being laid, that is, before the arraignment. Furthermore, the defendant had no obligation to plead one way or the other if public infamy had not been established by the court. Interrogations were recorded by notaries, and the details of depositions were taken down but not necessarily verbatim, and these

---

27. C.2 q.7 p.c.26 *Sed queritur*, in Friedberg, vol. 1, col. 489, where Gratian cites the *novella*.

28. Maisonneuve, pp. 62–63.

29. Vallerani, pp. 106, 113; and the recent study by Julien Théry, "*Fama*: L'opinion publique comme preuve judiciaire. Aperçu sur la révolution médiévale de l'inquisitoire (XIIᵉ–XIVᵉ siècle)," in *La preuve en justice de l'Antique à nos jours*, ed. Bruno Lemesle (Rennes: Presses Universitaires de Rennes, 2003), pp. 119–147.

amounted rather to a sum and substance of testimony aimed at illuminating truth as determined by the court.[30]

Defendants were permitted to supply to the court a specified number of witnesses on their behalf. A defendant could not be judged according to conscience but only on what was actually proven.[31] Ecclesiastical courts could not judge something that exhibited no manifestation. That principle laid down by Innocent II has been studied.[32] Secret defamations could not be used to initiate an inquisition. Accusations had to be public.[33] As noted, the accused underwent formal interrogatory examination, and the substance of the testimony was recorded by a duly appointed notary before witnesses. The court hoped to establish guilt by confession or by means of evidence.[34] The presiding judge had considerable discretion in terms of deciding the validity of individual witnesses.[35] Publicity was essential. In concert with that principle, the defendant had to be present when the inquisition was begun, unless the defendant absented himself or herself deliberately on account of contumacy. This became a critical factor in the Jan Hus trial, despite the fact that attorney Jan Jesenice attempted to persuade the court that Hus's presence was not necessary and should be excused. The matter of contumacy appears to have been a central consideration in the judicial procedures in heresy cases and likewise critical in processes leading to conviction and punishment. Contumacy carried the weight of conviction inasmuch as medieval lawyers and criminal courts did draw an equation between contumacy and confession. Contumacy led to conviction, and the consequences were severe.[36] Defense lawyers (procurators, defenders, or advocates) were not permitted. Here we encounter a striking difference from modern criminal proceedings, wherein each

---

30. Gui, *Practica*, pp. 188, 214, 243. See also G. R. Evans, "Notoriety: A Mediaeval Change of Attitude," *Ecclesiastical Law Journal* 4, no. 20 (1997): 629–638.

31. Johannes Andreae, *Novella super sexto Decretalium* (Venice: Philippus Pincius, 1499), on X 5.3.33, *Sicut* (5.32, no. 8), citing Hostiensis.

32. Stephan Kuttner, "Ecclesia de occultis non iudicat: Problemata ex doctrina poenali decretistarum et decretalistarum a Gratiano usque ad Gregorium PP. IX," in *Acta Congressus iuridici internationalis Romae 1934* (Rome: Apud Custodiam Librariam Pont. Instituti Utriusque Iuris, 1936), vol. 3, pp. 225–246.

33. Innocent III, decretal X 5.1.21 *Inquisitionis negotium*, in Friedberg, vol. 2, cols. 741–742.

34. Gui, *Practica*, pp. 189–191, 214–215.

35. Ibid., p. 215

36. Carraway, p. 110.

defendant has the right to an attorney, and, if necessary, defense counsel is provided by the court. Witnesses might be anonymous, and the depositions of unidentified testimonies did not need to be conveyed in full to the defendant. This also represents a difference from modern court proceedings. The court did preclude known enemies of the suspect from giving testimony.[37] In keeping with papal and canonical mandates, torture was permitted if persuasion failed to elicit testimonial confession. However, there were limits on this to the extent that physical mutilation and bloodshed were prohibited.[38] The matter of torture is tenuous inasmuch as it was prohibited in canon law with cause for considering it illegal in ecclesiastical trials.[39] The judicial sentence or the judgment of the court, called the *sententia*, could only be passed if there was confession or if the charges were sustained through due process. At this stage, the individual was considered *infamis* (infamous). This legal status (*infamia*) had social consequences.

Once a verdict of guilt had been returned, sentencing followed by means of a publicly delivered general sermon (*sermo generalis*).[40] Inquisitors were often episcopal legates, which eliminated the necessity of securing the consent of the bishop when rulings were made.[41] Repentant heretics were sentenced to any number of penalties. This might include incarceration in a prison cell, where the penitent might be chained up.[42] Heresy inquisitors did not own prisons, but many bishops did, and the latter were obliged to share their facilities with the former.[43] In some cases, we know that the decision of the court required the accused to wear special clothing as a mark of his or her crime.[44] Other court decisions mandated levying a fine or specified that appropriate penitence should be the undertaking of a pilgrimage to a place such as Rome, Cologne, Canterbury, or Santiago de

---

37. Gui, *Practica*, pp. 214–215.

38. Ibid., p. 284. Kenneth Pennington, "Torture and Fear: Enemies of Justice," *Rivista Internazionale de Diritto Comune* 19 (2008): 203–242.

39. C.15 q.6 a.c.1 "Quod vero confessio cruciatibus extorquenda non sit," in Friedberg, vol. 1, col. 754.

40. For a description of the sermon, see Gui, *Practica*, pp. 82–86.

41. Ibid., p. 30.

42. Ibid., pp. 101–102, 105, 152, 154, 159.

43. Clem. 5.3.1 *Multorum querela*, in Friedberg, vol. 2, cols. 1181–1182.

44. Gui, *Practica*, pp. 150–159.

Compostela.[45] Gui sentenced 930 individuals, and almost 900 of these judgments were to something other than death.[46] In the event of conviction, the penalty for impenitent heretics was capital punishment.[47] Handing over the defendant to secular authorities normally included the odd requirement that the convicted felon not be harmed.[48] The death penalty was often implemented. Bernard Gui tells us that recalcitrant heretics were turned over to secular authorities for execution of sentence, which generally implied burning at the stake.[49] Gui regarded the fire that consumed the physical body a metaphor for eternal fire that destroyed the soul.[50]

The medieval appeal process and ecclesiastical court system consisted of four levels: the court of the archdeacon; the court of the bishop, often called the consistory; the court of the archbishop, or provincial court; and the apostolic see. In terms of an appellate process, an appeal might be made from the court of the archdeacon to either the consistory, the provincial court or the Curia. Cases before the consistory might lodge an appeal with the provincial court or the Curia. Appeals from the provincial court might be filed with the apostolic see. But there was no legal provision for appeal from the papal court. The medieval appeal process allowed for either one of two procedures to unfold. Either the appellant could appeal to the next superior court or authority until eventually reaching the Holy See, or the appellant might appeal directly to the pope at any time in the legal process. The latter option was permissible because canonists generally agreed that the pope was *ordinarius cunctorum*—the universal ordinary. The right of appeal from the court to the pope was allowed if the defendant believed that his or her rights had been or were being violated. However, "frivolous" appeals were prohibited.[51] It is unclear exactly

---

45. Ibid., pp. 36–44, 50, 60, 94–98, 100.

46. *Le Livre des sentences de l'inquisiteur Bernard Gui (1308–1323)*, ed. Annette Palès-Gobillard, 2 vols. (Paris: CNRS Éditions, 2003), presents judgments declared during seventeen years in eighteen separate proceedings.

47. Gregory IX, X 5.7.13 *Excommunicamus*, in Friedberg, vol. 2, cols. 787–789; and 4 Lat c.8 *De inquisitionibus*, in Tanner, DEC, vol. 1, p. 238.

48. Gui, *Practica*, p. 127.

49. Ibid., pp. 218–219.

50. Ibid., p. 351.

51. Innocent III, decretal X 2.28.53 *Pastoralis*, in Friedberg, vol. 2, col. 432.

how or by what process an appeal might be adjudicated and dismissed as "frivolous." It is impossible to exclude subjective assessments. A comparison with modern appellate court procedures provides a useful means of reference. A defendant dissatisfied with the outcome of a trial may file an appeal with a higher court. Appellate courts do not retry cases, evaluate new evidence, hear witnesses, or make determinations on factual evidence in the original case. The appellate court limits itself to legal principles. Its work is concerned with finding an error on the part of the lower court that would justify overturning the original verdict. The court of appeals reviews the original process to determine if the law was properly applied and evaluates whether the court proceedings were conducted fairly. General arguments normally are limited to claims that the trial was not conducted fairly or the law was improperly applied. Thus, the appellate court is limited to a consideration of legal principles in dispute. The entire process is predicated on written arguments (called briefs), which are submitted by both sides. In the modern system, interested third parties may obtain permission from the court to file an *amicus curiae* (friend of the court) brief. After all briefs have been received, the case is scheduled for oral argument, wherein each side presents statements to the judges hearing the case. It is incumbent upon the appellant to convince the court of appeals that a legal error led to an unsatisfactory verdict at the lower court level. Modern appeals courts generally will not consider an argument based on a theory raised for the first time in the appeal. The appellate court either upholds the original verdict or orders a remand. Remand is when an appeal is successful and the matter is referred back to the lower court for retrial or reconsideration. The Curia in the Middle Ages possessed the power of discretionary review (like modern supreme courts), meaning that it could decide whether or not even to hear the appeal. It is important to recognize that defendants in medieval courts had the right of appeal.

With reference to Jan Hus, the consideration of an appellate process becomes less important, because by the end of the thirteenth century, that statute was subverted by Pope Boniface VIII, who ruled that appeals were forbidden to heretics.[52] The property of heretics was subject to confiscation, descendants of the accused were barred from holding public office, and a certain level of suspending civil rights

---

52. Sext. 5.2.18 *Ut inquisitionis*, in Friedberg, vol. 2, col. 1077.

occurred.[53] Houses previously occupied by heretics were summarily destroyed.[54] This general procedure—the *ordo iudiciarius*—had to be followed by all judges, including inquisitors. In 1179, Pope Alexander III declared that no one was authorized to engage in interdict, excommunication, or suspension apart from the provisions of the *ordo iudiciarius*.[55] Technically and legally, no special powers were afforded to judges of heresy proceedings according to medieval law. However, this point is mitigated by papal decrees relating to the power granted to inquisitors, and this must be taken into account before definitive conclusions are drawn about the legality of heresy trials.[56] What is critical according to the medieval *ordo iudiciarius* is that the judge established *publica fama* and laid specific charges against the defendant. In modern parlance, the accused has the right to a proper and fair trial with adequate representation and lawfully determined protections guaranteeing the rights of the defendant.

Of course, there are cases wherein the accused failed to appear in court in response to a proper summons. This was a relevant issue during the papal court proceedings against Jan Hus between 1410 and 1412. From the late twelfth century, we find evidence that an automatic excommunication, *latae sententiae*, could be imposed, and this was generally accepted by canon lawyers. This was a ban, without trial, and its provisions might be applied by those aware of the offense.[57] There were dissenters. The canon lawyers Placentinus (d. 1192) and Baldus de Ubaldis (d. 1400) considered conviction *in absentia* for capital crimes problematic inasmuch as, technically, such an individual might thereafter be apprehended and executed without standing trial. They urged that in such cases, an interlocutory

---

53. Gui, *Practica*, pp. 19–25, 120–123, 182–184; and Henry C. Lea, "Confiscation for Heresy in the Middle Ages," *English Historical Review* 2 (April 1887): 235–259.

54. Gui, *Practica*, pp. 59, 160.

55. Walther Holtzmann, ed., *Papsturkunden in England*, 3 vols. (Göttingen: Vandenhoeck & Ruprecht, 1952), vol. 3, p. 392.

56. On this point, see the careful study by Albert Clement Shannon, *Popes and Heresy in the Thirteenth Century* (Villanova, Pa.: Augustinian Press, 1949), pp. 48–49.

57. Relevant here is Josephus Zeliauskas, *De excommunicatione vitiata apud Glossatores, 1140–1350* (Zurich: Pas Verlag, 1967), pp. 100–110. On excommunication in general, Elisabeth Vodola, *Excommunication in the Middle Ages* (Berkeley: University of California Press, 1986); and Titus Lenherr, *Die Exkommunikations- und Depositionsgewalt der Häretiker bei Gratian und den Dekretisten bis zur "Glossa Ordinaria" des Johannes Teutonicus* (Sankt Ottilien: EOS Verlag, 1987), are useful.

sentence might be issued but not a definitive one.[58] In such matters, it seems that the relevant *consuetudo* (customary law or tradition) in a given region or jurisdiction would prevail. With the development of legal procedure between the eleventh and thirteenth centuries, the process became lengthier, and witnesses increasingly were questioned secretly.[59]

In addition to the *ordo iudiciarius*, there were a number of relevant statutes and practices pertaining to heresy trials in the medieval period. We can be confident that Jan Jesenice was fully cognizant of these laws and advised his client accordingly. The definition of heresy, which evolved and changed to some degree during the Middle Ages, always retained its core meaning. Central to the concept of heresy is the idea advanced by Jerome of human choice in making decisions determining correct doctrine. Heresy is generally understood in its Augustinian sense as erroneous doctrine, contrary to scripture, stubbornly defended.[60] Equally broad is the assumption that those disagreeing with the church could not be regarded as faithful Christians.[61] Canon legislation in its early stages as collected by Gratian in the twelfth century followed the definitions and opinions of church fathers such as Jerome and Augustine in defining heresy.[62] Previously, it was noted that the precise canonical statute outlined heresy as "views chosen by human will, contrary to scripture, publicly declared, and defended contumaciously."[63] The fourth element cannot be overstated. The matter of contumacy—"contumax in causa fidei"—plays an important aspect in late medieval heresy trials.[64] In the thirteenth century, leading theological thinkers considered heresy to exist in the denial of any article established by the church. Those engaging in such beliefs or practices were heretics.[65] According to the canonist Hostiensis, whoever refused to accept a papal

---

58. See Carraway, pp. 110–111, 115.

59. As shown by Litewski, *Der römisch-kanonische Zivilprozeß.*

60. Augustine, *De utilitate credendi*, in CSEL, vol. 25.1, pp. 37–40.

61. Gregory VII, *Dictatus papae*, in *Das Register Gregors VII*, ed. Erich Caspar, in MGH, *Epistolae*, vol. 2, pp. 201–208.

62. C.24 q.3 c.27 *Heresis grece* and C.24 q.3 c.31 *Qui in ecclesia*, in Friedberg, vol. 1, cols. 997–998. See also Anders Winroth, *The Making of Gratian's Decretum* (Cambridge, U.K.: Cambridge University Press, 2000), pp. 34–76.

63. C.24 q.3 c.26 *Inter heresim*, in Friedberg, vol. 1, col. 997.

64. Gui, *Practica*, p. 285.

65. Thomas Aquinas, *Summa theologica*, vol. 4, 2a, 2ae, q. xi, art. ii, *ad tert.*, p. 72.

decretal was a heretic, and a Christian who doubted aspects of the faith might be denounced as heretical, even if that doubt resulted in only slight deviation from accepted teaching. By the thirteenth century, medieval law considered deviation of any margin sufficient to justify a charge of heresy.[66] Thirteenth-century canonists elaborated the idea of heresy in a number of distinctions. These included perversity in terms of the sacraments, separation from the unity of the church, excommunication, error in the interpretation of scripture, inventing or following a new sect, understanding the faith differently from how it was decreed by the church, and holding malignant views of the sacraments.[67] Any of these issues indicated heresy. Geoffrey of Trani, another thirteenth-century canonist, added to the list the charge that removing the Roman church from the place of priority among all other churches likewise implied heresy.[68] By the same time, heretics and their followers were subjected to the ecclesiastical censure of excommunication, and this penalty can be found throughout the twelfth century.[69] Canon law rulings limited the penalty of excommunication to individuals, which grave censure bound the soul, thereby placing the excommunicate in eternal peril. The connection between legislation and the enforcement of law with respect to heresy may be located in the commentaries of the canon lawyers and in the actual legal proceedings wherein the courts prosecuted heresy suspects.

The decretal of Pope Lucius III in 1184 seems to be a watershed in the official legal campaign of the Latin church against heresy. By the end of the twelfth century, heresy became attached to treason.[70] Heretics were then subject to the new legislation and could be punished accordingly.[71] The legal ramifications of heresy extended farther. Belief in heresy or

---

66. Hostiensis, SA, 5, cols. 1529–1530. Offenders created new heresies. C.2 q.24 p.c.4 *Nouam heresim*, in Friedberg, vol. 1, cols. 967–968.

67. Ordinary gloss to the *Liber extra* of Gregory IX as compiled by Raymond of Peñafort in 1234, commenting on X 5.7.3.

68. Noted in Edward Peters, *Inquisition* (New York: Free Press, 1988), p. 63.

69. Canon 27, Lateran III, 1179; Pope Lucius III, 1184, decretal, *Ad abolendam*, in PL, vol. 201, cols. 1297–1300, with precedents from the Councils of Toulouse 1119, Lateran II 1139, Reims 1157, and Tours 1163. An abbreviated version of *Ad abolendam* appears as X 5.7.9 in Friedberg, vol. 2, cols. 780–782, where it appears incorrectly as *Ab abolendam*.

70. Innocent III, 1199, decretal, X 5.7.10 *Vergentis in senium*, in Friedberg, vol. 2, cols. 782–783.

71. Innocent III, 1207, decretal, *Cum ex officii nostri*.

in heretics was considered an offense.[72] Moreover, any person following teachings or practices already condemned as heretical automatically were subject to the same condemnation of that particular heresy.[73] The presumed relationship between Jan Hus and John Wyclif is relevant here. If convicted and found guilty, condemned heretics were handed over to secular authority for execution of sentence, since the *res iudicatae* of the church courts in such matters were observed by the secular courts. Increasingly, secular authorities were expected to seek out and exterminate heresy. All defenders of heretics were to be excommunicated. As noted, an excommunicate who remained out of communion with the church longer than twelve months automatically incurred *infamia* without the need to judicially establish the mandatory *fama publica*. This canonical provision was applied in the case against Jan Hus. Negligent excommunicates placed themselves passively in grave danger. An individual willfully remaining excommunicate for more than one year (for nonappearance) resulted in serious legal and ecclesiastical judgment. This fate befell Hus in February 1411. Legal statutes such as this were not empty threats, as we learn from the work of Bernard Gui. Failure to respond to a summons within the nominated twelve months meant that the verdict of guilt might be applied without any legal requirement of evidentiary guilt to prove the judgment.[74] Theoretically, this implied that a heresy suspect might be relaxed to the secular arm for punishment as a convicted heretic. In the rare instances when an excommunicate elected to make satisfactory purgation after the twelve months had elapsed, thirteenth-century canonists were divided on the matter. Vincentius Hispanus admitted that it was an option, while Damasus Hungarus denied this, noting that canon law mandated that after a year, no voice could be heard, which he took to mean excluded the possibility of reconciliation.[75] Authorities possessed the power to compel the denunciation of suspected heretics, and those found negligent in such duty were subject to deposition.[76] On the other hand, a trial might

---

72. X 5.7.13 *Excommunicamus* and X 5.7.15 *Excommunicamus et anathemtizamus*, in Friedberg, vol. 2, cols. 787–789.

73. C.24 q.1 cc.1–3 *Quod autem ab heretico*, in Friedberg, vol. 1, col. 966.

74. Alexander IV, Sext. 5.2.7 *Cum contumacia*, in Friedberg, vol. 2, col. 1071.

75. C.11 q.3 c.36 *Rursus constitutum*, in Friedberg, vol. 1, col. 654.

76. 4 Lat c.3, *De haereticis*, in Tanner, DEC, vol. 1, pp. 233–235. The fifteenth-century canonist Abbas Siculus (d. 1445), also known as Panormitanus or Nicolaus de Tudeschi, submitted that bishops negligent in the pursuit of heresy should be removed from office.

be declared void if the judge failed to charge the defendant formally or questioned witnesses about matters of guilt *before* infamy had been established.[77] Today, a mistrial might be declared if the judge determines that an interlocutory order has been violated, the rules of evidence contravened, or the rule of law brought into disrepute. Canonists such as Hostiensis argued for the possibility of invalid heresy trials. That point of law and the commensurate legal safeguards against abuse were invalidated by Boniface VIII in his *Liber sextus* of 1298 in two statutes. According to the first statute, *Postquam*, the opinion of Hostiensis on the invalidity of a criminal proceeding could be set aside if the defendant confessed to the charges.[78] In the second statute, *Si is*, a trial was not invalid if the defendant did not object to the proceedings.[79] By 1242, the canonist Raymond of Peñafort drew up guidelines at the instigation of the archbishop of Tarragona for the purpose of enabling authorities to deal more accurately with "the fact of heresy" *(factum heresis)*.[80] His categories of heretical depravity were incorporated into canon law.[81] Based on other legislation in the *Decretum*, if the offense was indisputable, notorious, or public or if the accused remained contumacious, the courts might proceed to judgment without a formal trial. Jurists such as Hostiensis defended this interpretation. Such legal procedure *(actiones)* was controversial.[82]

Inquisitorial procedures were outlined as early as 1248. The earliest exemplar is the *Processus inquisitionis* produced upon the order of Pope Innocent IV. This became a model for similar books during the next century.[83] Inquisitorial manuals had no official legal status. Although they were based on law, they were not legally binding. But their existence

---

77. Hostiensis, *Commentaria in Decretales Gregorii IX* (Venice: Apud Juntas, 1581), on X 5.1.24, no. 15.

78. Sext. 5.1.1 *Postquam*, in Friedberg, vol. 2, col. 1069.

79. Sext. 5.1.2 *Si is*, Friedberg, vol. 2, col. 1069.

80. José Rius Serra, ed., *Sancti Raymundi de Penyafort opera omnia* (Barcelona: Universidad de Barcelona, 1954), vol. 3, pp. 74–82.

81. Sext. 5.2.2 *Quicunque haereticos*, in Friedberg, vol. 2, cols. 1069–1070; Sext. 5.2.6 *Praesidentes regimini*, in Friedberg, vol. 2, col. 1071; and Sext. 5.2.11 *Ut officium inquisitionis*, in Friedberg, vol. 2, cols. 1073–1074.

82. C.2 q.1, in Friedberg, vol. 1, cols. 438–449.

83. Madrid, University Library, MS 53; translation in Walter L. Wakefield, *Heresy, Crusade and Inquisition in Southern France 1100–1250* (London: George Allen & Unwin, 1974), pp. 250–258.

demonstrates the application of law. Moreover, it should not be forgotten that canon law existed as a system based on precedent. The *stare decisis* doctrine ("to stand by that which is decided") is the legal procedure wherein courts and judges adhere to previous judicial rulings.[84] In the Middle Ages, the legal term was *consuetudo*, meaning that a repeated tradition or custom took on the form of legal precedent without specific legislation. This is an assumption in medieval canon law that speaks of *consuetudo* as *lex non scripta*, which is to say, "the law which is not written" or the shorthand phrase "unwritten law."[85] Inquisitorial procedure can be extrapolated from a number of extant manuals between the thirteenth and fifteenth centuries, including the *Processus inquisitionis* (1248), Bernard Gui's *Practica inquisitionis hereticae pravitatis* (1323/1324), and Nicholas Eymeric's "directions for inquisitors" (1376).[86] We have already noted a number of procedural elements enumerated by Gui. His *Practica* is an indispensable tool. Some scholars consider it a virtual *summa* of inquisitorial procedure.[87] Within its pages, we find a listing of the varieties of heresies at the end of the Middle Ages. Gui sets forth protocols for questioning potential witnesses and delineates the prerogatives and responsibilities of those conducting inquisitorial inquiries and investigations. His manual describes instructions and procedures for actual examinations. Based on his years of work as an inquisitor, the *Practica* cannot be seen as merely a theoretical guide. Altogether, Gui's manual is a useful summary of legal procedure in late medieval heresy trials.

In the text by Nicholas Eymeric, the second part of the *Directorium* focuses on the identity of heretics. Over the course of fifty-eight questions (*Quaestiones Quinquaginta Octo de haeretica pravitate ad officium Inquisitionis pertinentes*), Eymeric draws attention to the troubling history

---

84. This does not mean that medieval canon law was structured as in other modern common law jurisdictions.

85. See D.1 c.5 *Consuetudo autem*, in Friedberg, vol. 1, col. 2, where Isidore is cited; and D.12 c.11 *Illa autem*, in Friedberg, vol. 1, cols. 29–30. On the latter, there is useful comment in Rudolf Weigand, "Das Gewohnheitsrecht in frühen Glossen zum Dekret Gratians," in *Ius populi Dei: Miscellanea in honorem Raymundi Bidagor*, ed. Urbano Navarrete, 3 vols. (Rome: Università Gregoriana, 1972), vol. 1, pp. 91–101.

86. Gui, *Practica*; and Eymeric, *Directorium*.

87. Antoine Dondaine, "Le manuel de l'inquisiteur (1230–1300)," *Archivum Fratrum Praedicatorum* 17 (1947): 116.

of improper belief through the ages.[88] The existence of such manuals indicates a desire and a willingness for correct legal procedure in heresy trials. Eymeric's text might be considered the high point of the medieval inquisitor's manual.[89] From a medieval canonical and ecclesiastical point of view, heresy was a *crimen exceptum*, an exceptional or extraordinary offense or crime, which constituted a special legal category of offense considered a threat to vital social structure.[90] The classification of heresy as *crimen exceptum* is expressed in the *Liber extra* even more keenly than in the *Decretum*, which reflects the growing alarm over the spread of serious dissent in the later Middle Ages.[91] Established canonical process prevailed in western Europe until the fourteenth century.[92] The *Clementines* of 1317 authorized the adoption of summary procedure in the courts.[93] The development is sufficiently important that the statute deserves to be quoted in *extenso*:

> It frequently happens that we commit cases and order them to be processed simply and plainly without the noise and shape of a trial. The meaning of these words is disputed by many and it is doubtful how one ought to proceed. However, desiring to settle this doubt, we authorize in perpetuity with a valid constitution, that the judge, to whom we commit a case, need not complete the *libellus*, or demand the *litis contestatio* at times which include feastdays permitted for the necessities of the people, and the procedure can remain valid. He should curtail the causes of delays, cause the *litis* to be as brief as

---

88. Eymeric, *Directorium*, pp. 230–388.

89. Dondaine, p. 124.

90. Edward Peters claims that the use of the *ordo iuris* and inquisitorial procedure in the prosecution of so-called *crimen exceptum* was dubious. Its existence as a legal category made possible the elevation of any offense to the level of an extraordinary crime. See Edward Peters, "*Crimen exceptum*: The History of an Idea," in *Proceedings of the Tenth International Congress on Medieval Canon Law*, ed. Kenneth Pennington, Stanley Chodorow, and Keith H. Kendall (Vatican City: Bibliotheca Apostolica Vaticana, 2001), p. 194.

91. *Constitutis* X 2.20.45 and *Licet heli* X 5.3.31, in Friedberg, vol. 2, cols. 334–336, 760–761.

92. Pennington, *The Prince and the Law*, pp. 132–164, provides a helpful outline.

93. Clem. 2.1.2 *Dispendiosam prorogationem* and Clem. 5.11.2 *Saepe contingit*, in Friedberg, vol. 2, cols. 1143, 1200. The distinction is succinctly drawn in James A. Brundage, *Medieval Canon Law* (New York: Longman, 1995), pp. 139–140. Evidence for summary procedure can be found as early as 1255 in Pope Alexander IV's bull *Cupientes*. Paul Frédéric, ed., *Corpus documentorum inquisitionis haereticae pravitatis neerlandicae*, 5 vols. (Ghent: Vuylsteke, 1889–1902), vol. 1, pp. 123–124.

possible, repelling dilatory and frustrating exceptions and appeals, the contentious arguments of advocates and proctors, while limiting a superfluous throng of witnesses. However, the judge should not abbreviate the *litis* so as to eliminate admitting necessary proofs and a legitimate defense. We also intend by this commission that citation and the giving of oaths pertaining to calumny and malice, or of telling the truth not be restricted so that truth is either concealed or excluded.[94]

Dispendiosam prorogationem made the concept of summary procedure quite clear, while *Saepe contingit* brought together disparate aspects of summary procedure and details its constituent parts. *Saepe contingit* clarified the rules of summary procedure, especially that codified in the common legal phrase "simpliciter et de plano, ac sine strepitu et figura iudicii procedi mandamus," meaning "simply and plainly, without the noise of the usual forms of procedural order." Therefore, an abbreviated process was introduced into the canon law courts. Numerous statutes were eliminated, and objections, appeals, and witness might also be limited. The required time needed to reach a definitive judgment was reduced, while the *libellum* and holidays were further aspects of the *ordo iudiciarius* set aside by the new constitution. *Saepe contingit* strove to ratify an expeditious process while maintaining the concept of a fair trial within the medieval framework of due process.[95] Summary procedure gave the presiding judge fairly wide discretionary powers, though legal safeguards were preserved. It is possible to say that *Saepe contingit* is the single most important piece of medieval law in terms of the history of summary procedure.[96] *Saepe contingit* codified procedural rules that very nearly paralleled the modern legal doctrine of due process. While there are some inherent difficulties in using the summary procedure of canon law in heresy cases (*Saepe contingit* sought to clarify these), this did not prevent its application. Summary procedure in heresy trials provided the judge with responsibility to maintain proper procedural order, formal instructions to the participants, and,

---

94. Clem. 5.11.2 *Saepe contingit*, in Friedberg, vol. 2, col. 1200.

95. Kenneth Pennington, "Due Process, Community and the Prince in the Evolution of the *Ordo iudiciarius*," *Rivista Internazionale de Diritto Comune* 9 (1998): 9–47.

96. Stephan Kuttner, "The Date of the Constitution 'Saepe,' the Vatican Manuscripts and the Roman Edition of the Clementines," in *Mélanges Eugène Tisserant*, vol. 4, *Archives Vaticanes Histoire Ecclesiastique*, pt. 1 (Vatican City: Biblioteca Apostolica Vaticana, 1964), p. 427.

of course, the verdict. By the end of the thirteenth century, summary procedures for the inquisitorial process were legalized.[97] This meant it governed heresy trials. The theologian Jan Hus may not have known this, but the lawyer Jan Jesenice was certainly well informed. When grave presumption of guilt prevailed in heresy proceedings, there were tendencies to abbreviate summary procedure even further. To what extent due process was violated becomes a matter of dispute.

Exceptional crimes were offenses regarded as so dangerous to the community, or the faith, that once an accusation was advanced, a suspension of the traditional procedural protections allowed a defendant sometimes occurred. Thorough and sometimes ruthless prosecutorial practices were employed in order to protect the community. In instances in which authorities considered certain cases severe public security risks or in instances of the crime of lèse-majesté, summary procedure might be invoked, all previous privileges or protections revoked and stripped from the defendant, authorization for arrest granted with incarceration, and torture permitted.[98] These measures are not unlike the wide-ranging practices introduced by the American Patriot Act (2001) in the interests of national security even when such provisions come dangerously close to infringing on constitutional rights. I do not think heretics in the later Middle Ages caused the same immediate panic or social alarm as alleged witches in the sixteenth and seventeenth centuries, but the connections between the two phenomena are evident.[99] The presumption of guilt in a heresy trial remained high in the Middle Ages though not absolute. With heresy being an exceptional crime, normal rules pertaining to witnesses and testimony could be suspended upon the authority of the presiding judge.[100] For example, witness identities *could* be suppressed in heresy cases, although this was a later development.[101] Canonists such as Vincentius Hispanus thought it pernicious for

---

97. Sext. 5.2.20 *Statuta quaedam*, in Friedberg, vol. 2, col. 1078.

98. Auguste Coulon and Suzanne Clémencet, eds., *Lettres secrètes et curiales du pape Jean XXII (1316–1334) relatives à la France* (Paris: Boccard, 1967), fasc. 9, pp. 59–60.

99. Edward Peters, *The Magician, the Witch and the Law* (Philadelphia: University of Pennsylvania Press, 1978), pp. 152–153; and Sext. 5.2.8 *Accusatus de haeresi*, in Friedberg, vol. 2, cols. 1071–1072.

100. Innocent III, X 5.3.31 *Licet Heli* (1199) and clarified in the decretal X 5.3.32 *Per tuas*, 1204, in Friedberg, vol. 2, cols. 760–762.

101. Trusen, "Der Inquisitionsprozeß," p. 214.

the defendant not to be present.[102] The question of legal advocacy is a matter of significance. Early comment on this aspect of procedure made clear that lawyers were not to assist heretics in any way, under penalty of *infamia* and loss of office.[103] Shortly thereafter, a modicum of allowance seems to have entered the legal sphere, when a decretal ruled that lawyers normally were not permitted in criminal proceedings.[104] That implied an exception to the rule clause. A distinction seems to have been introduced into law. An accused heretic (*suspectus*) had the right to legal counsel, but convicted heretics did not. For legal advocates considering making their services available to heretics, the papal decretal issued a stern warning: "we strictly forbid lawyers and notaries from assisting in any way by counsel or support any heretic or those who adhere to them or believe in them or giving them any assistance or defense in any manner."[105] However these rulings and distinctions were applied, it seems clear that a defendant's right to an attorney diminished after the mid-thirteenth century in heresy processes. For example, the Council of Albi in 1254 prohibited advocates in heresy proceedings.[106] Two years later, the Council of Béziers ruled that defendants should be allowed adequate defense.[107] Later inquisitors commented that lawyers in heresy trials could be suspected of heresy themselves for defending someone accused of heresy.[108] Nevertheless, it is possible to find cases in which accused heretics did have legal council. In 1323, a defendant had been remanded to prison by the inquisitor in Tours and was not permitted counsel. An appeal overturned the court's decision.[109] There are other situations in which similar cases were not challenged or verdicts were vacated, and in

---

102. Gloss on *Qualiter et quando* 1210/12, cited in Frank R. Herrmann and Brownlow M. Speer, "Facing the Accuser: Ancient and Medieval Precursors of the Confrontation Clause," *Virginia Journal of International Law* 34, no. 3 (1994): 524.

103. X 5.7.10 *Vergentis in senium* (1199), in Friedberg, vol. 2, cols. 782–783.

104. X 5.1.15 *Veniens* (1202), in Friedberg, vol. 2, col. 737.

105. X 5.7.11 *Si adversus* (1205), in Friedberg, vol. 2, cols. 783–784. On lawyers, see James A. Brundage, "The Medieval Advocate's Profession," *Law and History Review* 6, no. 2 (1988): 439–464.

106. Mansi, vol. 22, col. 838.

107. Ibid., vol. 23, cols. 689–702.

108. Eymeric, *Directorium*, p. 565.

109. Jean-Marie Vidal, ed., *Bullaire de l'inquisition française au xiv siècle et jusqu'à la fin du grand schisme* (Paris: Letouzey et Ané, 1913), pp. 77–83.

still other proceedings, a defendant refused legal counsel.[110] In even further instances, a request for counsel was denied on the basis of legal statute.[111] By the fifteenth century, in the aftermath of the Hus trial, Pope Martin V ruled that suspected heretics could not have lawyers.[112] There is little indication even in early inquisitorial records and registers that accused heretics had lawyers.[113] This is my reading of the sources, although there are scholars who disagree on this point.[114] There were statutes in canon law effectively excluding attorneys for heretical defendants: "We grant in matters concerning heretical depravity, one may go about that business without the noise of qualifications and the appearance of lawyers and judgments."[115] In terms of incarceration, suspected heretics might be remanded pending trial or during trial, but imprisonment had the aim of being custodial, not punitive or a form of punishment.[116] One hundred years before the trial of Jan Hus, the Council of Vienne mandated that those held on criminal charges of heresy "may not be committed to harsh or close imprisonment which seems more like punishment than custody."[117] In other words, the judicial doctrine of *peine forte et dure* (severe and hard punishment) was inapplicable. Early-fifteenth-century sources declared penal incarceration illegal.[118]

---

110. The trial of Jerome of Prague at Vienna in 1410 is one example. Ladislav Klicman, ed., *Processus iudiciarius contra Jeronimum de Praga habitus Viennae a. 1410–1412* (Prague: Česká Akademie Císaře Františka Josefa Pro Vědy, Slovesnost a Umění, 1898), p. 2.

111. As in the case of Jan Hus at the Council of Constance. Novotný, *Correspondence*, p. 246. In this letter written by Hus sometime after January 19, 1415, he notes that in the presence of witnesses and notaries, his request for a "procurator and advocate" was refused.

112. *Inter cunctas*, 1418, Hardt, vol. 4, cols. 518–531; Mansi, vol. 27, col. 1213.

113. Louis Tanon, *Histoire des tribunaux de l'inquisition en France* (Paris: Bloud, 1893), p. 401.

114. For example, Ullmann, "The Defense of the Accused," pp. 481–489; and Henry Ansgar Kelly, "Inquisition and the Prosecution of Heresy: Misconceptions and Abuses," *Church History* 58 (1989): 445; and Henry Ansgar Kelly, "Inquisitorial Due Process and the Status of Secret Crimes," *Monumenta Iuris Canonici, Series C: Subsidia* 9 (1992): 408.

115. Sext. 5.2.20 *Statuta quaedam*, in Friedberg, vol. 2, col. 1078.

116. Clem. 5.3.1 *Multorum querela*, in Friedberg, vol. 2, cols. 1182. On prisons in the Middle Ages, see G. Geltner, *The Medieval Prison: A Social History* (Princeton, N.J.: Princeton University Press, 2008); Jean Dunbabin, *Captivity and Imprisonment in Medieval Europe, 1000–1300* (New York: Palgrave Macmillan, 2002), especially pp. 144–158; and Edward M. Peters, "Prison before the Prison: The Ancient and Medieval Worlds," in *The Oxford History of the Prison: The Practice of Punishment in Western Society*, ed. Norval Morris and David J. Rothman (New York: Oxford University Press, 1995), pp. 3–47.

117. Clem. 5.3.1 *Multorum querela*, in Friedberg, vol. 2, cols. 1181–1182.

118. The anonymous *De carceribus*, discussed in Geltner, *The Medieval Prison*, pp. 46–47.

In practice, however, we learn from Bernard Gui, Archbishop Guillaume of Narbonne, and Jacques Fournier that prisons frequently were utilized to induce confession and in that sense were mediums of punishment in addition to being custodial.

Interrogatories were often standardized. Handbooks possessed by judges and inquisitors frequently included set interrogatories, official documents, outlines of power delegated to heresy prosecutors, and instructions for conducting heresy trials.[119] A specific example of the questioning of deponents and witnesses can be traced to the Council of Vienne in 1311–12, which published a canon, *Ad nostrum*, later found as a widely used interrogatory in German territories in the fourteenth and fifteenth centuries.[120] Occasionally, entire locales were subjected to legal deposition and evidence taken from large numbers of deponents. In Toulouse in 1245–46, between eight thousand and ten thousand witnesses are reported to have provided testimony during a heresy inquiry. Even if the figures are grossly inflated, the example indicates the wide purview of investigations into heresy. Responses to interrogatories technically cannot be added to prior charges or accusations. As previously noted, contumacy is equivalent to heresy in medieval legal opinion, and the church viewed this with as much gravity as for dogmatic deviation.[121] This is apparent in the Hus trial. Defiance of ecclesiastical authority—*contumacia*—is clearly as central a component in the crime of heresy as ideas or specific teachings that are inconsistent with received conventional orthodoxy determined by the church. Contumacy emerged as an integral element in the later medieval legal curriculum. Court records in some European jurisdictions in the fourteenth century show a high rate of contumacy.[122] The use of the ordeal was condemned in 1212 by Innocent III, although there are examples of its use persisting into the 1220s in some heresy trials.[123] Torture was permitted in cases of heresy.[124] The practice likewise had approval in

---

119. Dondaine, pp. 85–194; and more recently, Riccardo Parmeggiani, "Un secolo di manualistica inquisitoriale (1230–1330): Intertestualitè e circolazione del diritto," *Rivista Internazionale di Diritto Comune* 13 (2002): 229–270.

120. Tanner, DEC, vol. 1, pp. 383–384.

121. Johannes Teutonicus, *Si papa*, Dist. 40, c.6, "contumacia dicitur heresis."

122. Carraway, p. 101.

123. Robert Bartlett, *Trial by Fire and Water: The Medieval Judicial Ordeal* (Oxford: Clarendon Press, 1986), pp. 22–23, 39, 52, 80, 95.

124. Innocent IV, X 5.41.6 *Ad extirpanda* (1252), in Friedberg, vol. 2, col. 928, confirmed and renewed by Alexander IV in 1259 and Clement IV in 1265.

secular jurisdiction.[125] Predictably, abuses followed. Therefore, Clement V regulated its usage in ecclesiastical trials, but this did not eliminate the practice altogether.[126] It is noteworthy that inquisitorial manuals and registers seldom refer to the practice. By way of clarification, judicial torture was not punishment in the strict sense. Although it was allowed by canon law, its purpose lay in the solicitation of evidence that otherwise remained difficult to access. One might draw a parallel with the controversial practice of waterboarding employed by the United States government during the Bush administration (2000–2008) on extrajudicial prisoners in the so-called war against terrorism. For repentant heretics, the normally applied punishment was life imprisonment.[127] Inquisitorial sources often called for sentences of *carcere perpetuo* to be commuted after three years if the prisoner showed signs of repentance.[128] Thus, sentences of life imprisonment (*carcere perpetuo*) might be vacated after three years, sentences referred to as "unforgivable life imprisonment" (*carcere perpetuo irremissibile*) occasionally extended only to eight years of detainment, and even penalties meant to imply literal life sentences (*immuratio*) were sometimes known to have been commuted and were, in any event, not necessarily to be understood as having someone walled up.[129] Medieval canonists were quite clear that heretics desiring to return to the church were entitled to be heard on the matter and received, because the church had no desire to refuse those wishing to be in fellowship, and it was considered improper to deny pardon for sin to those earnestly seeking it. Those persisting in contumacy were necessarily handed over for punishment, but otherwise the truly penitent were neither abandoned nor handed over to secular authorities.

---

125. For example, the *Constitutiones Regni Siciliani* of Frederick II in 1231 and *Fuero Juzgo* of Ferdinand III in Castile in 1241, among others.

126. *Clementines*, 1317, especially Clem. 2.1.1–7 *De iudiciis* and Clem. 5.3.1–3 *De haereticus*, in Friedberg, vol. 2, cols. 1143–1156 and 1181–1184.

127. X 5.7.15 *Excommunicamus et anathematizamus*, in Friedberg, vol. 2, col. 789.

128. Iacobo de Simancas, *De Catholicis Institutionibus liber, ad praecavendas et extirpandas haereses admodum necessarius* (Rome: In Aedibus Populi Romani, 1575), p. 113; Iacobo de Simancas, *Enchiridion Iudicum Violate Religionis, ad extirpandas haereses, theoricen et praxim summa brevitate complectens* (Antwerp: Plantini, 1573), ch. 57, p. 293; and Eymeric, *Directorium*, pp. 641–642.

129. John Tedeschi, *The Prosecution of Heresy* (Binghamton: Medieval & Renaissance Texts and Studies, 1991), p. 147.

For those convicted of heresy but choosing to remain impenitent, the penalty was death by burning at the stake. This can be witnessed as early as 1197 with Peter II, king of Aragon, followed by Emperor Frederick II in 1224 and most famously by Pope Gregory IX in 1231.[130] When Sigismund threatened to drown all heretics in Bohemia in 1418, the bishop of Passau corrected the king, pointing out that the proper sentence in such cases was burning.[131] The application of the principle of burning was sometimes broad and severe. For example, there were medieval authorities who argued that if there were proven heretics in a particular city, theoretically everyone in that city might be burned.[132] During the twelfth and early thirteenth centuries, the term *animadversio debita* (debt of hatred) can be found often with reference to the punishment for heresy. The term seems rather imprecise and appears to have implied whatever penalty the local authorities deemed appropriate. It clearly did not retain a universal understanding of the death penalty. That all changed in 1231, with the publication of Gregory IX's bull *Excommunicamus*, when the term became regularized as a synonym for capital punishment.[133] There were canonists and legal authorities who disagreed with the death sentence for heresy and argued for life imprisonment as the preferred application for all heretics, penitent and impenitent alike.[134] That perspective did not gain wide acceptance, and a preference remained for the execution of the impenitent heretic. In terms of final appeal, the law allowed for this right, which was legally permissible only from the period following conviction but lapsed prior to formal sentencing. Once the sentence had been passed by the court, appeals could no longer be considered. In a modern criminal trial, of course, the appellate process does not commence until the cessation of the initial judicial procedure. It is evident that medieval canonists in general accepted existing heresy legislation.[135] There were few major

---

130. James M. Powell, ed., *The Liber Augustalis* (Syracuse, N.Y.: Syracuse University Press, 1971), pp. 7–10; and Gregory IX, 1231, X 5.7.13 *Excommunicamus*, in Friedberg, vol. 2, cols. 787–789. See also G. G. Coulton, *The Death Penalty for Heresy* (London: Simpkin, 1924).

131. An additional manuscript note in a letter sent to King Václav in *Documenta*, p. 684.

132. Johannes Teutonicus, *Glos. ord.* to C.23 q.5. c.32.

133. For example, the term is found a dozen times in Gui, *Practica*, pp. 178, 195, 219, 220, 221, 228, 305, 306, 315, 351, 352. See also Maisonneuve, *Études sur les origines de l'inquisition*, pp. 245–249.

134. Hostiensis, SA, 5, cols. 1537–1538.

135. Ibid., cols. 1528–1542.

disagreements on points of heresy legislation and summary procedure by the time Jan Hus went on trial. Those that did persist were doubtless within the purview of Jan Jesenice.

By the fifteenth century, law and procedure relating to heresy seem well defined. In terms of practice, there were mitigating circumstances. Heresy could be notoriously difficult to prove from a legal point of view, especially in terms of dogmatic deviance, and it often proved easier to identify by action. Therefore, canon law declared that heretics might be identified *de visu* (by seeing) or *de auditu* (by hearing).[136] As we have seen, heresy is relative; it can be detected, identified, or otherwise made meaningful only in relation to agreed-upon orthodoxy administered by a recognized authority. Facing those difficulties, it is important to keep in mind that inquisitors were subject to the pope and ordinarily were exempt from episcopal oversight. Inquisitors and judges in heresy trials might proceed against suspects without waiting for formal accusations to be advanced. In other words, the *ordo iudiciarius* did not apply.[137] Pierre Cauchon, bishop of Beauvais and canon lawyer, served as chief judge in the 1431 Joan of Arc trial. If Cauchon violated trial procedures, he seemed unaware of this, and even more notably, the bevy of canonists and legal experts in Rouen also seemed oblivious.[138] One might argue for a conspiracy to contravene law and legal procedure in the interests of a speedy conviction, but this argument seems suspect. The motivations for the appellate verdict twenty-five years later are a separate consideration. Irregularities in criminal procedures against heretics are evident. In many cases defamation is asserted but not proven. The suspect is arrested, imprisoned, and sometimes interrogated before formal charges have been laid. In many instances there is no explanation of defenses or opportunity to call defense counsel, subpoena witnesses, or present evidence to rebut the charges. Judges may order purgation without evidential proof of guilt or the establishing of ill fame. In the records of medieval history, there is plenty of legal history and procedural precedent for these judicial irregularities, which sitting judges and attending jurists did not regard as problematic. In an examination of

---

136. X 2.20.27 *Praeterea quum*, in Friedberg, vol. 2, col. 324.

137. Point made by James Given, *Inquisition and Medieval Society: Power, Discipline, and Resistance in Languedoc* (Ithaca, N.Y.: Cornell University Press, 1997), p. 15.

138. The best source is François Neveux, *L'évêque Pierre Cauchon* (Paris: Denoël, 1987).

nearly a dozen treatises on the prosecution of heresy, a tendency toward legal deviation can be seen. In a modern criminal court case, a mistrial would almost certainly be declared, or, failing that, the judicial verdict would be referred to a court of appeals based on a writ of mandamus. Of the sources in question, the earlier treatises seem perfectly in accord with the *ordo iudiciarius*, but the later ones appear to have embraced procedural innovations that fall outside the guidelines of the *ordo iudiciarius*.[139] Moreover, later canon law accepted that since the pope held and controlled all law in the "chamber of his heart," theoretically, he could alter or modify existing law as he determined proper.[140] Since God is the source of all power, then by extension, so is the vicar of Christ.[141] In certain jurisdictions, the administration of justice came under the firm control of papal legates.[142] Controversy over the decretal of Boniface VIII aside, there is reasonable doubt that proper procedure achieved Europe-wide status and may be found in regular and uniform application. The pervasive presence of canon law can be established, but evidence is lacking to prove that a modicum of orthodoxy existed on the matter of inquisitorial procedure. Any study of trials in the thirteenth through the fifteenth centuries reveals variations in practice and application. The variants can be traced to time and place, custom, episcopal presence, and reliance on one inquisitorial tradition or another. It is apparent that the rights or powers of judges in 1230 were different from those in 1300.[143] Even if the assumption of universal procedure could be established, the question remains: is judicial irregularity necessarily legal invalidity? One of the consequences of *Ad abolendam* and *Vergentis in senium* in cases where priests or the religious came under condemnation for heresy was degradation from holy orders.[144] This meant specifically the loss of *privilegium fori*, the right to trial in an ecclesiastical court, and *privilegium canonis*, the right to special protection. No longer could there be privilege in terms of shielding from secular authorities. Under

---

139. Dondaine, pp. 85–194.

140. Sext. 1.2.1 *Licet Romanus pontifex*, in Friedberg, vol. 2, col. 937.

141. Hostiensis, SA, 5, col. 1533.

142. Vallerani, p. 304.

143. Dondaine, p. 86.

144. X 5.7.9 and X 5.7.10, in Friedberg, vol. 2, cols. 780–783.

canon law, the condemnation of a priest necessitated the presence of six bishops.[145] The ritual of degradation was carried out in the presence of secular officials, indicating that *privilegium fori* and *privilegium canonis* were now forfeit, and the convicted priest was thereby stripped of holy orders, cast out of the church, and handed over to Satan.[146] Bishops would be present as witnesses during this solemn assembly.[147] Earlier, the church took the view that it did not, and could not, judge hidden offenses—"ecclesia de occultis non judicat." With the introduction of the inquisitorial procedure and use in heresy trials, the church did reverse this policy in practice and began to judge in this area. In part, this is because inquisitorial method deviated from the *ordo* by virtue of a trial that did not require an accuser, that was predicated upon the notion of *fama*, and in which facts or criminal activity could be established by a judge by whatever means possible, thereafter proceeding to punishment. In other words, by definition, inquisitorial procedure was *extra ordinem* and contrary to civil law.[148]

Excommunication was generally restricted in application to the living. However, the crime of heresy presented an exception to that rule. Canon law allowed for the posthumous condemnation of those considered and judged heretical by the church.[149] At the head of the relevant canon, the statement is unambiguous that even after death, heretics may be excommunicated. Cardinal Robert Courson (d. 1219) wrote on the matter of posthumous condemnations.[150] Moreover, by the later Middle Ages, the canonical allowance for such judgments had significant support from

145. Erwin Jacobi, "Der Prozeß im Decretum Gratiani und bei den ältesten Dekretisten," ZRG KA 3 (1913): 223–343, but especially 241–244, where he delineates the relevant passages in legal sources.

146. C.11 q.3 c.32 *Omnis Christianus*, in Friedberg, vol. 1, col. 653.

147. On the cooperation of ecclesiastical and secular courts in this matter, see Bernhard Schimmelpfennig, "Die Absetzung von Klerikern in Recht und Ritus vornehmlich des 13. und 14. Jahrhunderts," in *Proceedings of the Fifth International Congress of Medieval Canon Law*, ed. Stephan Kuttner and Kenneth Pennington (Vatican City: Biblioteca Apostolica Vaticana, 1980), pp. 517–532, but especially pp. 517–521.

148. Vallerani, pp. 101–102, 228–230.

149. C.24 q.2 c.6 *Sane profertur*, in Friedberg, vol. 1, cols. 986–987.

150. Relevant passages from his *Summa* have been edited in J. M. M. H. Thijssen, "Master Amalric and the Amalricians: Inquisitorial Procedure and the Suppression of Heresy at the University of Paris," *Speculum* 71 (1996): 61–5.

consuetudo, and the annals of Christian history reveal numerous examples of this practice from the late antique period to the fifteenth century.

Paramount in the juridical prosecution of heresy and the guiding principle in its legal procedures remained papal authority.[151] There were two notable exceptions. The first consisted in the procedures latent in the conciliar challenges of the fifteenth century. On account of the papal schism, the sovereignty of the general council seemed certain.[152] This applied especially to the Councils of Pisa (1409) and Constance (1414–1418). This did not mean that councils innovated legal precedent or procedure when it came to the matter of heresy. However, declarations such as *Haec Sancta*, promulgated at Constance, transferred ultimate authority from the papal office to a general council. *Haec Sancta* was a solution prompted by an extraordinary situation posing great danger to the Latin church. Thus, *Haec Sancta* should be viewed as an emergency measure, although, of course, differences of opinion on this remain. The other exception to the rule relates to the soundness of the sitting pope. In the first instance, the conclave of 1378, which precipitated the papal schism, is problematic. Canon law regards as illegal an election wherein a person of unsound mind is promoted. The case against Urban VI has been made on this basis. Strictly speaking, a pope may be removed from office for heresy. It is the single offense by which a pope may be deposed. There is a longer history to this point, but it appears that Ivo of Chartres and Gratian incorporated the exception-to-papal-immunity provision into canon law. A finding of heresy against a pope had to be predicated on proof that the pope was negligent in matters of personal and corporate salvation. Further, it had to be shown that the holy father proved remiss in his duties and demonstrably led others from the path to salvation. Should a pope be guilty of such behavior, he was regarded as liable to suffer forever in the eternal torments of hell. The text warns that "no mortal should presume to argue his guilt. Though [the pope] judges everyone he is not subject to judgment by anyone except if he

---

151. Boniface VIII, *Unam sanctam*, 1302, on papal authority, is a striking example. The Latin text appears in Carl Mirbt, *Quellen zur Geschichte des Papsttums* (Freiburg: Mohr, 1895), pp. 88–90.

152. A helpful overview is in Karl August Fink, "Das Konzil von Konstanz: Martin V," in *Handbuch der Kirchengeschichte*, 2nd ed., ed. Hubert Jedin (Freiburg: Herder, 1973), vol. 3, pp. 545–572.

deviates from the faith."[153] In the matter of heresy, many canon lawyers gave the pope absolute jurisdictional authority. Aspects of medieval law, legal procedure, and practice can be found vividly in the acts of the Council of Constance. In the space of thirty-nine days, Pope John XXIII was deposed on a variety of charges, including heresy, and Jan Hus was sent to the stake as a contumacious heretic.

At the same time as lawyers and theologians were drawing up legislation and legal procedure for dealing with heresy, the medieval church was engaged in prosecuting and punishing heretics.[154] The dictum *Roma locuta, causa finita est* constituted the first line of defense against the onslaught of heresy: "Rome has spoken, the question is decided." For those who objected and found the principle unsatisfying, being charged with heresy was often the result. Discussion was usually out of the question. As the inquisitor Bernard Gui put it, "one should not engage in disputation with heretics."[155] Lucas, the thirteenth-century bishop of Túy in northwest Spain, was even more blunt: "we should not listen to heretics, rather we should kill them."[156] Those who persisted in disobedience to the authority of the official church were denounced as heretical. By refusing to avoid the danger of heresy, these men and women placed themselves beyond the communion of the church. This meant naturally that they were no longer subject *de iure* to the positive provisions or protections of the law, either civil or ecclesiastical. In this posture, they automatically incurred the disadvantages of a heresy investigation and possible legal prosecution. Hence, Jan Jesenice labored to convince the court that his client Jan Hus was not, on any probable-cause suspicion, a heretic. The argument had enormous implications. In a circular letter of 1208, Innocent III placed a fine point on this matter when he wrote, "there can be no obligation to keep faith with the one who keeps not faith with God."[157] It was to this principle that Jan

153. Ivo of Chartres, Decretum, V, 23, in PL, vol. 161, cols. 329–330; and D.40 c.6 *Si papa*, in Friedberg, vol. 1, col. 146.

154. I suggested some of the following in Thomas A. Fudge, "Image Breakers, Image Makers: The Role of Heresy in Divided Christendom," in *Christianity in East Central Europe*, ed. Paweł Kras and Wojciech Polak (Lublin, Poland: Instytut Europy Środkowo Wschodniej, 1999), pp. 205–223.

155. Quoted in Malcolm Lambert, *The Cathars* (Oxford: Blackwell Publishers, 1998), p. 202.

156. Lucae Tudensis, *De altera vita*, ed. Emma Falque Rey [Corpus Christianorum Continuatio Mediaevalis, vol. 74A] (Turnhout: Brepols, 2009), bk. 3, ch. 22.

157. "Et cum juxta sanctorum Patrum canonicas sanctiones qui Deo fidem non servat fides servanda non sit," in PL, vol. 215, col. 1357.

Hus fell victim at the Council of Constance in 1414, when his imperial safe conduct from Emperor-elect Sigismund was summarily set aside and he was thrown into prison. His refusal to submit wholeheartedly to the decisions of the Council precipitated his eventual condemnation. In response, the conciliar fathers noted, "we see now how obdurate he is in his wickedness and obstinate in heresy."[158] Pertinacity in error as defined by the official church became grounds for punishment. Heresy was an ecclesiastical and legal matter, although chiefly the former. Its implications, however, were legal, religious, and social. By the time of Hus, the distinctions were blurred to the extent that stubbornness in refusing to conform to prevailing ecclesiastical authority generally resulted in denunciation on charges of heresy. The implications were summed up in the words of the canonist Huguccio, who said that heretics were thieves who robbed the church and, by extension, stole from God.[159] Outcomes were often predictable. Jesenice was faced with a Herculean task in representing Hus.

Now that heresy was defined, repression began in earnest, and prosecution and punishment followed in exacting detail. Heretics could not be tolerated; they were to be feared. If they could not be turned from the dark side of depravity, they had to be destroyed. The effective demonization of the heretic saw to that. Savary de Mauléon, a thirteenth-century Cathar in Languedoc, achieved a representative, though most unsavory, reputation:

[the] most depraved apostate, that iniquitous transgressor, son of the Devil, servant of Antichrist...worse than any infidel, assailant of the Church, the enemy of Christ...most corrupt of mortals...prime mover of heresy, architect of cruelty, agent of perversity, comrade of sinners, accomplice of the perverted, a disgrace to mankind, a man unacquainted with manly virtues, devilish— himself the devil incarnate.[160]

Operating on the conviction that heresy was a dangerous element in society, the cooperative rulers, both ecclesiastical and civil, sought ways

---

158. *Relatio*, p. 116.

159. Maisonneuve, pp. 84–88.

160. Peter of les-Vaux-de-Cernay, *Historia Albigensis*. Critical edition in *The History of the Albigensian Crusade*, trans. W. A. Sibley and M. D. Sibley (Woodbridge, U.K.: Boydell Press, 1998), p. 130.

and means to eliminate the danger. Heresy was a corrosive element. Simon de Montfort's attitude during the Albigensian crusade reflects common opinion; he asserted that should he abandon the siege of Toulouse and fail to conquer that heretical city, the church would suffer and the true faith be destroyed. So Simon soldiered on until the heretics killed him.[161] Where actual wars were not engaged, anathemas and excommunications followed frequently.[162] In some cases, special units were formed to protect rulers from the threat of heresy. For example, in 1408, Sigismund founded the Order of the Dragon at Buda. This foundation was to defend the Hungarian royal house against political enemies, but also, and with no less importance, to provide a shield against the dangers posed by pagans and heretics.[163]

The process of dealing with heretics was a gradual one, in terms of procedure, as we have seen, and also extent and intent. Before much legislation was passed and practiced, heretics were in danger of being lynched and put to death by mobs of vigilantes.[164] Peter Abelard feared this fate at both his trials. At Soissons, he recounted how he had come close to being stoned.[165] At Sens, he wisely did not argue for his views, ostensibly on the grounds that there might be a popular rising against him.[166] His fears were not unfounded. Guibert of Nogent told the story of townspeople breaking

---

161. Janet Shirley, ed. and trans., *The Song of the Cathar Wars: A History of the Albigensian Crusade* (Aldershot, U.K.: Scolar Press, 1996), pp. 164–165, 172. Simon died June 25, 1218.

162. The anathematizing of heretics has a long history. See Lester K. Little, *Benedictine Maledictions: Liturgical Cursing in Romanesque France* (Ithaca, N.Y.: Cornell University Press, 1993); or the late-fourteenth-century compilation of Serbian Orthodox Church anathemas in John V. A. Fine, Jr., *The Bosnian Church: A New Interpretation* (Boulder, Colo.: East European Quarterly, 1975), pp. 212–213.

163. For a description of the *Sáskanyrend*, see the fifteenth-century Eberhart Windecke, *Denkwürdigkeiten zur Geschichte des Zeitalters Kaiser Sigmunds*, ed. Wilhelm Altmann (Berlin: R. Gaertners Verlagsbuchhandlung, 1893), p. 130; and the statutes of the Order in György Fejér, ed., *Codex diplomaticus hungariae* (Budapest: Regiae Vniversitatis Vngaricae, 1841), vol. 10, pt. 4, pp. 682–693.

164. On these frequent occurrences, see Hermann Theloe, *Die Ketzerverfolgungen im 11. und 12. Jahrhundert, ein Beitrag zur Geschichte der Entstehung des päpstlichen Ketzerinquisitionsgerichts* (Berlin: Rothschild, 1913), pp. 23–24, 28, 31–39, 43–55, et al.

165. Related in his *Historia calamitatum*, in *The Letters of Abelard and Heloise*, trans. Betty Radice (Hammondsworth, U.K.: Penguin, 1974), p. 79.

166. Otto of Freising, *The Deeds of Frederick Barbarossa*, trans. Charles Christopher Mierow (New York: W. W. Norton, 1966), p. 84.

into the city jail in Soissons and executing heretics in 1114.[167] Ivo of Chartres essentially concluded that such activity was justified.[168] Abelard himself related how his former teacher Roscelin was nearly killed in England.[169] This was not the only time Roscelin had almost been lynched. In the eleventh century, a preacher named Ramihrdus was shut in a hut at Cambrai by a mob and the building set ablaze.[170] Heretics at Cologne in 1143 were dragged to the stake before their case had been legally resolved.[171] It is possible to argue that the earliest executions for heresy in the West were informal, in some cases carried out by vigilantes operating on the unwritten premise and *consuetudo* of lynch law.[172]

Augustine favored rehabilitation and discouraged the use of force. He advocated that healing heretics was preferable to destroying them and persuasion more profitable than coercion.[173] Bishop Wazo of Liège echoed this sentiment in the eleventh century, saying that weeds and wheat ought to grow together until the harvest.[174] Hostiensis agreed. But as noted already, such milder policies were generally eschewed by the medieval church. Heretics throughout the early Middle Ages were treated in most cases better than they were in later medieval history. In 1022, a group of heretics at Orléans were burned to death as a consequence of their heresy.[175] This

167. Guibert of Nogent, *Monodiae*, bk. 3, ch. 17, in *A Monk's Confession: The Memoirs of Guibert of Nogent*, ed. Paul J. Archambault (University Park: Pennsylvania State University Press, 1996), p. 198.

168. PL, vol. 162, col. 17.

169. *Peter Abelard, Letters IX–XIV*, ed. Edmé Renno Smits (Groningen, Neth.: Rijksvniversiteit, 1983), p. 280.

170. Pope Gregory VII expressed concern over the event. Ostensibly, Ramihrdus preached only against simony and clerical fornication. Gregory was outraged and called for the punishment "with canonical severity" of those who had burned the preacher. See his letter to Bishop Joseph of Paris in *The Correspondence of Pope Gregory VII*, ed. Ephraim Emerton (New York: W. W. Norton, 1960), pp. 116–118.

171. Our knowledge of this trial comes from a letter written by Abbot Evervin of Steinfeld to Bernard of Clairvaux. PL, vol. 182, cols. 676–680, especially col. 677.

172. See Coulton, *The Death Penalty for Heresy*, p. 2.

173. See his *Contra epistolam quam vocant fundamenti*, CSEL, vol. 25.1, pp. 193–194. The other text of note is Sermon 62 in PL, vol. 38, col. 423.

174. Anselm of Liège, *Gesta episcoporum Leodiensium*, in MGH, *Scriptores*, vol. 7, pp. 226–227; and Moore, *The Birth of Popular Heresy*, p. 23.

175. The account of the encounter between heretics and churchmen is in Wakefield, *Heresies*, pp. 74–81.

punishment and sentence were not based on legal precedent or canonical directive.[176] There seems to be no reasonable explanation for this type of condemnation. Indeed, heretics had not been executed for centuries, and there was utterly no legal jurisdiction or justification available to the authorities who pronounced and carried out the sentence. The repression of heresy in eleventh-century Orléans must be regarded as a historical anomaly.

After the events at Orléans, the official church moved to consolidate its position on the prosecution and punishment of heresy. In 1048, the Council of Rheims excommunicated heretics in Gaul.[177] A synod at Toulouse in 1119 also legislated that heretics be driven from the church and repressed by civil authorities and that their defenders treated likewise.[178] The Council of Montpellier in 1162 and the Council of Tours in 1163, under Pope Alexander III (1159–1181), established harsh measures against heresy. Authorization was given for searching out heretics, imprisoning them, and confiscating their belongings.[179] At the same time, the canons of the third Lateran Council (1179) were coming into force. Canon 27 took the significant step of declaring that all heretics and their defenders were subject to excommunication, and should they die in their heresy, such persons were denied proper Christian burial and were also not to be prayed for.[180] There are several canonical statutes on the prohibition of burying heretics in consecrated ground.[181] If heretics have already been buried, they must be exhumed, because their mortal remains pollute the ground and contaminate the church.[182] Innocent

---

176. Comments in Milan Loos, *Dualist Heresy in the Middle Ages* (Prague: Academia, 1974), p. 153; and Lambert, *Medieval Heresy*, p. 17. The definitive study of the heresy at Orléans seems to be Robert-Henri Bautier, "L'hérésie d'Orléans et le mouvement intellectuale au début du XIe siècle: Documents et hypothèses," *Actes du 95e Congrès National des Sociétés Savantes Reims, 1970* (Paris: Bibliothèque Nationale, 1975), vol. 1, pp. 63–88.

177. Mansi, vol. 19, col. 742.

178. Ibid., vol. 21, cols. 226–227.

179. Ibid., cols. 1159–1160, 1177–1178.

180. 3 Lat c.27 *Sicut ait beatus Leo,* in Tanner, DEC, vol. 1, pp. 224–225, issued by Pope Alexander III.

181. 3 Lat c.27, in ibid., p. 224; 4 Lat c.3 *De haereticis,* in ibid., p. 234; C.24 q.2 c.1 *De communione,* in Friedberg, vol. 1, col. 984; and X 3.28.12 *Sacris est,* in Friedberg, vol. 2, col. 553.

182. X 3.40.7 *De homine,* in Friedberg, vol. 2, col. 640.

III allowed that outlaws might be killed by those seeking to defend the church.[183] Jurists dealt with this question.[184] The aforementioned decretal by Lucius III in 1184 legitimized active interrogation of entire neighborhoods, if necessary, in order to determine who belonged to the heretical faction. Power was also granted to examine these individuals and then proceed to judgment. Those who favored and defended heretics were excluded from holding public office and serving as witnesses or advocates and were consigned to perpetual infamy.[185] Steps were taken to curb unauthorized popular preaching, and in some cases, penalties were handed down to people who listened to wandering preachers.[186] A papal bull forbade laypeople from preaching and mandated that secret assemblies were illegal.[187] Papal policies in the identification, definition, and prosecution of heresy find a staunch defender in the person of Innocent III.[188]

On April 1, 1198, Innocent outlined his conviction that the church required the aid of secular power and authority in order to carry out a successful campaign of suppressing heresy.[189] The following year, he enumerated his prescriptive penalties for heretical transgressors: banishment for heretics, confiscation of property, disinheriting the convicted person's heirs, and an equation of heresy and lèse majesté, while penalties for treason applied to heretics had the most serious social implication.[190] When heresy became equated with treason, new rules were introduced that some scholars regard as violation of due process. When secular lords declined to assist the Holy See in its antiheresy campaign, Innocent was prepared to invest

---

183. The decretal *Ut famae* was issued on December 10, 1203. Hageneder, *Die Register Innocenz' III*, pp. 301–302, and later incorporated into canon law.

184. Carraway, p. 125.

185. Mansi, vol. 22, cols. 476–478.

186. A Paris synod of 1207/1208 determined this to be an offense. Mansi, vol. 22, col. 683. Date given incorrectly in Mansi; correction in Grundmann, p. 66.

187. X 5.7.12 *Quum ex iniuncto*, in Friedberg, vol. 2, cols. 784–787.

188. For a helpful survey of the period, see Brenda Bolton, "Tradition and Temerity: Papal Attitudes to Deviants, 1159–1216," in *Schism, Heresy and Religious Protest*, ed. Derek Baker (Cambridge, U.K.: Cambridge University Press, 1972), pp. 79–91.

189. Correspondence addressed to the archbishop of Auch. PL, vol. 214, col. 71.

190. X 5.7.10 *Vergentis in senium* (March 25, 1199), in Friedberg, vol. 2, cols. 782–783. See Walter Ullmann, "The Significance of Innocent III's Decretal *Vergentis*," in *Etudes d'histoire du droit dédiées à Gabriel Le Bras*, 2 vols. (Paris: Sirey, 1965), vol. 1, pp. 729–741.

authority in other foreign secular rulers to intervene.[191] Initially, Innocent attempted to persuade heretics through preaching to return to the church.[192] He warned of the danger inherent in a complete refusal to consider seriously alternative ideas whereby people might unnecessarily be driven into heresy.[193] He also made efforts to reintegrate certain types of heretics into the faith by encouraging them to join reform movements within the official church.[194] The strategy worked in terms of the Humiliati and similar movements based on convictions of apostolic poverty, such as the Franciscans and the Dominicans and women's movements, were grafted into the body of the official church.[195] Ultimately, the policy failed. After Lateran IV, this ceased altogether when the Council declared that there should no longer be new religious orders created. Innocent enumerated the chief duties of the church, which were twofold: lead the erring from their errors and heresies back to the church, and preserve the faithful in the true religion. Of these two, Innocent declared the second more important.[196] In 1207, with measures to curb heresy now in place, Innocent announced the passage of a "perpetual law" on the matter of heresy. All known heretics were ordered seized, delivered to the court, and prosecuted according to prevailing legal jurisdiction. The goods of the heretic were subject to confiscation and disposal. The dwelling of the heretic was torn to the ground and future construction on that site forbidden. All defenders, followers, or persons favoring the condemned heretics were to be fined one-quarter of the value of their goods.[197] Similar measures regarding confiscation were mandated by regional councils, including the Synod of Albi in 1254. When these measures ultimately proved unsatisfactory, Innocent called for the preaching

---

191. Two early-thirteenth-century letters from Innocent support this notion. See those of May 1204 and February 1205 in PL, vol. 215, cols. 361, 526–528.

192. In 1204, he issued the bull "Etsi nostri navicula," confirming the appointment of several Cistercians to preach to Cathar heretics. PL, vol. 215, cols. 355–360.

193. PL, vol. 214, cols. 698–699.

194. Grundmann provides an overview of Innocent's attitudes toward heretics. Herbert Grundmann, *Ketzergeschichte des Mittelalters*, vol. 2, in *Die Kirche in ihrer Geschichte: Ein Handbuch*, ed. Kurt Dietrich Schmidt and Ernest Wolf (Göttingen: Vandenhoeck & Ruprecht, 1963), pp. 34–39.

195. Grundmann, pp. 89–137, on women.

196. PL, vol. 216, col. 74.

197. This is in Innocent's decretal *Cum ex officii nostri*, in Edward Peters, ed., *Heresy and Authority in Medieval Europe* (Philadelphia: University of Pennsylvania Press, 1980), p. 178.

of a crusade against the incorrigible Cathar heretics and their protectors in Languedoc. From at least the time of Lateran IV through the Hussite period, those who helped exterminate heresy through the preaching of the cross were awarded indulgences equal to those offered to crusaders waging war against the infidel in the Near East. In letters to archbishops and bishops in southern France, Innocent III refers to the well-earned rewards of the faithful through the extermination of heretics.[198] Needless to say, all such crusaders were placed under the protection of the Holy See.[199]

The fourth Lateran Council, in 1215, identified a common theme among the heretics of medieval Europe. The strictures called for by Lucius III were repeated in the canons of the Lateran Council, where they received the impetus of Innocent's doctrine, and the formulations on the repression of heresy made it clear that secular rulers were obliged to assist the church in the hunt for heretics. Those refusing to aid the church in this matter were threatened with the loss of their lands or incurred other penalties.[200] Canon law ruled in favor of this stance, making the requirement a binding obligation and having the effect, noted earlier, of turning heresy into crime.[201] There was both support and disdain for such policies.[202] Repression of heretics often was fueled by political motives.[203] There were no clear lines of demarcation between the prevailing justice system and the motives and agendas of the various parties to a conflict. Criminal proceedings, and heresy trials especially, often played out in the "highly charged political atmosphere" of the times.[204] The canons of Lateran IV as they relate to this

---

198. See, for example, letter 136, dated autumn 1204, in PL, vol. 215, cols. 426–427.

199. Similar indulgences were offered to heresy fighters in the vicariate of Bosnia in the 1230s by Gregory IX. See Fine, *The Bosnian Church*, p. 139, with references to the primary sources.

200. Mansi, vol. 22, cols. 986–990; and Maisonneuve, pp. 73–79, based on *Preterea* C.23 q.5 p.c.25, in Friedberg, vol. 1, col. 938.

201. C.23 q.4 *Tollerandi sunt*, C.23 q.5 *Circumcelliones illos*, and C.23 q.6 *Scismatici dicunt*, in Friedberg, vol. 1, cols. 899–950.

202. The correspondence of Innocent III reveals both positions. In 1205, he demanded that people in Viterbo stop sheltering heretics. PL, vol. 215, cols. 654–657. The following year, he congratulated authorities in Prato for expelling heretics. PL, vol. 215, col. 815. See the instructive article by Peter D. Diehl, "Overcoming Reluctance to Prosecute Heresy in Thirteenth-Century Italy," in *Christendom and Its Discontents: Exclusion, Persecution, and Rebellion, 1000–1500*, ed. Scott L. Waugh and Peter D. Diehl (Cambridge, U.K.: Cambridge University Press, 1996), pp. 47–66.

203. Lambert, *Medieval Heresy*, pp. 20, 198.

204. Carraway, p. 102.

matter of heresy involve several pertinent social implications. Lateran IV marked a turning point in the prosecution of heresy and the development of criminal procedure in Europe.[205] Elsewhere, ecclesiastical authorities were becoming serious about putting down heresy, and the aid of secular power was essential. Between October 14 and 17, 1234, Gregory IX sent six letters to Duke Coloman of Croatia, the Bosnian bishop, and others, demanding military action against unspecified recalcitrant Bosnian heretics. A number of antiheresy crusades were proclaimed in that region during the next decade.[206] Charges of heresy were always taken seriously. Like later specific witchcraft charges, general accusations of heresy that came to trial were most often successful prosecutions. In what presumably was a facetious comment, the Franciscan Bernard Délicieux told Philip IV in 1319 that if Saints Peter and Paul were to appear before the heresy tribunal, they would undoubtedly be convicted of heresy.[207] Unlike for certain other crimes, the right of asylum was denied to heretics. During the Middle Ages, churches and religious houses were granted the privilege of serving as sanctuaries. Criminal heretics, however, could not find shelter in the church. Indeed, the medieval church routinely cast them out both spiritually and physically.

Certainly, the great heretical battle the church had to wage in the thirteenth century was against Cathars in southern France. The work of several scholars, most notably Malcolm Lambert, proves how terribly mistaken Gordon Leff was in his conclusion that the Cathar heresy played an insignificant role in later medieval Europe.[208] Much of the antiheretical legislation dates from this monumental struggle. It was the Cathars who inadvertently shaped so much of the ecclesiastical posture vis-à-vis heresy. Canon 24 of the provincial Council of Narbonne, in 1227, regulated that there be an informer in every parish to report on heretics to the bishop.[209] We know of spies in fifteenth-century Prague filing reports on Jan Hus.

---

205. Karl Blaine Shoemaker, "Criminal Procedure in Medieval European Law: A Comparison between English and Roman-Canonical Developments after the IV Lateran Council," ZRG KA 85 (1999): 174–202.

206. Fine, *The Bosnian Church*, pp. 139, 146–147.

207. Paris, Bibliothèque Nationale, MS Lat. 4270 fol. 139[r-v].

208. Gordon Leff, *Heresy in the Later Middle Ages: The Relation of Heterodoxy to Dissent c.1250–c.1450*, 2 vols. (Manchester, U.K.: Manchester University Press, 1967), vol. 1, p. vii; irrefutably answered in Lambert, *The Cathars*.

209. Mansi, vol. 23, cols. 21–24.

The formation of this spy network played a key role in the prosecution of heresy, and the formal inquisitions later developed successfully made use of the informer system. In 1229, the Council of Toulouse adopted this idea in its first canon and applied the rule that every parish establish a committee of informers. Once heretics had been exposed and brought out into the open for punishment, their houses were to be destroyed, and anyone harboring or protecting a heretic on his or her property, whether land or dwelling, would forfeit that land or dwelling. Heretics could not be doctors.[210] If heretics voluntarily submitted to ecclesiastical authority and returned to the official faith, they were obliged to wear crosses on their garments for a determined length of time as a symbol of their former heretical sinfulness.[211] No one was exempt. Elsewhere, wealthy heretics in Italy saw their houses demolished.[212] Decisions made and passed by provincial, regional synods might have had no lasting effect whatsoever if canonists and theologians had not taken up these and other ideas and codified them. The great Catholic doctor of the Middle Ages, Thomas Aquinas, concluded his deliberations on the matter of heresy by stating that once individuals have been convicted of heresy, they ought to be immediately excommunicated and put to death.[213] On the authority of Saint Jerome, Aquinas advocated an unequivocal remedy and made his point through historical example: "Cut off the decayed flesh, expel the mangy sheep from the fold, lest the whole house, the whole paste, the whole body, the whole flock burn, perish, rot, and die. Arius was but a single spark in Alexandria, but as it was not at once put out, the whole world was laid waste by his flame."[214] We have already seen that canon law endorsed the theory of a single source of contamination. The history of heresy in the later Middle Ages bears grim witness to the fact that the rhetoric of thinkers such as Thomas Aquinas all too soon became widespread and lasting reality. The influence of Aquinas aside, as we have previously noted, death penalties for heresy were formalized in the late

210. On heretics serving in medical capacities, see Walter L. Wakefield, "Heretics as Physicians in the Thirteenth Century," *Speculum* 57, no. 2 (1982): 328–331.

211. Mansi, vol. 23, cols. 191–205.

212. Lambert, *The Cathars*, pp. 275–276.

213. *Summa theologiae*, vol. 4, 2a, 2ae, q. 11, art. 3 pp. 90–91.

214. Ibid., p. 90. For Jerome's original context, see PL, vol. 26, col. 430.

twelfth and early thirteenth centuries.[215] This helps to explain the secrecy of the activities of the suspected heretics, which often occurred surreptitiously under the cover of night.[216]

The recommendations of fourteenth-century synods (and even earlier) were implemented, groups of informers were formed, and heretics by the thousands were betrayed into the hands of their enemies. Where heretics seemed absent, they were invented, and political, social, and economic motivations and uses of heresy vied with religious and theological ones. These spiritual police forces infiltrated communities, neighborhoods, and even families in their quest to detect and eliminate all semblance of heretical inclination. Even dogs were used to flesh out the hiding places of heretics.[217] Heretics were hunted down, forced to recant, or destroyed. One convalescing heretic at Toulouse in 1234, refusing to abjure, was carried to a nearby field on her bed and burned.[218] Other heretics were spirited away under the cover of night and disposed of. In places at the end of the Middle Ages, heretics were secretly dropped into the sea, weighted down by large stones, and drowned.[219] For once, there was little gulf between rhetoric and reality. The twelfth-century canonist Rolandus said that the punishment of heretics was less vengeance than a "correction of love" (*amor correctionis*).[220] This may have been true in some cases, but generally, in the prosecution and punishment of heresy, three things were motivational factors: scandal, hatred, and fear, and the greatest of these was fear.

In medieval court cases, the "existence of a procedure at multi-levels that was constructed every time along pragmatic pathways, often backed

---

215. Coulton, *The Death Penalty for Heresy*, p. 2; for his contention that Innocent III did decree the death penalty for heresy, see pp. 2–19. The conclusion is that Innocent's decree of 1215 differs only verbally rather than substantively from the 1231 decree of Gregory IX.

216. Alexander Patschovsky, *Quellen zur Böhmischen Inquisition im 14. Jahrhundert* (Weimar: Hermann Böhlaus Nachfolger, 1979), pp. 209–211.

217. Sophia Menache, *The Vox Dei: Communication in the Middle Ages* (New York: Oxford University Press, 1990), p. 231.

218. Noted in the thirteenth-century chronicle of William Pelhisson, *Chronique (1229–1244): Sulvie de récit des troubles d'Albi*, ed. Jean Duvernoy (Paris: Editions du Centre National de la Recherché Scientifique, 1994), pp. 62–63, and translated in Wakefield, *Heresy, Crusade and Inquisition*, pp. 215–216.

219. John Martin, *Venice's Hidden Enemies: Italian Heretics in a Renaissance City* (Berkeley: University of California Press, 1993), p. 69.

220. Maisonneuve, pp. 79–80.

by ad hoc legislation or by exceptional rules that permitted the temporary adoption of particular solutions" cannot be ruled out.[221] Among the
debated issues is the question of whether the inquisitorial system worked
from a procedural point of view when applied to heresy trials. The question can be meaningfully answered only with reference to a specific or individual context.[222] By the time Jan Hus appeared before all the sage men of
Christendom at the Council of Constance, at the climax of his legal ordeal,
canon law, legislation pertaining to heresy, legal procedure, and ecclesias-
tically sanctioned practices aimed at the repression of heretics were well
established across western and central Europe. Heresy was understood as
both sin and criminal mischief within the categories of medieval criminal
definition.[223] An emphatic history of heresy hunting and prosecution in
the Czech lands formed an important context for the Hus trial. Zealous
heresy hunters such as Gallus of Neuhaus (Jindřichův Hradec) and
Peter Zwicker tried at least five thousand suspects in fourteenth-century
Bohemia. Sometimes entire communities were hereticated, and a palpa-
ble reign of terror descended on the land.[224]

The prosecution of Jan Hus as a heresy suspect did not begin in
November 1414 when he arrived at Constance. Indeed, the formal court
case had commenced more than four years earlier. Prior to this, the commission of an alleged crime had been reported. An investigation followed.
The suspect was identified. The proper authorities decided there was sufficient evidence to file charges and proceed. The defendant was cited to
appear in court. Attorneys on both sides prepared cases. The defendant
was arraigned on formal charges and given the opportunity to enter a plea.
Preliminary hearings were held. Pretrial motions were entered, interlocutory orders were handed down, a discovery process ensued, evidence was

---

221. Vallerani, p. 219.

222. Anne Gilmour-Bryson, in "The Templar Trials: Did the System Work?" *Medieval History
Journal* 3 (2000): 41–65, argues that it was successful procedurally but a failure on account
of the licit use, or threat, of torture.

223. Stephan Kuttner, *Kanonistische Schuldlehre von Gratian bis auf die Dekretalen Gregors
IX. Systematisch auf Grund der handschriftlichen Quellen dargestellt* (Vatican City: Biblioteca
Apostolica Vaticana, 1935), pp. 7–12.

224. The work of Alexander Patschovsky is crucial. See his *Quellen zur Böhmischen Inquisition
im 14. Jahrhundert*, pp. 19–23; *Die Anfänge einer Ständigen Inquisition in Böhmen ein Prager
Inquisitoren-Handbuch aus der ersten Hälfte des 14. Jahrhunderts* (New York: Walter de Gruyter,
1975), pp. 90, 130–132; and "Ketzer und Ketzerverfolgung in Böhmen im Jahrhundert vor
Hus," *Geschichte in Wissenschaft und Unterricht* 32, no. 5 (1981): 261–272.

gathered, witnesses were deposed, and testimony was recorded, while various evidence issues were handled on the basis of medieval *in limine* motions. Judges were appointed to hear the case. Hearings were scheduled. Arguments by prosecutors and defense lawyers were submitted to the court. The relationship between the defendant, Jan Hus, and his attorney, the legal expert Jan Jesenice, became crucial. A legal impasse caused the trial to be suspended and its proceedings deemed pending. All of this transpired between 1410 and 1412. Even so, the matter of the Latin church versus Hus had an immediate point of departure at least seven years prior to the convocation at Constance. Having constructed a portrait of the medieval heretic and outlined the legal theory behind the repression of heresy, we now turn to the trial of Jan Hus and its constituent parts.

4

Beginnings of the Hus Trial from Prague to the Papal Curia

> *When the existence of hidden crime is suspected there are three stages in the process of its suppression—the discovery of the criminal, the proof of his guilt, and finally his punishment. Of all others the crime of heresy was the most difficult to discover and to prove, and when its progress became threatening the ecclesiastics on whom fell the responsibility of its eradication were equally at a loss in each of the three steps to be taken for its extermination.[1]*

"IN THE YEAR of the Lord 1403, there arose a notable dissension" among the priesthood in the kingdom of Bohemia involving university masters and clerics.[2] The comment refers to the "forty-five articles" prepared against John Wyclif presented to the Prague cathedral chapter for assessment, although the chronicler pointed out that some of the controversial articles had been extracted improperly from the writings of Wyclif. The brief was submitted to the chapter's official Jan Kbel and to Archdeacon Václav Nos because the newly elected Archbishop Zbyněk, who had been appointed in November 1402 to the see of Prague, did not assume full duties until August 1403. The extracted articles from Wyclif's work were censured at a university convocation on May 28, 1403.[3] These consisted of twenty-four articles previously condemned at the Blackfriars synod in London in 1382 and twenty-one further articles selected by Johannes Hübner, a German

---

1. Henry Charles Lea, *A History of the Inquisition of the Middle Ages*, 3 vols. (New York: Harper, 1887), vol. 1, p. 305.

2. Chronicle of the University of Prague, FRB, vol. 5, p. 569.

3. *Documenta*, pp. 327–331.

university master at Prague. Jan Hus later claimed that some articles were simply manufactured by Hübner, and another university master, Mikuláš of Litomyšl, confirmed this.[4] The articles consisted of statements concerning the Eucharist, the priesthood, monasticism, aspects of ecclesiastical authority, and the nature of the church, especially with regard to wealth, property, and possessions. The tenor of the extracts was critical and negative. The initiation of heresy charges against Wyclif brought renewed heresy concerns to Prague and ultimately swept Jan Hus into an orbit spanning a dozen years. At the annual university Quodlibet in 1404 (January 3), Johannes Hübner declared Wyclif heretical and accused those reading his books as suspected heretics. Hus answered Hübner, insisting that the "forty-five articles" had been falsified and did not properly reflect the teachings of Wyclif. Apparently in reply, Hübner asserted that the pope ought to be obeyed absolutely. Hus expressed reservations.[5] The exchange seems not to have escalated, and we hear no more of the matter. Hus's initial defense of Wyclif does not appear to have had immediate repercussions. Enjoying the patronage of the new and young archbishop, Hus delivered the sermon at the annual synod of the diocesan clergy in Prague on October 19, 1405, seizing the opportunity to castigate the wickedness of priests.[6] Preaching on John 15:27, Hus argued that the characteristics of the true priests of Christ could be confirmed in matters such as poverty, chastity, obedience to the law of God, and humility. "But many of you are like dogs who should be put out of the house of God." The preacher claimed the priesthood was full of immorality, causing abomination. Concubinage was rife, and priests burned with lust so much that Hus said they constituted "unholy vessels," defiled with whores and cultivating unwholesome desires. More than this, he alleged that the priesthood had more drunks in its ranks than the general population and that greed for wealth and political power was more evident than concern for the cure of souls. He called upon Archbishop Zbyněk to purify the corrupt and unclean Prague priesthood with the "fire of prison."[7] In response, there were distinct rumblings of discontent from the chastened clergy.

---

4. Ibid., p. 178.

5. Hus, letter to Hübner, January 1404, in Novotný, *Correspondence*, pp. 11–15.

6. HM, vol. 2, pp. 39–47.

7. These denunciations were all noted in the records of a previous archiepiscopal visitation. Ivan Hlaváček and Zdeňka Hledíková, eds., *Protocollum visitationis archidiaconatus Pragensis annis 1379–1382 per Paulum de Janowicz archidiaconum Pragensem, factae* (Prague: Academia, 1973).

If moral reform concerned Hus, the salient theological issue was the doctrine and practice of the Eucharist. On June 15, 1406, in article 20, the Prague synod prohibited the Wyclifite teaching of remanence.[8] A theologically faulty mandate from Zbyněk to the same effect followed. He forbade the teaching of Wyclif's doctrine of remanence, called for affirmation of the doctrine of transubstantiation to be read from all Prague pulpits, but went astray in forbidding mention of "bread" or "wine" in discussions of the sacrament. Violators were ordered punished.[9] From this time on, the Eucharist became a flashpoint of controversy in Prague. At the autumn convocation of the synod, on October 18, 1406, limitations were placed on those who wished to preach, and it was declared necessary for all preachers to hold specific ecclesiastical authorization.[10] Canon law already provided legislation against lay preaching, and earlier synods in Prague (June 16, 1374) had mandated punishment for parish priests who allowed unauthorized preaching to occur.[11] Hus delivered a sermon in Bethlehem Chapel on July 17, 1407, in which he attacked the practice of simony and continued clerical irregularity. This homily was later a point of controversy, and certain Prague priests complaining to Archbishop Zbyněk specifically referred to this sermon.[12] Despite his opposition to the archbishop and his strident calls for reform, Hus continued to enjoy the patronage of Zbyněk and was again selected to preach before the Prague synod of the diocesan clergy on October 18, 1407. The sermon, based on Ephesians 6:14, condemned clerical vice and immorality, and we find in the homily an echo from the synodal statutes of September 18.[13] In his address to the synod, Hus urged his colleagues to join all true popes, cardinals, archbishops, bishops, abbots, priests, and friars in the front lines of the spiritual

---

8. Kadlec, *Synods*, p. 261. On Wyclif's eucharistic theology, see Ian Christopher Levy, *John Wyclif: Scriptural Logic, Real Presence, and the Parameters of Orthodoxy* (Milwaukee, Wis.: Marquette University Press, 2003), pp. 217–326.

9. *Documenta*, p. 335.

10. Kadlec, *Synods*, p. 263 (art. 7).

11. C.16 q.1 c.19 *Adicimus*, in Friedberg, vol. 1, col. 765; X 5.7.9 *Ad abolendam*, in Friedberg, vol. 2, col. 780; X 5.7.12 *Quum ex iniuncto*, in Friedberg, vol. 2, cols. 784–785; X 5.7.13 *Excommunicamus*, in Friedberg, vol. 2, cols. 787–788; and X 1.31.15 *Inter cetera*, in Friedberg, vol. 2, col. 192. Jaroslav V. Polc, "Statutes of the Synods of Prague, 1362–1377," *Apollinaris* 52 (1979): 519–20; see art. 8.

12. *Documenta*, p. 154.

13. HM, vol. 2, pp. 47–56; and Kadlec, *Synods*, pp. 266–267, art. 3.

conflict. Those who neglect spiritual duties were heretics. Simoniacs were denounced as the greatest heretics, and Hus warned offenders that all who dispensed the grace of God in such fashion were liable to the "leprosy of Gehazi" as followers of Judas Iscariot. Pluralist priests in this life were destined to be pluralists in eternal torment. The church could not be excused. "She shines resplendent in the walls of the church, and the poor go in need; she puts gold on her stones, but leaves her children naked."[14] All denials aside, the main thrust of the sermon parallels many of the themes evident in the outlawed "forty-five articles" of John Wyclif.

The impulse for reform exhibited by Hus now encountered resistance. Formal charges complaining of Wyclifism were lodged in early 1408 at the papal Curia by Ludolf Meistermann, a member of the Prague university theology faculty. Pope Gregory XII referred the matter to Cardinal François of Bordeaux, and a ruling was made on the matter that spring (April 20). Three rather firm points were made: teaching the doctrines of John Wyclif was forbidden, debating Wyclifite tenets was outlawed, and the owning of Wyclif's books was deemed illegal.[15] On an indeterminate date, Gregory XII dispatched a special nuncio to Prague, the bishop of Lodi, Jacob Balardi Arrigoni, who later appeared at the Council of Constance during the climax of the Jan Hus trial.[16] Meanwhile, Gregory XII, in a letter addressed to Zbyněk on May 15, 1408, called for reconfirmation of Bethlehem Chapel and vernacular preaching therein. The pope noted that the chapel had been founded for the purpose of preaching in the Czech language. This declaration effectively conferred on Hus's Bethlehem Chapel all the rights of a parish church.[17] It may be assumed that a request for this action had been made by Hus or one of his colleagues.[18] Hus claimed that hostile priests in Prague asked Archbishop Zbyněk to have the chapel destroyed.[19] This proved impossible as a result of Hus's popularity and royal support,

---

14. Hus is effectively quoting Bernard of Clairvaux, *Apologia ad Guillelmum Sancti-Theodori Abbatem*, in PL, vol. 182, col. 915.

15. Decision text in František M. Bartoš, "V předvečer Kutnohorského dekretu," *Časopis Českého Musea* 102 (1928): 107–108.

16. For references, see Bartoš, *Čechy*, p. 278.

17. *Documenta*, pp. 340–341.

18. Suggested by Kejř, *Husův proces*, p. 33.

19. Novotný, *Correspondence*, pp. 123–124.

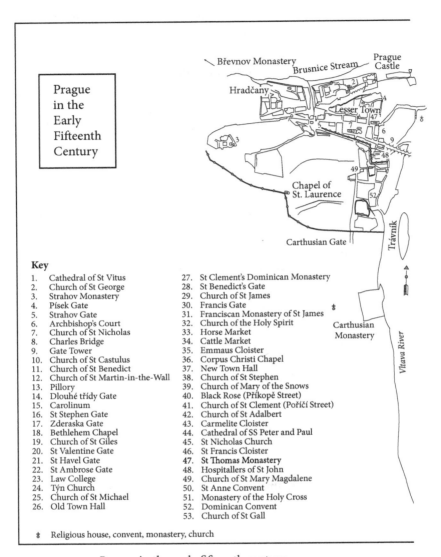

Prague
in the
Early
Fifteenth
Century

Břevnov Monastery Brusnice Stream Prague Castle

Hradčany

Lesser Town

Chapel of St. Laurence

Carthusian Gate

Carthusian Monastery

Trávník

Vltava River

Key

1.	Cathedral of St Vitus	27.	St Clement's Dominican Monastery
2.	Church of St George	28.	St Benedict's Gate
3.	Strahov Monastery	29.	Church of St James
4.	Písek Gate	30.	Francis Gate
5.	Strahov Gate	31.	Franciscan Monastery of St James
6.	Archbishop's Court	32.	Church of the Holy Spirit
7.	Church of St Nicholas	33.	Horse Market
8.	Charles Bridge	34.	Cattle Market
9.	Gate Tower	35.	Emmaus Cloister
10.	Church of St Castulus	36.	Corpus Christi Chapel
11.	Church of St Benedict	37.	New Town Hall
12.	Church of St Martin-in-the-Wall	38.	Church of St Stephen
13.	Pillory	39.	Church of Mary of the Snows
14.	Dlouhé třídy Gate	40.	Black Rose (Příkopě Street)
15.	Carolinum	41.	Church of St Clement (Poříčí Street)
16.	St Stephen Gate	42.	Church of St Adalbert
17.	Zderaska Gate	43.	Carmelite Cloister
18.	Bethlehem Chapel	44.	Cathedral of SS Peter and Paul
19.	Church of St Giles	45.	St Nicholas Church
20.	St Valentine Gate	46.	St Francis Cloister
21.	St Havel Gate	47.	**St Thomas Monastery**
22.	St Ambrose Gate	48.	Hospitallers of St John
23.	Law College	49.	Church of St Mary Magdalene
24.	Týn Church	50.	St Anne Convent
25.	Church of St Michael	51.	Monastery of the Holy Cross
26.	Old Town Hall	52.	Dominican Convent
		53.	Church of St Gall

☦ Religious house, convent, monastery, church

FIGURE 4.1 Prague in the early fifteenth century

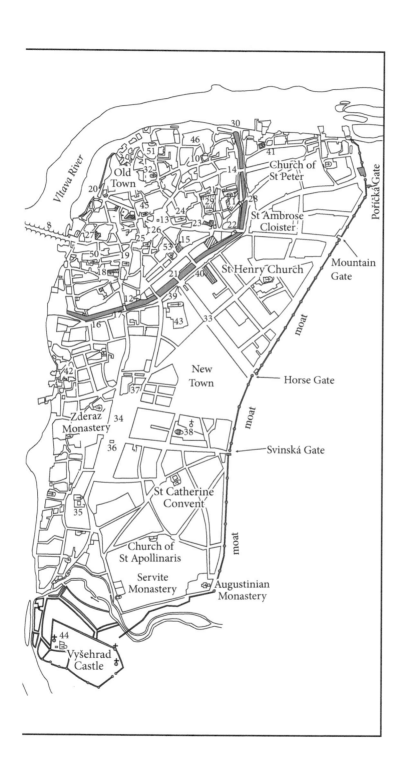

Vltava River

Old
Town

20

51
46
30
32
10
14
Church of
St Peter
41

29
43
24
11
28
St Ambrose
Cloister
13
23
22
27
26
25
15
53

50
19
St Henry Church
Mountain
Gate

18
21
40
12
39
moat
16
43
33

42

37

Zderaz
Monastery
34
Horse Gate

36
38
moat

New
Town
Svinská Gate

St Catherine
Convent
35

Church of
St Apollinaris
moat

Servite
Monastery
Augustinian
Monastery

44
Vyšehrad
Castle

Poříčká Gate

to say nothing of the pope's mandate. Later, Hus pointed out that the order to stop preaching in Bethlehem Chapel was contrary to its foundation charter, which carried with it confirmation of privilege authorized by the apostolic see.[20]

This brief triumph notwithstanding, efforts to rein in the reform movement continued apace. On May 14, 1408, university master Matěj Knín was placed on trial at the archbishop's court, before Zbyněk, on charges of holding the heresy of remanence. The case was examined by the vicar general of the Prague archbishopric, Jan Kbel.[21] The proceedings reveal that Kbel violated legal procedure previously established in *De accusationibus* by refusing, upon request, to establish the charges against Knín, which called for the judge or the court to provide to the defendant in writing details of the charges and supporting evidence.[22] Zbyněk was complicit in this violation by ordering Knín to adhere to the ad hoc procedures. Kbel told Knín he was obligated to recant heresy and undertake a formal abjuration, even if he had never held it. This is a precedent for the stance later assumed at Constance during the last stages of the legal proceedings against Hus. Knín was remanded by Kbel for further questioning by inquisitors, namely, Jaroslav of Bezměř, bishop of Sarepta, and in the end, Knín submitted. In response, an assembly of Czech university masters convened on May 24 at the house called the Black Rose in Příkopě Street in the New Town of Prague. Those in attendance included Stanislav of Znojmo, Jan Hus, Štěpán Páleč, Jan Eliášův, Ondřej of Brod, Jakoubek Stříbro, and Jan Příbram. These men passed a resolution refusing to submit to the anti-Wyclifite climate fostered by the Germans and Zbyněk.[23] This constituted open defiance. Acutely aware of the rising conflict, the Prague synod, at its spring meeting on June 15, declared that there were no heresies in the realm. At the same time, the synod forbade all preachers to make negative statements about priests in sermons (article 3), adopted Zbyněk's prohibition on remanence (article 2), and issued a warning that violators would be reported to the archiepiscopal court as heretics.[24]

---

20. *Defensio articulorum Wyclif*, in Hus, *Opera omnia*, vol. 22, p. 150.

21. *Documenta*, pp. 338–340; Chronicle of the University of Prague, FRB, vol. 5, p. 570.

22. X 5.1.27 *De accusationibus, inquisitionibus et denunciationibus*, X 5.1.24 *Qualiter et quando*, in Friedberg, vol. 2, col. 746.

23. For discussion, see Novotný, *M. Jan Hus*, vol. 1, pp. 221–222.

24. Kadlec, *Synods*, pp. 268–269.

Two weeks later, on June 30, Mikuláš called Abraham, born Martin of Velešovice, a priest at the Church of the Holy Spirit, along with the presbyter Zikmund of Jistebnice, appeared before Jan Kbel on charges of preaching without authorization. Kbel declared the matter heresy and remanded the defendants to appear before inquisitor Jaroslav of Bezměř. This business of needing authorization to preach has a longer history. At the Council of Verona in 1184, unauthorized preaching was considered heresy.[25] This harsh stricture was loosened under Innocent III, and while preaching without official approbation was forbidden and penalized in the heresy statute of the fourth Lateran Council, it no longer qualified as heresy per se.[26] Kbel's characterization of the offense is therefore questionable.[27] Regardless of the technical legal definition, Hus defended Abraham, who was released on July 1.[28] The official record says the inquisitor was Jaroslav of Bezměř, but Hus and other sources note the involvement of Mařík Rvačka in the inquisitorial role.[29] At this stage, Hus had openly defended someone in the face of rulings codified in canon law and ratified by the Prague synod. Acting on this defiance, Prague priests filed a boilerplate complaint with Zbyněk either in August or September against Hus.[30] The charges nominated three concerns, all chiefly related to his unrelenting criticism of the abuses practiced by Prague priests. Hus's reply to the charges of excessive criticism of Prague clergy was dismissive.[31] Notably, Czech chroniclers claimed Hus's troubles began when he attacked the irregular lives of priests.[32] Under pressure from King Václav, Zbyněk claimed there were no heresies in Bohemia. Hus later stated explicitly that on July 16, 1408, a special synod convened at the archiepiscopal court wherein

---

25. Mansi, vol. 22, col. 477; and thereafter in canon law X 5.7.9 *Ab abolendam*, in Friedberg, vol. 2, col. 780.

26. 4 Lat c.3 *De haereticis*, in Tanner, DEC, vol. 1, pp. 234–235.

27. See an overview of limitations on preaching and concerns with heresy in Richard H. Rouse and Mary A. Rouse, *Preachers, Florilegia, and Sermons: Studies on the* Manipulus florum *of Thomas of Ireland* (Toronto: PIMS, 1979), pp. 43–64.

28. *Documenta*, pp. 342–343.

29. Novotný, *M. Jan Hus*, vol. 1, p. 241; and *Documenta*, pp. 184–185.

30. *Documenta*, pp. 153–155.

31. Novotný, *Correspondence*, pp. 30–41.

32. SRB, vol. 3, p. 7.

this declaration was made.³³ No records exist of this convocation, but Hus refers to it in his appeal. This was altogether fortuitous inasmuch as envoys of King Václav appeared before cardinals in Pisa (somewhere between July and November 1408), asserting that an investigation in Bohemia revealed no heresies or eucharistic irregularities whatsoever.³⁴ Meanwhile, troubles in Prague continued to brew and gain momentum. Formal synods, on June 15 and October 18, 1408, issued prohibitions against remanence, repeated the 1406 synodal decision limiting preaching to those holding authorization, and banned preaching except in appointed places. The synod also passed a general ban on Wyclif, which was announced in terms of owning Wyclif's books, divulging their contents, and defending their teaching. Furthermore, the synod declared that one was allowed to preach only what was in agreement with the official church.³⁵ By this stage, Hus had lost the favor of the archbishop, and this became public when Zbyněk suspended Hus from preaching in October 1408 on account of controversy over which pope should be obeyed. Hus's rejoinder appears in a letter to the archbishop sometime late in 1408.³⁶ Ostensibly, the archbishop posted on church doors in Prague orders that Hus and his disciples and supporters were prohibited from all priestly activities.³⁷ This dispute was inflamed over the politics of allegiance during the papal schism. Zbyněk remained faithful to Gregory XII, but in 1409, the king and many university masters (including Hus) supported the Pisan policy, which meant acknowledging Alexander V.

Behind the controversy and discontent was an evident and ongoing preoccupation with heresy, especially in its Wyclifite manifestations. This continued. The first order to hand over copies of Wyclif's books was announced either in late 1408 or early 1409. The text is not extant, and therefore the date is uncertain and cannot be determined with

---

33. *Documenta*, p. 392. Hus's affirmation comes in his June 25, 1410, appeal, in *Documenta*, pp. 387–396, and Novotný, *Correspondence*, p. 63.

34. *Deutsche Reichstagsakten*, 22 vols. (Munich: Historische Kommission bei der Bayerischen Akademie der Wissenschaften, 1867–1973), vol. 6, p. 577.

35. Kadlec, *Synods*, pp. 268–270, 270–273, especially noting art. 2, pp. 268–269; art. 3, p. 271; art. 8, pp. 271–272; and art. 5, p. 271.

36. Novotný, *Correspondence*, pp. 42–44; also reported by Hus in a letter to the cardinals, dated September 1, 1411, pp. 101–102.

37. Ibid., p. 101.

any precision.[38] In response to this demand, five university students at Prague (Přibík of Húžné, Hroch of Podvek, Peter of Valencia, Michael of Drnovice and Jan of Lanstein) filed an appeal with the Pisan Curia against Archbishop Zbyněk's order to surrender Wyclifite books. The text is not extant, but it may reasonably be assumed to have been filed shortly after the initial demand to turn over all known copies of Wyclif's works.[39] The attorney for the students was Marek of Hradec. The appeal was submitted to one of the *auditores generales* (papal auditors) Heinrich Krumhart of Westerholz, who on December 8, 1409, cited Zbyněk for appearance at the Curia to answer the complaint.[40] Efforts at reform in Prague had now escalated into legal considerations.

While this was going on, the momentous decree of Kutná Hora was issued on January 18, 1409, in which control of the university passed from the German minority to the Czech majority.[41] This political move allowed the reformers associated with Hus to exert greater influence within the halls of Prague academe. Later, Hus was accused of inciting the king against the Germans. This came up in his trial as evidence of less than salutary motivations. The protracted schism at the highest levels of the Latin church continued to have direct and serious implications in Prague. On January 22, 1409, King Václav limited papal power in Bohemia, an overt policy aimed at containing residual obedience to Gregory XII, by forbidding any and all payment to Gregory and conducting any transactions with him.[42] The royal decree is similar to the 1353 statute *Praemunire* in England, which Henry VIII later used so effectively against the English clergy in 1530. The controversy generated by the king's policies prompted the lawyer Jan Jesenice to defend the decree of Kutná Hora in his *Defensio mandatum*, which appeared in February or March 1409.[43] In an effort to

---

38. Hints suggesting a time frame can be extrapolated from Kejř, *Husův proces*, p. 23; Höfler, vol. 2, pp. 123–124; and testimony given at the heresy trial of Jerome of Prague in Vienna in 1410, in Ladislav Klicman, ed., *Processus iudiciarius contra Jeronimum de Praga habitus Viennae a. 1410–1412* (Prague: Česká Akademie Císaře Františka Josefa Pro Vědy, Slovesnost a Umění, 1898), pp. 15, 23, 25, 30, 32, 33.

39. Referred to in the *Ordo procedendi*, p. 226. I cite from the edition in Novotný, *Correspondence*, pp. 225–234. A similar reference is in the Chronicle of the University of Prague, FRB, vol. 5, pp. 570–571.

40. Leipzig Chronicle, in Höfler, vol. 1, p. 11.

41. *Documenta*, pp. 347–348.

42. Ibid., pp. 348–350.

43. Text in ibid., pp. 355–363.

solve the papal schism, the Council of Pisa cited Popes Gregory XII and Benedict XIII to appear. They declined. The Council then deposed and excommunicated both pontiffs during session fifteen on June 5, 1409, denouncing the feuding popes as notorious and contumacious schismatics, heretics, and criminals who were deviant from the faith. The statement was read by Simon of Cramaud. On June 26, the Council elected Alexander V as the new pope.[44] Behind the scenes, as political and ecclesiastical struggles in Prague and at the Curia continued, the enemies of Jan Hus mobilized against him.

The first formal charges in the Hus case were put forward by Jan Protiva, priest of St. Clement's in Poříčí Street, who lodged accusations against Hus somewhere around midyear 1409.[45] The charges consisted of alleged statements made by Hus between 1399 and 1409. The accusations should have been alarming to Hus, but he appears to have dismissed their import. The charges are concerned with simony, abuses of the priestly office, and allegations of Wyclifism, but, most important, with ecclesiastical authority. It appears Jan Protiva used this method of denunciation to position Hus as a challenger of church authority and by this strategy to suggest that Hus was a disobedient heretic. It is not possible to make any firm connection, but Protiva may have had in mind conciliar mandates on the rules and limitations for bringing accusations against church administrators.[46] Protiva alleged that Hus disseminated heresies and incited people to act against the priesthood, while scorning the disciplinary powers of his superiors. Protiva's brief creates a prelude to formal heresy accusations soon to come. This was both clever and a strategic means to discredit Hus by suggesting that his activities were carried out in defiance of prevailing polices and practices in the late medieval church. The limited effectiveness of Protiva's formal accusations was bolstered by the more aggressive actions of others. If Protiva's initiative was designed to curb reform in Prague, that action was supported by the Prague synod, which on June 16, 1409, implemented Zbyněk's order for the confiscation of Wyclifite books, which were to be turned over by the feast day of Saint Prokop (July 4) for

---

44. Martène and Durand, vol. 7, cols. 1095–1098; and Mansi, vol. 26, col. 1146.

45. *Documenta*, pp. 164–169. On Protiva, see Kamil Krofta, "Kněz Jan Protiva z Nové Vsi a Chelčického 'Mistr Protiva,'" *Časopis Českého Musea* 74 (1900) : 191–209.

46. See Canon 6 *Quinam ad accusationem* of the Council of Constantinople (381) and Canon 21 *De accusatoribus* of the Council of Chalcedon (451), in Tanner, DEC, vol. 1, pp. 33–34, 97.

examination in Prague.[47] With his authority at issue, Zbyněk dispatched two envoys to the Curia—Jaroslav of Bezměř, bishop of Sarepta, and canon Jakeš Jinoch from Plzeň—around September of that year to plead his case. This delegation worked to obtain a favorable decision for the archbishop, codified in a bull issued by the Curia in December.[48] That same autumn, we find evidence that Zbyněk switched papal allegiance to Alexander V, ostensibly forced to do so by the king and for reasons of political expediency.[49] On the other hand, Hus was disinclined to buckle in the face of criticism, and, although he was questioned by the inquisitor Mařik Rvačka in September, having been ordered by Zbyněk to appear to respond to the charges filed by Protiva, he held his ground. It appears none of the charges preferred by Protiva were sustained by Rvačka. Unfortunately, the responses made by Hus to the interrogatories are not extant. At the same time, Zbyněk filed a complaint with Pope Alexander alleging that all the troubles in Bohemia were rooted in Wyclifism, the result of widespread disobedience to ecclesiastical authority. The charge completely contradicted Zbyněk's 1408 declaration, in which he stoutly affirmed, "there are no heresies in Bohemia."[50] The rising tide of antireform sentiment did little to harm Hus at this point, for he was elected chancellor of the university on October 17, 1409, and installed three days later.[51]

Having cast aside allegiance to Gregory, Archbishop Zbyněk turned wholeheartedly to the newly elected Alexander V, who advised prompt action against heresy in a bull dated December 20, 1409. The bull called for Zbyněk to appoint a commission to examine the books of Wyclif, to remove said books from the purview of the faithful, to uproot Wyclifism from his jurisdiction—"that heretical depravity and wickedness which creeps in like a cancer"—to actively punish those practicing such "damnable heresies," and to take steps to prohibit preaching except in approved locations. Moreover, the bull expressly forbade any appeal from

---

47. Kadlec, *Synods*, p. 273, art. 1.

48. Chronicle of the University of Prague, FRB, vol. 5, pp. 570–571; and *Postil*, in Hus, *Opera omnia*, vol. 2, p. 165. Both envoys later signed as witnesses to the action taken by Cardinal Colonna against Hus on August 25, 1410. *Documenta*, p. 408.

49. *Documenta*, pp. 372–373.

50. Chronicle of the University of Prague, FRB, vol. 5, pp. 570–571.

51. See text of his inaugural address in Jiří Daňhelka, ed., *Výbor z České literatury husitské doby* (Prague: ČSAV, 1964), vol. 1, pp. 105–110.

its directives upon pain of interdict, suspension, and excommunication.[52] When this decision reached Hus, he claimed that envious Prague priests colluding with Zbyněk had solicited the bull from Alexander as a deliberate strategy in a campaign to curtail his preaching activity in Bethlehem Chapel.[53] The plot thickened on Christmas Day, when Alexander appointed Zbyněk as his representative to deal with Wyclifite heresy via ecclesiastical censures.[54] From a legal perspective, this is problematic, since the auditor for the protest filed by the Prague students, Heinrich Krumhart, had cited Zbyněk to the Curia, and the appeal was pending, meaning an appellate process was now effectively subverted by the action undertaken by Alexander. An appeal was designed to suspend the proceedings of the lower court so that no sentence might be executed until the appellate court either dismissed the appeal or overruled the lower court. The papal bull effectively appointed Zbyněk to take charge of a situation in which he was a named defendant. Hus suspected bribery. At this stage, forces in Prague and at the Curia had joined against Hus, and several factors had coalesced to create a confrontation between the Prague priest and the Latin church.

The momentous December papal bull was delayed and did not arrive in Prague until around March 9, 1410, but even so, for reasons not altogether clear, it was not widely disseminated until June.[55] It was later alleged that Hus arranged for Alexander's bull to be tied to the tail of a horse and dragged through the streets of Prague in contempt.[56] The suggestion sounds more like propaganda, but we have no way of knowing whether any truth can be attached to the allegation. Acting on the provisions of the bull, Archbishop Zbyněk appointed a kangaroo commission to investigate Wyclif's works. The members, including Ondřej of Brod, Jan Eliášův, Jan Hildessen, Hermann Schwab of Mindelheim, Adam of Nežetice, and Záviš of Zap, were implacably opposed to the reforms of the

---

52. *Documenta*, pp. 374–376.

53. Novotný, *Correspondence*, p. 123.

54. Chronicle of the University of Prague, FRB, vol. 5, p. 570.

55. Leipzig Chronicle, in Höfler, vol. 1, p. 11.

56. *Liber diurnus de gestis Bohemorum in Concilio Basileensi*, in František Palacký, ed., *Monumenta conciliorum generalium seculi Decimi Quinti*, 2 vols. (Vienna: Typis C.R. Officinae Typographicae Aulae et Status, 1857–1873), vol. 1, p. 311. On the usefulness of this source, see Thomas A. Fudge, "Prokop in the Bath: Some Observations on the *Liber diurnus de gestis Bohemorum in Concilio Basileensi*," in BRRP 7 (2009), pp. 139–155.

Hus party.[57] It cannot be supposed that this commission was assembled with any intent to assess objectively the controversial writings. That said, shortly after the arrival of the papal bull, Hus appealed "from the pope ill-informed to a pope better-informed." It is regrettable that the text is not extant. The appeal is mentioned by Hus elsewhere in his writings. This was Hus's first appeal.[58] A legal anomaly followed.

Pope Alexander placed Hus's appeal on the docket of a papal auditor for action.[59] Hus's writ constituted an appeal from a papal decision. We noted previously the four levels constituting the medieval appeal process and the ecclesiastical court system. These included the courts of the archdeacon, the bishop (consistory), the archbishop (provincial court), and the apostolic see. An appellate process either moved from one court to the other or might be lodged directly with the papal Curia. There were no legal provisions for appealing from the papal court. For reasons not altogether clear, Alexander allowed Hus's appeal against his decree to be considered. Without waiting for a judicial outcome, Hus preached a sermon on March 20, 1410, in which he critiqued the archbishop's prohibition against using the word *bread* with reference to the Eucharist, set down in 1406. This was, on the part of Zbyněk, an extreme reaction to remanence and theologically problematic.[60] The appeal process was interrupted by the sudden and untimely death of Alexander V on May 3, 1410. John XXIII was elevated in his stead. Hus immediately submitted the identical appeal to John that he had submitted to Alexander.[61]

Unwilling to await passively the application of episcopal power, sometime before June 16, university chancellor Jan Šindel convened a meeting of university faculty in which a condemnation of any forthcoming action against Wyclif's books was agreed upon and made public.[62] This indicates resolve to oppose the archbishop, and we may suspect Hus's

---

57. Novotný, *M. Jan Hus*, vol. 1, pp. 400–401.

58. *De ecclesia*, p. 231; and Novotný, *Correspondence*, p. 124. The quotation appears often in Hus historiography. Where does it come from? In the document just noted, we find the phrase "a qua bulla appellavi ad informacionem meliorem ipsius Allexandri." See also the *Ordo procedendi*, p. 226. It is not a literal quote as such but rather an inferred sentiment.

59. *Ordo procedendi*, p. 227.

60. Sermon text in ST 1, pp. 482–491. See *Documenta*, p. 335, for Zbyněk's faulty eucharistic statement.

61. We learn this from Hus in a sermon for Trinity V. *Postil*, in *Opera omnia*, vol. 2, p. 320.

62. Höfler, vol. 2, p. 187.

involvement in this initiative. The reformers and university faculty had not long to wait. Zbyněk's new initiative against Wyclifism, dated June 16, was published as a synodal statute and certified by the notary Petr of Mokrsk. Wyclif was denounced as a "heresiarch" multiple times, numerous books (at least seventeen) written by Wyclif and identified by title were noted as unacceptable "on account of heresy, error, and blasphemy," and all of Wyclif's books were ordered surrendered to Zbyněk upon penalty of excommunication. Beyond this, preaching in private chapels was now formally suspended, and those ignoring the provisions of the mandate were to be indicted as suspects and summarily excommunicated.[63] The most severe penalty the medieval church could administer was the censure of excommunication.[64] Being cut off from the church was tantamount to being separated from God. The eternal implications were rather precipitous. Clearly, both pope and archbishop were serious about putting down the threat of heresy in the Bohemian province. Marek of Hradec, attorney for the students, was forced to accept the unsuccessful appeal against Zbyněk. This development was reported at the diocesan synod on June 16. It appeared Archbishop Zbyněk had triumphed.[65]

Jan Hus seems to have taken little note of such developments, and on the same day these announcements were made, he mounted the pulpit and preached a defiant sermon, pointing out that Christ preached out-of-doors and that wherever people were, preaching should occur. In other words, he had no intention of obeying the papal mandate to cease his activities.[66] With these public remarks, Hus threw down the gauntlet. Opposition of the university in Prague to Zbyněk's latest initiative remained undeterred, and on June 21, representatives asked the king to prevent the proposed action.[67] It must have galled Zbyněk that on the same day, Hus was elected leader for the 1411 Quodlibet.[68] Noting that the archbishop intended to physically destroy the writings of suspected heretics, Hus wrote a book opposing such policies.[69] The short piece reveals that Hus was disinclined

---

63. Kadlec, *Synods*, pp. 275–291.

64. C.24 q.3 c.17 *Corripiantur itaque*, in Friedberg, vol. 1, col. 995.

65. Kadlec, *Synods*, pp. 276–277.

66. Text in Sedlák, pp. 159*–164*.

67. *Documenta*, pp. 386, 734.

68. Bohumil Ryba, ed., *Magistri Iohannis Hus Quodlibet* (Prague: Orbis, 1948), p. 2.

69. *De libris hereticorum legendis*, in Hus, *Opera omnia*, vol. 22, pp. 21–37.

to avoid suspected books and material thought by some to be heretical and went on to argue that it was perilous to ignore such literature, suggesting that "one must read the books of heretics and not burn them."[70] Hus argued that real heretics were not the ones who wrote such books but those who censured the same books. Faithful Christians were obligated to be acquainted with such writings.[71] He took his thesis a step farther: "One is permitted to read and to have in one's home the books of authors some containing, in spite of certain false or heretical opinions, much truth useful to the church."[72] This approach was troubling to church authority, and later this perspective formed aspects of formal accusations leveled against Hus with the force of law. Hus appeared unmoved and replied that "one should not invoke imperial laws in ecclesiastical controversies."[73] Oddly, perhaps, there are no direct references to either the archbishop or the synod, but it is significant that Hus's text is filled with legal references, both Roman and canonical, and this may suggest the hand of the lawyer Jan Jesenice, who shortly appeared as counsel for the defense in the legal case involving Hus. The matter came to the brink of legal action when Hus announced his intention to appeal during a sermon on June 22, while at the same time, he openly condemned the decision of the Zbyněk commission investigating Wyclif's books and denounced the order to stop preaching.[74]

We have already noted the nature of legal appeals at the end of the Middle Ages. In canon law, there were quite specific rules governing the appellate process. For example, appeals were to be filed within ten days.[75] Thereafter, a determination on the validity of the decision against which an appeal was lodged should be ascertained.[76] The appellant could expect the judge to issue an *apostoli* or a considered opinion on the appeal. A formal request for the decision document had to be lodged

---

70. Ibid., pp. 21, 33–34. On the history of burning books, see the dated but suggestive essay by Louise Fargo Brown, "On the Burning of Books," in Christabel Forsyth Fiske, ed., *Vassar Mediaeval Studies* (New Haven, Conn.: Yale University Press, 1923), pp. 247–271.

71. *De libris hereticorum legendis*, pp. 30, 36.

72. Ibid., p. 31.

73. Ibid., p. 33.

74. Sedlák, pp. 168*–170*.

75. X 2.27.15 *Quod ad consultationem*, in Friedberg, vol. 2, col. 400.

76. C.2 q.6 c.31 *Post appellationem interpositam*, in Friedberg, vol. 1, cols. 477–478.

within thirty days.[77] Refusal on the part of the judge to produce the document could not derail an appeal.[78] Moreover, the execution of the sentence specified in the original pronouncement could not be implemented if an appeal was pending.[79] Further, any anathema or interdict applied after an appeal had been lodged was invalid.[80] There was, however, an exception. The legal suspension generated by an appeal had no legal effect in cases of excommunication. Even if the excommunicate had appealed the decision, he or she remained under the sentence of excommunication and was liable for denunciation per se.[81] Innocent III adjudicated that this was the case because there could be no meaningful distinction between the sentence and the execution thereof in cases of excommunication.[82] Canonists generally agreed with the provisions of the early-thirteenth-century papal decretal *Pastoralis* because excommunication constituted a spiritual offense, the penalty was confirmed by Christ, and there was no possibility of appealing from Christ. Beyond this, excommunication ultimately was only leveled against one who was contumacious, and it was impossible for a contumax to appeal.[83] There is considerable attention devoted to appeals in medieval canon law, indicating that the matter was complex and exacting. Church lawyers went to some lengths to systemize a catalogue of legal procedure governing the process.[84]

On June 25, 1410, Hus and associates—Master Zdislav of Zvířetice, who was later university chancellor; Jan of Brandýs; Beneš of Lysa; Petr of Sepekov; Peter of Valencia, Michael of Drnovice, and Jan of Lanstein—filed an appeal against the prohibition issued by Pope Alexander V aimed

---

77. Sext. 2.15.6 *Ab eo, qui allellat*, in Friedberg, vol. 2, col. 1017.

78. Clem. 2.12.2 §1 *Quamvis rigor*, in Friedberg, vol. 2, col. 1154.

79. X 2.28.37 *Ad haec*, in Friedberg, vol. 2, col. 422.

80. X 2.28.55 *Dilectis filiis*, in Friedberg, vol. 2, cols. 433–435; and Sext. 5.11.20 *Is, cui est*, in Friedberg, vol. 2, cols. 1104–1105.

81. See Eugène Vernay, *Le "Liber de Excommunicatione" du Cardinal Bérenger-Frédol précédé d'une introduction historique sur l'excommunicatione et l'interdict en droit canonique, de Gratien à la fin du XIIIe siècle* (Paris: Rousseau, 1912), pp. lviii–lxiv.

82. X 2.28.53 *Pastoralis*, in Friedberg, vol. 2, col. 432.

83. See the thirteenth-century Dominican canonist Raymond of Peñafort, *Summa sancti Raymundi de Peniafort* (Rome: Sumptibus Ioannis Tallini, 1603), 3.33.55, p. 433.

84. In the decretals of Gregory IX, for example, X 2.28 *De appellationibus* has seventy-three chapters, in Friedberg, vol. 2, cols. 409–443.

at stopping preaching.[85] In this appeal, Hus denounced decisions made by Zbyněk, claiming they breached the privileges of the university, while asserting that only the jurisdiction of the pope was relevant. Hus protested the seizure of Wyclif's books and the threat of burning them. The text of the appeal pointed out that Pope Alexander had ruled a moratorium on book burning until a decision had been made at the papal level. The appeal claimed the papal bull of December 20 by Alexander V was extracted by dishonest means and was erroneous in assuming that Bohemia was filled with heresy. Hus and his colleagues argued that the books in question had been obtained at considerable cost and effort. Moreover, there was plenty in the said volumes that could not be construed as heresy, and it was a travesty to destroy books of logic, philosophy, and mathematics. With directives such as this, Hus suggested that they might as well collect Aristotle, Averröes (Ibn Rushd), Peter Lombard, Origen, and others and burn them, too. Moreover, the command to cease preaching constituted a capital sin. There is no reason to think Hus's appeal was not executed squarely within the canonical rules for a legitimate appellate process. The appeal was formalized before a notary public in the presence of seven witnesses. This action was Hus's second appeal. This started a legal process and must be regarded as the formal beginning of the trial of Jan Hus. It is not accurate to claim that Archbishop Zbyněk initiated the legal process.[86] On the same day as the appeal, Hus preached a defiant sermon. The text has not survived, but Zbyněk reported excerpts of it to the Curia.[87] Apparently, Hus asserted that Alexander claimed many Czechs were infected with heresy. Hus went on to say that the action of the late pope fulfilled a prophecy that in the year 1409, the gospel of Christ would be subjected to persecution. Hus said he could not be sure if Alexander was now in heaven or hell, but the fact that he permitted Zbyněk to burn books constituted an offense against the faith. Therefore, Hus boldly declared that he had appealed and wanted to know if the congregation would support him. When shouts of support rang out, Hus thundered that the time had come for those

---

85. *Documenta*, pp. 387–396. Of the latter six, all are obscure except Petr of Sepekov. For details, see Josef Tříška, *Životopisný slovník předhusitské Pražské Univerzity* (Prague: Univerzita Karlova, 1981), p. 461. On the others, see Novotný, *M. Jan Hus*, vol. 1, p. 411. The last three were also among the students appealing the call to turn over Wyclifite literature.

86. Matthew Spinka, "Hus' Trial at the Council of Constance," in *Czechoslovakia Past and Present*, ed. Miloslav Rechcigl (The Hague: Mouton, 1968), vol. 2, p. 1211.

87. *Documenta*, pp. 404–406.

who wished to defend the law of God to take up swords. Hus had thrown down the gauntlet. In a later writing, he explained the rationale behind his disobedience to the directives of the pope and Zbyněk.[88] His *apologia* amounted to a statement that the commands of the pope and the archbishop contravened the law of God and therefore constituted sin. Faithful Christians were obligated to resist.

It comes as no surprise to learn that once Hus took this public stand of defiance, numerous denunciations on the grounds of heresy sprang up.[89] The archbishop wasted little time putting into practice the provisions allowed in the papal bull. With the active assistance of Zdeněk of Chrást, archdeacon of Žatec, Zbyněk conducted the burning of Wyclifite books on July 16, 1410, resulting in the destruction of approximately two hundred volumes.[90] Chroniclers noted the ensuing uproar in Prague over the book burning, which consisted of dignified protests and outright hooliganism. Considerable conflict broke out. Songs were sung against Zbyněk "everywhere in Prague," and there was much hostility between the Prague canons and Hus. It was reported that many other volumes besides the condemned Wyclif books had been destroyed. Ostensibly, those who followed Hus were assaulted by choristers who lived in the castle, and some were dragged away to suffer the indignity of an unmerciful thrashing.[91] The canon lawyer Jiří Bor was nominated as the main cause of the troubles in Prague. He was a colleague of Michael de Causis, a man who shortly thereafter emerged at the front of the Hus case. We find evidence that three years later, use of the medium of song had escalated to significant proportions. Opponents of Hus complained: "The disgusting and slanderous songs which have been recently forbidden and are offensive to the reputation of some should not be sung in the streets, in taverns, or in any other place."[92] Unrest continued. A mob invaded the cathedral and chased the priest from the altar, while six men with drawn swords entered St. Stephen's Church in the New Town and threatened the

---

88. *Výklad desatera*, in Hus, *Opera omnia*, vol. 1, p. 151.

89. Novotný, *Correspondence*, pp. 69–70, 72, 82–83, 90, 96–98.

90. Chronicle of the University of Prague, FRB, vol. 5, pp. 571–572; song text in NK, MS III G 16, fol. 18ʳ.

91. SRB, vol. 3, pp. 12–13.

92. Art. 11 in the *Confessio doctorum contra Hus*, in Jan Sedlák, ed., "Několik textů z doby husitské," *Hlídka* 1 (1911): 48–49.

incumbent priest with death. These acts occurred on July 22.[93] Perhaps surprisingly, King Václav seems to have taken exception to the archbishop's action and ordered all book owners compensated for their losses.[94] Already, on July 18, Zbyněk had excommunicated Hus as a corrupter of the faith. This was the first censure of excommunication. The writ suggested that Hus's appeal was frivolous and that the appellants were rebellious and disobedient. Moreover, these men were enemies of the faith.[95] Zbyněk's attempt to cast doubt on the appeal is questionable. The right of appeal from a court to the pope is permitted if the defendant believes his or her rights have been or are being violated. Only "frivolous" appeals were prohibited.[96] Of course, those were the precise grounds for dismissal on which Zbyněk denounced the appellate action. The pronouncement of excommunication established a presumption of offense, namely, sin or crime. Appeals were subject to judicial investigation to determine if the writ was valid and whether the original case should be upheld. Such inquiry would also produce a finding on whether the appeal was frivolous. Implicit in Zbyněk's characterization of Hus was suspicion of theological heresy, which was subject to punishment under canon law (*de iure*) with automatic excommunication.[97] Full excommunication could only be applied legally after three warnings.[98] Had there been the requisite admonitions? It is hard to say. It is possible to argue against this action on the grounds that Alexander V's bull became invalid upon his death. Indeed, Hus did not miss the opportunity in his appeal to advance that very point. He argued that everything Zbyněk had done on the authority of the papal bull was null and void. Pursuant to common law, Hus alleged, the authority behind an order expired upon the death of the one who authorized the order, except to the extent that the mandate had been put into practice during the lifetime of the one who originally authorized it.[99] Had that judgment been recognized by curial authorities, than by consequence,

---

93. Chronicle of the University of Prague, FRB, vol. 5, pp. 571–572.

94. Štěpán of Dolany, *Antihussus*, in Pez, vol. 4, cols. 417–418.

95. *Documenta*, pp. 397–399.

96. X 2.28.53 *Pastoralis*, in Friedberg, vol. 2, col. 432.

97. C.17 q.4 c.29 *Si quis*, in Friedberg, vol. 1, cols. 822–823.

98. C.17 q.4 c.21 *Quisquis inventus*, in Friedberg, vol. 1, col. 820.

99. *Documenta*, p. 392.

Zbyněk lacked proper authority to proceed, leaving his condemnation of Hus without foundation. That argument did not find traction, so the case against Hus proceeded.

Two important events followed. University faculty members, among them Hus, Jakoubek Stříbro, Prokop Plzeň, Zdislav Zvířetice, Šimon Tišnov and Jan Jičín, protested the book-burning exercise by holding a two-week-long disputation during late July and early August in which they defended Wyclif's works.[100] Hus stated the obvious by declaring that he disagreed with book burning and remained opposed to the prohibition against preaching.[101] The other development took place when Zbyněk sent new charges to the Curia against Hus and requested approval for his actions to date via his representatives Bishop Jaroslav of Bezměř and Canon Jakeš Jinoch. These and possibly other reports reached Pope John XXIII alleging that Hus was a heresy suspect and should be cited to the Roman court. The call by Zbyněk for curial intervention in the Hus case appears fueled by bribery, and the possibility cannot be ruled out.[102] The archbishop's envoys at the Curia prompted Cardinal Odo Colonna to write to Zbyněk on August 25. Since Alexander V had died, his successor, John XXIII, verbally instructed Colonna to handle the matter, with *auxilium brachii secularis* (the aid of secular authority) if needed. Appeals were strictly prohibited. The letter, which arrived in Prague on September 20, clearly reflects the assumption that Colonna approved of Zbyněk's actions, especially the excommunication of Hus, and urged further immediate action, noting that Hus must be regarded as the "author of errors" circulating in Prague.[103]

While Zbyněk and his supporters were doubtless celebrating their apparent victory, four cardinals met at Colonna's house at Bologna in August under the chairmanship of the Dominican Thomas of Udine, dean of the Bologna university theological faculty. A number of masters and doctors from Paris and Oxford universities also attended that meeting. Perhaps surprisingly to all principals in the affair, they adjudicated that the books should not have been destroyed. A notarized report of this

---

100. Ibid., pp. 399–400.

101. "Defensio libri de trinitate," in Hus, *Opera omnia*, vol. 22, pp. 41–56, esp. pp. 49–50.

102. Chronicle of the University of Prague, FRB, vol. 5, p. 571; and *Knížky proti knězi kuchmistrovi*, in Hus, *Opera omnia*, vol. 4, p. 321.

103. *Documenta*, pp. 401–408.

meeting reached Prague on November 25, 1410.[104] The moral victory of the Bologna report must have been a boost for Hus and his colleagues, but this was even more meaningfully supplemented by a variety of protests from King Václav, Queen Žofie, various Czech barons, Prague city councilors, and the university. These were sent between September 12 and October 2 to the Curia concerning the prohibition against preaching and the book burning.[105] We know from other sources that such letters were dispatched.[106] One in particular demonstrates the nature of support that Hus enjoyed in some quarters of the royal house. In this missive, King Václav defended Hus as "a faithful, devout and beloved chaplain." He insisted that the controversy about the books was nonsense, insofar as he knew that no one in Bohemia had fallen into heresy on their account. The matter should be resolved completely, since Václav made clear that the kingdom would not tolerate continued discord. Bethlehem Chapel should be allowed to continue according to its foundation charter, and Hus should be permitted to preach unhindered. Moreover, the king asked the pope to cancel the requirement for Hus to appear personally in Bologna. If charges were to be preferred against Hus, it was better for them to be heard before a competent authority in the Czech realm. Forcing Hus to go abroad to defend himself was tantamount to confounding the entire nation.[107] This last point was legally problematic; Hus had appealed to the papal court, and it was he who had thereby transferred the case out of Bohemia. Meanwhile, news of the aforementioned decision from the Bologna meeting reached Prague. When he learned of the leaked report, Colonna became very angry. We hear of details in a letter Hus wrote to an unnamed priest sometime in the spring of 1411. In this communication, Hus claimed that there was disagreement among the cardinals pursuant to his legal case. Opinion held that King Václav should resolve the matter, and one of Hus's attorneys, Marek of Hradec, advised John XXIII that it would be desirable if the Hus case was referred to another cardinal.[108] The opinion of the Bologna doctors seems to have been blown out

---

104. Ibid., pp. 426–428.

105. Ibid., pp. 409–415, 422–425. The reliability of these texts is qualified in Fudge, *Jan Hus*, p. 117, with reference to Czech scholarship.

106. Jesenice, *Repetitio*, pp. 408–419; and *Ordo procedendi*, pp. 227–228.

107. Letter of late September or early October, *Documenta*, pp. 422–423.

108. Novotný, *Correspondence*, p. 89.

of proportion by the reform party in Prague. It had no binding authority and no official weight. As part of his support for the reform effort, Prague university chancellor Jan Šindel wrote to John XXIII on September 12 asking facetiously for permission to use Wyclif's books.[109]

Feeling threatened and motivated to assert his authority in the face of Hus's flagrant disobedience, and encouraged by the instructions of Colonna, Archbishop Zbyněk placed Hus under aggravated excommunication on September 24.[110] This was the second anathema. With the legal case moving ahead, we have no record of a surviving verdict on the appeal against the book burning. Correspondence from the royal house indicates the margin of separation between the king and the archbishop. Separate letters from Queen Žofie, dated October 1, and King Václav to Pope John (noted above), dated September 30, contain requests for a change of venue, stating that Hus should not be tried elsewhere and accusations against him ought to be lodged in Prague. The same thing was communicated by the king to Colonna, and the queen wrote a second letter to Colonna on October 2.[111] Canonical convention of the times agreed that legal proceedings normally should take place in the jurisdiction wherein the offense or crime was committed.[112] This point of procedure was eventually raised by Hus or Jesenice in the *Ordo procedendi*. However, the argument is mitigated by the fact that it was Hus, not Zbyněk or someone else, who transferred the case from Bohemia to the Holy See in the first place. At this stage, the disturbances in Prague had definitely assumed the shape of a formal legal case. In the midst of arguments over who should now oversee the Hus case, Colonna questioned witnesses to see if allegations against Hus were true. We are told that as many as two hundred deponents submitted testimony about Hus during legal proceedings.[113]

On an indeterminate date in the autumn of 1410, Colonna summoned Hus to the papal Curia in Bologna by means of a formal *citatio*.[114] Medieval

---

109. Sedlák, p. 197*.

110. *Documenta*, p. 202.

111. Ibid., pp. 422–425; noted also in *Ordo procedendi*, pp. 227–228.

112. C.3 q.6 c.1 *Ibi semper* and *Ulta prouinciarum* c.4, in Friedberg, vol. 1, col. 519.

113. *Ordo procedendi*, p. 227. Flajšhans, *Sebrané spisy*, vol. 1, pt. 1, p. 31, gives the number of deponents.

114. Leipzig Chronicle, in Höfler, vol. 1, p. 12; *Documenta*, p. 734 gives the date as October 1; also *Ordo procedendi*, p. 227.

law insisted that a summons and a citation of the defendant were so absolutely essential that not even a pope could neglect these steps. If a defendant
had not been properly cited, witnesses were not technically permitted to
give testimony against the accused.[115] The legal citation was often exactingly
precise upon danger of the case being dismissed.[116] Colonna's summons is
theoretically problematic. In 1203, Innocent III addressed the problem that
an excommunicate could not be a plaintiff in a church court. The question,
then, has to do with the appeal against the excommunication. Such appeal
may be filed on the grounds that it is unfair or considered invalid.[117] If the
appeal was lodged on the basis of unfairness, the validity remained, and
the appellate would require absolution before proceeding with the appeal.
If the appeal was on the basis of an invalidity claim (because sentence was
passed *after* appeal or there was an error), this raised a legal question. It
was incumbent upon the pope to absolve the appellant before hearing the
case. Precedent suggested that such absolution might be denied only if the
judge in the first instance demonstrated that the excommunication was
for cause or if it could be demonstrated that the excommunication came
after an appeal had been filed.[118] Further grounds for appeal against a writ
of excommunication could be claimed if the authority issuing the excommunication lacked proper jurisdiction for taking such action.[119] Absolution
on these grounds was routinely granted in the later Middle Ages.[120] None
of this mattered, because Hus refused to attend all prospective hearings at
the Curia, citing personal danger. He provided a fairly detailed explanation
later for his refusal to comply.[121] In that extended narrative, Hus pointed
out that he had dispatched a legal team to the Curia to represent him, but
his lawyers were refused a proper hearing and were imprisoned because of
their persistent demands for justice. Moreover, the distance from Prague

---

115. X 4.17.13 *Per venerabilem*, in Friedberg, vol. 2, cols. 714–716.

116. Vallerani, pp. 260–261.

117. X 5.39.40 *Per tuas*, in Friedberg, vol. 2, cols. 906–907.

118. On the former, see constitution 20, *De eodem*, of the first Council of Lyons (1245), in
Tanner, DEC, vol. 1, pp. 291–292, a Council enacting reform measures with respect to ecclesiastical litigation.

119. Raymond of Peñafort, *Summa sancti*, 3.33.33, p. 413.

120. Vernay, *Le "Liber de Excommunicatione,"* pp. 4–7.

121. Initially in *Ordo procedendi*, pp. 228–231, and then in the 1413 *Postil*, in Hus, *Opera omnia*,
vol. 2, pp. 164–166.

to the papal court (some eight hundred miles) was deemed prohibitive. Further, Hus advanced the claim that the citation was contrary to the law of God. Even if he had agreed to go, Hus asserted, divine truth was dishonored in the papal courts, and any hearing resulting from his appearance could only be regarded as unproductive. Hus was also reluctant to abandon his priestly charge at Bethlehem Chapel in order to litigate his case personally. He further noted the enormous financial burden such an undertaking would incur. Moreover, he pointed out that since his grievance was directed at the ecclesiastical hierarchy, it made no sense whatever for those same people to preside over the appellate process. In other words, Hus expected the judges to recuse themselves from the case, citing conflict of interest. After all, these same popes and cardinals were the ones opposing Bethlehem Chapel, calling for its destruction, demanding the cessation of preaching outside authorized venues, and adjudicating Hus himself a heretic. In sum, he believed that should he go to Rome, he would be summarily executed. All things considered, Hus said he preferred to commit himself to the grace of God.

Upon examination, Hus had some legal grounds for refusing to comply with the order to appear personally at the papal court. Canon law allowed for appeal if the subject could not safely travel to the court.[122] Hus made this point, citing fears for his safety should he agree to travel to the papal court at either Bologna or Rome. Hus's representation was problematic, because those who refused to appear could be charged with contumacy and disobedience, both serious matters in heresy cases.[123] It was possible that those in such circumstances, suspected of heresy, could be sentenced *in absentia*.[124] This was a calculated risk on Hus's part. Of course, the aggrieved party could appeal against any judgment handed down if the defendant considered it unjust.[125] However, no one excommunicated for contumacy could appeal once the sentence had been issued,[126] and appeals were forbidden to heretics.[127] In the patristic age, contumacy

---

122. X 2.28.47 *Ex parte tua*, in Friedberg, vol. 2, col. 428; X 2.6.4 *Accedens*, in Friedberg, vol. 2, col. 262; and Clem. 2.11.2 *Pastoralis*, in Friedberg, vol. 2, cols. 1152–1153.

123. C.24 q.3 c.6 §1 *De illicita*, in Friedberg, vol. 1, cols. 990–991.

124. Sext. 5.2.7 *Quum contumacia*, in Friedberg, vol. 2, col. 1071.

125. Johannes Andreae, *In quinque decretalium libros novella commentaria*, X 5.40.23.

126. C.2 q.6 c.41 *Si quis appellat* §11, in Friedberg, vol. 1, col. 482.

127. Sext. 5.2.18 *Ut inquisitionis*, in Friedberg, vol. 2, col. 1077.

meant deliberate opposition to church authority. By the high Middle Ages, the term had come to imply disobedience.[128] The gravity of the offense meant that those judged contumacious were at the mercy of the full legal force of the medieval church. This seems not to have unduly disturbed Hus, who took to his pulpit on December 20 and preached a sermon in which he openly acknowledged that he would not obey his ordinary.[129] He exhibited no hesitation in the assertion "I will not obey." However, as we have seen, Hus did send three legal representatives—Jan Jesenice, Marek of Hradec, and Mikuláš Stojčín—to the Curia to offer explanation and arguments to the court for why he could not appear and simultaneously filed an appeal against the summons.[130] It must be acknowledged, however, that lawyers can only ask for exemption from appearance by the client; they cannot answer charges on behalf of the defendant. In criminal matters (i.e. heresy), representation was disallowed.[131] The law required the accused to appear in person.[132] Procedurally, the defendant in a criminal case was required to attend the preliminary hearing and subsequent trial unless he or she chose to remain absent on account of contumacy.[133] That noted, Jesenice hired five lawyers familiar with curial processes to assist in the case. These were Peter of Ancharano, Giovanni Scribanis (or Scrivanis), Augustinus, Marcus of Caniculo, and Ardicin.[134]

The legal affairs concerning Hus may have shifted south to the papal Curia, but Archbishop Zbyněk had not given up his quest to reassert authority, suppress the reform movement in Prague, and curtail Hus's activities. Therefore, in the autumn of 1410, he produced further

---

128. Pierre Torquebiau, "Contumacia, Contumax," in *Dictionnaire de droit canonique*, ed. Raoul Naz, 7 vols. (Paris: Librairie Letouzey et Ané, 1935–1965), vol. 4, cols. 507–525.

129. Flajšhans, *Hus Sermones*, vol. 2, pp. 100–104. See especially pp. 102–103.

130. *Ordo procedendi*, p. 228. The latter procurator, later in the legal proceedings, appeared against Hus; Novotný, *Correspondence*, pp. 244–245. I can find no support for the claim that on three separate occasions, Hus dispatched attorneys to the Curia. Spinka, *Constance*, p. 38.

131. X 5.1.15 *Veniens*, in Friedberg, vol. 2, col. 737.

132. C.2 q.6 c.39 §1 *Si autem* and C.2 q.6 c.40 *Si quando*, in Friedberg, vol. 1, cols. 480–481.

133. 4 Lat c.8 *De inquisitionibus*, in Tanner, DEC, vol. 1, p. 238; and X 5.7.13 *Excommunicamus*, in Friedberg, vol. 2, cols. 787–789.

134. *Ordo procedendi*, p. 228. One of the two promotors at Constance (along with Henry of Piro) was Giovanni Scribanis (or Scrivanis) of Piacenza (Mansi, vol. 27, col. 532; and Hardt, vol. 4, p. 142), a well-known curial promotor. His role at Constance was unrelated to the Hus case.

depositions against Hus from hostile Prague priests.[135] These are the sworn testimonies of deponents. Eight of these priests included in the charges are identified as Jan Protiva, John Peklo, Beneš (a preacher in Prague Castle), Pavel (preacher at the Church of St. Castulus in the Old Town), Ondřej of Brod, Mikuláš of Podviní, Mikuláš (parish priest in Všetaty), and Václav of Voděrady (public notary). Protiva once again functions as the main plaintiff. In places, the accusations are a pastiche of hearsay and rumor. Other allegations appear rooted in statements Hus apparently made more than a decade earlier. Some testimony relates to theology, especially the Eucharist, and so-called Wyclifite doctrine. But there is more. Two of the more serious components emerging from these depositions characterize Hus as opposed to the pope, with the extravagant claim that he identified particular popes with Antichrist and heresy. The testimonies of Protiva, Brod, and the notary public Václav of Voděrady portray Hus as an inciter of racial hatred against Germans. Here we see the political and social overtones of heresy accusations come into focus. Hus is represented as a "rabble-rouser" known as "Judas." It would appear that the archbishop's motivation in collecting this dossier supports a strategic agenda aimed at presenting Hus as a subversive presence in the ecclesiastical province of Bohemia. Placing Hus in such a disadvantageous place was probably contrived in hopes of securing maximum papal attention. Hus was not just a preacher of questionable ideas; he posed a threat to the social and ecclesiastical security of the church in the Czech lands.

František Palacký dates the extant document to 1414, but this was when Hus wrote answers to the allegations. Therefore, the earlier date is preferred. This is the first time Hus is formally accused of heresy. Hus's legal team promptly submitted a second appeal to the examining magistrate of the court, questioning the partiality of the judge and effectively framing a motion asking *iudicis recusatio*—for the magistrate to be recused from the case.[136] The law considered that a partial judge should not preside over a case.[137] The appeal was lodged by Marek of Hradec, one of Hus's representative attorneys, with John XXIII on the grounds of irregular

---

135. *Documenta*, pp. 174–185. The names are noted in Novotný, *M. Jan Hus*, vol. 1, pp. 464–466.

136. *Ordo procedendi*, p. 228.

137. C.3 q.5 c.15 *Quia suspecti*, in Friedberg, vol. 1, cols. 518–519.

proceedings.[138] This appeal was referred to the papal auditor and canon lawyer John de Thomariis of Bologna, who had the brief to examine the complaint. Presumably, the auditor would consider both the issue of the objectivity of the judge and concerns about irregular procedures.[139]

The Curia was unmoved by these efforts, and by February 1411, Cardinal Colonna found Hus in contempt of court and excommunicated him for contumacy and nonappearance.[140] This is the third excommunication of Hus. The matter of contumacy has already been underscored. It was a legal matter and could be incurred for at least three reasons, including refusing the summons of a court, ignoring the court's decisions, or generally circumventing the legal process, for example, by leaving before the case was settled.[141] Hus was guilty of the first two causes and potentially in breach of the third, given his approach later to the supreme court of Bohemia. The issue was contempt of court, more specifically, contempt of ecclesiastical authority. Canon law ruled that contumacy in the face of excommunication engendered suspicion of heresy.[142] The penalty for contumacy in canon law was excommunication.[143] Hus claimed that the excommunication was secured through the malice and ex parte efforts of Michael de Causis.[144] From the standpoint of canon law, the action by Colonna might be classified as malfeasance and illegal, inasmuch as the second appeal should have been heard before further action on the initial summons took place. A papal ruling stated that no one should dare condemn one who had appealed to the apostolic chair.[145] It might have been possible to mount a legal rebuttal arguing that Colonna's action was valid on the grounds that Hus's appeal had no judicial basis for effecting a legal suspension in the application of a sentence because the appeal was rooted in a response to a previous writ of excommunication. Medieval

---

138. Novotný, *Correspondence*, pp. 88–89.

139. *Ordo procedendi*, p. 228.

140. *Documenta*, p. 202.

141. C.11 q.3 c.43 *Certum est*, in Friedberg, vol. 1, col. 656.

142. X 5.37.13 *Graven dilectorum*, in Friedberg, vol. 2, col. 884.

143. C.11 q.3 c.41–c.64, in Friedberg, vol. 1, cols. 655–661, an assumption that appears to have gained unofficial status as a legal canon by the thirteenth century.

144. *De ecclesia*, p. 231.

145. Gregory VII, *Dictatus papae*, in *Das Register Gregors VII*, ed. Erich Caspar, in MGH, *Epistolae Selectae*, vol. 2, pp. 202–208.

canon law allowed that excommunication created an exception-to-the-rule clause.[146] Be that as it may, we have no record of the obligatory *canonica monitione* preceding the verdict, which would also call into question its validity.[147] Technically, as noted earlier, full excommunication could only be applied after three warnings.[148] Colonna's action was "at the very least controversial and problematic." The procedure can be criticized on three counts, namely, Colonna did not rule on the reasons invoked by Hus for failing to appear, the sentence had been passed by a judge who was himself the subject of an appeal, and finally, there was the alleged problem of corruption in terms of judicial bias and suspicion of bribery.[149] Since a reason was not given for rejecting Hus's petition to avoid appearing, an appeal could have been lodged that would have suspended legal proceedings and by consequence referred the matter back to an appellate court based on the medieval equivalent of a writ of mandamus.[150] There is no extant evidence that Hus or any of his attorneys attempted this legal challenge. Those who remained incorrigible, according to canon law, could be subject to force via the secular authorities.[151] Despite the obvious irregularities, it is incorrect to argue that the ban issued against Hus was invalid. It could certainly have been challenged, but it was not. The auditor John de Thomariis did not replace Colonna but instead was appointed to investigate the complaint against him. The critical point is that Colonna was still in charge of the legal process.[152] As these matters were unfolding, on March 6, 1411, curial official Dietrich Niem, incited by Michael de Causis, published his vitriolic tract against Hus and his followers. Niem argued that legal procedure at the Curia was irregular for even having received Hus's appeals. According to this argument, Zbyněk was the final authority in such matters. Suspicion of heresy was sufficient for condemnation, and the church should act to eliminate heresy, with the use of crusade if necessary, and heretics should be imprisoned, degraded, and handed over

---

146. X 2.28.53 *Pastoralis*, in Friedberg, vol. 2, col. 432.

147. X 2.28.26 *Reprehensibilis*, in Friedberg, vol. 2, col. 418.

148. C.17 q.4 c.21 *Quisquis inventus*, in Friedberg, vol. 1, col. 820.

149. Kejř, *Jesenice*, pp. 48–49.

150. X 1.29.27 §5 *Super quaestionum articulis*, in Friedberg, vol. 2, col. 172.

151. C.11 q.1 c.20 *Istud est*, in Friedberg, vol. 1, col. 632.

152. Novotný, *M. Jan Hus*, vol. 1, p. 470, incorrectly assumes that Colonna was removed. Kejř, *Jesenice*, p. 49, and de Vooght, p. 169, have it right.

to the secular arm.[153] It is possible that Niem's argument was predicated upon the alleged irregularity of Hus's transfer of the case from Prague to the Curia. Niem's position was contrary to earlier legal opinion, which held that even heretics deserved the opportunity to mount a defense.[154]

Legal questions aside, Zbyněk had Colonna's anathema against Hus proclaimed in Prague churches on March 15, 1411, although two churches in the city (St. Michael's and St. Benedict's) refused to make the announcement.[155] Earlier, a priest was attacked at St. Stephen's in the New Town when he attempted to announce an interdict against Hus.[156] At this stage, Hus considered himself disobedient, hereticated, and excommunicated, although he refused the suggestion that he was an evildoer.[157] Sensing that Hus was now in a weakened position, Michael de Causis lodged further articles of accusation against Hus in March 1412.[158] Formerly a priest in Prague at St. Adalbert's, succeeded by Jakoubek Stříbro, Michael had been appointed by Pope John XXIII as advocate in matters of faith (*procurator de causis fidei*) and thereafter worked as a lawyer in the papal courts. In terms of the Hus case, he functioned tirelessly in the role of *promovens*. The tenor of these articles shifts Hus into a confrontation with church authorities. Hus appears in this legal document as a dangerous and cunning preacher of heresy. Points of theology are raised, especially about the Eucharist and indulgences, but once more, Hus is presented deliberately as a man standing in opposition to the church. It is alleged that he denounced "the Roman Church as the synagogue of Satan" and also encouraged parishioners to actively disobey the ecclesiastical hierarchy. De Causis went on to present Hus as favoring violence against priests and prelates and as a radical who did not hesitate to incite common people to seize properties of clerics, going so far as to encourage their physical harm. The articles include accusations that Hus was a "heretic" and

---

153. *Contra damnatos Wiclifitas Prage*, in ST, 1, pp. 45–55.

154. Hostiensis, SA, 5, col. 1468.

155. Leipzig Chronicle, in Höfler, vol. 1, p. 12.

156. Kateřina Horníčková, "Memory, Politics and Holy Relics: Catholic Tactics amidst the Bohemian Reformation," in BRRP 8, pp. 136–137.

157. Novotný, *Correspondence*, p. 90. On de Causis, see Fudge, *Memory and Motivation*, chap. 5; and Thomas A. Fudge, "The Role of Michael de Causis in the Prosecution of Jan Hus," forthcoming.

158. *Documenta*, pp. 169–174.

a "heresiarch." It is not difficult to agree with the careful assessment of these articles of accusation as "patently absurd," with some quite false and others lacking necessary nuance.[159] Clearly unsettled by this vitriolic attack, Hus defiantly and repeatedly called de Causis a "liar" and the "manufacturer of lies." Hoping to stymie the work of Hus's advocates at the Curia, de Causis moved to have Jan Jesenice disqualified from the Hus case by filing a motion amounting to a complaint that included accusations of heresy against Jesenice. The process was interrupted to some extent when the papal Curia at Bologna under John XXIII relocated to Rome in the first half of April 1411. That spring, John took charge of the Hus case (sometime after June 6) and assigned it to a committee of four cardinals. These were Francesco Zabarella, cardinal-deacon of Florence; Cardinal Rainaldo Brancacci; Antonio Caetani, former patriarch of Aquileia (but at this time bishop of Porto and Santa Rufina), and an obscure "de Veneficiis."[160] Their brief was to examine and clarify legal procedure. During the autumn of 1411, this commission made no ruling on Colonna's anathema but undertook a legal review of the submissions of Hus's legal team, concluding with a finding that arguments for Hus's exemption from personal appearance must be admitted.[161]

Despite three excommunications and pending legal action, Hus preached a sermon on April 23, 1411, defiantly stating that he would not stop preaching.[162] Hus told his congregation that preaching must continue even in the streets if necessary. The prelates who worked to restrict the proclamation of the gospel were characterized as "false witnesses" whom no one should listen to. Hus declared that he could be prevented from preaching only by death. So far, Hus had the king on his side, although this may have only been apparent inasmuch as the archiepiscopal see and the royal house remained locked in a power struggle. King Václav issued an order that

---

159. De Vooght, vol. 1, pp. 167, 169.

160. *Ordo procedendi*, pp. 228–229. He may possibly have been Francesco Lando (or Landi), who died in 1427, popularly known as the cardinal of Venice. He was a renowned canon lawyer who was promoted by Pope Gregory XII. He attended the Council of Constance. Alfonso Chacón, *Vitae, et res gestae Pontificvm Romanorum et S.R.E. Cardinalivm ab initio nascentis Ecclesiae vsque ad Vrbanvm VIII. Pont. Max*, 2 vols. (Rome: Typis Vaticanis, 1630), vol. 2, cols. 797–798; Conrad Eubel and Guglielmus van Gulik, *Hierarchia Catholica Medii Aevi*, vol. 1 (1198–1431) (Munich: Sumptibus et Typis Librariae Regensbergianae, 1913; reprint Padua: Il Messagero di S. Antonio, 1960), pp. 32, 38, 41, 207, 266.

161. Jesenice, *Repetitio*, pp. 416–417.

162. Flajšhans, *Hus Sermones*, vol. 4, pp. 67–71.

because Zbyněk had not followed his directive to compensate owners of the confiscated Wyclif books, he intended to take steps. He promptly suspended the salaries of the clergy on April 28.[163] Zbyněk retaliated on May 2, threatening anathema upon those obeying the king's decree. He followed this up by excommunicating royal officials and councillors.[164] Riots then broke out across Prague, in which many churches and priests were attacked.[165] In an effort to thwart the king, establish order, and reassert his crumbling episcopal authority, Zbyněk imposed interdict on the city of Prague and its immediate environs around June 19, 1411.[166] The censure of interdict was a tremendous weapon in the arsenal of the medieval church. Hus was the cause of its implementation in Prague, but Zbyněk regarded the entire city as culpable and responsible in the matter of Hus. That being the case, one could argue for the collective guilt of the entire community.[167] The sentence of interdict legally was required to follow the normal procedures of *monitio* and citation before implementation. This allowed opportunity for appeal. An appeal had suspensive effect. If an appeal was launched in good time, the interdict could not be imposed. Appeals made after imposition were heard while the interdict remained in effect. The archbishop clearly breached those legal provisions, but it hardly mattered when King Václav forbade the observation of interdict. Štěpán Páleč wrote a denunciation of the interdict, noting several points in which it was invalid.[168] Hus preached a sermon for the second Sunday in Trinity, on June 21, defending the king and justifying royal action against the archbishop.[169] Hus stated unequivocally that the king's action was consistent with the power and authority given to him by God. By contrast, the imposition of interdict on Prague and within a two-mile radius was nothing other than an exercise in resisting the power of God. Hus noted grimly that "every priest who resists God in this manner, along with him [Zbyněk] are heading for damnation unless they repent."

---

163. Chronicle of the University of Prague, FRB 5, p. 572.

164. *Documenta*, pp. 429–432.

165. Ibid., pp. 415, 429–432, 735–736.

166. Ibid., p. 736; but see also Miroslav Černý, "Interdikt nad Prahou roce 1411: Na okraj jednoho mocenského střetu," *Právněhistorické Studie* 35 (2000): 225–230.

167. This has been argued generally by Peter D. Clarke, *The Interdict in the Thirteenth Century: A Question of Collective Guilt* (Oxford: Oxford University Press, 2007).

168. *Documenta*, pp. 432–433.

169. HM, vol. 2, pp. 73–75.

Things improved for Hus and the reform party on July 3, when the chancellor of the university, Šimon Tišnov, and a representative assembly of the arts faculty met in the Franciscan monastery of St. James in the Old Town and announced their decision to side with the king against the archbishop. At the same time, another group convened in a back room in the archiepiscopal palace and sided with Zbyněk. These included Adam Nežetice, Záviš of Zap, Jan of Kolín, Zdeněk of Chrást, Jan of Dubá and Jan Protiva.[170] Realizing that he had overreached himself, Zbyněk submitted to the king on July 3 and was formally defeated on July 6.[171] An arbitration committee was appointed to resolve the conflict between king and archbishop. That commission included Konrad of Vechta, bishop of Olomouc; Václav Králík, titular patriarch of Antioch; Rudolf, duke of Saxony; Stibor of Stibořice, an emissary of King Sigismund; Petr Zmrzlík, master of the mint; and a number of others. Unsurprisingly, the committee sided with the king. Zbyněk was forced into a retraction of his allegations about Hus. The archbishop was pressured to reassert his findings of 1408 and declare Bohemia free of heresy. The anathema against Hus was to be annulled, Zbyněk was instructed to request cancellation of the papal censure against Hus, and so on. It should be noted that Hus's name was nowhere used, and the suggestions were, in fact, generic. There could be little doubt that the active force in all of this was the matter of Jan Hus. A draft letter to the pope from Zbyněk reflecting the aforementioned points was produced by royal officials.[172] In this document, the defeated archbishop declared that he had been unable to detect any heresy anywhere in Bohemia. Not a single person could be identified as holding any punishable opinion. Zbyněk declared that he and Hus had been reconciled and all previous disputes and disagreements had been resolved. Therefore, the letter requested that the pope withdraw all ecclesiastical censures and excommunications leveled against the country and, moreover, cancel any obligation incumbent upon Hus to appear at the papal court.

The cost of defeat was high. For five weeks, the archbishop sought an audience with the king. This never occurred. Václav remained deaf to the entreaties of the vanquished prelate. The submission of Zbyněk in no sense implied that Hus's enemies were now silenced. An anonymous critique of

170. *Documenta*, pp. 434–437.

171. Ibid., pp. 437–439.

172. Ibid., pp. 441–442.

Hus's August 16 sermon was left in the Bethlehem Chapel.[173] It is likely the response was written by Mařik Rvačka. The accusation claimed that Hus was trying to destroy the priesthood and the law of God by alleging that Hus approved of secular powers disciplining the clergy.[174] Hus took the opportunity to write to John XXIII on September 1, 1411, submitting to his authority and asking for a suspension of all proceedings against him, an informal motion for acquittal *sine die*, noting that he had been fully reconciled with Zbyněk.[175] The letter was notarized and confirmed with the seal of the university.[176] Hus also wrote to the college of cardinals on the same date to the same effect.[177] In his letter to Pope John, it is notable that Hus affirmed his commitment to eucharistic orthodoxy as defined by the church.[178] Hus requested both John XXIII and the college of cardinals to absolve him from a personal appearance at the curial court. The request was never granted. According to law, excommunication was automatic after one year for nonappearance and thereby made a suspect guilty of heresy.[179] That legal statute mirrored the position taken by ecclesiastical councils.[180] Despairing of any form of desired justice, Zbyněk fled Prague at the beginning of September, intending to find shelter at the court of Sigismund in Buda. From the east Bohemian town of Litomyšl, upon the advice of Bishop Jan Železný, he wrote to the king on September 5, complaining of his treatment and refusing to follow the royal injunctions, especially in requesting that the Holy See absolve those under anathema, declaring that doing so would be false, dishonorable, and contrary to conscience.[181] The archbishop's letter was filled with bitterness. Zbyněk complained that he had been made to wait five weeks, during which time he had exhausted all avenues in an effort to secure a hearing before the king.

---

173. Flajšhans, *Hus Sermones*, vol. 4, pp. 339–343.

174. Details of its reception, its text, and Hus's reply are in *Contra occultum adversarium*, in Hus, *Opera omnia*, vol. 22, pp. 73–107, written in October 1411.

175. Novotný, *Correspondence*, pp. 95–98.

176. Details have been recorded. *Relatio*, pp. 63–64.

177. Novotný, *Correspondence*, pp. 101–102.

178. Ibid., pp. 96–97.

179. Sext. 5.2.7 *Quum contumacia*, in Friedberg, vol. 2, col. 1071.

180. See, for example, 4 Lat c.3 *De haereticis*, in Tanner, DEC, vol. 1, p. 233.

181. *Documenta*, pp. 443–445.

He noted that his enemies appeared to have free access to the king's ear. Moreover, his authority and office had been maliciously mistreated. Those teaching error persisted with impunity. One priest whom the archbishop had ordered arrested on charges of wickedness was summarily released. Disobedient priests were shielded from accountability and punishment, and in consequence, archiepiscopal authority was prevented from prosecuting any semblance of ecclesiastical discipline. Zbyněk complained that scurrilous letters written against him circulated around Prague. He complained of royal interference in depriving clerics of property and income. He pointed out that the priest at the Church of St. Nicholas had been robbed and thrown into prison though innocent of any misconduct. The archbishop had desired to discuss all of this with the king. But these grievances and the king's refusal to grant a hearing forced Zbyněk to turn to Hungary for redress, in hopes that Sigismund might be able to intercede with Václav, with the result that Zbyněk might be restored to office and the contempt now heaped upon the see of Prague removed. The letter went unheeded. The hopes of the archbishop went unfulfilled. Zbyněk died, unexpectedly, on September 28 in Bratislava, possibly murdered.[182] Hus is reported to have rejoiced at the news.[183] The claim is both malicious and untrue.

Meanwhile, Hus's persistence in refusing to appear at the papal court as ordered brought him condemnation from some of his peers, who regarded his position as effectively contempt of court.[184] Hus remained unmoved. When Cambridge University master John Stokes visited Prague and reportedly made derogatory comments about Wyclif, Hus challenged him to a public debate on September 13. The notice was posted on church doors. Stokes declined. Hus went ahead anyway.[185] Immediately thereafter, he wrote his treatise "Against John Stokes," in which he refused to admit that Wyclif was a heretic, expressed hope that Wyclif was saved, admitted that he was drawn to the English thinker, and claimed that

---

182. František Šimek, ed., *Staré letopisy české z vratislavského rukopisu novočeským pravopisem* (Prague: Historické Spolku a Společnosti Husova Musea, 1937), p. 8. Zbyněk's body was returned to Prague and buried in the lower-tower chapel in St. Vitus's Cathedral. Klára Benešovska and Ivo Hlobil, *Peter Parler & St Vitus's Cathedral 1356–1399* (Prague: Správa Pražského Hradu, 1999), p. 126.

183. Štěpán of Dolany, *Antihussus*, cols. 153, 383.

184. Štěpán of Dolany, *Dialogus volatilis*, in Pez, vol. 4, cols. 464–467.

185. Novotný, *Correspondence*, pp. 102–104.

Wyclif had tried only to bring people into conformity with the law of God and encouraged clerics to adopt the life of Christ. Hus went on to say that just because "multitudes of prelates and clerics" in England, France, Bohemia, and elsewhere considered Wyclif a heretic, that did not make him so. Moreover, book burning was so much nonsense and contrary to the law of God. If Stokes and anyone else insisted that Wyclif was heretical and therefore damned, Hus challenged them to show cause and prove it.[186] In a move that may be considered inconsistent, Hus preached on Saint Václav Day, September 28, declaring his willingness to appear before the papal court and, if need be, to die.[187] The university continued to support Hus and on October 10 issued a statement of support, which amounted to a testimonial about his faith and conduct.[188] The death of Zbyněk created a vacancy, which was filled by Albík of Uničov, who was elected archbishop of Prague on October 29 and confirmed on January 25, 1412. In the midst of this transition, John XXIII announced a crusade against King Ladislas of Naples.[189] This declaration worked to isolate Hus further. On December 2, a papal bull authorizing the sale of indulgences in Prague appeared.[190] This initiative was designed to financially underwrite the crusade against Ladislas. The bull promised not a comprehensive *a culpa et poena* (plenary indulgence) but remission only to the truly penitent, although this was contradicted by the absolution formula, which suggested forgiveness for all sins without referring to repentance, confession, or penance. Hus had grave reservations about the initiative. Inasmuch as it stigmatized John's enemies as "perjurers, schismatics, blasphemers, relapsed heretics, defenders of heretics, guilty of the crime of lèse majesté, [and] conspirators against the church," Hus considered such broad, sweeping judgments contrary to the teachings and ethics of Christ. He concluded that it was unwise to call for Ladislas,

---

186. Hus, *Opera omnia*, vol. 22, pp. 59–70, especially pp. 62–66.

187. Flajšhans, *Hus Sermones*, vol. 5, p. 138; Hus, *Postil*, 1411–1412, Prague, KNM, MS XII F 1, fol. 86ʳ; Kejř, *Husův proces*, p. 92, n. 132.

188. *Documenta*, pp. 146–149; also in Hus's letter to the cardinals, Novotný, *Correspondence*, p. 102.

189. HM, vol. 1, pp. 212–213. The announcement came on September 9, 1411.

190. Ibid., pp. 213–215. Helpful discussion of context is in Eva Doležalová, Jan Hrdina, František Šmahel, and Zdeněk Uhlíř, "The Reception and Criticism of Indulgences in the Late Medieval Czech Lands," in *Promissory Notes on the Treasury of Merits: Indulgences in Late Medieval Europe*, ed. R. N. Swanson (Leiden, Neth.: Brill, 2006), pp. 101–145.

his colleagues, and their followers to be punished as heretics.[191] Sometime in late 1411, recalcitrant Prague canons hostile to Hus retained Michael de Causis as their advocate at the papal Curia, and through his ex parte efforts eventually secured the condemnation of Hus.[192] It is possible that de Causis was involved in this respect earlier.[193] Canon law allowed for the possibility that the public denunciation of an excommunicate (Hus) could be achieved by a prosecutor (de Causis) via legal and court procedures.[194] It was assumed that once the *libellus* had been presented, the accuser would tell the truth. There is little doubt that de Causis was motivated by malice toward Hus. However, canon law did not disqualify such witnesses in cases of *crimen exceptum*.[195] That provision allowed de Causis to remain active at the Curia in the case against Hus, and he did so with considerable success and aplomb. There is no evidence that Hus or his attorneys invoked the *exceptio criminis* to disqualify such persons from the legal proceedings.

A year and a half into the Hus case, the main legal matters were centered no longer in Prague but at the Curia. Sometime after January 10, 1412, the commission of cardinals placed the Hus case in the hands of Francesco Zabarella.[196] Former commission member Antonio Caetani died in early January. Zabarella undertook a review of the case to date and offered a dissenting opinion on the procedures thus far that must have heartened Hus and outraged de Causis. Zabarella made an interlocutory judgment that appears to agree with the appeal of Hus. He admitted previously excluded "evidence," set a new deadline for submission of evidence, and, perhaps shockingly for the prosecution, concluded that Colonna's decision not to allow a hearing of Hus's attorneys was inappropriate. Therefore, the excommunicating of Hus was unjustified because there was an appeal pending. Zabarella's findings rested on solid legal precedent. Canon law allowed admission of all relevant evidence and mandated that essential and necessary defenses should not

191. *Contra octo doctores*, in Hus, *Opera omnia*, vol. 22, p. 450.

192. Letter of Hus to the supreme court of Bohemia, in Novotný, *Correspondence*, p. 157.

193. *Postil*, Hus, *Opera omnia*, vol. 2, p. 166; and Novotný, *M. Jan Hus*, vol. 1, p. 468.

194. X 5.39.46 *In praesentia*, in Friedberg, vol. 2, col. 908.

195. X 5.3.31 *Licet heli*, in Friedberg, vol. 2, cols. 760–761; and X 5.3.32 *Per tuas*, in Friedberg, vol. 2, cols. 761–762.

196. *Ordo procedendi*, p. 229.

be excluded.[197] Whatever hope Zabarella's report may have given Hus's attorneys was quickly nullified. Crucially, from a legal point of view, Pope John XXIII did not act positively on these findings, and we have no record that either Hus or Jesenice filed an *exceptio* (formal objection), pressed the matter on appeal, or introduced a motion based on a writ of mandamus. This seems curious, and one can only speculate about why Jesenice did not seize this opportunity to argue the finer points of law on behalf of his client. The handling of the Hus case by Zabarella in January and February 1412 provided the best legal decisions for Hus thus far. Contemporary opinion referred to Zabarella as "a man of great and unique knowledge."[198] There is a strong case to be made for considering Zabarella the most astute canon lawyer of his time.

Politics appear at this stage to have intruded. Inexplicably, in February, Pope John ordered the findings of the Hus inquiry submitted to Cardinal Rainaldo Brancacci, thereby effectively removing the case from Zabarella.[199] We do not know why the pope undertook this course of action or the thinking that prompted it, but the possibility of lobbying by Michael de Causis cannot be excluded. Brancacci did little with his legal responsibility, and some sources allege that he stalled the case for a year and a half. This is exaggeration, but it is true that the Hus case was bogged down for four or five months. Brancacci rebutted efforts from Hus's representatives, some of whom were arrested and imprisoned. Hus and his followers were anathematized, and a personal interdict (*interdictum ab ingressu ecclesiae*) was imposed upon Hus that theoretically barred him from entering a church and thereby deprived him of certain ecclesiastical ministrations such as the Eucharist. Personal interdict had to do with excommunication and was not related to a local interdict. Personal interdict for all intents and purposes was equivalent to "minor excommunication," once the distinction between "major" and "minor" excommunication attained legal status. This distinction within the censure of excommunication was drawn by canonists from the thirteenth century on. What is strikingly evident is that Brancacci did not follow the legal recommendations of Zabarella, he postponed making a verdict, and he claimed that the pope ordered him

---

197. Clem. 2.1.2 *Dispendiosam prorogationem*, in Friedberg, vol. 2, col. 1143; and Clem. 5.11.2 *Saepe contingit*, in Friedberg, vol. 2, col. 1200.

198. According to Fillastre, in Finke, *Acta*, vol. 2, p. 146.

199. *Ordo procedendi*, p. 229.

not to hear appeals any longer from Hus's advocates.[200] The results of Brancacci's oversight of the Hus case were effectively a confirmation of the decisions made by Colonna. Brancacci's handing of the case and allegations of interference on the part of the pontiff constitute grounds for concerns about malfeasance. Gratian said that an offender could be anathematized after conviction by a judicial procedure.[201] This obstacle—in this case, the trial—was gradually overcome, and by the thirteenth century, this requirement does not seem to have retained binding force in legal practice.

Meanwhile, we find evidence of continued attack on Jan Jesenice's involvement in the Hus case by the indefatigable Michael de Causis, who cunningly worked to introduce the suspicion of heresy and also filed a motion for the pope to subsume all cases concerning Jesenice under a single judge. Jesenice was ordered to answer charges. Investigations carried out by de Causis revealed other legal matters involving Jesenice and an otherwise obscure cleric named Šimon Burda. These matters had been presided over by Zdeněk of Chrást, archdeacon of Žatec, whom earlier we found implicated in the book-burning affair in Prague.[202] The auditor in charge of this complaint, Jean Belli, did nothing so de Causis tirelessly lobbied for action, and the matter was committed to the papal auditor Berthold Wildungen.[203] As a result of this initiative, Jesenice was imprisoned in Rome by March 1412, with the outcome that he was removed from the Hus case.[204] This, of course, had been the strategic intention of de Causis all along, for Jesenice was altogether too shrewd an advocate, and cunning legal strategy was to have him eliminated from representing the defendant Hus. Canon law stated clearly that a lawyer under anathema could not practice law.[205] Church councils ratified the same ruling.[206] Hus

---

200. Ibid., p. 229.

201. C.11 q.3 c.24 *Evidenter itaque*, in Friedberg, vol. 1, cols. 651–652.

202. Kejř, *Husův proces*, pp. 65, 74.

203. Novotný, *M. Jan Hus*, vol. 2, p. 58. See also Emmanuele Cerchiari, *Capellani papae et apostolicae sedis auditores causarum sacri palatii apostolici: Seu sacra Romana rota* (Rome: Typis Polyglottis Vaticanis, 1920), p. 46.

204. Chronicle of the University of Prague, FRB 5, p. 571.

205. X 5.7.13 §5 *Excommunicamus*, in Friedberg, vol. 2, col. 788; and Sext. 5.11.8 *Decernimus ut iudices*, in Friedberg, vol. 2, col. 1101.

206. 4 Lat c.3 *De haereticis*, in Tanner, DEC, vol. 1, p. 234.

had just lost his best asset at the Curia. Complicating this development at Rome were concurrent events back in Prague. Sometime in April, the German Wenceslas Tiem of Mikulov in Moravia, who was dean of Passau, along with Pax de Fantuciis of Bologna, a licentiate in canon law, arrived in Prague. These two men were indulgence commissioners, and on May 22, during the feast of Pentecost, they issued a public proclamation for the implementation of the indulgences campaign announced by John XXIII. However, they did not follow the terms of the bull but preached the benefits from the sale of indulgences as relief from the penalty and guilt of all sins (*a culpa et poena*), with salvation for the buyers, damnation for those who declined, and so on. Tiem had been appointed for the dioceses of Salzburg, Magdeburg, and Bohemia. We know nothing about the second fellow and his whereabouts, but Tiem remained in Prague and at least on one occasion had a confrontation with Hus. Large fortified boxes for collections were placed in the Týn Church in the Old Town, where the incumbent priest, the German Johannes Vartemberk, vocally opposed reform, and also at the Capitular Church of Saints Peter and Paul at Vyšehrad and at St. Vitus's Cathedral in Prague Castle.[207]

The indulgences campaign become controversial, and the fallout was swept up into the trial of Jan Hus. Štěpán Páleč initially resisted the indulgences campaign, noting that supporting arguments were flawed.[208] Hus engaged in two strident critiques of the bull.[209] In the latter document, Hus addressed the clergy and listed twelve reasons the bull should be condemned. Explicit in this action was a rejection of the sale of indulgences. Hus claimed that the thrust of this particular indulgence was simony, argued that the claims of the preachers constituted falsehood, insisted on the impossibility of the *a culpa et poena* claim, and did not fail to underscore the commensurate greed he thought the sale revealed. More than a year later, he continued to ridicule the operative phrase, parodying it as *a pera et bursa* (of the pocket and the purse), underscoring his thesis

---

207. SRB, vol. 3, p. 15; and Šimek, *Staré letopisy české*, p. 10.

208. Both his *Antihus* in Sedlák, *Miscellanea*, p. 498, and *Tractatus de ecclesia*, in Sedlák, p. 280, use the phrase "articulis errores manu palpabiles." Some think the latter text was authored by Stanislav of Znojmo. Pavel Spunar, *Repertorium auctorum Bohemorum provectum idearum post universitatem Pragensem conditam illustrans*, 2 vols. (Wrocław: Institutum Ossolinianum, 1995), vol. 2, pp. 291–292.

209. "De indulgentiis sive de cruciata papae Joannis XXIII" and "Contra Bullam Papae Joan. XXIII," in HM, vol. 1, pp. 215–237.

that indulgences were more about economics than salvation.[210] The whole affair was unpalatable. Hus wrote that it was nonsense that papal commissioners could determine the amount of money or property required in order to obtain a pardon. On top of this, priests had to purchase licenses from the indulgence sellers in order to sell the pardons. Hus claimed that nowhere else was simony more obvious.[211] Páleč refused to allow proclamation of the indulgences sale at his parish in Kouřim.[212] In similar fashion, Hus preached against the indulgences on May 29 in Bethlehem Chapel.[213] Elsewhere, we learn from contemporary reports that Hus in a great many sermons influenced people against buying indulgences.[214] In the later stages of his legal ordeal, Hus was accused of preaching against the crusade and its associated indulgences. Hus admitted that this was correct. In response to the accusation, Hus claimed that Wenceslas Tiem had modified aspects of the crusade indulgences that created drastic problems demanding redress. To facilitate his trade, Tiem rented out churches, deaneries, and archdeaneries in the same manner as a landlord might rent out a house or a pub. This nefarious practice, Hus argued, created considerable ignorance, chaos, sexual immorality, and gambling among wicked and greedy priests, who created much disorder and, to raise the necessary money to take advantage of the available opportunities advertised by Tiem, began charging exorbitant fees for confession. According to Hus, these clerics made considerable money, but in doing so, they "stained their souls with simony and greed." This is the explanation provided by Hus for why he preached against the crusade and its indulgences. Hus ended his explanation by declaring that if his opposition was wrong, he was prepared to plead guilty as charged.[215]

---

210. Novotný, *Correspondence*, p. 165.

211. "Utrum secundum legem Jesu Christi licet, & expedit, pro honore Dei & salute populi, ac pro commodo Regni Bullas Pape de erectione Crucis contra Ladislaum Regem Apulie, & suos complices Christi fideliter approbare," in HM, vol. 1, pp. 222–223.

212. *Tractatus de ecclesia*, in Sedlák, *M. Jan Hus*, p. 281.

213. Sermon for the Tuesday of Holy Week in Hus, *Opera omnia*, vol. 2, pp. 203–205.

214. Šimek, ed., *Staré letopisy české*, p. 10.

215. *Documenta*, pp. 222–223. He said much the same thing about Tiem's tactics in a letter at the time, in Novotný, *Correspondence*, p. 124. Instructions for the sale of indulgences appear in Johann Loserth, ed., "Beiträge zur Geschichte der Husitischen Bewegung: Gleichzeitige Berichte und Actenstücke zur Ausbreitung des Wiclifismus in Böhmen und Mähren von 1410 bis 1419," AÖG 82 (1895): 367–370.

Despite attempts on the part of the theological faculty to prevent the event, Hus conducted a university debate condemning the crusade bull of John XXIII on June 17, 1412, after posting public notices challenging detractors.[216] The university disputation of June 17 featured Hus opening the discussion by posing the query: "Whether it is permissible according to the law of Jesus Christ, and advantageous for the salvation of the people and the honor of God, and for the comforts and piety of this kingdom, to approve the papal bull for the raising of the cross against King Ladislas of Naples and his adherents, and to recommend it to the faithful of Christ?" Hus attacked the idea that money could produce "complete acquittal from the guilt and penalty" of sin.[217] He cited the pope's bull, wherein the phrase "I grant to you the complete remission of all your sins including all guilt and punishment" appeared. Hus demanded to know with what gall the pope presumed to usurp the place of God and grant plenary pardons. How could this be done unless "God has expressly commanded him to do this"?[218] Priests and bishops had no business taking up physical weapons. Instead, prayer, intercession, and the weapons of the spirit were preferred.[219] The two swords should not be confused. Now that John XXIII had acted improperly, Hus argued that he must not be obeyed.[220] The whole business was another example of simony.[221] Arguing for the right and power of the pope to undertake such action on the grounds that the pope was immune from error was, according to Hus "not only false but blasphemous."[222] Therefore, when it was apparent that the pope was exercising ecclesiastical power contrary to the law of God, it was required to take a stand against the pope, to disobey and remain faithful to God.[223] Not only was the papal crusade bull contrary to the law of God, but it also contravened canon law. Indulgences bought and sold were useless, because selling spiritual gifts accomplished nothing.[224] Elsewhere, Hus

---

216. "Utrum secundum legem Jesu Christi licet," in HM, vol. 1, pp. 215–235.

217. HM, vol. 1, pp. 216, 217, 223, 224, 225, 226, 228, 229, 234.

218. Ibid., pp. 226–227.

219. Ibid., p. 218.

220. HM, vol. 1, p. 219.

221. Ibid., vol. 1, pp. 222, 223, 224.

222. Ibid., vol. 1, p. 232.

223. Ibid., vol. 1, p. 234.

224. *Contra cruciatam*, in Hus, *Opera omnia*, vol. 22, pp. 131, 134.

drew attention to legislation that forbade any person under holy orders pronouncing a "sentence of blood," or implementing such an order, and furthermore ruled that no priest should be present when it was carried out.[225] Hus's speech seems to have had a positive response. A note turned up in the indulgences collection box at St. Vitus declaring that "it is better to believe Master Hus who tells the truth than great prelates, who keep concubines and are simoniacs, who lie to the people." This theme apparently caught on in Prague and was often repeated. The leaflet included the line "you [followers of] Asmodeus and Belial, and especially all you teachers of greed."[226] An anonymous treatise appeared, attacking the scoundrels who prevented Tiem from carrying out his indulgences sale.[227] The indulgences controversy only made blatant the matter of disobedience that now featured prominently in the Hus case.

On July 10, the theological faculty at Prague, under the deanship of Štěpán Páleč, who had undergone a dramatic volte-face and reversed his initial position, filed a protest with the king against Hus on account of his stance against indulgences.[228] Hus was required to submit his position on indulgences. He refused. Páleč had already written a defense of indulgences in June, accusing Hus of wishing to obey scripture only while ignoring tradition and law.[229] Hus retorted that "the Roman Curia does not take a sheep without its wool."[230] The text of Páleč's argument was read at a meeting convened by the king in Žebrák, about thirty-five miles southwest of Prague, in the house of Šimon Voděrady, the parish priest. We are not informed of how the gathering proceeded.[231] However, an apparent lack of

---

225. *Contra octo doctores*, in Hus, *Opera omnia*, vol. 22, p. 458, citing X 3.50.9 *Sententiam sanguinis*, in Friedberg, vol. 2, cols. 659–660.

226. Text in Höfler, vol. 2, pp. 201–203, corrected in Doležalová et al., "The Reception and Criticism of Indulgences," p. 134.

227. Hardt, vol. 3, p. 9. See Pavel Soukup, "Mařik Rvačka's Defense of Crusading Indulgences from 1412," in BRRP 8, pp. 77–97, with an edition of the treatise, "Articuli contra impedientes dominum Wenceslaum Thyem," based on Nürnberg, Stadtbibliothek, Cent. I, 78, fols. 176ᵛ–178ʳ, on pp. 90–97.

228. *Documenta*, pp. 448–450.

229. Text of his *Tractatus gloriosus* in Johann Loserth, ed., "Beiträge zur Geschichte der Husitischen Bewegung," AÖG 75 (1889): 333–339.

230. *Contra Palecz*, in Hus, *Opera omnia*, vol. 22, p. 237. The line comes from a Latin satire two centuries before Hus and may be found in Hans Walther, *Initia carminum ac versuum medii aevi posterioris Latinorum* (Göttingen: Vandenhoeck & Ruprecht, 1959), p. 199.

231. See the account in *Contra octo doctores*, in Hus, *Opera omnia*, vol. 22, pp. 371–372.

consensus prompted the king to seek resolution to the squabble, and on July 10, he convened a second meeting at Žebrák Castle. The theologians passed a resolution (known as the Žebrák Articles) reaffirming the condemnation of the "forty-five articles" from 1403 but adding seven additional articles and explicitly calling Hus and his party heretical.[232] The display of relics with attached indulgences in Prague led to protest and violence.[233] Hus later claimed that faithful Christians tried to warn certain priests about the perils of speaking falsehood in their sermons about indulgences. Already, Hus had enumerated those errors as sinfulness on the part of those priests who told their congregations that "the one who puts his or her money here will have their sins forgiven" and that it was possible to redeem loved ones by means of indulgences.[234] Hus complained that those who took up this theme opposing the sale were not simply ignored but were seized and beaten by priests in the churches, abused, and in some cases dragged away and whipped. The monks at the Carmelite monastery of the Mother of God of the Snows in the New Town were involved in this nefarious activity, as were monks resident in other religious houses.[235] Hus wanted to know how it was possible for anyone to escape judgment at the court of Christ by buying a papal pardon.[236] The uproar generated by the dispute led to the martyrdom of indulgences protesters on July 11. Hus blamed the furor on Štěpán Páleč and Stanislav of Znojmo, who had abandoned the truth and now opposed the reformers. The most striking and tragic outcome of the upheaval was the beheading of three men who withstood the indulgences preachers. Hus also claimed that there were others who were arrested, tortured, and incarcerated.[237] There is some evidence the deaths occurred at the order of King Václav. This assumption was advanced by Jan Náz, a lawyer and diplomatic representative of King Václav, and confirmed by Páleč. It was disputed by Hus.[238] The truth is shrouded in the past. A controversial funeral of the three martyrs at Bethlehem Chapel was conducted not

232. *Documenta*, pp. 451–455.

233. Štěpán of Dolany, *Antihussus*, in Pez, vol. 4, cols. 380–382.

234. "Utrum secundum legem Jesu Christi licet," in HM, vol. 1, p. 232.

235. Sermon for Lent V, in *Postil*, in Hus, *Opera omnia*, vol. 2, p. 175.

236. "Utrum secundum legem Jesu Christi licet," in HM, vol. 1, p. 228.

237. SRB, vol. 3, pp. 16–19; and *Postil*, in Hus, *Opera omnia*, vol. 2, pp. 114–115.

238. *Relatio*, p. 107.

by Hus, as was reported, but instead by Jan of Jičín, a university master. The chapel thereafter was referred to by some as the chapel of the three saints.[239] Another meeting called on July 16 convened at the Old Town Hall in hopes of settling the indulgences controversy. The sessions were chaired by Bishop Konrad of Olomouc and Václav Králík. Hus was not present. The Žebrák Articles were reaffirmed, and those questioning them were judged worthy of exile. On the authority of the king, all further disputations about Wyclif were forbidden.[240] Undeterred, the next day, university chancellor Marek of Hradec, having called for a subsequent meeting, convened a discussion at the Carolinum in which the "forty-five articles" were discussed, in violation of the royal decree. Hus refers to the gathering in his *Postil*.[241] Elsewhere, Hus tells us that Marek of Hradec, along with Friedrich Eppinge and Prokop Plzeň, signed a petition opposing the royal decree.[242] But his opponents on this occasion could hardly have been Master Blažej Vlk and Jan Kbel, as asserted by the Vratislav manuscript, since the former had died in 1410 and the latter was also likely deceased. Nevertheless, issues revolving around heresy continued. The main outcome of the indulgences controversy in Prague during the summer of 1412 resulted in Hus losing the support of the king, falling victim to political and economic factors. It is also of considerable consequence that Štěpán Páleč defected from the reform party and by the autumn of 1412 had become one of Hus's greatest foes.

The indulgences controversy cannot be separated from the legal affairs of Jan Hus. His stance on the matter not only cost him the support of the royal house, but it added even more fuel to the fire being fanned by his enemies. Indeed, the tumultuous events in Prague did nothing to divert ongoing legal action in the papal court. In terms of the Hus case at the Curia, Michael de Causis submitted an ex parte petition to the pope calling for the replacement of the papal auditor Berthold Wildungen, who had been assigned oversight of the Hus case. We do not know the reason. The influence held by de Causis cannot be in doubt, especially when yet another of his legal motions was granted and George Fleckel was appointed to

239. Štěpán of Dolany, *Antihussus*, in Pez, vol. 4, col. 381.

240. "K dějinám českého viklefství r. 1411 a 1412," ST 1, pp. 55–65, is a notarized record of the meeting.

241. Hus, *Opera omnia*, vol. 2, pp. 114–115; and Šimek, *Staré letopisy české*, pp. 9–10.

242. *Contra Stanislaum*, in Hus, *Opera omnia*, vol. 22, p. 277.

replace Wildungen. During these developments, Jan Jesenice escaped from prison. He was promptly anathematized on July 29 and thereafter considered contumacious on the basis of established legal statute.[243] During that same tumultuous summer, Jiří Bor wrote against Hus, claiming that since Hus was a defendant in a heresy suit, he had no right of appeal, because he was excommunicate and contumacious.[244] Regardless of the gathering legal storm, in late July, Hus and other university masters conducted a defense of Wyclifite articles in the university in further defiance of the royal prohibition. Eight of the outlawed "forty-five articles" were selected. Hus defended six of these (numbers 4, 13–16, and 18). Jakoubek Stříbro defended one (number 32), arguing that clerical endowment violated the law of God, while Friedrich Eppinge defended yet another (number 11) on the matter of unjust excommunication.[245] Eppinge's speech was praised by Hus.[246] Hus's position, enumerated in his defense of these articles, sheds further light on issues that continued to emerge throughout the remainder of the judicial trial. Defending the thirteenth article, Hus announced that it was insufficient for the "forty-five articles" to have been theoretically condemned when, in fact, it was essential that the alleged errors therein be demonstrated. Hus submits that neither he nor his colleagues will accept the unsubstantiated condemnation of Wyclif. Elsewhere, Hus denounced as "foolish temerity" the action to condemn without proof.[247] On the fourteenth article, Hus asserted that those who stopped preaching in fear of the threat of excommunication were already excommunicated and that when the day of judgment came, these mute preachers would be numbered among the "betrayers of Christ." The issue became heresy. Priests who would not oppose the heresies promulgated by the papacy were mute dogs who could not open their mouths to bark against the wolves who came to kill the sheep.[248] On the fifteenth article, Hus used the

---

243. Kejř, *Jesenice*, p. 61.

244. *Replicatio contra Hus*, in Sedlák, *Miscellanea*, pp. 234–237.

245. Texts of Hus's "Defensio articulorum Wyclif" are in Hus, *Opera omnia*, vol. 22, pp. 143–232. Jakoubek's and Eppinge's defenses are in S. Harrison Thomson, ed., *Mag. Johannis Hus Tractatus Responsivus* (Princeton, N.J.: Princeton University Press, 1927), pp. 28–54, 103–133, the latter based on Prague Castle Archive, MS C 116, fols. 279ʳ–291ᵛ.

246. *De ecclesia*, pp. 216–217.

247. Novotný, *Correspondence*, p. 124.

248. Hus, *Opera omnia*, vol. 22, pp. 143–150. Hus cites canon law on excommunication.

analogy of marriage and children to drive his point home. Once a man and a woman marry, they were allowed to engage in procreation and have children without special permission from any authority. Priests were engaged in the practice of begetting spiritual children and they needed no additional mandate to do this through preaching.[249] Obstruction of preaching could be put down to the work of "false prophets" who accomplished nothing except the "blaspheming of Christian truth" and the unhindered proclamation of lies. It was the "subtleties of Antichrist" that attempted to "extinguish the true preaching of the gospel."[250] Turning to article 17, Hus argued that the priesthood should in no way live contrary to the rule of Christ. If they did, they should be corrected, their possessions seized, and, if need be (citing Hostiensis), people might lawfully "withhold the alms of their tithes." Moreover, if it could be demonstrated that possessing wealth and worldly goods hindered the priesthood from fulfilling its duties, then it was proper for the secular authorities to remove those things from the priests.[251] "Pope Silvester and Emperor Constantine made a mistake by enriching the church."[252] Hus continued in the same vein, defending article 18 and concluding that priests were the stewards of goods but should not be lords or owners. If the church abused this duty, Hus declared, the guilty priests were "thieves, robbers and sacrilegious who, unless they repent, are condemned by God's righteous judgment."[253] These and other statements made during the defense of the Wyclif articles reveal Hus as an independent thinker, unwilling simply to accept decisions made by church authority, and he moreover presented himself as unafraid to challenge the church itself. Naturally, there were consequences.

At the height of the debates, controversies, and legal procedures in the summer of 1412, Jan Hus set out to summarize his legal case to date. In particular, he noted the establishment of Bethlehem Chapel for preaching to the people, Zbyněk's animosity, the papal bull against preaching, his appeal against the bull of Alexander, and how he had also tried to appeal to Pope John. Hus noted that he had preached against avarice, simony, luxury, and pride of the clergy and therefore had come under attack. However,

---

249. Ibid., vol. 1, p. 153.

250. Ibid., p. 164.

251. Ibid., pp. 177–182.

252. Novotný, *Correspondence*, p. 125.

253. Hus, *Opera omnia*, vol. 22, pp. 206–208.

he claimed to have undertaken such preaching on account of conscience and the distress he felt "because of the moral decay of the church." Hus called attention to the "envious parish priests of Prague," who agitated against him and ultimately charged him with heresy and arranged for him to be summoned to Rome. This was a short, incomplete narrative of the difficulties between him and the church. Some of this covered legal issues.[254] Logically, it would have appeared before the better-known *Ordo procedendi*, which is taken up in detail in chapter 6 below. However, it cannot be earlier than the controversy over the crusade bull and indulgences of 1412. Hus defended some of the "forty-five articles," (but erroneously referred to them thrice as "42 articles") and claimed that his stance against the irregular lives of Prague priests caused his citation to the Curia. He was quite mistaken in this assertion, since it was he who appealed from Zbyněk to the Holy See. This is a curious but important slippage. At this stage, it is alleged that Hus appealed to a future council. At least, this was claimed in the *Ordo procedendi*, but the assertion is manifestly untrue. We might account for this spectacular claim on the grounds that it must have been Jan Jesenice's method of obfuscating the legally indefensible appeal to Christ that Hus elsewhere did announce.

The personnel in charge of the Hus case continued to shift, and during the summer of 1412, Cardinal Peter degli Stephaneschi replaced Brancacci on the legal case and wasted no time in issuing an affirmation of Colonna's anathema against Hus on July 29, 1412.[255] He, too, chose to ignore the legally defensible findings of Zabarella. Of importance from a legal point of view is the conclusion of the writ, which states that the censures against Hus could only be lifted by the pope. Once more, suspicion was voiced that the action of Cardinal Stephaneschi may have been motivated by bribery.[256] Questions of money predictably dominated aspects of the case, with both sides alleging improprieties. Hus's enemies suggested that his attorneys had at least eleven hundred florins at their disposal with which to bribe curial officials.[257] Those baser assumptions aside, a papal order in

---

254. Prague Castle Archive, MS D 50, fols. 237ʳ–238ʳ; and Novotný, *Correspondence*, pp. 123–125. The text is undated. Flajšhans suggests 1413. Novotný thinks it is July or August 1412. I follow Novotný. Flajšhans, *Sebrané spisy*, vol. 1, pt. 1, p. 63; and Novotný, *Correspondence*, p. 123.

255. *Documenta*, pp. 461–464.

256. Jesenice, *Repetitio*, p. 418.

257. Štěpán Páleč, *Antihus*, in Sedlák, *Miscellanea*, p. 376.

the late summer for the destruction of Bethlehem Chapel issued by John XXIII reached Prague before the end of September.[258] This resulted in an unsuccessful attack on the chapel led by an otherwise unknown fellow named Bernard Chotek. Hus provided details.[259] The assault on the chapel was undertaken by a group of men wearing armor and carrying cross-bows, halberts, and swords. The attack took place while Hus was in the pulpit preaching. The attempt came to naught on account of poor plan-ning, although Hus said the malevolent gang was confused on account of divine intervention. A second plan was put in motion following a meet-ing at the Old Town hall, and on this occasion, the Germans attempted to enlist the help of the Czechs and had a man named Holubář act as mediator between the two sides. Holubář's entreaties were of no avail, for the Czechs would not consent. Meanwhile, on September 4, Cardinal Stephaneschi issued a writ of major excommunication against Hus, which was the aggravation of the previous excommunication, meaning that the full implementation of the legal and ecclesiastical sanction—the *aggrava-tio*—had now finally and formally arrived in Prague. This was the fourth condemnation of excommunication issued against Hus. This constituted the *sententia*, the formal judgment of the court. As noted above, canon law made distinction between minor and major excommunication; the former barred one from the Eucharist, the latter from the community of the faithful.[260] The provisions were intended to isolate Hus in the most comprehensive sense imaginable. Under penalty of excommunication, no good Christian was to speak to Hus or engage in any conversation. There could be no greeting, eating, drinking, buying, or selling that involved the excommunicated heretic. No one could offer him anything whatsoever, favors might not be granted, comfort could not be extended, shelter could not be provided, and no human exchange on any level was permitted. In any place Hus might come seeking shelter, all church services and ecclesi-astical functions were ordered suspended immediately, and these spiritual offices could not resume for a period of three days after the excommuni-cate departed. Should Hus die, he could not be granted burial. If he had

---

258. Spinka, *John Hus*, p. 162.

259. *Postil*, in Hus, *Opera omnia*, vol. 2, pp. 166–167.

260. C.11 q.3 p.c.24 *Ad mensam*, in Friedberg, vol. 1, col. 651; C.23 q.4 c.27 *Inter querelas*, in Friedberg, vol. 1, col. 912; X 5.38.12 *Omnis utriusque*, in Friedberg, vol. 2, cols. 887–888; X 5.39.15 *Quum desideres*, in Friedberg, vol. 2, cols. 894–895; and Sext. 5.10.2 *Quum medicinalis sit excommunicatio*, in Friedberg, vol. 2, cols., 1093–1094.

already died and been buried, his remains were to be disinterred without delay. Canon law already viewed the defenders of heresy and those who received them as ineligible for burial.[261] Canon law allowed that an outlawed person might be killed with impunity. After all, the punishment of crimes was in the public interest.[262] Those aiding the condemned faced severe consequences. In 1400, a tavern keeper in northern Italy was executed for ignoring such strictures in extending aid and comfort to the enemy by providing hospitality.[263] All of this came to bear upon Hus. These drastic measures had been prompted by Michael de Causis and Mařík Rvačka. The two were now haunting the halls of the papal court in Rome and actively collaborating against Hus.[264] A second bull (ostensibly procured by Michael de Causis) also arrived in Prague, and in this decree, Hus was ordered seized by the faithful and turned over either to the archbishop of Prague or the bishop of Litomyšl to be condemned and burned according to law. The Bethlehem Chapel (described as a "nest of heretics") was again ordered destroyed to prevent the continued congregation of heretics.[265] Hus and his followers were to stand down and abjure. Otherwise, they were to appear at the Curia to answer the outstanding charges of contumacy before appropriate judges, including Michael de Causis.

On October 18, the major excommunication of Jan Hus was announced to the annual Prague diocesan synod by Cardinal John of Lisbon (João Alfonso Esteves, ca. 1340–1415), papal legate and titular prelate of the church of St. Peter in Chains in Rome. This was the formal notification that Stephaneschi had reaffirmed the sentence of Colonna, on top of the double anathema of Zbyněk and the tacit judgment passed by Brancacci. The provisions of the writ followed canon law in the requirement that heresy suspects were required to clear themselves of suspicion within one year; otherwise, the faithful were obligated to avoid them.[266] Major

---

261. X 5.7.8 *Sicut ait*, in Friedberg, vol. 2, cols. 779–780, based on Lateran III. See also X 3.40.7 *De homine*, in Friedberg, vol. 2, col. 640.

262. X 5.39.35 *Ut famae*, in Friedberg, vol. 2, col. 904.

263. Carraway, p. 109.

264. Writ against Hus, in *Documenta*, pp. 461–464.

265. Chronicle of the University of Prague, FRB, vol. 5, pp. 574–575; Chronicle of Prokop the Notary, in Höfler, vol. 1, p. 912.

266. X 5.7.13 §2 *Excommunicamus*, in Friedberg, vol. 2, cols. 787–788; X 5.7.10 *Vergentis in senium*, in Friedberg, vol. 2, cols. 782–783.

excommunication referred to the application of the penalty by an ecclesiastical judge. Anathema was its solemn imposition.[267] In order to stress the gravity and severity of the matter, an *Interdictum locale* (local interdict) was imposed on all of Prague (including Vyšehrad) on account of Hus's continued presence in the city.[268] This was an effort to impress upon the citizens of Prague their collective guilt in the heresy of Hus and the sin of continuing to tolerate him within their midst. The traditional ceremonies of announcing the eviction of one from the community of the faithful accompanied the declaration of excommunication. The writ of excommunication against Hus ordered all abbots, priors, and priests everywhere in churches, chapels, and monasteries to intone a solemn mass and follow the ritual of excluding one from the household of faith. This might include a bell being rung, a candle being lit and then extinguished and knocked to the floor, a cross being raised, foot stamping, spitting, the closing of a door, and three stones thrown at the house of the excommunicate.[269] The broad thrust of the ban, the writ of excommunication, and the relevant laws on which the censure was based aimed to isolate offenders from the community, to aid in the capture of the accused, and to render contumacy more difficult.[270] It is challenging to prove that the writ issued by Stephaneschi against Hus was legally invalid.[271] At this stage, with all obvious legal avenues exhausted, Hus appealed to Christ on October 18 and publicly announced his intention to do so in a sermon. He apparently nailed a written text of the appeal to the gate of the bridge tower in the Lesser Town.[272] It must be said that Hus's action had no precedent or provision in canon law and presented

---

267. Hostiensis, SA, 5, col. 1880.

268. Noted in Šimek, *Staré letopisy české*, pp. 12–13, but the chronicler erroneously applied the interdict to the summer of 1413. Canon law provisions are summarized in Sext. 5.11.16–20 *De sententia excommunicationis, suspensionis et interdicti*, in Friedberg, vol. 2, cols. 1104–1105.

269. See Genevieve Steele Edwards, "Ritual Excommunication in Medieval France and England, 900–1200," PhD dissertation, Stanford University, 1997. Some of these elements are specifically mentioned in the writ of excommunication against Hus promulgated by Zbyněk, *Documenta*, p. 399, and in the writ of excommunication issued by Cardinal Stephaneschi, *Documenta*, p. 463.

270. Carraway, p. 108.

271. De Vooght, p. 269.

272. Novotný, *Correspondence*, pp. 134–136. The public display is recorded in the chronicle of Jan Długosz, *Historia Polonicae libri xii*, 2 vols., ed. H. von Huyssen (Leipzig: Gleditoch & Weidmann, 1711–1712), vol. 1, col. 335.

a judicial conundrum, inasmuch as there was no possible legal option to transfer the case to a court or authority higher than the Holy See.[273] Hus never accepted that legal distinction and held to the validity of this appeal right up to the day of his death.[274] At this stage, with the issuing of the aggravated anathema, the case against Hus, from a legal point of view in terms of the court proceedings at the Curia, was suspended and could be regarded as "pending" until the Council of Constance two years later. In the face of unrelenting ecclesiastical censure, Hus voluntarily went into exile sometime after October 18 in order to spare Prague the blunt consequences of the interdict that was now being enforced. This did not cause Michael de Causis to scale back the prosecution of Hus. By the end of the year, he had initiated new inflammatory charges against Hus, prompted by Prague canons.[275] In these accusations, Hus was called a "son of iniquity," a "heretic," a "Wyclifite," and one who "despises the keys." The charges claimed that "all heretics and schismatics deserve a place with the devil and his angels in the flames of eternal hell."[276] The sentiment simply reflected canon law, which affirmed that heretics would burn forever in hell.[277] Hus was characterized as the initiator of heretical depravity, responsible for numerous souls lost in the depths of error. De Causis insisted that the poison of Hus had filled Bohemia and spread to Moravia and could be found as far afield as Poland and Hungary. Even more drastic was the fact that Hus continued to act with impunity, so much so that the church of God suffered severe oppression, and many of the faithful had died as a result. De Causis begged the pope to act against these wolves who had rushed in a frenzy among the faithful. Elsewhere, we find evidence that de Causis and Jan Cifra filed new charges at the "Roman Curia," which disgraced King Václav and the kingdom of Bohemia.[278] New to the prosecution of Hus, Cifra has elsewhere been identified as a Prague canon.[279]

---

273. C.9 q.3 c.16 *Ipsi sunt canones*, in Friedberg, vol. 1, col. 611.

274. *Relatio*, pp. 113–114.

275. *Documenta*, pp. 457–461.

276. Ibid., p. 457.

277. X 5.7.3 *Firmissime tene*, in Friedberg, vol. 2, col. 750.

278. Chronicle of the University of Prague, FRB, vol. 5, p. 571.

279. *Documenta*, p. 731.

Later that autumn, Hus informed the supreme court in Bohemia about the nature and proceedings of his case and openly acknowledged his disobedience to higher clergy, while tacitly suggesting that the court might intercede.[280] Arguably, this constituted willful legal violation of procedure by attempting to transfer the case from an ecclesiastical to a secular court. Whatever Hus's intentions may have been, the approach to the supreme court did not go unnoticed. Around this time, Jan Jesenice reappeared in Prague, and on December 18, he defended Hus at the university, arguing for the invalidity of the sentence against Hus, claiming in part that Pope Boniface IX had granted the university privilege in 1397 wherein legal authorities could not proceed against members.[281] Jesenice further suggested that the anathema was contrary to canon law.[282] This assertion was predicated mainly on the premise that without a specific admonition (*monitio canonica*) to the person in question, before witnesses, the anathema had no legal standing.[283] The admonishment was obligatory in order for the excommunication to be valid.[284] As noted, full excommunication could only be legally and properly applied after three warnings.[285] The anathema issued by Peter Stephaneschi mentioned *monitio canonica*, but there is no record of its having been issued separately in advance of the anathema itself as required, unless the references in Cardinal Colonna's letter to Zbyněk two years earlier qualify.[286] Excommunication was invalid if predicated on procedural errors that were deemed unfair or if such errors resulted in procedural inequity.[287] Jesenice was now powerless to submit any motions personally, but it is unclear whether he advised Hus to do so perhaps via another advocate. In the defense of his former client, Jesenice's arguments are predicated on a single issue: Jan Hus did not refuse to go to Rome.[288] The

---

280. Hus letter, early December 1412, Novotný, *Correspondence*, pp. 157–158.

281. *Repetitio*, pp. 408–419. On the university privilege, see *Monumenta historica universitatis Carolo-Ferdinandae Pragensis*, 3 vols. (Prague: Spurny, 1830–1848), vol. 2, p. 371.

282. Sext. 5.11.9 *Constitutionem felicis*, in Friedberg, vol. 2, cols. 1101–1102.

283. See also X 5.39.48 *Sacro approbante*, in Friedberg, vol. 2, cols. 909–910.

284. X 2.28.26 *Reprehensibilis*, in Friedberg, vol. 2, cols. 418–419.

285. C.17 q.4 c.21 *Quisquis inventus*, in Friedberg, vol. 1, col. 820.

286. *Documenta*, p. 407.

287. Sext. 5.11.9 *Constitutionem felicis*, in Friedberg, vol. 2, cols. 1101–1102.

288. See de Vooght, p. 270.

presentation made by Jesenice constituted a tour de force executed by a legal virtuoso. But the reality remained. Hus was formally an excommunicate and an accused heretic. Further legal representation of such an individual in the early fifteenth century was doubtful. Jesenice's *Repetitio pro defensione causae Magistri Joannis Hus* was submitted to Bishop Konrad of Olomouc in late December 1412.[289] A few weeks earlier, Albík of Uničov had signaled his intention to step down from the archiepiscopal see. Konrad was poised to succeed him, having purchased the office (simony), and was already at this date functioning as the administrator. Hence Jesenice submitted his argument for Hus to Konrad rather than Albík.

Hus may have left the capital, but the investigation into heresy had not ended. On January 3, 1413, King Václav ordered a meeting of the Prague clergy to convene at Český Brod on February 2 under the leadership of Konrad of Vechta and Jan Železný, the redoubtable bishop of Litomyšl. This meeting was convened by Konrad for the purposes of reconciliation and uprooting heresy.[290] The convocation did not take place on the date or at the place specified by the king. It met instead on February 6 at the archbishop's residence. The February synod referred everything back to the king, who appointed a pro-Hus commission consisting of university chancellor Křišťan of Prachatice, university master Zdeněk of Labouň, former Prague Archbishop Albík of Uničov, and Jakub of Dubá, protonotary of the royal chancery and dean of Vyšehrad, to negotiate a settlement. Both sides bound themselves to accept the decision of the commission under penalty of fine and exile.[291] Why should the king appoint a pro-Hus commission if he and Hus had a falling out the previous summer? The answer must be political. Around this time, Štěpán Páleč composed his polemical tract *Antihus*, which stridently critiqued Hus for disobedience to ecclesiastical authority.[292] He argued that the legal maneuvers and appeals undertaken by Hus were merely attempts to obfuscate ecclesiastical authority, because the defendant did not wish to be subjected to earthly judgment, and his legal appeal to the law of God was nothing other than an effort by a heretic to avoid evaluation and accountability.[293] *Antihus* underscored the

---

289. *Documenta*, p. 499.

290. Ibid., pp. 472–474.

291. Chronicle of the University of Prague, FRB, vol. 5, pp. 575–579.

292. Text in Sedlák, *Miscellanea*, pp. 366–507.

293. *Antihus*, in Sedlák, *Miscellanea*, pp. 457, 377, 459, 466.

perceived problems with Hus. These included disobedience, violation of church orders, rejection of indulgences, adherence to Wyclif, criticism of the priesthood, and a steadfast refusal to submit to church authority. This attack on Hus was supported by a brief anonymous rebuttal to Jesenice's university defense of Hus, which also appeared in early 1413.[294]

As both sides in the legal struggle sought stability and focus, we note two statements that emerged from the February meeting aimed at unifying the clergy in Bohemia. The antireform party led by Páleč and Stanislav of Znojmo produced a document that condemned the "forty-five articles" and called for each member of the university to swear not to uphold any of the articles. The text argued that since Hus upheld the sanctioned articles, he was rightly placed under ecclesiastical censure and personal interdict by the church, and the local interdict on Prague was likewise justified. Moreover, the authors insisted, Hus should not preach again until he had received papal absolution, and his continued presence in Prague should not be tolerated, since it hindered authorized preaching.[295] This last point goes some distance toward proving Hus's assumption that the papal bull of 1409 restricting preaching in Prague to certain locations was nothing other than a crass attempt to limit his preaching function at Bethlehem Chapel. With Hus formally excommunicated, the city under interdict, and Hus in exile, his detractors now wanted preaching resumed. A second document, more delicate in approach, called for obedience to the official church, defined by the papacy and the college of cardinals, in opposition to views maintained by "some of the clergy in the Kingdom of Bohemia." The *Concilium* pointed out that while "some of the clergy in the Kingdom of Bohemia" remain opposed to ecclesiastical decisions on the "forty-five articles," it was necessary to support a renewed condemnation of Wyclif. Further, in spite of the teachings of "some of the clergy in the Kingdom of Bohemia," views contrary to Rome should not be tolerated. This document, dated February 6, also asserted that the name *heretic* was worse than all evil names. The repeated reference "quidam autem de clero in regno Bohemiae" must be understood as referring to Hus and his colleagues and supporters. Finally, the document made an unambiguous statement that it was not appropriate for the Prague clergy to decide if the excommunication of Hus and its aggravation by the Roman Curia was either

---

294. *Motiva ad Hus fulminatos*, in Sedlák, *Miscellanea*, pp. 77–79.

295. *Confessio doctorum contra Hus*, in Sedlák, "Několik textů z doby husitské," pp. 48–49.

right or wrong. Instead, the priests were bound to accept the procedural rulings from the Roman court that had been received in Prague. The apostolic rulings were binding on the clergy and should neither be challenged nor ignored.[296] The document referred to the obscure and provincial fourth-century Council of Sardica, which was represented later as ratifying a canon effectively claiming that decrees of the apostolic see should be regarded as legally binding and by consequence privileging the pope with appellate jurisdiction. The interpretation is both wrong and anachronistic.[297] Hus did not consider the argument compelling.

These developments caused Hus to spring back into the fray, and he lost little time preparing his own proposal for reconciliation consisting of nine articles.[298] Hus challenged his detractors to show cause and said that should they fail to sustain allegations of heresy or error, they should suffer the appropriate consequences as their case falters (article 3). In this work, he repeated his conviction that he and Archbishop Zbyněk had been reconciled (article 1) and that such agreement should govern all discussions. He argued for the right of the king to judge decisions made by the Holy See (article 8). Moreover, the imposition of interdict should not be permitted (article 9). In this general stance, Hus was supported by Jakoubek Stříbro.[299] In his short but highly academic treatise, Jakoubek argued that peace could only be meaningful in the context of reform and that true peace came from observing the law of God. Jakoubek was quite specific at this juncture, calling upon King Václav and all inhabitants of the realm to put an end to the "heresy of simony," licentiousness, sexual immorality, concubinage, ecclesiastical wealth, and the secular power of the clergy. Malicious accusations of heresy against Hus should simply be ignored. This was a de facto appeal for enforcing the reform program in the entire Czech church. Hus also composed a critique of the clergy's meeting and its proposals, repeating many of his previously expressed arguments.[300]

---

296. *Consilium doctorum facultatis theologicae studii Pragensis*, in *Documenta*, pp. 475–480. Reference to the term *heretic* is on p. 478, and the urge to accept the legal findings is cited on p. 480.

297. Hamilton Hess, *The Early Development of Canon Law and the Council of Serdica* (Oxford: Oxford University Press, 2002), provides an up-to-date analysis of the synod and its canons. See especially pp. 180–189. Ancient Sardica is today Sofia, Bulgaria.

298. *Conditiones concordiae*, in *Documenta*, pp. 491–492.

299. *Documenta*, pp. 493–494.

300. *Contra falsa consilia doctorum*, in *Documenta*, pp. 499–501.

Hus and Jakoubek were supported by Jan Jesenice, who rebutted the proposal of the theologians, arguing that the matter had not been investigated thoroughly and was in consequence in violation of canonical statutes that required care in determining guilt or innocence. Jesenice argued that the foundation for the work of the theologians was questionable.[301] He went on to allege that the prelates were falsifiers of scripture and canon law. The papal court was filled with simoniacs and heretics, and these men were the principal cause of dissension. Here, Jesenice surely had in mind Michael de Causis and his associates. Nevertheless, he built his case to a climax and suggested it was naive and indefensible to claim that the judicial process against Hus must be obeyed simply because legal rulings were handed down by the court in Rome. With biting sarcasm, Jesenice suggested that sort of logic was rather like claiming people should obey the devil because Adam and Eve had done so. As an experienced lawyer, Jesenice was convinced that the legal process against Hus was frivolous and contrary to law. Those who persisted in applying the illegitimate sanctions should be considered "blasphemers, sacrilegious, heretics, and excommunicates."[302] The religious history of Bohemia during the previous decade had caused the realm to gain a reputation for heresy. Hus referred to "the sinister and false infamy" that enveloped Bohemia, while Jesenice described the nation as blackened by infamy.[303] There were expected rejoinders to these proreform writings. Stanislav of Znojmo wrote a treatise taking issue with Hus and especially with Jesenice's *Replicatio contra false consilia doctorum*.[304] Štěpán Páleč joined Stanislav in opposing Jesenice and Hus in another literary blast.[305] Neither side was prepared to budge, and the salvos continued. The polemics between Hus and Páleč may be characterized as "merciless and mutually inconsiderate."[306]

---

301. *Replicatio contra false consilia doctorum*, in *Documenta*, pp. 495–499, drawing upon C.11 q.3 c.4 *Si episcopis*, in Friedberg, vol. 1, col. 643; X 1.3.5 *Si quando*, in Friedberg, vol. 2, col. 18; and X 3.5.6 *Quum teneamur*, in Friedberg, vol. 2, cols. 465–466.

302. *Documenta*, pp. 497–499.

303. Hus, *Conditiones concordiae* in ibid., p. 491; and *Replicatio magistrorum Pragensium contra conditiones concordiae a facultate theologica latas*, in ibid., p. 495.

304. *Alma et venerabilis*, in Johann Loserth, ed., "Beiträge zur Geschichte der Husitischen Bewegung," AÖG 75 (1889): 361–413.

305. *Replicatio contra Quidamistas*, in Loserth, "Beiträge zur Geschichte," pp. 344–361.

306. "M. Štěpán z Pálče a Husův proces," in Kejř, *Počátků*, p. 115.

While Hus continued to be under attack in Prague, Wyclif was formally condemned by the papal authority of John XXIII on February 2, 1413, at a Lateran council, and his books were burned on February 10 in Rome in front of St. Peter's Basilica. The bull of condemnation is extant.[307] A glossed copy of John XXIII's bull condemning Wyclif later turned up. These comments were thereafter attributed to Hus, who denied writing them.[308] They are more likely from the pen of Jesenice, who underscored the irrelevance of the Roman council, the nepotism of the Curia, the ignorance of those who condemned the books, and the questionable motives of those involved.[309] He characterized the synod as just "a few monks and simoniacs gathered in a corner." The destruction of Wyclif's books in Rome was reported to Jiří Bor in a brief undated communication from Olan, one of the lawyers at the Curia.[310] Given Hus's association with aspects of Wyclif and his out-spoken defense of some of the "forty-five articles," the fact that Wyclif had now been formally condemned by the pope and his books destroyed by papal order had direct legal consequences for the Hus court case and trial proceedings. Anyone deemed to be following a condemned heresy was automatically associated with the condemnation.[311] In short, the develop-ments in Rome strengthened the case for the prosecution. Hus's sworn enemies continued to press the Czech authorities, calling for even further measures to eradicate the threat of heresy. Bishop Jan Železný wrote to Konrad of Vechta on February 10, urging that Hus never again be permit-ted to preach at Bethlehem Chapel, that all preaching by those sympa-thetic to Hus be curtailed, and that his books be declared contraband and their publication and circulation stopped. He urged the appointment of an official to search out and punish all errors, characterizing the works of Hus as "the stalks of accursed tares and schism," scattered in great mea-sure among the common people, which should be placed under anath-ema. He railed against the "wolves" associated with Bethlehem Chapel. Moreover, Železný argued, Hus had erred in attempting to escape the

---

307. *Documenta*, pp. 467–469. Brief notice in NK, MS III G 16, fol. 98. The papal action had been incited by Canterbury archbishop Thomas Arundel.

308. *Relatio*, p. 106; and in his reply to the forty-two articles prepared by Páleč, in *Documenta*, pp. 222–223. Discussed in detail in Kejř, *Jesenice*, pp. 74–84.

309. *Documenta*, pp. 470–471.

310. Ibid., p. 469.

311. C.2 q.1 a.c.1 *Quod autem ab heretico*, in Friedberg, vol. 1, col. 966.

verdict of the papal court by asking for a decision from the high court of Bohemia. The action suggested, at the very least, additional evidence of contumacy on the part of Hus.[312] The work of the February commission continued, and there was a request for submissions from both sides in the ongoing dispute. Sometime in April, a meeting was convened in the rectory of St. Michael's Church in the Old Town of Prague. No agreement emerged. Jesenice, Jakoubek, and Šimon Tišnov appeared for the Hussite side. Determined to rid his realm of heresy accusations and suspicion and now fed up with the protracted arguments and lack of consensus, the king expelled Stanislav of Znojmo, Petr of Znojmo, Páleč, and Jan Eliášův from the realm because they refused to sign a letter addressed to the Curia stating that Bohemia was free of heresy.[313] The king also deprived them of their positions and instructed the University to execute his wishes.[314] The king then demanded revenues from the clergy. With surprisingly little complaint, they complied on April 23.[315] It appeared that King Václav had scored a convincing victory, but the annual Prague diocesan synod declared on June 16 in article 6 of its resolutions that it was erroneous to argue that the pope could not summon someone to a judicial examination (*cognitio*). The resolution had the stance of Hus clearly in mind. The exile of his enemies had settled nothing.[316] Even Hus went to the bother of once again explaining his decision. He recorded a conversation with the indulgence vendor Wenceslas Tiem, which in all probability occurred in the spring of 1412, wherein Hus drew a distinction between apostolic and papal commands, noting that he would obey the latter only if they conformed to the former and that he was prepared to die rather than submit to the pope against Christ:

I know the difference between commandments of the pope and apostolic commandments. When I was asked by the legates of the Roman Pope John XXIII in the presence of Albík, the Archbishop of Prague if I would obey apostolic commands, I replied that I greatly desired to obey the commandments of the apostolic Church.

---

312. *Documenta*, pp. 501–504.

313. Ibid., pp. 510–511.

314. Ibid., pp. 540–1 and Chronicle of the University of Prague, FRB, vol. 5, p. 576.

315. *Documenta*, p. 501.

316. Kadlec, *Synods*, p. 291.

The legates considered the commandments of the apostles and the commandments of the Pope to be the same thing and thought I would agree with raising the cross against Ladislaus, King of Naples and against the other people subject to him and to preach thus to the people against [Pope] Gregory XII. Therefore the envoys said, "behold, Archbishop, he is now willing to obey the commandments of our Lord." But I said, "masters, you have not understood me. I said I was willing to obey all of the commandments of the apostles. But I consider the Roman pope's commandments and doctrines apostolic [only] if they are consistent with the message and teaching of the law of Christ. If so, I very much want to be ready to obey. But if I think there is difference in those commands, then I will not obey, even if the fire for the burning of my body is prepared before my eyes."[317]

Here was the expression of an unequivocal point of view. It elicited comment when his trial resumed. The same perspective can be found in Hus's book against Páleč, in which he argues that a judge must decide cases in conformity with the law of God.[318] The appeal to the law of God indicated a different authority paradigm from that of the late medieval church. Indeed, the two philosophies presented significant challenge, and the collision was strikingly revealed in the trial of Hus. During this time, a transition occurred that had little bearing on the Hus case. Albík of Uničov, having indicated his intention to resign as archbishop of Prague, relinquished all duties, responsibilities, and powers, in accordance with his announcement in late 1412. This meant that from June 1413 and for the duration of the Hus trial, the principal ecclesiastical authority in Bohemia was Konrad of Vechta, who was installed as archbishop of Prague on July 17, 1413.

The trial of Jan Hus continued to present legal anomalies as it wound its way toward formal hearings and court appearances. The papal auditor Konrad Conhofer secured an agreement for the prosecution of Hus by a secular court, although the details are shrouded in mystery. Even the dating is uncertain. This may have occurred in December 1413, but it may have been a year earlier, since precise dating is impossible. What is certain

---

317. *Contra octo doctores*, in Hus, *Opera omnia*, vol. 22, pp. 375–376.

318. *Contra Palecz*, in Hus, *Opera omnia*, vol. 22, pp. 259–260.

is that this arrangement transpired before Hus went to Constance.[319] Such initiatives and political machinations are legally problematic, because heresy cases are restricted to ecclesiastical courts.[320] In medieval law, heresy was considered a *crimen mere ecclesiasticum*, which meant it was an offense reserved for judgment by the church. The right of the church to judge heresy could not be intruded upon even if secular legislation ruled otherwise.[321] Conhofer's strategy remains a mystery. Meanwhile, from exile, Hus continued to work, preach, explain himself, and comment on legal affairs. In a sermon prepared for the fourth Sunday in Lent, he again explained why he refused to appear at the papal court.[322] In another sermon, for the second Sunday in Trinity, based on Luke 14:16–24, Hus referred to the prohibition against preaching as an act of Antichrist and said that priests supporting the initiative (Michael de Causis, Zbyněk, et al.) constituted the "crew of Antichrist." Hus noted that he continued preaching anyway, first in Prague and then in exile, specifically mentioning his activity at Kozí Hrádek.[323] Elsewhere, in his sermon for the fifth day after Trinity, Hus mentioned efforts to stop preaching outside approved places but noted that he withstood the bull, appealed to the pope, and, when Alexander died, submitted a second appeal to John XXIII. When this failed, he appealed to Christ and continued to preach up to the present in cities, castles, fields, and forests, and were it possible, he would imitate Christ and preach from a boat.[324] The appeal to John suggests that Hus considered the death of Alexander as having no consequence. Obviously, Jesenice must have agreed that such understanding was legally defensible. If this were the case, arguments against Zbyněk's actions would be invalid. In the late spring, Hus wrote his opinion stating that the death penalty was inappropriate in matters of faith.[325]

The legal case involving Jan Hus was only one matter in the ecclesiastical affairs of Latin Christendom in the early fifteenth century. The wider

---

319. *Documenta*, p. 203.

320. Sext. 5.2.18 *Ut inquisitionis*, in Friedberg, vol. 2, col. 1077.

321. *Glos. ord.* to Sext. 5.2.18.

322. *Postil*, in Hus, *Opera omnia*, vol. 2, pp. 164–167.

323. Ibid., pp. 298–289.

324. Ibid., p. 320.

325. *Contra octo doctores*, in Hus, *Opera omnia*, vol. 22, pp. 464–465.

picture of concerns prompted those in places of authority to contemplate a venue for dealing with matters such as the protracted papal schism and issues related to heresy. Therefore, Pope John XXIII and Sigismund agreed that a general council should be held, commencing in one year.[326] In the official summons to Constance, it is significant that the emperor declared that the performance of the imperial office included the safety and security of each and every person of whatever rank who attended the convocation and guaranteed each person's complete liberty. No one should fear to attend, for the imperial office promised to do everything to maintain the complete freedom and safety of each person, whether traveling to the Council, staying in the city, or returning to one's home. All who came to Constance were guaranteed freedom of speech and movement. Sigismund never mentioned any exceptions to that imperial rule or promise. The same commitments are noted in the apostolic brief drawn up by the pope and notarized. Sigismund and John XXIII met in northern Italy at Lodi to talk about details of the planned council. They were in Lodi for a month, from late November through December 1413. Cardinal Zabarella was also there.[327] This meeting may have caused John to take the rather tolerant attitude toward Hus that he initially assumed at Constance. Although it cannot be proven, perhaps Sigismund had an ameliorating influence on the pope in this regard. After all, Sigismund's political aspirations in Bohemia would be enhanced with a successful conclusion to the matter of Jan Hus.[328]

Meanwhile, at the behest of Michael de Causis and the bishop of Litomyšl, Jan Železný, Pope John XXIII applied pressure on church officials—namely, Konrad, archbishop of Prague; Václav Králík, bishop of Olomouc; and bishop and inquisitor Nicholas of Nezero, who is not specifically named in the bull—to enforce the terms of interdict against Hus under threat of punishment and sanction. As noted previously, canonists, such as the fifteenth-century Abbas Siculus, argued that bishops who did not diligently pursue heresy should be censured. The initiative against officials in the Bohemian province was prompted by the fact that Hus continued to preach openly in the countryside and tried to do so occasionally

---

326. Edict of Sigismund, October 30, 1413, in Hardt, vol. 4, pp. 5–6; John's call, October 31, in *Documenta*, pp. 515–518; the bull of convocation, December 12, in Loomis, pp. 75–78.

327. Hardt, vol. 1, p. 540. Zabarella left the papal Curia in October and met Sigismund at Lodi.

328. Richental, *Chronik*, pp. 6–7; Finke, *Acta*, vol. 1, pp. 174–179.

in Prague, though under aggravated excommunication and interdict. In a letter addressed to Jan the Iron, Hus and his accomplices were called "twisting snakes" and there was allusion to the tails of heretics being tied together, a common image of heretics from Lateran IV onward.[329] There were other calls for action. Paris university chancellor and canon of Notre Dame Jean Gerson wrote to Archbishop Konrad on May 27, 1414, urging the eradication of heresy entirely from his province.[330] Pope John XXIII continued to press the matter and wrote to King Václav (either on June 15 or 17) asking that he uproot all "miserable and lamentable" heresy from his realm, which the pope insisted was rumored to exist in many places and still continued to spread and flourish.[331] The entrance of Gerson into the Hus process became crucial both in the preparations for the Council of Constance and during the legal procedures against Hus during the Council. Archbishop Konrad replied to Gerson on August 2, claiming hyperbolically that he was prepared to do everything in his power to uproot heresy in Bohemia, even at the risk of his own life. As a token of his commitment to that task, he dispatched his emissary Petr of Prague to Paris with copies (or extracts) of the works of Hus for Gerson to examine.[332] Evidently, Gerson examined the writings put into his hand and replied to Konrad on September 24, noting that Hus had erred in several ways. He suggested that the best procedure for dealing with such problems involved fire and sword rather than reason. That policy echoed the suggestions of Dietrich Niem, which had been expressed in 1411.[333] On the same day, Gerson filed a series of twenty articles taken especially from Hus's *De ecclesia* that he regarded as manifestly heretical.[334] Gerson identified two particularly troubling concerns. The first was Hus's insistence on moral purity, while the other related to the idea that legitimate secular and spiritual authority was contingent on this premise (articles 1–5, 8, 16). Gerson concluded that

---

329. Text in Kamil Krofta, "Zur Geschichte der husitischen Bewegung: Drei Bullen Papst Johanns XXIII. aus dem Jahre 1414," *Mittheilungen des Instituts für österreichische Geschichtsforschung* 23 (1902): 605–606. The dating is a matter of conjecture but may be assigned to April 30, 1413 or 1414. I suspect the latter, agreeing with de Vooght, p. 316.

330. *Documenta*, pp. 523–526.

331. Finke, *Acta*, vol. 4, pp. 507–509. Finke gives June 11 as the date.

332. *Documenta*, pp. 526–527.

333. Ibid., pp. 527–528.

334. Ibid., pp. 185–188.

this constituted a grave misunderstanding, which he described as utterly "rash, seditious, offensive, pernicious and subversive." Beyond this, Gerson discovered evidence that Hus actively maintained views that could only be characterized as antipapal (articles 7–8, 11–12, 17). Worse still was evidence that Hus encouraged laypeople to voice their opinions concerning the vices of priests and spiritual superiors (article 10). Gerson opined that he regarded that perspective as "a pernicious and offensive error," which incited "rebellion, disobedience, sedition and malediction." Gerson also found that Hus permitted the withholding of tithes from priests considered unworthy (article 15). This prompted Gerson to issue a stiff denunciation, calling the practice "a most pernicious and offensive error which encouraged secular people to commit sacrilege thereby interfering with ecclesiastical liberty." In a similar vein, Štěpán of Dolany, abbot of the Carthusian abbey in Moravia, accused Hus of effectively invalidating the priesthood.[335] In addition, Gerson noted ruefully that Hus maintained that preaching did not require official permission (article 6) and that a writ of excommunication issued by the pope might be appealed to Christ. This was evaluated as a positively "reckless and arrogant error" (article 19). Finally, Gerson pointed out, Hus did not believe heretics should be burned (article 9). Two days later, on September 26, Simon Cramaud, cardinal and archbishop of Reims, also advised Archbishop Konrad to deal with heretics without delay.[336]

And so it came to pass that Hus was invited by Emperor Sigismund to attend the forthcoming Council of Constance. He agreed to go.[337] He secured a promise of safe conduct from Sigismund through the knight Jan Chlum initially in April, but he was later given a revised assurance in more promising terms through Jindřich Lacembok, an advisor to King Václav, confirmed by Sigismund's emissary Mikeš Divoký of Jemniště in August. At this stage, Hus wrote a short summary of legal events at the Curia in 1410–1411.[338] Thereafter, on August 26, Hus offered to appear before a special session of the diocesan synod in Prague to debate anyone challenging him as a heretic. Public notices in Latin, Czech, and

---

335. Štěpán of Dolany, *Antihussus*, in Pez, vol. 4, col. 400.

336. *Documenta*, pp. 529–530.

337. Letter to Sigismund, September 1, 1414, Novotný, *Correspondence*, pp. 197–199.

338. *Knížky proti knězi kuchmistrovi*, in Hus, *Opera omnia*, vol. 4, pp. 312–323, but see pp. 320–322.

German to this effect were posted.³³⁹ There are differences between the first two versions, with the Czech being more detailed. In the Latin notice, reference is made to retaliation against plaintiffs; to wit, if allegations could not be sustained, the accusers were liable to judgment. Canon law described a form of prosecution, the so-called *accusatio*, wherein a private person (*actor*), on the basis of evidence or knowledge, voluntarily accused another (*reus*) and was therefore party to the prosecution. Should the case fail, the accuser or plaintiff was liable for *pena talionis*, meaning that he or she was legally forced to accept *lex talionis* or retaliatory punishment commensurate to the penalty of the offense.³⁴⁰ As noted previously, the law required that an accusation rest on *infama* (infamy or bad reputation). This was established either by *clamosa insinuatio* (notorious suspicion), *validus clamor* (strong outcry), or *fama* (common report).³⁴¹ No one accepted Hus's challenge. Hus had also noted this "retaliatory penalty" in previous letters, which must indicate that he believed no one would dare oppose him for fear of suffering the severe retribution of the *talio*.³⁴² This suggests rather firmly that Hus believed none of his teachings or writings was heretical. He did not seem to take any note of contumacy in relation to medieval canon law and heresy accusations. This was a fatal oversight.

When a special meeting of the synod convened in the archbishop's court in Prague on August 27, 1414, Hus's former lawyer, Jan Jesenice, petitioned to appear and attempted to do so—along with Šimon Tišnov, Šimon Rokycany, Prokop Plzeň, Mikuláš Stojčín, Jan Příbram, and a number of others—by "pounding on the door of the gate" but was denied entrance at the order of Ulrich, known as Šváb Švábenice, the marshal of Archbishop Konrad.³⁴³ Nevertheless, Jesenice secured a notarized announcement

---

339. See Novotný, *Correspondence*, pp. 192–195, for the various texts (pp. 192–193 for the Latin, pp. 193–194 for the Czech, and pp. 194–195 for the German).

340. C.2 q.3 c.2 *Si accusator*, in Friedberg, vol. 2, col. 451; X 5.1.1–16 *De accusationibus*, in Friedberg, vol. 2, cols. 733–738; X 5.1.24 *Qualiter et quando*, in Friedberg, vol. 2, cols. 745–747. For the Roman roots, see Walter Ullmann, "Some Medieval Principles of Criminal Procedure," *Juridical Review* 59 (1947): 1–28; and Louis Tanon, *Histoire des tribunaux de l'inquisition en France* (Paris: Bloud, 1893), pp. 255–263.

341. Supported in canon law at X 5.1.21 *Inquisitionis negotium*, in Friedberg, vol. 2, col. 742; and C.2 q.3 c.1–c.6, in Friedberg, vol. 1, cols. 450–451.

342. September 1, 1411, to Pope John XXIII, Novotný, *Correspondence*, p. 98; and the Bohemian supreme court, December 1412, Novotný, *Correspondence*, p. 158.

343. *Relatio*, p. 28.

about the convocation.³⁴⁴ During the special meeting of the diocesan synod, financial arrangements were made for supporting a delegation to go to Constance, led by Jan "the iron."³⁴⁵ Elsewhere, we find further details claiming that this was the main point of the special session of the synod and further specifying that the sum of fifty-three thousand gulden had been collected for the purpose of securing Hus's death, funded by a voluntary tax imposed by the higher clergy.³⁴⁶ An anonymous Hussite preacher lamented that this was the price for the flesh of Hus. Elsewhere, we find the figure of two hundred thousand florins specified as the sum raised to aid in the prosecution of Hus.³⁴⁷ Both money and testimony were provided by the cathedral chapters of St. Vitus and Vyšehrad in Prague. These pieces of evidence indicate a high level of animosity among the priests of Prague with respect to Hus and a determination to see him prosecuted to the full extent of the law, not only silenced but permanently eliminated.

In preparation for his appearance at the continuation of his trial, Hus approached Nicholas Nezero, inquisitor of Prague, who provided references on August 29 regarding Hus's innocence and lack of heretical depravity.³⁴⁸ Nezero affirmed that he had known Hus for some years, had spoken with him on many occasions, had shared meals and heard him preach, but never detected in him any trace of evil or error. Hus also appealed to King Václav and Queen Žofie around August 30, pleading for justice.³⁴⁹ In a deliberate effort to ensure his security at the Council, Hus's friend and canon lawyer Jan "Cardinal" of Rejnštejn composed a treatise addressed to Sigismund, arguing for the superiority of the emperor over the pope. The tract is buttressed by numerous legal citations, biblical references, and examples of historical precedent. The work may be reliably dated to the early autumn of 1414.³⁵⁰ In addition to these documents and

---

344. Ibid., pp. 59–60.

345. Šimek, *Staré letopisy české*, p. 14, dated incorrectly to 1415; and the *Hussite Chronicle*, FRB, vol. 5, pp. 338–339.

346. Details from an anonymous sermon, FRB, vol. 8, p. 371; with comment also in George the Hermit, FRB, vol. 8, p. 379.

347. Czech *Acta* in the Freiburg Codex, FRB, vol. 8, p. lxxv.

348. *Relatio*, p. 28; text has been included on pp. 64–65, with a notarized statement of the same on pp. 57–59.

349. *Relatio*, pp. 92–93.

350. František M. Bartoš, "Reformní program M. Jana Kardinála z Rejštejna: Vyslance Karlovy university pro Koncil kostnický," JSH 38 (1969): 99–118.

efforts, we also have a second-hand report obtained through the efforts of Jesenice reflecting that Archbishop Konrad testified he personally knew of no heresy in Hus. That account comes from the period around September 19–22.[351] Altogether, these witnesses and documents made up a hopeful dossier for Hus to take with him to the next stage of his legal ordeal. In the autumn of 1414 and before departure for the Council, a summary of the Hus case to date, the so-called *Ordo procedendi*, was prepared either by Jesenice or by Hus or perhaps by both.[352] Additionally, Hus prepared three specific documents for use at the Council. The first was a sermon, *De pace*; the second was an essay on faith, *De fidei suae elucidatione*; and the third was a reflection on the sufficiency of the law of Christ, *De sufficientia legis Christi*.[353] Supporting all of this, Jesenice wrote yet another account of Hus's legal case, called *Summaria de iusticia et nullitate sentenciarum contra Hus*.[354] Unfortunately, it is no longer extant. What has survived and may be considered of some importance is a document the Czech barons Čeněk of Vartenberk, Boček of Kunštát, and Vilém of Vartenberk wrote to Sigismund on October 7, in which they summarized Archbishop Konrad's position on Hus, namely, that he knew of no heresy in Hus and did not personally accuse Hus of holding any heretical opinions. The letter pointed out that Archbishop Konrad noted it had been the pope, and not he, who had accused Hus of heresy and conducted judicial procedures in the matter; therefore, Hus would have to answer to the pope.[355] The posture assumed by the archbishop is at the very least mildly astonishing.

The promised safe conduct for Hus was prepared and dated October 18, 1414. It was issued by Canon Michael of Přestanov, at Speyer.[356] Predictably, there was controversy over the imperial safe conduct. Hus believed it implied round-trip protection, and other witnesses confirm this.[357] We have previously noted that security for all Council attendees was

---

351. *Relatio*, p. 65.

352. *Documenta*, pp. 188–193, and discussed in chapter 6 below.

353. HM, vol. 1, pp. 55–71.

354. Noted in Jiří Kejř, "O některých spisech M. Jana z Jesenice," *Listy Filosofický* 86 (1963): 81–83.

355. *Documenta*, pp. 531–532.

356. *Relatio*, pp. 25–26.

357. Letters of January 3 and June 13, 1415, Novotný, *Correspondence*, pp. 238, 276. See also Richental, *Chronik*, p. 60.

guaranteed by the emperor, and this included travel to and from the venue. Hus later confused his imperial document with a papal safe conduct.[358] At no time during his trial did Hus possess any form of papal immunity. The position of the Latin church with respect to suspected heretics was later revealed in a statement released by the Council of Constance that confirmed that no safe conduct could interfere with the administration of church authority.[359] Canon law noted that no promise extended to a heretic need be observed.[360] We have already noted papal precedent for such policy.[361] Regardless of the church's view about the safe conduct issued to Hus or the intended meaning of Sigismund's security policy outlined in the edict and summons to the Council, it is critically important to consider the simple fact that none of the ecclesiastical censures against Hus issued by Zbyněk (twice), Colonna, Brancacci (implied), and Stephaneschi between 1410 and 1412 was withdrawn or declared invalid by a higher authority. In the same period, Hus continued to perform the functions of a priest, namely, preaching and sacramental celebration. According to canon law, this was not only irregular but also explicitly illegal. Priests who continued performing sacramental functions while under interdict or anathema (major excommunication) were ordered permanently deposed from office.[362] At the very least, as a consequence of minor excommunication, offenders were considered to have committed a serious sin.[363] Hus already had commented on this matter. "From this it may be concluded that an excommunicated person, a schismatic, the degraded, a manifest heretic or one joined with a concubine, who knowingly receives the sacrament of the eucharist sins grievously."[364] Tweaked ever so slightly, Hus appears to have already condemned himself. Hus lacked papal absolution, which was the only remedy against the aforementioned censures.[365]

---

358. Novotný, *Correspondence*, pp. 220, 246.

359. Hardt, vol. 4, col. 521.

360. X 5.7.16 *Absolutos se*, in Friedberg, vol. 2, cols. 789–790; X 5.7.13 §5 *Excommunicamus*, in Friedberg, vol. 2, col. 788.

361. Innocent III, circular letter, 1208, in PL, vol. 215, col. 1317.

362. X 5.27.3 *Clerici autem*, in Friedberg, vol. 2, col. 827.

363. X 5.27.10 *Si celebrat*, in Friedberg, vol. 2, col. 832.

364. *Super IV Sententiarum*, in *Mag. Jo. Hus Opera omnia: Nach neuentdeckten Handschriften*, 3 vols., ed. Václav Flajšhans (Osnabrück: Biblio-Verlag, 1966), vol. 2, p. 585.

365. X 2.28.16 *Ad praesentiam*, in Friedberg, vol. 2, cols. 414–415; Sext. 2.15.7 *Non solum*, in Friedberg, vol. 2, col. 1017.

Did Jan Jesenice warn him about this? We have no way of knowing. Hus believed his appeals granted him immunity from prosecution or consequence. We learn elsewhere that Hus celebrated Mass daily.[366] Moreover, Hus continued to believe he had been reconciled to Zbyněk. However, Pope John XXIII never issued any ruling withdrawing or modifying any of the ecclesiastical censures against Hus. Papal absolution returned the appellant to his or her standing prior to the sentence and in Hus's case would have permitted him to continue the work of divine office without charges of irregularity. However, Hus could not claim this. The clear dictates of canon law and ecclesiastical precedence were firmly against the defendant in this court proceeding. Hus was walking into a legal and procedural trap that had been set by his enemies, especially the cunning and clever Michael de Causis. It is absolutely specious to suggest that Hus was going to Constance as a guest of the Council or as a delegate to a dialogue or academic debate. It would be unfair to argue that he had no choice but to attend. He was invited. He accepted. There were suggestions that he had been pressured by King Václav to attend the convocation. We cannot know how valid that claim is. Notwithstanding, there is firm evidence that members of the Czech nobility were prepared to shield and protect Hus from harm. Given the relative ineptness of Václav's rule, there is no reason to think that Hus could not have survived in relative peace had he declined to go to the Council. He chose to leave Bohemia. The church had not connived to lure the unsuspecting priest to Constance. Hus was not unaware of the dangers that awaited him in Germany. Indeed, he was up against a solid body of legal opinion, precedent, and the virtually unassailable rulings of medieval canon law.

Beyond this, there remains the ominous fact that Hus's lawyer, Jan Jesenice, would not be accompanying him to Constance. The excommunication leveraged against him through the efforts of Michael de Causis made Jesenice ineligible for continued representation of Hus. It was in the face of this troubling legal reality that Hus departed from Bohemia for Constance on October 11 with an escort of two knights, Jan Chlum and Václav Dubá, provided by Sigismund. The Hus entourage included Petr Mladoňovice, Jan "Cardinal" Rejnštejn, possibly Oldřich of Znojmo, and several other people. Curiously, the Hus party left Krakovec Castle in Bohemia without waiting for the imperial safe conduct to arrive. It is possible to regard that as a tactical error on Hus's part. The travelers

---

366. Novotný, *Correspondence*, p. 222.

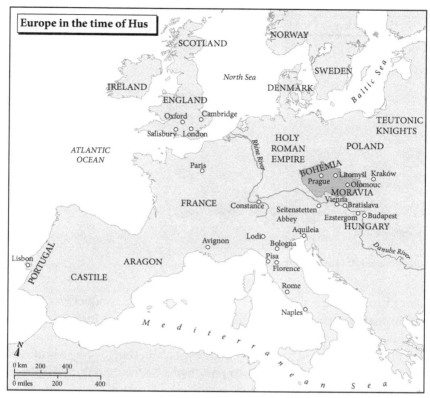

FIGURE 4.2 Europe in the time of Jan Hus

made their way along the Mže River valley to Plzeň and then to the Czech frontier and came to Bärnau in German territory. From there, Hus and his companions went through Neustadt, Weiden, Sulzbach, Hirsweld, Hersbruck, Lauf, and Nürnberg. Along the travel route, Hus posted public notices inviting dialogue.[367] A second decision made en route to the Council may also be considered an even more serious error. At Nürnberg around October 20, Hus elected to travel directly to Constance rather than joining the emperor's entourage at Aachen, for, as he wrote, "we consider it useless to add an additional sixty miles" to the journey.[368] Václav Dubá left the Hus party to join Sigismund. This was perhaps a fatal decision, since Hus did not have the safe conduct in hand when he arrived. Sigismund

---

367. Ibid., pp. 211, 217–218.

368. Novotný, *Correspondence*, p. 214.

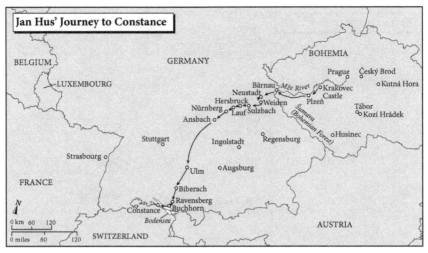

FIGURE 4.3 Jan Hus' journey to Constance

later grimly remarked on this.[369] In a sense, the safe conduct was a tech-
nicality, an assurance that Hus took far too seriously, too literally, and too
fatefully. It is doubtful that if Hus had the document in hand upon arrival
in Constance, it would have altered the course of events in any significant
fashion. From Nürnberg, the direct route to the Bodensee followed the road
to Ansbach, then to Ulm, and on to Biberach. From there, he journeyed
farther south to Ravensberg and reached Lake Constance at Buchhorn
(today Friedrichshafen). At Buchhorn, the travelers sent their horses back
to Ravensberg to sell. Hus sailed from Buchhorn to Constance, a distance
of twelve nautical miles, reaching his destination on November 3.[370]

Shortly after Hus departed from Bohemia, Jakoubek Stříbro began the
practice of utraquism for all the faithful in four Prague churches.[371] The

369. *Documenta*, p. 610.

370. There is some conjecture about the route. Several scholars assume Hus arrived at
Constance by ship. Franz Lützow, *The Life and Times of Master John Hus* (London: Dent,
1909), p. 196; Herbert B. Workman and R. Martin Pope, eds., *The Letters of John Hus*
(London: Hodder and Stoughton, 1904), p. 155. On the other hand, Hus referred to riding
into Constance. Novotný, *Correspondence*, p. 219. However, we read elsewhere that the Hus
party sent the horses back to Ravensberg with Jan Chlum, yet Chlum is later with Hus in
Constance. Novotný, *Correspondence*, p. 218. Either the horses were sent to Ravensberg upon
arrival in Constance (although we know Hus kept one horse), or Chlum took them from
Buchhorn. The reference to a distance of four miles may be the key.

371. *Hussite Chronicle*, FRB, vol. 5, pp. 329–330.

eucharistic cup for the laity was controversial, and although he was never a participant in the practice, Hus would be pulled into the orbit of debate and condemnation over the chalice during the next phase of his trial. Meanwhile, Dietrich Niem wrote his *Avisamenta* in the late summer or early autumn of that year, a treatise that included Hus in its recommendations to the Council on how to solve the conundrum facing Christendom.[372] These background factors had no immediate impact on Hus. His journey across western Bohemia and through German territories was uneventful. We have no evidence of sanctions, opposition, protests, or any apparent violence against Hus at any of his several stops. There is no hint that any official sought to enforce the terms of excommunication or interdict that had previously been applied to him. At Nürnberg, Albrecht Fleischmann, priest of St. Sebald's Church, and Master Johannes Helwel, pastor of the Church of St. Laurence, engaged Hus in a wide-ranging and lengthy discussion spanning four hours on matters of theology and rumors circulating about his trial. At the end, Fleischmann declared that he considered Hus's opinions entirely orthodox, claiming that they paralleled the teachings then current in Nürnberg. The German priest expressed his hope and expectation that Hus would be able to return from the Council with honor.[373] The next stop was Constance.

---

372. Finke, *Acta*, vol. 4, pp. 584–636. The term *avisamentum* in this context means advice or proposal.

373. *Relatio*, pp. 31–32, but note that at one stage, Fleischmann seemed unhappy that common people agreed with some of Hus's opinions.

5

An Extraordinary Motion to an Appellate Court

BEFORE ENGAGING WITH the trial of Jan Hus at the Council of Constance, it is essential to consider two pertinent documents. The first is Hus's formal appeal, and the second is a summary outline of Hus's legal affairs to date. This examination forms the basis for chapters 5 and 6. Recalling the nature of law, criminal procedure, and established judicial practice in medieval heresy trials as outlined in chapter 3, it is clear that a defendant or plaintiff had the legal right and recourse to appeal the verdict of a court and initiate an appellate process aimed at reversing the lower court decision. In late July 1412, Jan Hus became a formally excommunicated heretic for the fourth time, on the basis of the promulgation of the aggravated anathema published by Cardinal Peter degli Stephaneschi.[1] In that writ, Stephaneschi noted that this step was the natural extension of the curial court procedures, which were now exhausted. Hus had twenty days in which to appear at the court to plead his case. Beyond this, he had a scant twelve days more before all of Prague would suffer the ravages of interdict. The writ mandated that if Hus remained recalcitrant beyond this point, the stones thrown against his house in Prague as part of the ritual of excommunication were meant to signify "a sign of eternal malediction," in much the same way as when the earth opened and swallowed up the wicked men Dathan and Abiram, they were rejected by God and

---

1. Novotný, *Correspondence*, pp. 126–128.

cast out of the community of faith.[2] This decisive action brought to an end a chapter in the trial of Hus. The only recourse now was for the defendant to initiate an appellate process. In the modern criminal court system, the right of appeal is part of the judicial system. However, in the fifteenth century, the avenue of appeal by canonical mandate had to go back to the pope. Defendants had the legal right of appeal from a court to the pope.[3] There was a catch, however, inasmuch as it is impossible for a contumax to appeal.[4] Stephaneschi's writ of aggravated excommunication against Hus drew attention to the fact that there could be appeal and absolution only from the pope, and those who took exception to the legal processes thus far were warned that "they could be acquitted by no one save the pope alone."[5]

That autumn, Hus elected not to petition the pope for reconsideration in his legal ordeal. Hus was convinced such appeal could produce no desired outcome. Instead, on October 18, he took the unusual step of making an appeal to Jesus Christ. This was an extraordinary development.[6] In general terms, the appellate process should be understood as a formal legal appeal against the decision of a lower court. It was part of the medieval judicial process. At the time of the Hus trial, prevailing legal practice allowed appeals to be made from the court of the archdeacon to the consistory, or to the provincial court, or to the Curia, in that order. Alternatively, an appeal might be made directly to the pope from any of the lower-level courts. Having exhausted that standard legal process, and having received no *apostoli*, or reply from the relevant judge, Hus took his case to another extrajudicial level. Filing an appeal in the later Middle Ages was not unlike contemporary legal practice. The plaintiff or defendant, normally with the advice of counsel, drew up a written document

---

2. This alludes to a rebellion led by Korah against Moses in the Hebrew Bible book of Numbers 16:1–50; Novotný, *Correspondence*, p. 127. Interestingly, the main antagonist, Korah, is not mentioned. The stones are specifically mentioned in the writ of excommunication against Hus issued by Cardinal Stephaneschi, in *Documenta*, p. 463.

3. X 2.28.53 *Pastoralis*, in Friedberg, vol. 2, col. 432.

4. Noted by Raymond of Peñafort, *Summa sancti Raymundi de Peniafort* (Rome: Sumptibus Ioannis Tallini, 1603), 3.33.55, p. 433.

5. Novotný, *Correspondence*, p. 128.

6. Text in *Documenta*, pp. 464–466; and Novotný, *Correspondence*, pp. 129–133 (Latin) and pp. 134–136 (Czech). Translation in Spinka, *Constance*, pp. 237–240. I use the Novotný edition.

outlining the elements upon which a higher court might reconsider the original ruling. This document was lodged with the relevant court, and a scheduling order was then set to hear the appeal. Hus's appeal, like any other, was designed to demonstrate that errors or bias had prejudiced the lower court in some fashion, leading to an incorrect verdict. Appealing to God, however, introduced a legal anomaly. It was inconceivable that the Hus case would be subject to remand in any of the four courts recognized in medieval law. Therefore, there could be no retrial or reconsideration of the verdict. Inasmuch as the papal Curia possessed the power of discretionary review, and since Hus had taken his legal affairs outside canon law and ecclesiastical jurisdiction, it was impossible for the Curia to agree to hear this new appeal. The 1412 appeal of Hus constitutes an unusual chapter in the history of medieval canon law and criminal procedure.

Practically every scholar dealing with Hus's trial has noted the appeal to Christ and underscored its uniqueness and importance. There have been few careful analyses of the appeal, and those that do exist appear within the Czech historiography of the subject.[7] There is no adequate treatment in English. Some scholars regard the appeal engineered by Hus as the most revolutionary act in his unusual and extraordinary career. "In the whole of his extensive literary activity there is no more significant text than the famous 'appeal to Jesus Christ the supreme judge' from the year 1412. In his entire life, there is nothing any more crucial than this appeal 'to the valley of Jehoshaphat.'"[8] The step was "a piece of astonishing daring contrary to canonical provisions," invoking "extracanonical procedure."[9] I follow Kejř in seeing the main question as the need "to clarify the nature and the consequences of Hus' appeal to Christ."[10] Appealing from the papal court in such an unorthodox fashion to an imaginary heavenly court presided over by Christ and procedurally based on the law of God was exceptional, had no legal basis, and was indicative that Hus no longer believed in the integrity of the ecclesiastical court system, was prepared to

---

7. Flajšhans, *Odvolání*, pp. 237–258; Amedeo Molnár, "Husovo odvolání ke Kristu," in *Husův sborník: Soubor prací k 500. výročí M. Jana Husa*, ed. Rudolf Říčan and Michal Flegl (Prague: Komenského Evangelicka Fakulta Bohoslovecká, 1966), pp. 73–83; French version, "Hus et son appel à Jesus-Christ," CV 8 (1965): 95–104; and Kejř, *Odvolání*.

8. Flajšhans, *Odvolání*, p. 237. A reference to a place mentioned only once in the Hebrew Bible (Joel 3:2), where some believed the last judgment would be convened.

9. Spinka, *Constance*, p. 68.

10. Kejř, *Odvolání*, p. 23.

disregard the authority of the medieval church in this matter, was legally construed as disobedient and guilty of contumacy, and was also pursuing an action without precedent. From the perspective of the papal court and its officers, the appeal was a deliberate breach of legal procedure, an effort to obfuscate canon law, and an act of defiance against the jurisdictional authority of the church. The step could not pass without strident condemnation. The appeal created theological and legal complications.[11] In the Hus case, we find a variety of appeals against verdicts handed down by popes or church courts. The appeal to Christ was simply the last and the most extreme type of appellate process. In order to assess this action, it is important first to examine the actual content of the appeal.

The appeal text begins by nominating God as Lord of the oppressed and the ultimate reliable refuge. This provides us with a glimpse into the thinking and emotional state of Jan Hus. Drawing upon images and motifs chiefly found in the Psalter of the Hebrew Bible, the appeal sets up a construct implying that Hus has been sorely disadvantaged by the legal process and its findings. For example, God is the guardian of truth. Those who suffer wrong can expect to find justice in God. Those who call upon God from a perspective of truth will discover that God is near. Those who fear God will have their wishes realized, and prisoners will be freed. God will preserve those who truly love the Lord, but all incorrigible sinners will be destroyed. The historic ordeal of Jesus as characterized in the New Testament is described as one of distress in which the righteous man is surrounded by "pontiffs, scribes, Pharisaical priests, wicked judges and witnesses," all acting in concert for his destruction.[12] By the example of Christ, who delivered himself up to God, his followers should imitate that excellent example and commit their cause to God, who possesses all knowledge and power. When enemies arise, God is the infallible support and deliverance. The gentle lamb consigned to the slaughterhouse can be assured of justice in God, who will exercise vengeance on the wicked who conspire against the righteous. The innocent often find those who afflict them seeming to be arrayed in multitudes against them. The wicked conspire to destroy the righteous and assume that God has forsaken them, and they can therefore pursue and seize their prey with impunity, for there is no one who will intervene on their behalf. Therefore, God is implored to

---

11. Ibid., p. 8.

12. Novotný, *Correspondence*, p. 129.

deliver the helpless from the snares of the enemy when tribulation is near, and one is surrounded by dogs and those who work evil. When "many dogs" and a "malignant council" surround the righteous one, speaking "words of hatred" and attacking without cause, only God is a hopeful refuge.[13] This is the broad thrust of the appeal. Tellingly, the appeal to Christ makes no reference to canon law but refers at least fifteen times to scripture. By contrast, as we shall see in chapter 6, the *Ordo procedendi* cites legal sources ten times but does not refer to scripture.

Hus claims he has the full intention of following the salutary example of Christ in appealing to God from the serious situation he has been thrust into, which he describes as "grave oppression," an "unjust sentence," and the "pretended excommunication" leveled against him by the pope, scribes, Pharisees, and judges who unlawfully occupy the seat of Moses. To the one who can counteract their wickedness, Hus declares he has now committed his case. Hus enumerates three examples in which faithful Christians have previously taken such a step. He refers to John Chrysostom, bishop of Constantinople, who was twice deposed by unjust councils in 403 and 404. He refers to a lesser-known case in which a thirteenth-century bishop of Prague named Andreas ran into conflict involving both the sitting pope at the time, Honorius II, and King Přemysl I. The nature of his appeal is rather vague. A third example is the important bishop of Lincoln, Robert Grosseteste, whom Hus characterizes as having been "condemned unjustly" and who appealed away from the pope to God in 1253.[14] These examples are evaluated below. The text of the appeal describes God as the "most just judge," who cannot be bribed, influenced by gifts, manipulated, or deceived and who remains impervious to the testimony of false witnesses.

This action undertaken by Hus appeals in general to all faithful Christians but especially to "princes, barons, knights, their dependents, and all the rest in our Kingdom of Bohemia" to know and understand what has happened, because the "pretended excommunication," which was manifestly false and predicated upon malice and perjured testimony, resulted in great harm to both Hus and the realm. In this context, Hus nominates Michael de Causis as the "instigator and adversary" who caused

---

13. Hus uses texts from Psalms 3, 22, 59, 71, 109, 119, 145, and 146; Jeremiah 11; and Lamentations 19 to create a portrait of the helpless attacked unjustly and requiring extraordinary measures of intervention and deliverance.

14. Novotný, *Correspondence*, p. 131.

this injustice to occur, with the support of the canons of the Prague cathedral chapter. At this stage, the appeal digresses into a brief narrative of the legal proceedings. Hus begins with the publication of the aggravated excommunication declared by Stephaneschi but immediately points out that for a period of two years, Pope John XXIII refused to allow Hus's attorneys a hearing, and he claims this behavior was unfitting when even Jews, pagans, or heretics should be allowed a defense. Moreover, the pope declined to acknowledge the sealed and notarized testimony on behalf of Hus that had been submitted by the university in Prague. Hus denies the legitimacy of the contumacy charge, pointing out that he did not ignore the summons to the papal court. He cannot be held in contempt of court, for he refused the order on the grounds of "reasonable cause."[15] This follows a normal appellate process. Hus does not hesitate to explain himself. He alleges that there were conspiracies afoot to attack him when opportunity arose. He suggests that these were many and varied. Moreover, he cites the fate that befell his former colleagues Stanislav of Znojmo and Štěpán Páleč, who were robbed and imprisoned at Bologna when they obeyed a previous citation to appear at the papal court.[16] The two men were traveling to the papal court of Gregory XII in Rome but were apprehended by men loyal to Cardinal Baldassare Cossa (later Pope John XXIII) in Bologna and therefore never arrived at the papal court. This transpired in 1408, and the two were detained for the better part of a year. Hus writes that his colleagues were deprived of the benefit or legal right of a formal arraignment or preliminary hearing. Besides this, Hus had dispatched lawyers to represent his cause, but one of them, Jan Jesenice, had been jailed without cause. Furthermore, in his own defense, Hus makes the argument that he has been reconciled with the late Archbishop Zbyněk "of holy memory." He refers to the conflict of the previous year, in which the archbishop had been compelled by the king to contact the Curia and represent to the pope that all affairs of heretical inquiry in Bohemia had ended, there was no cause for alarm or concern in the Bohemian province, "full reconciliation" in the matter of Hus had been achieved, and it would therefore be appropriate to absolve Hus from the summons to appear, from the legal citations, and also from the writ of excommunication. These arguments

---

15. Ibid., pp. 131–132.

16. Hus specifically accused the pope of robbing the men of their horses and a total of 207 "gold coins." *Knížky proti knězi kuchmistrovi*, in Hus, *Opera omnia*, vol. 4, p. 321.

are precisely the elements expected in an appeal process. Hus is arguing that the original verdict be vacated.

Hus goes on to draw attention to what may be seen as an allusion to procedural law, although he does not make a specific citation. He says that according to all known laws, it is incumbent upon judges in legal proceedings to visit the place where the alleged crime occurred and make inquiries into the nature of the charges that have been laid against the defendant and exercise due diligence in assessing the validity of the accusations.[17] Hus goes further to suggest that this can only be accomplished by investigation that focuses on witnesses who the court can reasonably be assured are not party to the legal proceedings. The interrogatories must be put to such persons who are not "ill disposed, haters, or enemies of the accused or defamed, but honest men; not transgressors, but fervid lovers of the law of Jesus Christ; and finally that the cited or accused has convenient, secure, and open access to the place, and neither the judge nor the witnesses are his enemies."[18] Hus concludes that this criteria was lacking in his situation. Therefore, it was impossible for him to appear personally at the papal court as required, for there could be no reasonable expectation of fairness or justice. Herein we see the broad basis for the argument of a legal appeal. This being the case, Hus announces boldly that he is lawfully excused from a court appearance on the grounds that there was inadequate security to guarantee his safety. Therefore, he cannot be judged contumacious, and the verdict of excommunication is false and frivolous. Having laid out his case in this fashion, Hus makes a formal declaration. He sets forth his credentials as master of arts, bachelor of theology, and priest of Bethlehem Chapel before concluding with a terse statement: "I offer this appeal to Jesus Christ, who is the most just judge, who knows, protects and judges, and who reveals and rewards the just cause of every person without fail."[19] All of this amounts to a careful argument designed to call into question the integrity of the previous legal process and to argue, upon appeal, for a reconsideration of the verdict handed down by the lower court.

The date of Hus's appeal to Jesus Christ has been assigned as October 18, 1412.[20] It marked a crucial turning point in the legal proceedings.

---

17. Novotný, *Correspondence*, pp. 132–133.

18. Ibid., p. 133. Translation from Spinka, *Constance*, p. 240.

19. Novotný, *Correspondence*, p. 133.

20. Flajšhans, Odvolání, p. 247.

On that day, the major excommunication of Hus was announced to the annual Prague diocesan synod. According to canon law, an appeal had to be filed within ten days. Ostensibly, Hus anticipated the verdict and prepared his response and filed his appeal on the same day.[21] It is of some interest to note examples of those in peril, even at the point of death, who call their judges and those they consider false witnesses to accountability. According to some accounts, Jerome of Prague did this at the Council of Constance. On May 26, 1416, he called his judges to the bar of divine judgment.[22] However, it must be noted that Jerome was not appealing against a sentence, because in his case, none had been reached. Another documented example comes from the legal proceedings in the trial of Jacques de Molay, the last grand master of the Order of the Temple. In the end, after the great repression of the Order, there were four Templars (Molay among them) to be dealt with. Pope Clement V assigned three cardinals to try the case. At the end, Molay and one other Templar retracted everything. Feeling betrayed, Molay challenged King Philip the Fair of France and Pope Clement before God. This was on March 18, 1314. Molay and his colleague were condemned to die the same day. The others died in prison. Molay is reported to have said, "God knows who is in the wrong and who has sinned. Soon misfortune will come upon those who have unjustly condemned us. God will avenge our death."[23]

The appeal filed by Hus can only properly be understood if we come to terms with notional concepts of justice held in later medieval Europe, particularly those that focus on innocence, malicious prosecution, and unjust consequences, especially death. Justice, of course, had to do with a court order, judicial verdicts, the directives of a spiritual or secular superior, and related matters. Issues of power and authority came to bear on justice and its miscarriage. The strength of Kejř's analysis of the appeal may be attributed to the fact that he focuses on this question. Of course, it must be said that protests against ecclesiastical decisions, decrees of councils, and the orders of popes were not uncommon. To what extent Hus may have been aware of such appeals against decisions made by higher

---

21. X 2.27.15 *Quod ad consultationem*, in Friedberg, vol. 2, col. 400.

22. Hardt, vol. 4, col. 757; and see Kejř, *Odvolání*, p. 45, n. 143, for the citation.

23. *Chronique métrique attribuée à Geoffroi de Paris*, ed. Armel Diverrès (Paris: Société d'Edition, Les Belles Lettres, 1956), II, 5711–5742. The relevant passage has been translated in Alain Demurger, *The Last Templar: The Tragedy of Jacques de Molay Last Grand Master of the Temple*, trans. Antonia Nevill (London: Profile Books, 2004), pp. 197–198.

authorities is unknown. The argument from silence, as supported by the lack of reference in the appeal text, may not be strong determining evidence. Pursuant to the demand to establish a context for understanding Hus's appeal to Christ, Kejř has dealt with examples of appeals against a papal decision.[24] The thirteenth-century emperor Friedrich II launched an appeal on the grounds that he had been removed from the imperial throne by Pope Innocent IV at the first Council of Lyons in 1245. It is important to point out that the act was not a conciliar decision, but instead, Lyon was simply the venue where the verdict was announced. The emperor's lawyer, Thaddaeus de Suessa, concluded that the decision was null and void on the grounds that proper procedure had not been followed, resulting in an invalid verdict. An appellate process was directed to a future pope and a future council because the existing synod sitting at Lyon was not considered a general or universal council. The act was a definite appeal against a papal decision. Appealing to another synod likewise struck at the validity of the conciliar gathering. This case appears to be an example of medieval political machinations. In contrast to Hus's appeal, this one was addressed not to God but to another pope and council. The differences are important. We have mentioned already the case of Jacques de Molay, who appealed to God while standing at the stake on March 18, 1314. Molay believed the case against him was flawed and the verdict equally unjust. By implication, Pope Clement V was wicked, and a month later, the pope was dead, effectively fulfilling the appeal of Molay, who had said God would avenge the unjust deaths of the Templars. In 1376, controversy between Pope Gregory XI and the city of Florence simmered into open conflict. Interdict was pronounced on the city, along with other sanctions. Envoys of the city claimed the acts were unjust and appealed against the sentence to God.[25] It is not possible to say if Hus knew about any of these proceedings or, if he did, if they exerted any influence over his decision to appeal to God.

We have already noted legal difficulties in mounting an appeal against papal pronouncements. This was all the more difficult in cases of heresy and excommunication. The excommunicate might appeal a decision, but he or she remained under the sentence of excommunication, remained liable for denunciation, and was locked in an almost hopeless Sisyphean uphill battle. Innocent III had ruled that there was no meaningful distinction

---

24. Kejř, *Odvolání*, pp. 10–12.

25. Richard C. Trexler, *The Spiritual Power: Republican Florence under Interdict* (Leiden: Brill, 1974), pp. 40–43, 124–132.

between the sentence and the execution in such cases as excommunica-tion.[26] Canon lawyers generally agreed with the provisions and conclu-sions of *Pastoralis*, because excommunication was principally a spiritual response to a serious crime or offense against the church. The penalty was confirmed automatically by Christ, and there was no possibility of appealing from Christ. Appeals away from the pope, as vicar of Christ, to Christ made no sense. Nevertheless, this is precisely what Hus did. Pope Benedict XIII issued bulls in 1396 and again in 1407, claiming it was not permissible for one to appeal against a pope.[27] But theologians supporting conciliar theory defended in principle the legitimacy of an appeal directed to a general council in opposition to a pope. This was true of Jean Gerson and Pierre d'Ailly, men who played key roles in the latter stages of the Hus trial.[28] Indeed, the latter argued that if an appeal against papal decisions was disallowed, it would have serious and negative consequences for the church.[29] In May 1408, Pope Gregory XII violated promises made before coronation, created new cardinals, and in doing so extended the severity of the papal schism. Seven cardinals appealed against this action.[30] The car-dinals claimed that the standing papal order was contrary to law and there-fore illegal, nonbinding, and unenforceable. The cardinals filed a letter of appeal with Gregory, but going over his head, the appeal was directed to Christ, to a general council, and to a future pope.[31] This is a rather com-prehensive appeal to all possible higher authorities.[32] Of course, Gregory rejected the motion.[33]

It is fairly likely that Hus would have known about the controversy that erupted between Gregory and the cardinals, since the politics of the

---

26. X 2.28.53 *Pastoralis officii diligentia*, in Friedberg, vol. 2, col. 432.

27. Hans-Jürgen Becker, *Die Appellation vom Papst an ein allgemeines Konzil* (Cologne: Böhlau Verlag, 1988), pp. 406–412.

28. Paul de Vooght, "Jean Huss et ses juges," in *Das Konzil von Konstanz*, ed. August Franzen and Wolfgang Müller (Freiburg: Herder, 1964), pp. 152–173.

29. Clearly outlined in his *Tractatus de materia concilii generalis*, which may be dated between August 1402 and March 1403. In Francis Oakley, *The Political Thought of Pierre d'Ailly: The Voluntarist Tradition* (New Haven, Conn.: Yale University Press, 1964), pp. 244–342.

30. Mansi, vol. 27, cols. 33–36.

31. Howard Kaminsky, *Simon de Cramaud and the Great Schism* (New Brunswick, N.J.: Rutgers University Press, 1983), p. 279.

32. Kejř, *Odvolání*, p. 14.

33. Mansi, vol. 27, col. 36.

papal schism had direct bearing on affairs in Bohemia and were so acute that the nature of power in Prague was shaped to some extent by them. Additionally, the cardinals dispatched their appeal to temporal powers throughout Europe, revealing that the nature of the appeal had more to do with political disobedience than with ethical or theological issues relating to God strictly speaking. Of special interest is that among the cardinals who fled from Gregory to Pisa in supporting this appeal was Odo Colonna, who it should be noted would later complete a paradox when as Pope Martin V he issued a ban on appeals against papal decisions.[34] In between supporting an appeal from a pope and banning such actions, Colonna played a key role in the trial of Hus. Two lawyers, Antonius de Butrio and Peter of Ancharano, were involved in an appellate process in which the pope was rejected and the protections of God invoked. The appeal was directed chiefly to a general council. The second of these attorneys was later hired by Jan Jesenice as a consultant in the Hus trial during the process at the curial court.[35] Also in specific relation to the Hus case, we find among the cardinals in Pisa a latecomer, Peter degli Stephaneschi, who also disobeyed Gregory XII's summons and appealed to God and the general council. It was this cardinal whose action three years later prompted Hus to make an appeal to Jesus Christ. Altogether, the essence of these appeals and others is that they were directed away from a perceived erring or false pope to Christ but, more important, to a general council and to a future pope who would be considered the legitimate vicar of Christ. These cases illustrate the nature of unusual appellate procedures in the later Middle Ages.

In terms of appellate procedures, another case with connections to Bohemia occurred in the political realm. The German king and Palatine elector Ruprecht, through his representative Konrad of Soest, appealed to Christ and to another council after the king's proposals on papal legitimacy and the constitution of councils were rejected by the Council of Pisa. On March 23, 1409, Ruprecht openly broke with the Council, concluded that it was illegally convened, and therefore appealed to the Holy See, the

---

34. Less than three weeks after closing the Council of Constance (April 22, 1418), Martin drew up a constitution that explicitly forbade lodging appeals from the pope to a future council. The document of May 10 was read in consistory. Although never published, it reflects Martin's prevailing policy. See Peter Partner, *The Papal State under Martin V: The Administration and Government of the Temporal Power in the Early Fifteenth Century* (London: British School at Rome, 1958) for a reliable guide.

35. *Ordo procedendi*, p. 228.

true representative of Christ, and a legitimate council. Ruprecht's appeal indicates willing submission to divine protection, but this is not specifically an appeal to God in the same sense as that lodged by Hus. One might even go so far as to say Ruprecht's inclusion of God in his appeal is little more than third-party legal and political boilerplate language. The chief concern clearly lies with the legitimacy of the Council. Since King Václav of Bohemia recognized the Council of Pisa as a lawful assembly and was a principal antagonist in Ruprecht's affairs, there is every reason to conclude that the appeal of the German king reflects a wider political agenda at work. During the proceedings of the synod, Konrad of Soest explained why Ruprecht was opposed to the Council and its convocation. The delegates could hardly be expected to acquiesce in a negative judgment on them, and so when little enthusiasm was evident, Konrad announced that the king would appeal to Christ and to a legitimate general council. Ruprecht's delegation then promptly departed.[36]

It is entirely correct to say that if we compare the various late medieval appeals against papal decisions or policies, we find almost inevitably that these are generally political or administrative in nature and rarely, if ever, a response to criminal proceedings or verdicts of a court of law.[37] In other words, these examples of circumventing papal authority are fundamentally different in substance and intention when compared with the appeal to Christ filed by Hus. In order to assess the Hus appeal, it is necessary to evaluate it in light of the relevant legal norms and procedural court rules at the time. It has been pointed out that the greatest hurdle to overcome in the study of the trial of Jan Hus is the lack of sources and the gaps that occur in those that are extant.[38] Hus's first documented appeal, of which we have the text, came on June 25, 1410.[39] That was a formal response to the papal bull that reached Prague in March 1410. We find references to this act in several of Hus's works.[40] The basis for the appeal in 1410 was

---

36. *Deutsche Reichstagsakten*, 22 vols. (Munich: Historische Kommission bei der Bayerischen Akademie der Wissenschaften, 1867–1973), vol. 7, pp. 503–515, especially p. 514.

37. Kejř, *Odvolání*, p. 17.

38. Kejř, *Husův proces*, pp. 11–12; Kejř, *Odvolání*, p. 18; and chapter 1 above.

39. *Documenta*, pp. 387–396.

40. For example, *Defensio libri de Trinitate*, in Hus, *Opera omnia*, vol. 22, p. 48; *Defensio articulorum Wyclif*, in Hus, *Opera omnia*, vol. 22, p. 150; *Contra Stanislaum*, in Hus, *Opera omnia*, vol. 22, p. 359; *Contra octo doctores*, in Hus, *Opera omnia*, vol. 22, p. 373; *Ordo procedendi*, pp. 226–227 and elsewhere.

predicated on the assumption held by Hus that the pope had been poorly informed, indeed misinformed, to the extent that the papal bull lacked validity.[41] The appeal was intended to correct the misapprehension of the pope, clarify the egregious errors contained in the bull, and thereby clear up the matter entirely. It is rightly perceived that Hus's appeal was not an objection to law per se.[42] Therefore, from a canonical perspective, the appeal of Hus against the bull of Pope Alexander was perfectly legal and followed to the letter normal appellate procedures as understood in the fifteenth century. However, there are assumptions evident in the appeal that call into question some of the basis on which the appeal is predicated. The idea that Bethlehem Chapel had been established two decades earlier with papal approval cannot be taken as prima facie eternal guarantees, as Hus seems to have done. The chapel had been established for the purpose of vernacular preaching.[43] This foundation was ratified in writing by the senior prelate of the Bohemian province, Archbishop Jan Jenštejn, on June 27, 1391.[44] Hus claimed the archbishop had laid the foundation stone.[45] Moreover, we find evidence that in 1408, Pope Gregory XII gave official papal recognition to Bethlehem Chapel, effectively elevating it to the status of holding all the rights of a parish church.[46] These facts were held inviolable by Hus and formed part of the basis for his appeal against the papal bull.

There was another school of thought. Štěpán Páleč argued against Hus concerning the freedom of preaching in private chapels by pointing out that just because a pope had granted certain privileges to Bethlehem Chapel, that did not preclude another pope from revoking those same privileges if it was determined that the freedoms allowed initially were now being abused or misused.[47] The point was neither pedestrian nor frivolous, and in principle, Páleč was absolutely right. Those privileges were not beyond

41. See *Contra octo doctores*, in Hus, *Opera omnia*, vol. 22, p. 446; and *De ecclesia*, p. 165.

42. Kejř, *Odvolání*, p. 20.

43. Anton Dittrich, ed., *Monumenta historica universitatis Carolo-Ferdinandeae Pragensis*, 3 vols. (Prague: Spurny, 1830–1848), vol. 2, pp. 308–310, for the foundation charter.

44. Royal authorization in ibid., vol. 2, pp. 314–316.

45. *Documenta*, p. 169.

46. Ibid., pp. 340–341.

47. Páleč, *Tractatus de ecclesia*, in Sedlák, pp. 202*–304*, but especially pp. 287*–295*. Although this edition is the fullest that has been printed, it is nevertheless incomplete.

scrutiny, but Hus appears from time to time to have assumed that they were untouchable. Páleč somewhat forcefully hammered the point home. It is not true that the pope acted contrary to Christ when he issued the prohibition against preaching, especially in relation to Bethlehem Chapel. This was done to prevent the further spread of error and not to impede the proclamation of the word of God. The suspension was aimed at curtailing the assemblies and satanic schools of the wicked Wyclif. With the safety of the faithful in mind, the pope had an obligation to protect all souls redeemed by the blood of Christ from the poisonous infection of heresy. Anyone suspected of erroneous opinions had to be stopped from disseminating harm to the gospel. Since Wyclif had been condemned and Hus contemptuously ignored the ban and resisted its provision with much stubbornness, the pope was more than justified in taking action.[48] Páleč did have a point. Perhaps more important in the appeal of 1410 are the linkages between Hus's resistance to the papal bull and a wider opposition to the idea of unassailable authority exercised in papal politics.[49] The knife cut two ways. Since it was manifestly clear to Hus that popes were not infallibly powerful, this meant that the rights and privileges bestowed on Bethlehem Chapel in 1391 could not be summarily removed in 1410. The shrewd work of Jan Jesenice can be detected in the formulation of the June 1410 appeal.[50] This act eventually propelled Hus into a protracted court battle, which ultimately caused him to be excommunicated for failing to observe and follow established procedural rules. All of this forms the essential background for understanding how it came to pass that in the autumn of 1412, Hus initiated another appellate process.

The appeal to Christ was predicated on the implementation of the contumacy conviction. We have already noted the particulars surrounding the publication of that decree by Cardinal Stephaneschi in the summer and autumn of 1412. Nearly all scholars concerned with the legal ordeal of Hus note the appeal to God. Analysis of the text, especially in a legal context, is rare in Hus historiography. Salient issues are virtually overlooked in the major studies. For example, there are several obvious and striking problems with the declaration promulgated by Stephaneschi. From a strictly legal point of view, the precise wording of the text may be called

---

48. Ibid., pp. 287*–288*.

49. Kejř, *Odvolání*, p. 22.

50. Kejř, *Jesenice*, pp. 33–34.

into question on the grounds that the original is no longer extant. The two copies of the bull that do exist are not identical. We have information in a generally contemporary chronicle, but the edition of the writ based on manuscript sources is superior.[51] More serious is the absence of the entire protocol, including the intitulation. Moreover, we lack the conclusion of the document, which prevents us from knowing the exact date of the anathema. Kejř points out that for comparison, one might usefully refer to the surviving original text of the complete anathema against Jesenice, which has been preserved in Prague. Here we find a fairly wide band of familiar people to whom the document is addressed. This includes all the normal and usual forms of authority being stated that are generally required. Additionally, the reverse of the manuscript includes documents written by a notary who ratified the ban. The only thing missing is the date, which remains uncertain, because at that precise place, the manuscript has been damaged.[52] It is likely that the *aggravatio* shook Hus to the core. He was out of options. The law provided no further room for maneuver. In despair of any judicial remedy in his legal battle, Hus appealed to God.

The next question we must address in terms of Hus's bold action is the matter of whether there were precedents for such appeal. Of the appeals noted above, it appears that those motions for an appellate decision do not correspond with the action taken by Hus. Matthew Spinka says the appeal is "almost unprecedented," noting that Hus cited two previous examples.[53] In fact, the text of Hus's appeal reveals that he marshaled three examples to buttress his case. These were John Chrysostom in the fifth century, Bishop Andreas of Prague in the early thirteenth century, and Robert Grosseteste in the mid-thirteenth century. Inasmuch as there appears little to add by way of originality, I follow Kejř's examination and evaluation of these three cases in summary form. In appealing to Christ, Hus says he was following the example of John Chrysostom, the patriarch of Constantinople, who took issue with two congregations of bishops and

---

51. Chronicle of Prague University, FRB, vol. 5, pp. 573–574. The edition in Novotný, *Correspondence*, pp. 125–128, is based on Třeboň State Archives, MS A 16, fols. 91ᵛ–92ᵛ. Observation in Kejř, *Odvolání*, p. 24, n. 65.

52. Drawn up by the papal auditor Konrad Conhofer and preserved in Prague Castle Archive, MS XXV 26, which dates from 1413. The castle repository contains the medieval Cathedral Chapter Library. Kejř, *Odvolání*, p. 24. Kejř says the manuscript is essential for the biographical details of Jesenice. Kejř, *Jesenice*, p. 9.

53. Spinka, *John Hus*, p. 162.

priests.[54] Elsewhere in his work, Hus refers to these events.[55] More specifically, Hus says the reason Chrysostom was deposed can be attributed to his refusal to acquiesce in the condemnation of Origen.[56] Therefore, he suffered persecution as a result. More than this, Hus tells us Chrysostom was condemned when he continued to preach and to proclaim the truth and people were pleased to listen to him.[57] In his exposition of the church, Hus once more refers to Chrysostom and his condemnation, relying on a passage in canon law.[58] Hus notes that Chrysostom refused to join a group arrayed against him, for he did not agree with their point of view.[59] At this stage, it appears there are parallels between the case of Chrysostom and the legal ordeal of Hus separated by one thousand years. Elsewhere in his writings, we find Hus again referring to Chrysostom, although it is likely this reference is once more based on the canon law citation just noted.[60] Of significance is that while the two expulsions from his episcopal position are noted, Chrysostom was temporarily restored. We find further references to this fifth-century bishop in Hus's corpus.[61] Notably, in a prison letter, Hus points out that once Chrysostom was dead, God brought to light the falsehood of his enemies. Chrysostom did file an appeal with Pope Innocent I and with the presiding bishops of Milan and Aquileia.[62] But the protest can hardly be considered an appeal to the pope or a recognition of Roman supremacy. Instead, what seems clear is that Chrysostom was objecting to a breach of protocol and the perceived illegal removal from his episcopal see. He wanted an unbiased hearing aimed at securing a redress. The synod had acted improperly, and Chrysostom refused to

---

54. Novotný, *Correspondence*, p. 131.

55. *Contra Stokes*, in Hus, *Opera omnia*, vol. 22, p. 64; and *Defensio articulorum Wyclif*, in Hus, *Opera omnia*, vol. 22, p. 211.

56. *Defensio libri de trinitate*, in Hus, *Opera omnia*, vol. 22, p. 53.

57. *Defensio articulorum Wyclif*, in Hus, *Opera omnia*, vol. 22, p. 152.

58. C.3 q.5 c.15 *Quia suspecti*, in Friedberg, vol. 1, cols. 518–519.

59. *De ecclesia*, p. 156.

60. D.50 c.13 *Iohannes Crisostomus*, in Friedberg, vol. 1, col. 181.

61. *De libris haereticorum*, in Hus, *Opera omnia*, vol. 22, p. 21; and in a letter dated June 24, 1415 (from prison in Constance twelve days before his own death), in Novotný, *Correspondence*, p. 305.

62. Critical edition in Anne-Marie Malingrey, ed, and trans., *Palladois: Dialogue sur la vie de Jean Chrysostome* [*Sources Chrétiennes*, vol. 342] (Paris: Édition du Cerf, 1988), vol. 2, pp. 68–95.

recognize its jurisdiction in such matters. This was in 404. In response, Innocent sent letters of encouragement to the deposed bishop, refused to recognize the man elected in his stead, and tried to organize a council made up of objective men to investigate. When Innocent's envoys were mistreated, Innocent ceased diplomatic efforts with the bishops who had acted against Chrysostom.[63] Kejř points out the astonishing fact that while Hus referred to the sentence against Chrysostom promulgated by two synods, nowhere in his surviving work did he mention Chrysostom's appeal to Christ.[64] It is difficult to explain this remarkable fact apart from the possibility that Hus's knowledge of the fifth-century bishop was too slight to admit it. Be that as it may, the letter sent to Innocent I was not a proper appeal and in any event did not constitute an appeal to Christ. Instead, it is a request for intervention, which Innocent unsuccessfully attempted. Indeed, Chrysostom's grievance was predicated on the fact that he had been forcefully deposed without benefit of a legal trial or application of due process, which he argued even common criminals such as murderers and adulterers had the right to expect.[65] One can only conclude that Hus's use of Chrysostom in this regard was tenuous at best, drawing a parallel when, in fact, there was only a vague suggestion of similarity.

The second case Hus advanced relates to Andreas von Guttenstein, an early-thirteenth-century bishop of Prague. Prague was elevated to the status of an archbishopric in 1344.[66] Noting the trials of Bishop Andreas, Hus claimed the prelate had been unjustly condemned but in that state of adversity appealed from the pope to the ultimate and most just judge.[67] The conflict surrounding the bishop of Prague is well known and has been studied.[68] The case was somewhat odd. For example, there is ostensibly no

---

63. Essential books are J. N. D. Kelly, *Golden Mouth: The Story of John Chrysostom—Ascetic, Preacher, Bishop* (Ithaca, N.Y.: Cornell University Press, 1995); and Wendy Mayer and Pauline Allen, *John Chrysostom* (London: Routledge, 2000).

64. Kejř, *Odvolání*, p. 26.

65. Sozomen, *Historia ecclesiastica* 8.22, in PG, vol. 67, col. 1571.

66. Zdeňka Hledíková and Jaroslav V. Polc, *Pražské arcibiskupství 1344–1994: Sborník statí o jeho působení a významu v české zemi* (Prague: Zvon, 1994), pp. 10–15. The foundation bull has been published in Josef Emler, ed., *Regesta diplomatica et epistolaria Bohemiae et Moraviae* (Prague: Haase, 1892), vol. 4, pp. 566–568.

67. Novotný, *Correspondence*, p. 131.

68. Josef Žemlička, "Spor Přemysla Otakara I. s pražským biskupem Ondřejem," *Československý Časopis Historický* 29, (1981), pp. 704–730.

reference about any appeal. Furthermore, there are no references earlier than the fifteenth century wherein one can discover an account that in or around the year 1207, the bishop was disadvantaged by certain Czech lords and in consequence of this mistreatment appealed to Rome. Since the pope did nothing, Andreas appealed to Christ. He specified that within three days of his death, there would be a hearing before Christ on the matter. Three days after Bishop Andreas's premature death, the pope expired. The tale served its purpose in frightening other popes into judging properly. One might also note that Bishop Andreas was not actually elevated to the see of Prague until 1214.[69] Therefore, the reference to Andreas was based essentially on a legendary narrative and was in any event a protest against the lack of responsiveness of the court. It was not a formal legal appeal against a final sentence or judicial verdict. The two appeals, then, are dissimilar.

The third example presented in Hus's appeal had to do with Robert Grosseteste, bishop of Lincoln. Hus described him in the same manner as Bishop Andreas. Falsely persecuted, he appealed to Christ. The issue was politics and ecclesiastical administration, and Grosseteste came into conflict with the Curia. Evidently, Grosseteste wished for episcopal independence, but conflict broke out at mid-century when Pope Innocent IV unilaterally appointed one of his relatives to a canonry in Lincoln. Grosseteste protested. The bishop went to the papal court in 1250 with what amounted to a carefully prepared critique of prevailing papal policy. He also filed a letter with the pope in 1253. Apparently, he stated his willingness to be in obedience to the pope but appended a caveat that when issues like the one at hand suggested that the pope was unfaithful to God, an ally of the devil, and Antichrist, he would not obey. Such inflammatory convictions, which may not have actually been articulated as such by Grosseteste, nevertheless caused the bishop to communicate to the pope that accepting the papal decision would implicate Grosseteste in something contrary to Christ. Grosseteste enumerated a litany of abuses perpetrated by the papacy and recommended a series of reforms whereby these matters might be rectified. The outcome was predictable. The pope wanted to excommunicate the troublesome bishop but was persuaded not

---

69. Kejř, *Odvolání*, p. 27, with references to printed and manuscript sources. See also *Canonicorum pragensium continuations Cosmae*, in MGH, *Scriptores*, vol. 9, p. 170; Anton Frind, *Die Geschichte der Bischöfe und Erzbischöfe von Prague* (Prague: Tempsky, 1873), pp. 51–53.

to, and Grosseteste went back to England, although there is some evidence that he finished his life under a cloud of suspension.[70] Once again, upon inspection, the alleged appeal of Grosseteste was not strictly an appeal against a papal verdict. Grosseteste did disobey, but the matter cannot be construed as paralleling that of Hus. Once Grosseteste died—he expired shortly after his audience with the pope—a legend sprang up claiming that a voice was heard at the papal court calling the pope to an audience before the court of God. The next day, Pope Innocent IV was found dead, ostensibly stabbed with his own crozier. This story was used by Jan Jesenice in December 1412 while arguing a defense of Hus before a university audience at Prague.[71] As a matter of fact, Innocent died a full year after Grosseteste and not in the manner just described. The nature of the pope's demise aside, Grosseteste was opposing an order by the pope that he judged contrary to Christ. The issue was not a court verdict. No appeal was filed. No appeal to Christ was ever made by Robert Grosseteste in his struggle with papal policy. The fact that Hus believed the veracity of these alleged precedents for appealing to God means there is no real precedent at all for his action undertaken on October 18, 1412. "Hus's act is unique in that the appeal was expressed in an actual criminal matter, against the decision concerning the anathema, and that the possibility of addressing the council had been explicitly rejected because of the length of time required for such procedure."[72]

What seems clear thus far is that Hus's appeal to Jesus Christ at the height of his legal ordeal constituted a fundamental breach of the conventions laid down in canon law, because medieval legal procedures did not allow for this possibility, either in theory or in practice, any more than a modern court procedure would countenance an appellate process outside the established judiciary. In other words, the consequences of the appeal to Christ created a serious aggravating circumstance within the trial of Hus.[73] The outcome was as disadvantageous to Hus as transferring

70. Henry Richards Luard, ed., *Rerum britannicarum medii aevi scriptores* (London: Longmans, 1861), vol. 25, pp. 432–437. Of use are Servus Gieben, "Robert Grosseteste at the Papal Curia, Lyons 1250: Edition of the Documents," *Collectanea Franciscana* 41 (1971): 340–393; and R. W. Southern, *Robert Grosseteste: The Growth of an English Mind in Medieval Europe* (Oxford: Clarendon Press, 1986), pp. 272–295.

71. *Repetitio*, pp. 408–419, but see p. 418.

72. Kejř, *Odvolání*, p. 31.

73. Ibid., p. 31.

his case originally to the papal court. Of course, Hus took the view that his appeal was morally and legally defensible. This assumption has been investigated in some detail.[74] The moral dimensions are easier to detect and defend. From a strictly moral point of view, Hus's step in appealing his case to God might be considered a "courageous protest against ecclesiastical injustice."[75] However, the court hearing Hus's case and the judges who presided over those proceedings both at the Curia and at Constance were less interested in moral considerations than in law and procedure, and understandably, they focused on legal considerations. Those were in the end more salient. Investigating possible legal precedents for Hus's position is not a particularly fruitful pursuit. Thomas Aquinas acknowledged that higher appeals were acceptable and where a higher authority was unavailable or did not exist, the matter might be entrusted to God.[76] It cannot be maintained that Thomas considered such an appeal valid in a court context or in addition to canon law. The thirteenth-century "Golden Legend" of Jacobus de Voragine asserts the possibility of appealing beyond popes and emperors to God.[77] Regardless of what this reference can be made to say, it is manifest that the "Golden Legend" cannot be made a legal reference or indeed even reflective of a valid assumption or procedural rule anywhere in medieval law.

Of relevance also, as we have seen in some detail, remains the fact that canon law and prevailing legal practice and procedure did not allow for judgment to be made against popes.[78] The paucity of legal precedent for the practice and the rulings of canon law help to explain that when Hus attempted to support his appeal to Christ during the trial hearings before the Council of Constance, he was mocked.[79] It is difficult to assess emotions or characterizations like these from a distance of six hundred years, especially when the description comes from a tendentious source. Were

---

74. Ibid., pp. 32–39.

75. Spinka, *John Hus*, p. 162.

76. Commentary on the sentences of Peter Lombard, in Stanislas Éduard Fretté and Paul Maré, eds., *Doctoris angelici divi Thomae Aquinatis Opera omnia* (Paris: Apud Ludovicum Vivès, 1873), vol. 10, p. 558, where in dist. 19, quaest. 2, we find "vel si non habet superiorem, recurrat ad Deum, ut eum emendet, vel de medio subtrahat."

77. See the references in Kejř, *Odvolání*, p. 32.

78. C.9 q.3 c.13–c.15 *Nemo iudicabit*, in Friedberg, vol. 1, cols. 610–611.

79. This occurred during the third hearing on June 8. Petr Mladoňovice recorded that when Hus defended his appeal, "they laughed him to scorn." *Relatio*, p. 92.

the members of the Council poking fun at a man they now had in their power, or was their mockery a response to what they considered a ridiculous attempt to obfuscate the law and create a loophole whereby to avoid the consequences of disobedience and noncompliance? Michael de Causis certainly practiced malice toward Hus, and if he were among those laughing Hus to scorn, then the matter seems relatively straightforward. But does it seem proper to attribute to the entire Council the characteristics of one man or a handful of malevolent men? Canon law was unambiguous. Papal decisions could not be appealed, mainly on the grounds that the Holy See judges the entire church and is not and cannot be subordinate to any court.[80] Were this principle annulled, the ecclesiastical judicial system would face an endless stream of appeals from practically every ruling. The Roman church possessed the power and authority to judge all things, but its own rulings when rendered at the papal level could not be subject to judgment.[81] Hus regarded his protest as a moral and theological imperative. However, the conclusion seems unavoidable: Hus was confusing faith with law and moral conviction with legal procedure. The two were quite separate in the minds of ecclesiastical authorities presiding over aspects of the Hus case in Prague, at the Curia, and finally at Constance. The posture of morality that Hus assumed was incompatible with the posture of law and legal procedure that his judges defended. There was a total misunderstanding on the part of Hus and a complete inability of the lawyers and judges during the trial to understand him. The outcome seemed deceptively clear. As we have seen previously, canon law allowed for judgment against a pope only if there had been the obvious commission of an act contrary to the faith.[82] Medieval legal theory, along with most of its canonists, perceived a close relationship between the verdict of a pope and the will and decision of God.[83] All of this goes some distance toward showing that medieval judicature and Jan Hus were not compatible. The former was founded on formal statutes, rules of procedure, and limitations on appeal. The latter wished to subordinate such things to subjective considerations of truth, justice, morals, and personal theological convictions. Hus perceived an enormous gulf between the law of God and both

---

80. C.9 q.3 c.16 *Ipsi sunt canones*, in Friedberg, vol. 1, col. 611.

81. C.9 q.3 c.17 *Cuncta per mundum*, in Friedberg, vol. 1, col. 611

82. D.40 c.6 *Si papa*, in Friedberg, vol. 1, col. 146.

83. Kejř, *Odvolání*, p. 37, n. 113.

canon and civil law. Sometimes he posed it as starkly as "the law of the Lord, not Justinian."[84] Hus's position was admirable, ideal, even salutary, but ultimately naive and misguided. The appeal to Jesus Christ, though rooted in deep moral and ethical conviction, was unacceptable and inadmissible. It was both impracticable and illegal. A modern parallel might see a defendant file a motion with an appellate court, subsequently appeal to a supreme court, object to those rulings, and later ask for final judgment from a nonlegal entity. Such procedure would be dismissed as ludicrous, illogical, illegal, and intolerable. Laws and legal procedure cannot be made up by subjective criteria, whether in the Middle Ages or in the twenty-first century.

By contrast, Hus's rationale for continuing to celebrate Mass even though under anathema is sound and legally defensible. A legitimate appeal had been lodged in the proper fashion within the rules governing schedule. Technically, this should have caused a suspension in the original sentence of anathema.[85] That the Curia ignored those procedural rules cannot be taken to indicate that what happened next was legal. The initiation of an appellate process suspended the action or sentence of a lower court. The appeal took precedence. Once an appeal had been made and filed with the relevant court or authority, nothing further should be done with respect to the original case until a decision had been reached and announced.[86] In other words, the judgment of the lower court was withdrawn by the judge of the higher, appellate court, and the first judgment could not be executed while the appeal was pending.[87] In certain circumstances, this is also the case in modern judicial procedures. Applied to Hus's case, the imposition of excommunication and interdict after the filing of the motion on appeal was null and void.[88] While there were other rules governing appeals made after a ruling of excommunication, those were inapplicable, because Hus's appeal was lodged with the court

---

84. "Jan Hus sám o sobě," in Kejř, *Počátků*, p. 29, with references to sources in the Hus corpus.

85. The execution of the sentence pertaining to the original pronouncement cannot be implemented when an appeal is pending. X 2.28.37 *Ad haec*, in Friedberg, vol. 2, col. 422. By consequence, any anathema or interdict applied after an appeal has been lodged is invalid. X 2.28.55 *Dilectis filiis*, in Friedberg, vol. 2, cols. 433–435.

86. C.2 q.6 c.31 *Post appellationem interpositam*, in Friedberg, vol. 1, cols. 477–478.

87. Sext. 2.15.7 *Non solum*, in Friedberg, vol. 2, col. 1017.

88. X 2.28.55 *Dilectis filliis*, in Friedberg, vol. 2, col. 433.

before Colonna passed the anathema. The only grounds for assuming otherwise must be argued from the canon *Pastoralis*, which allowed for a legal exception to the rule with respect to excommunication.[89] In other words, since Hus was appealing against a sentence of excommunication, the normal suspension of a previous ruling had no effect. The argument is controversial.

Elsewhere in the appeal of 1412 to Christ, some scholars have argued the parts in the text about the reconciliation of Hus and Zbyněk are not original and must have been added by a later hand.[90] This has not been satisfactorily proven. Hus believed he had been reconciled to the archbishop. There is no compelling reason to think he omitted that from the appeal. In some ways, Hus considered that union a key part of his case. In that assumption, even if it were true, Hus was mistaken from a legal point of view. Further consideration draws attention to a critical legal distinction that mitigates the argument advanced by Hus and Jesenice that reconciliation with Zbyněk changed everything. In short, not even an effective reconciliation between the two foes would have changed the situation. This argument was put forward among the objections raised by Jan Železný, bishop of Litomyšl, on March 10, 1413, during the height of the most difficult period of polemical exchange between Hus and the Prague theologians. The bishop argued that in matters of faith, especially accompanied with a sentence passed down from the papal court, there could not possibly be any compromise allowed without the approval of the Holy See. This is evident because it is not permitted to discuss decisions made by higher courts at lower-level courts. Železný argued that by his appeal against the archbishop, which Hus had submitted to the Holy See, he now allegedly sought to avoid or nullify the curial decision by applying for a verdict within the kingdom of Bohemia.[91] The bishop also correctly recognized that Hus's defense in claiming that Archbishop Zbyněk did not accuse him of heresy or error was not justified, because a deadline had been set not for a decision but for an investigation.[92] This observation has been outlined by legal scholars to good and accurate effect.[93] Reconciliation

---

89. X 2.28.53 *Pastoralis*, in Friedberg, vol. 2, col. 432.

90. Flajšhans, *Odvolání*, pp. 251, 253.

91. *Documenta*, p. 503, art. 1.

92. Ibid., art. 3.

93. Kejř, *Odvolání*, p. 41.

with Zbyněk would not necessarily have caused any salutary effect in the trial of Hus.

It is somewhat astonishing that no one seems to have noted the obvious flaws in Cardinal Colonna's excommunication writ at the time the *aggravatio* was announced in 1412. This was a tremendous disadvantage to Hus. An appeal should have been filed immediately. There is no record that any appellate procedure was even contemplated. Where were Hus's lawyers? Unfortunately for the defendant, none of the members of his original legal team was available. Jan Jesenice had been imprisoned in Rome in March 1412. He escaped by May but did not return to Prague until December. By that time, the *aggravatio* had been proclaimed, Hus had filed his appeal to Christ, and the opportunity to challenge the validity of the final excommunication had passed.[94] As for the other attorneys, Marek of Hradec seems no longer to have been practicing law. By the time Stephaneschi's verdict was publicized in Prague, Marek had become university chancellor. The third of the three lawyers sent by Hus to the papal court in 1410 was Mikuláš Stojčín. At some indeterminate stage, he defected from the Hus legal team, and the next time we catch a glimpse of him is at the Council of Constance, where he aligned himself with the prosecution in the continuation of the trial of Hus.[95] We do not know the particulars of his defection. It would seem Hus had no legal representation in the summer and autumn of 1412. Bereft of legal advice, he unilaterally and independently appealed to Christ.

In repeating his rationale for not appearing in court as ordered, Hus referred to legal statute whereby he understood that the safety of the defendant must be guaranteed.[96] The real danger Hus faced, though, was not attack on the open road or assassination or an outbreak of general violence such as insurrection or war but malfeasance at the court itself on account of individuals such as Michael de Causis. This fear is different from an episode of military conflict. Since the venue is a papal court, Hus could not initiate a legally defensible appellate process elsewhere. Hus was clearly worried about judicial prejudice and bias in the proceedings. The law did allow for consideration of that concern.[97] Hus's appeal

---

94. X 2.27.15 *Quod ad consultationem*, in Friedberg, vol. 2, col. 400, specifies a ten-day period for filing a motion to inaugurate an appellate process.

95. Novotný, *Correspondence*, p. 245.

96. X 2.28.47 *Ex parte tua*, in Friedberg, vol. 2, col. 428.

97. C.3 q.5 c.15 *Quia suspecti*, in Friedberg, vol. 1, col. 518.

must be understood against concerns about bribery, the apparent illegality of Colonna's excommunication verdict, the question of judicial bias at the court, and the terminal *aggravatio*. The five-year legal ordeal under the lamp of scrutiny does reveal a number of procedural flaws that raise questions of fairness and objectivity.[98] But many of these shortcomings were either misunderstood or ignored by Hus. Those that were addressed by protest or appeal accomplished little. By the time the legal process restarted at the Council of Constance, the statute of limitations for appeal or legal challenge, in every instance, had expired. Issues of fairness and justice persisted, but these were now largely philosophical and existed outside the purview of renewed criminal procedure. Hus's decision to appeal to Jesus Christ as part of a court proceeding was not only irrelevant but counterproductive.

Something else that should be underscored is the fact that Hus consistently entrusted his case to God. We find considerable evidence of this throughout his writings. In replying to Archbishop Zbyněk at the end of the summer of 1408 in defense of the charges laid against him by members of the Prague clergy, Hus ended by saying he was prepared to commit his case to God, who judged righteously.[99] In the period encompassing late 1411 and early 1412, Hus again called witness to the fact that he had trusted his case to Christ, the just judge.[100] In his book on simony, Hus writes that it is better to appeal to God than to the pope or any other authority.[101] In writing to Sigismund on the eve of his departure for Constance, Hus committed himself to the "most just judge."[102] At this stage in his legal ordeal, it is reasonable to perceive of Hus as having no other viable option except what he conceived as the righteous judgment of God.[103] Therefore, in this emotional state and mental conviction, Hus repeatedly referred to committing his case to God, who is characterized frequently, as we have seen, as the most reliable and righteous judge. It remains a conundrum that having appealed to God, Hus would then agree to bring his case under

---

98. Brandmüller, *Konzil*, vol. 1, pp. 358–359.

99. Novotný, *Correspondence*, p. 41.

100. KNM, MS XII F 1 fol. 69ʳ. Comments in Novotný, *M. Jan Hus*, vol. 2, p. 174; references in Kejř, *Odvolání*, pp. 47–48.

101. *O svatokupectví*, in Hus, *Opera omnia*, vol. 4, p. 258.

102. Novotný, *Correspondence*, p. 198.

103. Flajšhans, *Odvolání*, p. 253.

the purview of the Latin church at the Council of Constance. Two weeks before the end, his commitment and conviction to this principle of Christ as judge remained steadfast and unshakable. "And because I appealed to Jesus Christ, the most powerful and most just judge and committed my case to him; for that reason I stand by his holy decision and opinion, knowing full well he will judge and reward every person not according to false witness or according to erroneous counsels, but consistent with the truth and the merits [of the case]."[104] This all adds up to a case for seeing the appeal as another example of Hus's desire to practice the imitation of Christ, which he had ardently pursued in his own life and had also encouraged others to do.[105] It is sensible to understand this motivation as the impetus for his appeal.

Accordingly, Hus announced his appeal publicly at Bethlehem Chapel. Whether he read the text or developed a homily around it is not known. Hus's enemies considered the initiative reprehensible. The Carthusian abbot Štěpán of Dolany wrote that Hus should blush to recall the "blasphemous rite" that he foisted upon his congregation in Prague. This was how the abbot characterized the appeal to God. We are provided with a graphic and doubtless tendentious account of the announcement. Apparently, Hus stood in the pulpit of Bethlehem Chapel and with a loud voice proclaimed, "I declare before you this day, that I appeal to Christ, away from this evil pope who claims [falsely] to be pope."[106] Because the appeal called upon all faithful Christians for support, a copy was nailed onto the bridge tower in the Lesser Town of Prague.[107] With Hus endeavoring to make his stand wider than himself, this action makes sense and is not an act of radicalism or revolutionary intent. Certainly, it could be perceived that way. I think Hus's intention was rather more benign.

Elsewhere, Hus stated that he wanted his case heard at the papal court. Indeed, that is why he originally lodged an appeal at that venue. However, as the legal process unfolded, Hus became convinced that the court was corrupt, its judges hopelessly biased and susceptible to bribery, and the

---

104. Novotný, *Correspondence*, pp. 282–283.

105. A clear theme and argument in Molnár, "Husovo odvolání ke Kristu."

106. Štěpán of Dolany, *Dialogus inter volatilis aucam et passerem*, in Pez, vol. 4, col. 492. The book was prepared in September 1414 and dedicated to Bishop Jan of Litomyšl.

107. Posting noted in Jan Długosz, *Historia Polonicae libri xii*, 2 vols., ed. H. von Huyssen (Leipzig: Gleditoch & Weidmann, 1711–1712), vol. 1, col. 335. The chronicle was written in the third quarter of the fifteenth century.

possibility of a fair hearing, or judicial examination (*cognitio*), not only gravely in doubt but out of the question. A judgment by Christ, however that might occur, would be more desirable than one by the pope.[108] Confiding his case to God brought Hus some measure of relief, for he believed that justice ultimately lay within the purview of the divine court constituted by the law of God. No one, popes included, could overthrow it.[109] Of course, this perspective codified succinctly in the appeal was considered treasonous. Štěpán Páleč claimed that whoever did not obey the pope was worthy of death. Hus objected.[110] Theological conviction caused Hus to use legal sources differently from how his judges in the court trial did. Hus often refers to legal sources, not to find support in their normative authority but to argue on the basis of their morally binding principle.[111] He focused almost exclusively on the latter while effectively ignoring the former. His judges and opponents in the court case took exactly the polar perspective. It seems as though Hus wanted to go behind the law and establish principles that would preserve order but reconcile the law of God with religious reform. He believed an appeal from an unjust sentence to a "better-informed" authority canceled the previous judgment.[112] For Hus to invoke Christ as judge in opposition to the judges of the criminal court was offensive to the fathers at Constance, and in terms of his trial, the appeal was utterly ineffectual.[113] The appeal to Jesus Christ was provocative from every imaginable perspective, achieving the opposite result Hus hoped for.[114] He had taken a stand on morals and ethics, but in terms of law and criminal procedure, he had doomed himself and his case.

---

108. *Contra Palecz*, in Hus, *Opera omnia*, vol. 22, pp. 259–260.

109. *Contra octo doctores*, in Hus, *Opera omnia*, vol. 22, p. 399.

110. *Contra Palecz*, in Hus, *Opera omnia*, vol. 22, p. 236.

111. Kejř, *Odvolání*, p. 52.

112. *Contra Palecz*, in Hus, *Opera omnia*, vol. 22, p. 260.

113. De Vooght, pp. 251–252.

114. Kejř, "Právo a právní prameny v Husově díle," in *Husův sborník: Soubor prací k 500. výročí M. Jana Husa*, ed. Rudolf Říčan and Michal Flegl (Prague: Komenského Evangelicka Fakulta Bohoslovecká, 1966), p. 87; and "Jan Hus sám o sobě," in Kejř, *Počátku*, p. 33.

6

The Ordo Procedendi *as a Political Document*

HAVING EXAMINED HUS'S appeal, the other document requiring analysis before taking up the remainder of the trial process has to do with with the procedural history of the court case involving Hus. The various lacunae that bedevil an investigation into the legal procedures and history of the trial of Jan Hus are alleviated in part by the existence and survival of a document known as the *Ordo procedendi*.[1] This "order of procedure" presents a summary outline of the legal proceedings involving Hus between 1410 and 1412. Its purpose is debatable. A number of options are offered in this chapter. The question of authorship remains open, although it is possible to advance a plausible hypothesis. The importance of the document has been recognized by most scholars dealing with the life of Hus, but curiously, like the appeal to God, it has not been subjected to detailed examination until recently. Václav Novotný and František Bartoš made passing references in their work.[2] Paul de Vooght noted that the *Ordo* had been prepared for Hus's use at the Council of Constance but made no effort to evaluate it.[3] In several books on Hus, Matthew Spinka did little more than refer to the existence of the

---

1. There are two editions: *Documenta*, pp. 188–193; and Novotný, *Correspondence*, pp. 225–234. I use the latter, designated *Ordo procedendi*. The former edition is incomplete, having omitted the series of legal citations that may have been incorrectly judged as not belonging to the text.

2. Novotný, *M. Jan Hus*, vol. 2, pp. 366–367; Bartoš, *Čechy*, pp. 351, 385.

3. De Vooght, p. 351.

Ordo.[4] Howard Kaminsky characterized it as an "interestingly tendentious" account of Hus's legal affairs.[5] Jiří Kejř has now provided us with
a comprehensive analysis of the *Ordo*, and his observations are both
sound and useful.[6] We can be quite certain about the proper name for
this document, for the manuscripts consistently use this term, and it is
present in all extant manuscripts.[7] This is true of both the Prague and
Vienna manuscripts.[8] The gaps that prevent a comprehensive review of
the Hus case are many and at times severe. The *Ordo* fills in some of the
blanks. A summary of its contents, then, is useful before turning to an
analysis and consideration of authorship, dating, intention, usefulness,
and reliability.

The document, as noted previously, did have something of a precursor.
In the St. Vitus Cathedral chapter library in Prague Castle, there is a brief
and incomplete outline of the controversy between Hus and the Latin
church.[9] In this fragment, Hus explains why he declined to obey papal
orders with respect to preaching and points out that he was forced before
a church court on account of mendacious articles advanced against him
by certain Prague priests. Here he has in mind the accusations brought
by Jan Protiva, Michael de Causis, and others from 1409 on. He notes his
opposition to the papal crusade of 1412 and the commensurate financial
support underwritten by the sale of indulgences. Hus outlines six points
of interest relating to the legal process. First, the matter began because
Hus's detractors wished to see Bethlehem Chapel pulled down and its
rector, Hus himself, silenced. Hus notes somewhat ruefully his ineffectual appeals to two successive popes and his inability to "achieve appropriate permission." So he disobeyed. Second, Hus argues that he had been

---

4. *John Hus and the Czech Reform* (Chicago: University of Chicago Press, 1941), *John Hus
at the Council of Constance* (New York: Columbia University Press, 1965), *John Hus' Concept
of the Church* (Princeton, N.J.: Princeton University Press, 1966), *John Hus: A Biography*
(Princeton, N.J.: Princeton University Press, 1968), and *The Letters of John Hus* (Manchester,
U.K.: Manchester University Press, 1972).

5. Kaminsky, HHR, p. 138, n. 144.

6. "K pramenům Husova procesu: tzv. Ordo procedendi," in Kejř, *Počátků*, pp. 132–145; also
published in *Právěhistorické Studie* 38 (2007): 57–67. I use the former.

7. *Ordo procedendi*, p. 234; Kejř, "K pramenům Husova procesu," p. 132.

8. Prague: KNM, MS VIII F 38, fols. 198ʳ–204ʳ; NK, MSS III G 8, fols. 101ʳ–103ᵛ, and IV F 25,
fols 197ʳ–200ᵛ. Vienna: ÖNB, MS 4524 109ᵛ–112ʳ. Kejř, *Jesenice*, pp. 165–166.

9. Prague Castle Archive, MS D 50, fols. 237ʳ–238ʳ.

urged by God and the testimony of scripture to withstand wickedness. "I preached against greed, simony, lust and the pride of the priests." Hence, he was subjected to criminal charges. Third, Hus regards the proclamation of crusade as nothing more than a cheap excuse to exact political revenge and engage in wholesale extermination "contrary to the law of God." Fourth, Hus announced that what was happening seemed to him against the law of God, when papal legates could set prices for indulgences as they saw fit, especially when the whole business was accompanied by much disorder, land dealing, and whoring. Fifth, the politically inspired opposition to Pope Gregory XII was unreasonable. Sixth, Hus was reluctant to join the chorus of condemnation directed against the "forty-five articles." He nominated seven of those articles that he considered salutary. However, this document was left unfinished, and there was no expansion of its points to include more critical aspects of the legal case. We may put this anomaly down to the fact that not long after its composition began, it was overshadowed and ultimately replaced by the longer and more definitive *Ordo procedendi.*[10]

Inasmuch as the constituent parts of the *Ordo procedendi* have been noted above, it will suffice to catalogue them here in chronological outline without commenting extensively beyond what the *Ordo* itself says. The summary is somewhat repetitive, but it seems useful to have the contents of the document all together in one place in order to make an assessment of the arguments and subject the work to some modicum of critical evaluation. According to the *Ordo procedendi*, the legal case of Jan Hus began with the appalling actions of Archbishop Zbyněk, when that prelate ordered the burning of books authored by John Wyclif in 1410 after having passed an unacceptable ruling on the Eucharist in 1406. The *Ordo* alleges that the former episcopal action was contrary to the freedoms and privileges of the university, while the writ on the sacrament contained "unbearable heresy."[11] Both actions required firm resistance. Hus appealed against these drastic measures. Stymied in Prague, Zbyněk sought papal support, first from Alexander V and then from John XXIII. The *Ordo* claims the papal office was "informed falsely and erroneously," which explains why the Latin church ordered repressive measures introduced in Prague, namely, the ban on unauthorized preaching. This papal

---

10. Flajšhans, *Sebrané spisy*, vol. 1, p. 63.

11. *Ordo procedendi*, p. 226.

order was obtained "surreptitiously," extracted from the pope "by concealing the truth and adding falsehood," to the detriment of the Czech kingdom. These convictions and perceptions formed the point of departure
for the outline of events in the *Ordo*. The perspective is both unique and
important. At this initial point, the document had assumed several stages
of development and was already outlining a formal legal cause well under
way in the courts. The matter of the legal proceedings was turned over
to a magistrate for examination. The *Ordo* then insists that Pope John
XXIII immediately entrusted the matter to four cardinals in Bologna who
were also doctors of theology. These men deemed the Prague book burning precipitous and unwarranted. Meanwhile, Hus was denounced to the
pope as a purveyor of heresies and thus presented as a criminal suspect
in these matters. Hus's detractors suggested that he should be remanded
to appear at the Roman court and arraigned on formal charges. The complaint was turned over to Cardinal Odo Colonna to handle. The *Ordo*
alleges that Colonna proceeded incorrectly and illegally by questioning
potential witnesses on the veracity of the initial charges laid against Hus,
suppressing evidence, and failing to allow the defendant recourse to legal
provisions which should have granted Hus permission to avoid a personal
court appearance as desired by his enemies. On the business of conducting interrogatories, the law was clear that a mistrial might be declared if
the judge failed either to formally charge the defendant or engaged in the
examination of potential witnesses about matters of guilt concerning the
accused *before* infamy had been established.[12] Back in Bohemia, the royal
house and the university filed appeals at the papal court against the citation of Hus to appear at the Curia. These documents were lodged by King
Václav, Queen Žofie, unnamed members of the Czech nobility, Prague
university, and the municipalities of the Old and New Towns of Prague.[13]
Envoys were dispatched to the papal court on several occasions, asking for
the citation to be canceled and the summons withdrawn. The reasoning
in these appeals was put down to the unjust accusations lodged by the

---

12. Hostiensis, *Commentaria in Decretales Gregorii IX* (Venice: Apud Juntas, 1581), on X
5.1.24, no. 15.

13. On problems concerning this correspondence, see Božena Kopičková and Anežka
Vidmanová, *Listy na Husovu obrana z let 1410–1412: Konec jedné legendy?* (Prague: Karolinum,
1999); and Aleš Pořízka, "Listy na obranu Husova ze 12. září až 2. října 1410: Konec druhé
legendy?" *Český Časopis Historický* 99, no. 4 (2001): 701–723. On the first, see the review
essay by Thomas A. Fudge in *Mediaevistik: Internationale Zeitschrift für Interdisziplinäre
Mittelalterforschung* 14 (2001): 402–405.

enemies of Hus and the commensurate dangers the defendant would definitely be exposed to while undertaking such a long and arduous journey from Prague to the papal court.[14] The *Ordo* implies the likelihood of kidnapping, assassination, or other violence being perpetrated against Hus.[15] The *Ordo* goes on to argue that sustaining charges against Hus was tantamount to slander against the kingdom of Bohemia. A request was made for canceling the prohibition against preaching. As an indication of good faith, the Czech envoys offered to pay all expenses for papal legates to come to Prague to set in order anything the pope thought useful in order to deal with the matter.[16] We have no evidence from any source that this overture was ever seriously considered.

Meanwhile, being unable to travel to the court personally, Hus dispatched three representative attorneys in his stead, who arrived at the nominated court prepared to argue his case. The attorneys are not named, but the *Ordo* does identify five additional lawyers contracted to aid in the defense of Hus.[17] These legal representatives personally appeared before Cardinal Colonna and submitted documents, evidence, and testimony in support of their client for the court's consideration. The *Ordo* specifically claims that the dossier submitted on behalf of Jan Hus was proper, permissible, and procedurally correct from a legal point of view. Beyond this, Hus's lawyers repeatedly told the court that their client was prepared to adhere to the rule of law in these matters. However, the *Ordo* alleges that Cardinal Colonna took no note of the brief submitted to the court on behalf of Hus. In the face of this obvious malfeasance, a second appeal was lodged with the pope. This resulted in a procedural appeal being placed in the hands of the examining magistrate of the court, John de Thomariis. While the appeal was under consideration by the court, the *Ordo* alleges, Cardinal Colonna acted illegally once again. He denounced Hus as contumacious, issued an anathema against him, and, "using a despicable method," publicly excommunicated him "in the Curia and also outside it."[18]

---

14. This is a clear reference to legal statutes in which the safety of a subpoenaed defendant must be guaranteed by the court. X 2.28.47 *Ex parte tua*, in Friedberg, vol. 2, col. 428.

15. *Ordo procedendi*, pp. 227–228.

16. Ibid., p. 228.

17. Ibid., p. 229.

18. Ibid., p. 228.

When news of this drastic measure came to the ears of the pope, he promptly removed Colonna from the case and placed the matter of Hus under the immediate purview of the papal office. The appeal Thomariis had taken under advisement was likewise suspended, and the entire case was turned over to four cardinals identified as Francesco Zabarella, Rainaldo Brancacci, Antonio Caetani, and an obscure fellow identified as "de Veneficiis," of whom we know nothing for certain. When Caetani died, Zabarella undertook a comprehensive review of the case and effectively reversed the decisions made by Colonna. The *Ordo* makes a clear effort to characterize Zabarella's findings as judging the various submissions by Hus's attorneys "proper, admissible and procedurally correct" in accordance with the law.[19] In other words, Colonna had erred so egregiously that Zabarella overturned the previous interlocutory ruling, admitted evidence hitherto ruled inadmissible, and assigned a new scheduling order for the examination of the previously excluded dossier in accordance with law. In other words, Zabarella was prepared to conduct an evidentiary hearing based on these probable-cause findings. Inexplicably, that never occurred. Instead, "when the aforementioned articles were sufficiently examined by proper witnesses and when the record of the case and its documents were completely and sufficiently written out, the pope ordered the record submitted to Cardinal Brancacci."[20] The silence or lack of commentary on this procedural development can be taken as consternation by virtue of the fact the *Ordo* pointed out that the Hus case languished in Brancacci's office for almost a year and a half. The *Ordo* specifically says Brancacci did not wish to proceed in the case but at the same time was reluctant either to cancel or to relax the initial summons demanding Hus's appearance at the papal court. The legal proceedings bogged down at this stage despite Hus's lawyers repeatedly arguing for action by submitting briefs to the court in accordance with the law, and even "defense lawyers authorized by the pope" were unable to gain any traction. When pressure continued to be applied by Hus's legal team, the *Ordo* alleges, Brancacci ostensibly acted contrary to the law and prevailing legal procedures and ordered lawyers for Hus to cease and desist making further application in this matter and to stop coming to his office, with the firm rebuke that he no longer wished to hear anything further by way of defending Hus. Brancacci claimed that

---

19. Ibid., p. 229.

20. Ibid.

his motion came upon the instigation of the pope. We are left with an implied sense that Brancacci's hands were tied specifically and intentionally by the papal office, and no amount of legal maneuvering could prevail in advancing the case. The fact that the *Ordo* repeatedly makes reference to the legality of the initiatives by Hus's attorneys suggests that there were no unethical ex parte efforts to sway the court case or influence Brancacci. All of this is information we cannot find elsewhere. The *Ordo*, then, is a crucial document for piecing together aspects of the curial process.

Lawyers for Hus persisted in seeking justice and were summarily immured in a "cruel prison," and "various things were taken from them."[21] With Hus's legal team sidelined, the *Ordo* pointed out, the prosecution began to advance its initiative ever more aggressively. Cardinal Brancacci now acted (allegedly under papal order) and took steps to aggravate the measures initiated by Colonna. The *Ordo* explicitly says these procedures were illegal and extravagant and not only violated the law but also contravened rules governing general councils. The consequences, therefore, amounted to the anathematizing of all followers of Hus; all of his relatives were subjected to the same censure (we know only of a brother and his two sons); and the city of Prague and various other places in Bohemia were placed under interdict. Hus was explicitly denounced as a heretic, even though he had not been heard as procedurally required in criminal cases. Hus was now an arch-heretic. Any persons connected to him were presumed guilty by association and therefore deemed heretical.[22] The *Ordo* concluded that none of these measures should have been permitted to happen in violation of the law and the church, not even if the pope had ordered such steps to be taken, because Hus had appealed to a future church council, which was permissible, and he intended to appeal against all of these illegal sanctions. This last statement is a deeply problematic claim, which is examined below.[23]

Anticipating a subsequent legal argument that all of these measures were, in fact, legal, justifiable, and necessary, the *Ordo* preempted this strategy by citing canon law in which a heresy suspect having been called to a court appearance and failing to show could be considered guilty of contumacy, and should the defendant continue in that resistance for a year,

---

21. Ibid.

22. Ibid., p. 230.

23. Ibid.

he or she could legally be sentenced as a heretic *in absentia*.[24] The *Ordo* addresses this legal argument by stating that Hus did not avoid appearing as summoned but endeavored to demonstrate his innocence pursuant to the charges, sent legal representatives to the Curia, and filed an appeal. None of this can be construed as contempt of court leading to a contempt citation formally constituted as contumacy.[25] All of Hus's actions, according to the *Ordo*, consisted of proper and legally justified conduct. In other words, Hus attempted to comply with the court order, but when his efforts, as mediated through his team of attorneys, were rebuffed, he initiated an appeal process based on a writ of mandamus. The *Ordo* goes to some lengths to demonstrate Hus's willingness to give account of his teachings and faith. Several names of ecclesiastical and imperial dignitaries are recorded.[26] The royal court is invoked as saying there was no unimpeachable evidence proving that Hus was a heretic. Moreover, the *Ordo* claims, Hus and Archbishop Zbyněk were completely reconciled, and the archbishop would have alerted the papal court to this important fact had he not suffered grave misfortune and suddenly died. The *Ordo* suggests that Zbyněk intended to inform the pope that he knew of no heresy in Hus and that it would be good and proper for the papal court to withdraw its summons ordering Hus to appear at the Curia, and, more important, that the archbishop fully intended to ask the pope to acquit Hus.

In the absence of the alleged letter from the see of Prague ever being sent or received at the papal court, the *Ordo* notes, Hus offered to appear before the general synod of the Prague archbishopric and also before the inquisitor of heretical depravity. Letters from both testifying to the innocence of Hus in the matter of heresy charges are available.[27] Archbishop Konrad evidently said he knew of no priest in the diocese who accused Hus of heresy. After these events, Hus was prepared to appear at the Council of Constance to resolve the matter.

The remainder of the *Ordo procedendi* is taken up with a dossier of legal citations.[28] These should be briefly delineated. We have alluded to one

---

24. Ibid. The relevant canon is Sext. 5.2.7 *Quum contumacia*, in Friedberg, vol. 2, col. 1071.

25. Jan Jesenice argued this point in his *Repetitio* of December 18, 1412, pp. 408–419.

26. *Ordo procedendi*, p. 231.

27. Text of the letter provided by inquisitor Nicholas Nezero has been included in the *Relatio*, pp. 64–65. We know of the existence of the other statement in the same source, *Relatio*, p. 65.

28. *Ordo procedendi*, pp. 232–234.

reference to canon law already. The *Ordo* shows evidence of some rather shrewd legal exegesis in its effort to strengthen the case for why Hus did not personally appear at the papal court. The legal point of departure was the argument for conviction on the grounds of contumacy, in which a heresy suspect could be sentenced even though he or she was not present in the court.[29] The legal rubric somewhat surprisingly appears neither in the surviving acts nor in the text of the anathema against Hus. As we have seen, the *Ordo* argues that the appeal to this statute is inapplicable in the Hus case. In all, there are ten references to legal sources in the *Ordo*. The final section of the document is definitely a legal outline. The legal brief argues from canon law that Hus had grounds for not appearing at the papal court as summoned.[30] The law allowed for a defendant to absent himself or herself if there was reasonable expectation of danger, harm, or violence. Further, the *Ordo* appeals to canon law to argue that enemies of the defendant could not act as judges in legal proceedings.[31] Persons reasonably close to the prosecution could be considered as having a conflict of interest. Therefore, material parties had to be excluded. Judges and prosecutors were obligated to recuse themselves in order for an objective hearing to transpire. This argument was used by the *Ordo* to support Hus's failure to appear in court. A third legal citation argued that accusations should be heard in the location or jurisdiction in which they were alleged.[32] A second supporting rubric underscored this question of jurisdiction and legal competence to hear a case.[33] A third reference on the same matter stated that the proper venue for a hearing had to follow the plaintiff.[34] Switching from the specific venue, the *Ordo* argues that if the location for the hearing was inaccessible for the accused, then the setting had to be changed.[35] Beyond this, and providing legal support for statements elsewhere in the *Ordo*, we find argument for why a legal proceeding could not be conducted in any place where the defendant was exposed to mortal danger or might fall into

---

29. Sext. 5.2.7 *Quum contumacia*, in Friedberg, vol. 2, col. 1071.

30. Clem. 2.11.2 *Pastoralis*, in Friedberg, vol. 2, cols. 1151–1153.

31. C.3 q.5 c.15 *Quia suspecti*, in Friedberg, vol. 1, cols. 518–519.

32. C.3 q.6 c.1 *Ibi semper*, in Friedberg, vol. 1, col. 519.

33. C.3 q.6 c.4 *Ultra prouinciarum terminos*, in Friedberg, vol. 1, col. 519.

34. C.3 q.6 c.16 *Neminem exhiberi*, in Friedberg, vol. 1, cols. 523–524.

35. X 1.29.35 *Quum R. canonicus*, in Friedberg, vol. 2, cols. 179–180.

the hands of his or her enemies.[36] Furthermore, the *Ordo* points out that adequate security for the case could not be ensured and delves into questions of guarantees that could not be given.[37] There is a single reference to Roman law which makes a similar point that on account of this frailty of caution the matter is questionable.[38] Kejř points out that neither allusion to the canon law specialist Hostiensis nor Roman law is related to procedural law, with the implication that both authorities are questionable and vague in relation to the trial of Hus. The *Ordo* concludes its legal outline by referring to the fact that the court was obligated to determine a scheduling order so the parties implicated in the proceedings could make the necessary arrangements in order to arrive safely at the court.[39] This is the sum and substance of the *Ordo procedendi*.

Any study of the trial of Jan Hus will necessarily have to take into account the several parts of the *Ordo*. Surprisingly, most treatments have not done due diligence with the *Ordo*. It is reasonable to conclude that this document was assembled about two years after the last events it records. As outlined, it consists of an overview of events, pertinent issues, and legal concerns. There is good argument for assuming that the narrative review of the chronological order of things in the *Ordo* was written sometime before the listing of the legal rules and norms that we find in the latter portions of the document.[40] This may explain why Palacký excluded this part of the *Ordo* from the version he edited and published.[41] The *Ordo* provides us with a particular version of what happened and why. It points out several problems that confounded the legal case, and it also underscores a number of procedural faults and issues that are presented as contrary to the rule of law. Of importance is the consistent fact that the *Ordo* draws attention to matters advantageous to Hus and his legal case.

---

36. X 2.6.4 *Accedens ad sedem*, in Friedberg, vol. 2, col. 262.

37. Hostiensis, *Lectura in quinque Decretalium Gregorianarum libros* (Paris: Rembolt, 1511), book 2, fol. 52, on the canon law statute X 2.13.13 *Literas v. alioquin*, in Friedberg, vol. 2, col. 288. I owe the Hostiensis reference to "K pramenům Husova procesu," Kejř, *Počátků*, p. 145.

38. Dig. 36.1.68 *Qui ita* 1 noted by Kejř, "K pramenům Husova procesu: tzv. Ordo procedendi," p. 145 with reference to the source collection.

39. C.33 q.2 c.4 *Siue de coniugii*, in Friedberg, vol. 1, col. 1151.

40. "K pramenům Husova procesu," Kejř, *Počátků*, p. 132.

41. *Documenta*, pp. 188–193.

One of the questions in dealing with this document revolves around the issues of authorship and the date of composition. We find in the *Ordo* a reference to Hus coming to the Council of Constance.[42] While it is possible to read this sentence to imply that Hus was already at Constance when the document was written, it seems more likely that the legal case summary was written down before he departed for Germany. There is no particularly compelling reason to think the *Ordo* was composed after he arrived in Constance. The likely candidate for authorship also precludes this assumption. The fact that Hus was not present at the papal court or personally privy to the legal process that unfolded at the Curia means either that the *Ordo* was written by someone other than Hus who was there or that the text is dependent on other informed sources. It seems likely that either Hus was briefed by his attorneys or the *Ordo* is the work of someone like Jan Jesenice. We know that Jesenice was Hus's lead attorney until he was taken off the case on charges of heresy and imprisoned in March 1412 at the initiative of the curial advocate Michael de Causis. Moreover, we know from a plethora of other sources that Jesenice labored to legally exonerate Hus and had endeavored to secure appropriate documents for him with which to more adequately defend himself as the legal process shifted to Constance.[43] It seems sensible to think that Jesenice is either the main author or the coauthor of the *Ordo*. The fact that the document is a brief history, or outline, of the Hus case from 1410 to 1412 allows for the possibility that Jesenice wrote it, since he had been intimately involved in the legal case during that time. This is not a new theory. Practically all scholars dealing with the *Ordo* have seen the hand of Jesenice at work in its constituent parts.[44] Previously, it was noted that Hus's work on the books of heretics is replete with legal references, both Roman and canonical, and it is possible to suspect the collaboration of Jesenice.[45] That book, written in 1410, demonstrates that Hus had an excellent command of canon law or was getting help from someone who did. The essential relationship between Hus and Jesenice in the legal process

---

42. *Ordo procedendi*, p. 232: "Magister Johannes Hus iam venit ad istud generale concilium."

43. Kejř, *Jesenice*, pp. 86–89.

44. Novotný, *M. Jan Hus*, vol. 2, p. 367; Flajšhans, *Odvolání*, p. 251; Bartoš, *Čechy*, p. 306; Kejř, *Jesenice*, p. 88; Hilsch, *Johannes Hus*, p. 244; "K pramenům Husova procesu," Kejř, *Počátků*, p. 133; et al.

45. *De libris hereticorum legendis*, in Hus, *Opera omnia*, vol. 22, pp. 21–37.

is again evident. It is clear that the author of the *Ordo* was well acquainted with medieval legal traditions. It seems beyond the scope of reasonable expectation to conclude that Hus was acquainted with Roman law and Hostiensis's use of the Gregorian decretals. Legal references of this sort go well beyond Hus's own legal purview.[46] Moreover, the case for Jesenice as author of the *Ordo* is advanced by the argument that the methodology displayed in the *Ordo* parallels that exhibited elsewhere in the corpus of Jesenice's work.[47] The firmest argument for attributing the *Ordo* to Jesenice has been advanced on the basis of manuscript evidence. Once more, we are indebted to Kejř for the hypothesis.[48] A lost manuscript once recorded a group of writings by Jesenice in which he defended the case for his client Jan Hus. These included the notarized statement concerning Hus from inquisitor Nicholas of Nezero, a copy of Jesenice's unsuccessful attempts to gain a hearing before the Prague synod in August 1414, a document called *Requisitio facta per M. Jessenicz* which incorporated the *Ordo*, and another lost work defending Hus that bore the title *Summaria Magistri Jessenicz de iusticia et nullitate sentenciarum contra Hus*.[49] The circumstantial evidence for including the *Ordo* among the works of Jesenice is compelling.

With or without the attribution of authorship to Jesenice, it remains sensible to date the *Ordo* to some period prior to October 1414. It seems likely that once Hus knew he was going to Germany, which was as early as April that year, he may have begun to consider more fully the nature and outcomes of the legal case while it had been before the papal court. Hus was invited to the Council of Constance by Emperor Sigismund. He accepted that invitation in a letter dated September 1, 1414. There were negotiations about an imperial safe conduct for Hus's journey to the Council. These took place between April and August. Therefore, once Hus

---

46. "K pramenům Husova procesu," Kejř, *Počátků*, p. 133. However, an investigation of Hus as a legal thinker has been neglected. Jiří Kejř, "Jan Hus jako právní myslitel," in *Jan Hus mezi epochami, národy a konfesemi*, ed. Jan B. Lášek (Prague: Česká Křesťanská Akademie, Husitská Teologická Fakulta Univerzy Karlovy, 1995), p. 203.

47. His *Auctoritates contra communionem parvulorum* has been nominated as a case in point. See "K pramenům Husova procesu," Kejř, *Počátků*, p. 144, n. 12. On this particular work by Jesenice, see also Kejř, "Auctoritates contra communionem parvulorum M. Jana z Jesenice," *Studie o Rukopisech* 19 (1980): 5–21.

48. "K pramenům Husova procesu," Kejř, *Počátků*, p. 134.

49. Kejř, *Jesenice*, p. 163.

knew for certain that he was going to attend the Council, the need for a
documentary summary of the legal process to date, like that contained in
the *Ordo procedendi,* became a matter of priority. We may assign the writing to the period between April and September 1414, but more likely, given
internal references to events in late August, a final version was completed
in September. This being so, it also suggests that Hus and/or Jesenice
were not ignorant of the fact that the case was a continuation of the curial
process.

Turning to the content of the *Ordo,* we find rather significantly a firm
stance against the accusation of heresy. This is also a recurrent theme
in other documents of the period that favored Hus. However, the *Ordo*
itself contains errors. The reference to the burning of Wyclif's books is
misplaced in the sequence of appeals lodged in the papal office. This
might be put down to faulty memory or that the *Ordo* was prepared in
some haste, as may have been true if the document was prepared or
finalized in September in the days leading up to Hus's departure for
Constance. Any reading of the *Ordo* itself against what we know of the
trial of Hus from other sources reveals immediately that the outline is
neither a fully accurate description of the course of the legal process
nor a careful interpretation of its legal aspects. This raises a number of
questions. If Jesenice is the author and the careful legal expert he has
been characterized as, how can these inaccuracies and deficiencies be
explained?[50] One must wonder about the strategy in the *Ordo.* Why are
certain fairly well-known things omitted, even issues that conceivably
were advantageous to Hus? Here one might recall King Václav's opposition to the book burning.[51] Moreover, why does the author of the *Ordo* fail
to mention the fairly significant body of law that might be used to defend
Hus's position in the legal proceedings? It has been said that the *Ordo* "is
a record *pro memoria* which should serve Hus not only as a reminder, but
also as a warning of what he should avoid and what he should not store
in his memory."[52] In other words, the *Ordo* was supposed to act as a legal
guideline for Hus as he defended himself. There were issues considered
advantageous to his case that the *Ordo* encouraged him to utilize. Here

---

50. The single great study of this lawyer is Kejř, *Jesenice,* which stands without antecedent
or peer in any language.

51. *Documenta,* pp. 409–415.

52. "K pramenům Husova procesu," Kejř, *Počátků,* p. 136; and Kejř, *Husův proces,*
pp. 66–67.

one thinks of Zabarella's examination of the procedures and his interlocutory ruling that evidence formerly excluded should be considered
by the court, a legally defensible ruling.[53] There were other issues that
Jesenice deemed a liability, and even though these were true or perhaps
beneficial to the Hus case from a particular point of view, they were
thought to create the possibility for disadvantage in the continuing legal
process, and so Hus was advised, by their omission, to leave those out of
his defense. But what can be said about confused chronology? The decision handed down at Bologna concerning the legality of the book burning occurred in August 1410, but the *Ordo* situates that event before the
commissioning of the four cardinals to consider the Hus case. We know
that the cardinals were given the brief after June 6, 1411.[54] This slippage
cannot have been intentional.

More serious, from the perspective of jurisprudence, is the fact that the
Ordo uses the inaccurate and inappropriate term *appellatio* when referring
to *iudicis recusatio*, which does not imply or mean an appeal but is concerned rather with the rejection of a judge.[55] Earlier, we noted that Hus's
legal team ostensibly had submitted an appeal to the examining magistrate of the court that called into question the objectivity and partiality of
the presiding judge. The language is problematic. What the *Ordo* refers to
as an appeal is accurately a motion requesting *iudicis recusatio*, meaning a
procedural application for the magistrate to be recused from the case. The
so-called appeal was not an effort to start an appellate process in opposition
to a verdict, for, indeed, no sentence had been passed. More important, the
deadline for Hus to appear at the court had not expired, and therefore, a
ruling could neither sensibly nor legally have been handed down. The
alleged appeal is more accurately a question about the impartiality of the
presiding judge.[56] The law ruled that an impartial judge should not preside
over a court case. The so-called appeal was lodged by Marek of Hradec,
one of Hus's representatives, with John XXIII on the grounds of irregular

---

53. As reflected in Clem. 2.1.2 *Dispendiosam prorogationem*, in Friedberg, vol. 2, col. 1143; and
Clem. 5.11.2 *Saepe contingit*, in Friedberg, vol. 2, col. 1200.

54. In addition to the witness in the *Ordo* itself, there is allusion to the work of these cardinals in Jesenice, *Repetitio*, pp. 416–417.

55. *Ordo procedendi*, p. 228.

56. Kejř, *Husův proces*, pp. 61–62. The relevant canons are X 1.29.27 §5 *Super quaestionum
articulis*, in Friedberg, vol. 2, col. 172; C.3 q.5 c.15 *Quia suspecti*, in Friedberg, vol. 1, cols.
518–519; and Sext. 1.14.5 *Iudex ab apostolica sede* in Friedberg, vol. 2, col. 979.

proceedings.[57] Would a lawyer of Jesenice's experience and acumen make such a mistake? It is possible, of course, but is it likely? Could this sort of thing indicate the presence of another hand in the final shaping of the *Ordo procedendi*? Might that second hand actually belong to the defendant, Jan Hus? It is true, as the *Ordo* makes clear, and there is canonical support for the assumption, that Colonna arguably lacked the authority to issue the anathema against Hus because an auditor had been appointed to investigate concerns raised by Hus's attorneys. The *Ordo* goes on to claim that Colonna undertook his initiative by means of a frivolous manner.[58] Later in the document, we find another reference to the four cardinals, and this time, it appears in the proper sequence. Did the author not proofread his own document? We encounter an error concerning the length of time in which the legal proceedings languished under the assigned supervision of Brancacci. The suggestion that nothing occurred for the better part of a year and a half is simply not defensible, as we know very well from other sources.[59] Presumably, this lapse can be related to faulty memory. Alternatively, the *Ordo*'s author may have wished to exaggerate the length of time the legal proceedings were held up, perhaps as an effort to show the inefficiency of the papal court, which had been grievously disadvantageous to Hus. The same might be said with respect to the fact that the judge at the time of the aggravation of the previous excommunication leveled against Hus by Colonna was not Brancacci, as assumed by the *Ordo*, but, in fact, Cardinal Peter degli Stephaneschi. There does not appear to be any purpose in deliberately allowing Brancacci to remain in the place of judgment unless the author of the *Ordo* hoped to imply that the *aggravatio* or the full implementation of the legal and ecclesiastical sanctions could be attributed to the illegal and unethical behavior of Brancacci, who refused to hear arguments from Hus's attorneys and inexplicably delayed the course of justice. This could be construed as shrewd lawyering. There is no reason to exclude the presence of Jesenice.

What was the purpose of the *Ordo procedendi*? Was this intended as a private document for Hus to use in his legal defense at Constance only,

---

57. Novotný, *Correspondence*, pp. 88–89.

58. *Ordo procedendi*, p. 228.

59. We know that by spring, Michael de Causis was able to have the papal auditor Berthold Wildungen replaced by George Fleckel. Meanwhile, Jesenice was arrested but later escaped from prison. Kejř, *Jesenice*, p. 61. So it is wrong to say nothing was happening with the Hus case while under the purview of Cardinal Brancacci.

or did the summary overview have some type of public role to play? If the purpose was solely to aid the memory of Hus, why make exaggerations on matters such as the length of time Brancacci allegedly hindered progress in the legal proceedings? On the other hand, if the document had some initial public function, then errors like those just mentioned could easily be corrected on the basis of other records, and there was a risk that such errors could be used to undermine the integrity or legitimacy of the entire document. It is sensible to agree with Jiří Kejř that there are almost certainly intentional inaccuracies in the *Ordo*. Suggesting that Hus's attorneys were imprisoned while at the papal court is not a sustainable allegation.[60] Kejř argues that we have no supporting evidence on this matter. It is true that Jesenice was imprisoned, but none of the others on Hus's legal team was ever arrested or incarcerated so far as the extant records show. We do have a comment on this issue elsewhere in Hus's writings, when he asserts that Pope John XXIII "captured my representatives and put them in jail; and when God helped them to get away from him, one of them was there a year and a half, the other as well, they returned home; the same happened to the third one."[61] Has Hus documented events in his legal affairs unrecorded elsewhere? In this instance, that possibility seems unlikely. By contrast, two years earlier, in his appeal to God, Hus noted only that Jesenice had been detained and imprisoned.[62] The narrative is deliberately misleading. This suggests the possibility that the *Ordo* is a political document. Jesenice was taken into custody not because he was acting as advocate for the accused seeking justice and judicial fairness (as the *Ordo* suggests) but because he was under suspicion of heresy on account of accusations lodged against him by Michael de Causis. However, the mention of heresy in connection with Hus's lead attorney in a document like the *Ordo* would have been injudicious. Indeed, the disadvantages of such reference for Hus in a criminal procedure would be, in effect, to aid the prosecution. It was deliberately omitted, and the facts were convoluted to suggest that all of Hus's lawyers were illegally interfered with to the detriment of the case for the defendant. Alterations

---

60. *Ordo procedendi*, pp. 229–230.

61. *Knížky proti knězi kuchmistrovi*, in Hus, *Opera omnia*, vol. 4, p. 321.

62. Novotný, *Correspondence*, p. 132. Jesenice is not named, but the reference reads, "meum procuratorem legittimum," denoting a single individual identified as Hus's lawful representative. The word *procurator* has been used traditionally of an agent representing another person or interest in a court of law.

to the legal account as recorded in the *Ordo* suggest that the document was prepared for wider circulation during the trial. Perhaps it was intended to be handed over to the judges in the course of the trial proceedings and not prepared exclusively as a reference for Hus. The *Ordo* claims that from the implementation of the legal and ecclesiastical sanctions against Hus, the *aggravatio*, sprang a series of malevolent outcomes.[63] The trial of Hus had been legally suspended, and yet while lawyers for Hus had effectively been silenced by the work of Michael de Causis and aided and abetted by the inactivity of Brancacci, illegal procedures had begun, excommunication had been announced, interdict had been imposed, and there was the even more serious and prejudicial assumption that Hus was a heretic despite the fact he had not been convicted according to legal procedures in a court of law. All of this is especially important for understanding the nature of heresy in the fifteenth century, along with the technicalities of ecclesiastical jurisprudence.

Among the most serious and obvious intentional editing of the legal process was the idea that Hus had filed an appeal with a future church council.[64] This was manifest falsehood. Some scholars have erred in assuming that this was a factual tactic encouraged by Jesenice that Hus took up to his ultimate detriment.[65] The fact is that in the absence of any known legal advice, Hus did appeal to Jesus Christ. Jesenice was not in Prague at the time. When he returned, it is likely he heard this news with consideration trepidation. The only recourse was to amend the appeal to keep it within the bounds of canonical procedure. It seems likely that this constituted the most compelling prima facie evidence for the intervention of Jesenice in the Hus case. Hus had, in fact, appealed to God, not to a future council. That, as we have seen, was legally impossible and contrary to canon law. Jesenice would never have advised it, aided in it, or defended it. The work of a shrewd attorney can be seen clearly in the effort to ameliorate the impact of Hus's appeal to God, which could be widely interpreted as a serious breach of legal procedure and canon law. Hus's action

---

63. *Ordo procedendi*, p. 230.

64. "A quibus omnibus gravaminibus ipse Magister Johannes Hus appellavit ad futurum concilium celebrandum." *Ordo procedendi*, p. 230.

65. Ferdinand Seibt, *Hussitenstudien: Personen, Ereignisse, Ideen einer frühen Revolution* (Munich: Oldenbourg, 1987), pp. 85, 237; and Ferdinand Seibt, "'Neodvolám!' Jan Hus před koncilem kostnickým," in *Velké procesy: Právo a spravedlnost v dějinách*, ed. Uwe Schultz (Prague: Brána, 1997), p. 94.

was tantamount to rejecting the jurisdictional authority and prerogatives of the church. Appealing to a future council was more palatable, because the appellate process remained within the purview of the church and provided evidence that the defendant was still acting within the limits of the rule of law and thereby willing to remain within the jurisdictional authority of the church. The papal court may have been displeased with such a move, but it could hardly be forbidden absolutely. Appealing to God was outright rebellion from a legal standpoint; appealing to a council indicated the continued possibility of submission to ecclesiastical authority. Legally, from a defense attorney's perspective, that was absolutely essential. The unavoidable mitigating factor in the novel clause introduced by Jesenice lay in the fact that nowhere can we find evidence that Hus ever acquiesced in the suggestion that he had or would appeal to a future council. In fact, quite to the contrary, we find Hus continuing to defend his appeal to God right up to the end.[66] The *Ordo* obviously did nothing to alter reality on this point. Surely, Jesenice knew that Hus would not lie to secure legal benefit. That being true, why include such manifest falsehood in a document if the text in question was intended never to be made public? If Hus would not go along with a legal strategy to avoid causing greater turmoil, why mention the appeal at all? Why not simply leave that fact out just as completely as the author omitted other issues? The answer may lie in the possibility that this fact provides the best evidence for arguing that the *Ordo* was in some intentional way a public document with a definite political motivation. That impulse might be characterized as the composition of a document intended to portray Hus in the best possible light, underscoring legal irregularities in the proceedings at the papal court but also presenting Hus as willing to submit to proper ecclesiastical judgment. Moreover, it had the brief to ameliorate the significant damage caused by Hus's appeal to God. Should the *Ordo* come into the hands of the court magistrates at Constance, the document itself contained the possibility of creating reasonable doubt on various matters to date, all in favor of the defendant. Once again, this suggests the presence of an experienced attorney.

In other ways, the *Ordo* altered essential facts in order to provide greater advantage to the defendant or, at the very least, to cast doubt on aspects of the case for the prosecution. An example of this is the reinterpretation

---

66. Mentioned in the definitive sentence of the court against Hus, July 6, FRB, vol. 8, p. 503.

of Hus's relationship to Archbishop Zbyněk.[67] Hus claimed that they had been reconciled and all semblance of disagreement and sanction had been removed. In other words, the ranking prelate in the Bohemian province had thrown his weight behind Hus. It is true that Hus appeared sincerely to believe this was the case. But Jesenice certainly knew better. Hus may well have clung to the naive and inaccurate belief that only death prevented Zbyněk from interceding with the pope and the court in relieving Hus from all charges of heresy and criminal conduct. Jesenice knew only too well that the late archbishop had been coerced and intimidated into his de facto posture of submission to the crown. Jesenice knew the prelate had been badgered into agreeing with the king but upon reflection was unable to escape the dictates of conscience that prevented him from sending the pro forma letter to Rome. Instead, the mounting stress caused the beleaguered prelate to flee Prague, hoping for sanctuary at the court of Sigismund at Buda, where he might have opportunity to regain his archiepiscopal seat with a certain level of support and protection from the man who already coveted the Czech crown. He had no intention of rehabilitating Hus. Zbyněk believed Hus to be a heretic and a dangerous presence in the Czech province. Had the archbishop been allowed to return to Prague, there should be no doubt he intended to prosecute Hus to the fullest extent of the law and perhaps even engage to the best of his ability the broad powers of the papal court and secular authorities to do so. Jesenice knew this was true. Hus's lawyer knew very well that the sudden and premature death of the prelate had nothing to do with prevailing policy concerning Hus. Had Zbyněk lived, Hus would not have been better off. Indeed, Hus would simply have had one more powerful enemy arrayed against him.

In similar fashion, we find evidence of good lawyering by which Jesenice fails to reveal that he was unable to gain entrance to the synod in Prague on behalf of his client.[68] This is omitted in the narrative overview, but we are told pointedly that Hus was prepared and ready to defend himself. Chronicling his own failure to gain an audience with the synod could be taken as prejudicial to the Hus case, for it would be interpreted in a negative light by Hus's detractors to know that Hus's lawyer had been rebuffed in his own hometown of Prague. In the latter parts of the *Ordo*, we find

---

67. *Ordo procedendi*, pp. 231–232.

68. Ibid., p. 232.

references to recent events before Hus's departure from Bohemia, which have been taken to allay suspicion about the nature or extent of Hus's heretical opinions. These consist of the manner of reporting attempts to obtain comments from the Prague synod or favorable expert evidence from the inquisitor. To this, the *Ordo* adds the archbishop's declaration that he knows nothing of heresy in Hus.[69] The greatest Achilles' heel in the effort to present a favorable account of the legal procedures in the trial of Hus is related to the transfer of the court case from Prague to the Curia. Hus was solely responsible, and in hindsight, the maneuver was a monumental error. It proved to be naive and nearsighted. It is possible Hus imagined he could obtain a fair and unbiased hearing at Rome before the bar of third-party objective men committed to legality, fairness, truth, and justice. When this turned out to be less than expected, Jesenice and his colleagues faced an uphill battle in their efforts to represent and defend their client. That said, the *Ordo* author takes the opportunity to outline a legal strategy aimed at making the best of a bad situation. It can be considered as sure that putting the *Ordo* together was the work of a lawyer. Clearly, the supplement to the *Ordo* is the work of an individual possessing knowledge of legal convention and *au fait* with canon law and legal procedure. It seems eminently sensible to point out that "the aim was to make the defense easier by making reference to the hostility of the court and the danger of local competence unfavorable to the accused."[70] Indeed, the legal statutes cited address the issues of local competence, the question of who had priority of jurisdiction in the case, and matters relating to the safety of the defendant. These legal arguments are also indirectly a suggestion of findings that in the trial of Hus, these legal norms and expectations were disregarded and breached during the proceedings at the papal court.[71] Features like these only further strengthen the assumption that the *Ordo* is almost certainly the work of a lawyer. Jesenice's efforts are entirely salutary but hopelessly defective in the simple fact that Hus, not the archbishop or anyone else, had transferred the case to the papal court. The legal arguments advanced by the *Ordo* were effectively nullified before they were collected and submitted. In terms of the previously mentioned narrative concerning the sentencing of a heresy suspect who refused to

---

69. Kejř, *Husův proces*, pp. 66–67.

70. "K pramenům Husova procesu," Kejř, *Počátků*, p. 142.

71. Kejř, *Husův proces*, pp. 66–67.

appear at the court venue, Jesenice's efforts to characterize Hus as willing to appear but fearing violence and extreme prejudice was thrown out of the case when the legal proceedings resumed in Constance.[72] Moreover, Hus had been derided on a number of fronts for not attending the proceedings at the papal court. The law requires the defendant to appear, but Hus refused to go there (*rebellas comparere*) in obedience and argue his case.[73] Of concern in the supplement is the unassailable fact that while there are ten references to or citations from legal sources, there are inaccuracies that are troubling. How can this apprehension be resolved? Is it reasonable to assume that Jesenice, as Hus's chief legal advisor, would be so sloppy? Even though one cannot characterize the legal section of the *Ordo* as anything more than an outline, the legal errors are glaring. It does not seem reasonable to assume that Hus himself undertook a revision of something so decidedly technical and legally precise.

Altogether, the *Ordo procedendi* presents a one-sided overview of the trial of Jan Hus between 1410 and 1412 and is a document that no one studying the Hus trial should overlook. The argument for the involvement of Jesenice in the composition of the *Ordo* is compelling, but questions and perplexing problems remain that are not easily resolved. The conundrums mitigate or call into question the thesis that Jesenice was the sole author of the document. The *Ordo* remains a puzzling albeit important document in the trial procedures involving Hus. Given its intentional manipulation of key events and procedural developments, together with boilerplate inventions such as Hus's alleged appeal to a future council, the *Ordo* is a quasi-public document with intentions extending beyond serving as a crib sheet for Hus as he went to Constance to defend himself against the amalgamated outstanding charges. It also reveals that Jesenice was shrewd enough to realize, as Hus did not, that what was about to unfold at Constance was a resumption of the legal proceedings initiated in Prague and then prosecuted at the papal court. The *Ordo* presents an outline that is incomplete and inaccurate in places, and sometimes these inaccuracies are deliberate. The document misplaces and misunderstands events and deviates from other records almost at will. This is not simply evidence of faulty memory or misinformation; it is rather indicative

---

72. Nowhere in the surviving records or sources from the trial proceedings at Constance is there any favorable comment on Hus's rationale for avoiding a court appearance at the Curia. But see the exchanges during the June 7 hearing. *Relatio*, pp. 78–79.

73. Štěpán Páleč, *Antihus*, in Sedlák, *Miscellanea*, p. 376.

of a well-intentioned strategy aimed at enabling Hus to mount the best defense possible in the court case set to reconvene at Constance. Kejř has presented the most compelling argument for a case of regarding the *Ordo* as the brainchild of Jesenice, who compiled the narrative and the legal outline as a document for Hus to use during the legal proceedings at the Council of Constance. This was intended to be used as a summary of things to emphasize in defense of his own case and as artillery with which to obfuscate some of the arguments certain to be advanced by the prosecution. By similar intention, Jesenice wished for Hus to leave particular things out and to avoid mentioning issues that could only complicate his case and create disadvantage. But the errors remain puzzling. Inasmuch as Hus was not a passive personality or a man detached from the world around him, it seems likely that he may have had a hand in shaping the *Ordo*. It is altogether possible to conclude that Jesenice prepared the outline and the essential content of the *Ordo* but Hus added to it, subtracted from it, or otherwise altered the text. However, it is doubtful that Hus introduced the legal errors, since his interests consistently were more ethical than legal, and if Hus did undertake a revision of the text, it remains unclear why he would not also correct glaring inaccuracies such as the suggestion that he had appealed to a future church council. None can deny the presence of a legal hand in the *Ordo*, and there is no reason to think that hand belonged to anyone other than Jesenice. But the *Ordo*'s specific function remains elusive. There seems to be little incentive for the document to have been turned over to the court in Constance. Curial authorities had their own records, which Michael de Causis claimed were kept in the apostolic see and in the papal court. Moreover, for reasons noted above, the *Ordo* could easily have been attacked for its one-sidedness and errors. Jesenice may have thought Hus needed to be equipped with a basic and concise legal awareness of the proceedings in the court case to date, so he drew up the *Ordo*. This may have been with a view to enabling Hus to rebut arguments Jesenice thought likely to be mounted against him. Did Jesenice imagine Hus would be so reckless as to blunder onto potentially dangerous grounds by raising issues such as his appeal to Christ? Did he think the *Ordo* would serve as a guide for Hus to follow around the pitfalls of defending oneself in a heresy litigation? We cannot know the answers. There is no evidence that Hus used or referred to the *Ordo* during his legal ordeal at Constance. There is no mention of it during his prison interrogations or during the numerous *in camera* sessions or in the three public hearings and court appearances. Beyond this, we find no trace of the *Ordo procedendi* in any of Hus's written responses to the various series of formal accusations filed against him during the Council of Constance. Nevertheless, the document remains a valuable, if flawed, account of the early stages in the trial of Jan Hus, a record of the prosecution of Hus up to the period when he departed for Constance. Now that the case of Hus has been considered in as much detail as possible, we turn our attention to the legal proceedings at Constance.

7

Legal Process at the Council of Constance

DURING THE DAYS of the Council, the city swarmed with tens of thousands of visitors, while secular and ecclesiastical dignitaries represented regions from all over Europe.[1] In the autumn of 1414, Constance became the virtual center of the world (see the map in figure 7.1). A veritable "who's who" could be found within its precincts. History-changing decisions were made, and we are also fortunate to know much of the social context and life at the local level. The dean of Constance Cathedral was so lame he had to be carried on a chair. Pope John XXIII fell from the papal carriage into a snow drift. A red and gold hat so large it required three horses to support its breadth was paraded through city streets. We catch glimpses of an archbishop arriving clad in full armor with six hundred horses, another bishop traveling with his own keg of beer, Mass celebrated with a doll (representing Birgitta of Sweden) on the altar, popes throwing candles from windows, a priest tossing small coins about, a provost murdered on the Preachers' Bridge, the execution of criminals, two suicides, King Sigismund arriving with two queens and five other ladies, 700 prostitutes working the streets (one source explicitly puts the number at "718 public whores") but as many as 1,500 in the city itself, medical doctors numbering 171 but unable to save the 500 people reportedly drowned in the lake.[2] And in the midst of all of

---

1. The oldest known view of Constance, from between 1458 and 1471, appears in Gebhard Dacher, *Konstanzer Chronik*, St. Gall, Stiftsbibliothek, Cod. Sang. 646, fol. 8ᵛ. One gets a sense of the cathedral, buildings, and walls.

2. Richental, *Chronik*, pp. 12–207; and Hardt, vol. 5, cols. 51–53. The precise figure is found in the *Hussite Chronicle*, FRB, vol. 5, p. 331. A caution on the problem of truth and fiction in

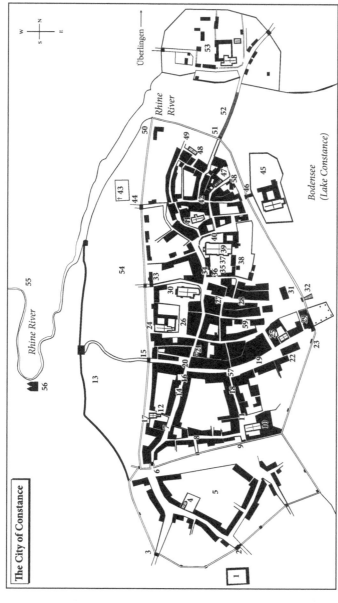

The City of Constance

1. Kreuzlingen Abbey (Augustinian Canons) 2. Kreuzlingen Gate 3. Emmishofer Gate 4. Church of St Jodok (Augustinian) 5. Stadelhofen District 6. Schnetz Gate 7. St Paul Street 8. New Street 9. Augustinian Gate 10. Monastery of the Augustinian Hermits 11. Holy Trinity Church 12. St Paul's Church 13. Brüel Field (Hus was burned here) 14. Pfister House where Hus stayed 15. Gelting Gate 16. Jerome of Prague stayed here 17. St Paul's Cemetery Tower 18. Mörder Street 19. Marketplace 20. Upper Market 21. St Laurence's Church 22. Granary 23. Aberhaken Tower 24. Franciscan Cloister 25. Hospital 26. Town Square 27. High House 28. Fishmarket 29. Merchants' Hall (Council Building) 30. St Stephen's Church 31. City Hall 32. St Konrad's Bridge 33. Upper Court 34. Picture House 35. Lanzenhof 36. Arsenal 37. Hus' books burned here 38. Bishops' Palace 39. Cathedral 40. Lower Court 41. St John's Church 42. Preacher's Street 43. Schotten Cloister (Benedictine Monastery of St James to the Scots) 44. Schotten Gate 45. Dominican Monastery 46. Preachers' Bridge 47. Zoffingen Cloister (Dominican Nuns) 48. St Peter's Church 49. Red light District (Ziegelgraben) 50. Powder Tower 51. Rhine Tower Gate 52. Rhine Tower Bridge 53. Benedictine Monastery of Petershausen 54. Village of Paradise 55. Reichenau 56. Gottlieben Fortress 57. Butchers Shop 58. Tümpfel House 59. Salmansweilerhof (Salem Abbey Townhouse, Cistercian)

FIGURE 7.1 The city of Constance

this was the continuation of a criminal proceeding. Prosecutors and those involved in the later stages of the trial of Jan Hus represented the crème de la crème of both legal and theological authorities of the day. Michael de Causis must have been quite satisfied.

Jan Hus arrived in Constance on November 3 without the *salvus conductus*, but he received it two days later.[3] It confirmed protection for Hus and his companions, saying they were "permitted to go freely, to stop, to stay and to return," for all impediments had been ordered removed. He had survived his long journey without evidence of imperial protection. He found lodgings in St. Paul Street, a thoroughfare providing southern access into the city from the Stadelhofen district through the Schnetz gate, at the Pfister House where the widow Fida lived.[4] That particular dwelling is now known as *Zur roten Kanne*—"The Red Can"— located at the modern address of Hussenstraße 22. Fida was considered an "honest and noble widow."[5] Even with the safe-conduct document securely in hand and the general guarantees contained in the official summons and apostolic brief, Hus's colleagues sought further confirmation that he was not in danger. Jan Chlum and his uncle Jindřich Lacembok were assured by John XXIII that Hus was safe in the city and that violence would not occur.[6] Nevertheless, there were questions and concerns. Some sources reported that since Hus had delayed so long in coming to Constance, the Council excommunicated him.[7] The assertion was wrong. However, Hus had already acquired the moniker *heresiarch*, and it is certain many of the conciliar fathers viewed him in that

---

the records can be found in Thomas Martin Buck, "Fiktion und Realität: Zu den Textinserten der Richental-Chronik," *Zeitschrift für die Geschichte des Oberrheins* 149 (2001): 61–96.

3. Text in Novotný, *Correspondence*, pp. 209–210; and *Relatio*, pp. 25–26. Hus tells us he had not received the imperial document prior to arrival in Constance in Novotný, *Correspondence*, pp. 207, 218, 220, 246.

4. Richental, *Chronik*, p. 60.

5. Šimek, ed., *Staré letopisy české z vratislavského rukopisu novočeským pravopisem* (Prague: Historické Spolku a Společnosti Husova Musea, 1937), p. 13. Gernot Blechner, "Wo in Konstanz war die Herberge des Jan Hus?—Eine Hauslokalisierung anhand zeitgenössischen Quellenmaterials," *Schriften des Vereins für Geschichte des Bodensees und Seiner Umgebung* 101 (1983): 49–71. There is controversy over this. The modern Hus Museum located at Hussenstraße 64 claims Hus was accommodated there. The point is not essential to our knowledge or understanding of the trial.

6. *Relatio*, p. 33.

7. Richental, *Chronik*, p. 60.

pejorative sense.[8] From a legal point of view, the fact that Hus was in Constance still under penalty of excommunication and interdict posed a dilemma. The issue was resolved when Pope John XXIII lifted the sentences of excommunication and interdict. This raises the question of whether there should have been new charges and a new summons. Jan "Cardinal" Rejnštejn claimed on November 10 that the sentences were lifted so that divine services need not be suspended in Constance during Hus's stay.[9] The letter in which we find this comment opens with the salutation "fautores et amici karissimi" (dear fellow suspects and friends), the first word being a technical term used in heresy proceedings. The letter states that the bishop of Constance and other representatives came to Hus to inform him of John's action. Štěpán Páleč and Michael de Causis arrived in Constance and immediately joined forces against Hus. Stanislav of Znojmo suffered a stroke and died en route to the Council, but Hus's other Czech enemy, Petr of Uničov arrived at the Council venue, as did Wenceslas Tiem, the indulgence vendor, who likewise aligned himself with this group. Clearly, these men considered the Council another stage in the fight against Hus. Hus claimed he would have few enemies in Constance were it not for the Czech priests deceiving people, motivated by gain and advancement.[10] De Causis immediately posted public notices against Hus, announcing the presumed indictment, repeatedly stating that the trial was being conducted against a contumacious excommunicate suspected of heresy.[11] The testimony of these two *promoventes*, de Causis and Páleč, went a considerable distance in establishing *fama publica* in the mind of the Council, that is, the belief by reputable persons that the defendant was guilty. This was part of the preliminary inquest in which the reputation of the suspect or defendant was investigated and established. Even before Constance, the work of de Causis and his colleagues aimed at establishing the nature of Hus's offense and detailing its notoriety. The result of this preliminary inquest (*inquisitio generalis*) had prompted Hus's citation to the papal court, where an *inquisitio specialis* was to follow. Inasmuch as Hus

---

8. See, for example, Ludolf of Żagan, "Tractatus de longevo schismate," chap. 50, ed. Johann Loserth, AÖG 60 (1880): 448.

9. *Relatio*, pp. 34–35.

10. Novotný, *Correspondence*, p. 224.

11. Ibid., pp. 218, 220.

refused to appear at the court, an actual trial—*inquisitio specialis*—could not take place and technically did not until Constance. In all of this, Hus claimed Páleč was the ringleader.[12] Both men continue to turn up in chronicles as inveterate enemies of Hus.[13] It is entirely possible to conclude that these men fulfilled the canonical requirement by which an inquisitor had to establish the *mala fama* (bad reputation) of the accused prior to legal proceedings. However, it was not always essential to establish *fama* before proceeding.[14] Notoriety in the Hus case was widespread in Bohemia by 1410 and throughout Europe by the time the Council convened as a result of legal procedures at the papal court. Hus believed Czechs were the source of "disgraceful accusations" brought against him.[15] In that assertion, he was on the mark.

The Council of Constance opened on November 5 in the Münster Unserer Lieben Frau (Cathedral of our Lady) with a three-point agenda. The first order of business was solving the papal schism, which some commentators described as an unprecedented event in world history.[16] The second brief was to eradicate heresy, especially those forms connected to John Wyclif and Jan Hus. The third matter involved reforming corrupt morals within the church. Although these points were at the top of the Council's agenda, there were also many legal cases under review at Constance, prompting one scholar to quip that there were more "ecclesiastical carpetbaggers" at the Council than "ecclesiastical statesmen."[17] At the opening session, Pope John XXIII celebrated Mass, a Cluniac monk preached the sermon, and Cardinal Zabarella announced that the first formal session would convene eleven days later, on November 16.[18] During these early days, the suggestion was privately circulated that Hus could resolve his case quietly. There are no extant details.[19] The only way this could be accomplished would be by means of a secret deal with the pope. How might this benefit John?

---

12. Novotný, *Correspondence*, p. 237.

13. *Hussite Chronicle*, FRB, vol. 5, p. 332.

14. Sext. 5.1.2 *Si is*, in Friedberg, vol. 2, col. 1069.

15. Novotný, *Correspondence*, pp. 271–272.

16. Ludolf of Żagan, "Tractatus de longevo schismate," p. 404.

17. C. M. D. Crowder, "Four English Cases Determined in the Roman Curia during the Council of Constance, 1414–1418," AHC 12 (1980): 316.

18. Mansi, vol. 27, col. 532.

19. Novotný, *Correspondence*, p. 220.

Might we assume Hus wanted his day in court? John told Hus he could do nothing about the case, since "it is your countrymen who are doing it."[20] The first formal session gathered as announced on November 16 in the cathedral. Zabarella read the convocation decree; John XXIII presided and then preached the sermon. Cardinal Giordano Orsini celebrated Mass.[21] With relevance for the trial proceedings, at the first session, Zabarella read the rules for the proceedings, citing a canon from the eleventh Council of Toledo (675) in which disturbances, tumults, loud talking, insulting language or behavior, mockery, loud noise or clamor, and laughter would not be tolerated. Zabarella insisted that silence and decorum should prevail. Offenders would be expelled and placed under sentence of excommunication for three days.[22] The decree later appeared in canon law.[23] Meanwhile, during the early days of November, Hus wrote a short opinion piece arguing that the laity should receive both bread and wine in the sacrament.[24] This is the earliest known firm support for the practice by Hus. A new list of charges was presented against Hus by de Causis, either in November or December.[25] These accused Hus of teaching utraquism, characterized as eucharistic irregularity. We might expect some elements of doctrinal deviance, but de Causis devoted more attention in these articles of accusations to presenting Hus as a dangerous subversive. The tenor of these charges depicts Hus as the spreader of disease in his persistent challenges concerning the nature and constitution of the church. De Causis also suggested that the disease had been disseminated because Hus worked to create strife between secular lords and prelates. Furthermore, the defendant encouraged laypeople to assume authority reserved for the priesthood by seizing the sacrament in any case in which they might initially be refused. Beyond this, we find Hus once more charged with urging a general divestment of ecclesiastical wealth. This concept had been controversial for

---

20. Ibid., p. 220. The comment seems disingenuous.

21. Mansi, vol. 27, col. 536.

22. The rubric has been preserved in a tenth-century manuscript. *Collectio Hispana Gallica Augustodunensis*, Rome, Vat Lat 1341, fols. 99ᵛ–100ʳ.

23. C.5 q.4 c.3 *In loco benedictionis*, in Friedberg, vol. 1, cols. 548–549. Fillastre's Diary, in Loomis, pp. 205–206. Hardt, vol. 4, pp. 16–17.

24. *Utrum expediat Laicis fidelibus, sumere sanguinem Christi sub specie vini?* in HM, vol. 1, pp. 52–54.

25. *Documenta*, pp. 194–199.

more than a century. On this issue, Hus was contrary to canon law. Prior papal bulls condemned the teaching of apostolic poverty as "erroneous and heretical."[26] De Causis was keen to exploit that divergence. If these accusations were not sufficient, Hus was again presented as an instigator of ethnic unrest. Because of this mischief, the entire kingdom of Bohemia had suffered, and there was looming danger that the disturbances would breach the Czech borders without warning and overrun the German lands. Somewhat astonishingly, these new charges suggested that the persecution of faithful Christians had no parallel or equal for an entire millennium. In other words, Hus had perpetrated more harm against the faithful than any heretic since the fourth century. The claim was extraordinary. De Causis took this opportunity to advise the Council that while "Jan Hus is dressed in the garments of a sheep, inside he is a ravenous wolf." The fathers were urged to move immediately against this dire threat to the faith. That many of these accusatory charges that de Causis applied to Hus were little more than exaggerated courtroom rhetoric was not unusual during heresy proceedings in medieval Europe. In fact, we find this normal policy in legal procedures against suspected heretics in the later Middle Ages. If only one accusation in a hundred could be sustained, that was more than what was required for conviction.[27] Other sources indicate that "Michael de Causis with considerable racket worked zealously" against Hus and hurried from place to place, politicking with ecclesiastical officials.[28] On November 17, Pierre d'Ailly, cardinal of Cambrai, arrived in Constance to be informed that legal proceedings against Hus had already begun or resumed.[29] Elsewhere, it is attested that the trial of Hus was in preparation prior to the opening of the Council.[30] D'Ailly has been described as a "priest-diplomat and theologian-politician." He played an essential role in the legal proceedings of the Hus case.[31]

---

26. Extrav. Jo. XXII 14.4 *Quum inter nonnullos*, in Friedberg, vol. 2, cols. 1229–1230.

27. By comparison, there were unscrupulous heresy hunters, such as the thirteenth-century Konrad of Marburg, who is reported in the *Annals of Worms* as declaring his willingness to burn a hundred suspects if this put an end to the career of only one heretic. *Annales Wormatienses*, ed. G. H. Pertz, in MGH, *Scriptores selectae*, vol. 17, p. 39.

28. Novotný, *Correspondence*, p. 222; *Relatio*, p. 33.

29. Giacomo Cerretano, *Liber gestorum*, in Finke, *Acta*, vol. 2, p. 203.

30. Dietrich Vrie, in Hardt, vol. 1, col. 123.

31. Novotný, *M. Jan Hus*, vol. 2, p. 362.

Two events in November altered the course of Hus's legal affairs. The first was a rumor suggesting that Hus had attempted to escape but had been captured before he could leave the city.[32] The tale is unreliable. Tellingly, it was never mentioned in the legal proceedings, where it might usefully have been used against Hus. There are no unimpeachable grounds for affirming its veracity. Immediately on the heels of this accusation, Hus was arrested on November 28, on the orders of John XXIII.[33] Officials came to the house in St. Paul Street where Hus was living to serve the arrest warrant, in order to prevent him from "teaching the wicked doctrine of Wyclif" any longer.[34] Hus was taken into the custody of William Challant, bishop of Lausanne, and held for eight days in the cathedral precentor's (choir master who was a canon) house. Clearly, the Council considered the matter of Hus a continuation of the curial legal process, and the previous verdicts of Zbyněk, Colonna, Brancacci, and Stephaneschi remained in effect. John XXIII initially denied any role in the Hus arrest, claiming it had been the unauthorized doing of hostile cardinals. The statement was a blatant lie. Later reversing himself, he admitted Hus had been arrested on his orders.[35] The rights of defendants in such cases were few, and some important medieval thinkers argued that heretics had no rights whatsoever.[36] Even in the mitigating circumstance of heresy accusations, this posture is in direct conflict with the legal doctrine enumerated by Johannes Monachus that the accused should be considered innocent until proven guilty. The agitations of Štěpán Páleč and Michael de Causis contributed to Hus's arrest, since it appears the cardinals were motivated by them.[37]

The case against Hus had been built on accusations chiefly constructed by Páleč and de Causis.[38] Once in custody, Hus was asked to give opinion

---

32. *Relatio*, p. 37; Richental, *Chronik*, p. 44.

33. Hefele and Leclercq, vol. 7, pt. 1, p. 200.

34. Cerretano, in Finke, *Acta*, vol. 2, pp. 188–189.

35. Hardt, vol. 2, col. 255.

36. Thomas, *Summa theologiae*, vol. 4, 2a, 2ae, q.10, art. 8, pp. 78–80.

37. *Relatio*, p. 37.

38. Anonymous fragment of a journal written by a Hus supporter, Rajhrad, Benedictine Monastery library, MS, edited in Johann Loserth, "Beiträge zur Geschichte der Hussitischen Bewegung: Gleichzeitige Berichte und Actenstücke zur Ausbreitung des Wiclifismus in Böhmen und Mähren von 1410 bis 1419," AÖG 82 (1895): 373.

on Wyclifite issues. This seems somewhat odd, inasmuch as he had publicly defended six Wyclifite articles at the Carolinum in July 1412, and this was a matter of record. This aspect of interrogation, however, played no role in the trial. One must wonder if Hus initially refused to reply and was advised that his refusal might be interpreted as an admission of guilt.[39] The rule of law often takes silence as consent, although defendants in medieval trials did have the right to silence in the same sense as the modern Miranda warning.[40] With the Council formally convened and the defendant behind bars, a committee of twelve was appointed on December 4 to examine Hus's books and teachings. Among that group were D'Ailly, Fillastre, Brancacci, Zabarella, Franciscan master-general Anthony of Pereto, and Dominican prior-general Leonard of Florence.[41] As the examining committee went to work, a commission to hear the Hus case assembled on the same day. The Hus commission was made up of three members: John of Rupescissa, titular patriarch of Constantinople; Jan of Bořenice, bishop of Lebus, near Frankfurt-an-der-Oder in Brandenburg; and Bernard, bishop of Castellamare. On December 4, John XXIII commissioned the three bishops to investigate the matter of Hus speedily and proceed to a definitive sentence. The pope referred to Hus as an "instigator of sedition," who had rashly asserted many errors and heretical teachings—"virulent poison"—through preaching and writing. The narrative betrays reliance on the charges filed by de Causis. John implied that the commission, and not necessarily the entire Council, would have access to full information in the Hus case, and its work would be to advise the pope and the Council on how to proceed.[42] It would seem that the "committee of twelve" and the "committee of three" constituted a division of labor. The former group investigated, while the latter group presided. While final authority rested with the pope in legal matters, it was impossible for individual pontiffs to preside over every case that came before the Curia. Hence, a delegation of jurisdiction became a routine feature of the later medieval church. One of the forms of this delegated authority is the *audiencia causarum sacri palatii*,

---

39. Considered a possibility in Spinka, *John Hus*, p. 236.

40. H. Ansgar Kelly, "The Right to Remain Silent: Before and after Joan of Arc," *Speculum* 68, no. 4 (1993): 992–1026.

41. Cerretano, *Liber gestorum*, in Finke, *Acta*, vol. 2, p. 189.

42. Document edited by Loserth in AÖG 82 (1895): 373–374.

also known by its shorthand, *Rota*.[43] The men handling the Hus case represented a form of delegated papal jurisdictional authority.

Following an initial period of incarceration, on December 6, Hus was remanded to a *sonder gemach* (special chamber), perhaps a cell in the dungeon of the Dominican monastery prison, situated on an island in Lake Constance.[44] This house of the *Ordo praedicatorum* had been founded in 1235. On the same day, he was examined by the panel of three judges on his position with respect to the "forty-five articles" of Wyclif.[45] This appears to have been a deliberate strategy on the part of the prosecution. Wyclif had been formally condemned and his books destroyed by papal order. Hus did not need his lawyer Jan Jesenice to advise him that his sworn affidavit in this matter left him in a legally precarious situation. If he answered the interrogatories with affirmation, his own condemnation could be expedited. If he rejected the "forty-five articles" completely, his previous public testimony could be used against him. Hus hedged. His judges pressed him. They required written answers to the controversial articles. Hus's extant replies indicate that he rejected outright thirty-two of the forty-five articles. Article 4 represented that a priest in mortal sin could not function properly. Article 8 claimed that the pope had no power over the faithful. Article 15 asserted that those in mortal sin could not hold office. In these three instances, Hus added the word *digne* (worthily) as a modification. Article 13 asserted that those who interfered with the freedom to preach were themselves excommunicates. Article 14 affirmed that there was no special requirement for deacons and priests to have additional authorization in order to preach. Article 16 suggested that secular authorities might confiscate wealth from the church if systemic sin persisted. Article 17 allowed the laity to correct sinful lords. Regarding these four articles, Hus declared they might be true. Article 5 denied that Christ ordained the Mass, while article 11 suggested that no one should be excommunicated apart from those whom God condemned. Here, Hus replied that since he was unfamiliar with the context wherein Wyclif may have made such claims, he was unable to answer. Article 19 denied that special prayers had more validity than ordinary prayers, while article 23 declared that members

---

43. Crowder, "Four English Cases," pp. 330–331.

44. The phrase is used by Richental, *Chronik*, p. 62.

45. Examination text in ST 2, pp. 1–19. Text with Hus's responses is extant and edited in Sedlák, *M. Jan Hus*, pp. 305*–310.*

of religious orders were not true Christians. Hus replied that since these statements were formulated incorrectly, they could not invite a meaningful response. Article 18 affirmed that tithes might be withheld, while article 33 concluded that Pope Silvester and Emperor Constantine had erred in endowing the church. Hus replied, "I can neither affirm nor deny." The judges and prosecutors must have been surprised at these responses.

Hus's responses to the interrogatories revealed some inconsistency.[46] They can also be interpreted as a clear backing away from previously held positions.[47] Other points of view acknowledge timidity but not a lack of truthfulness leading to perjury.[48] It is excessive to say that Hus was a liar, an egotist, and a hypocrite possessing a disreputable character.[49] The interrogation of Hus in prison was in accordance with medieval legal procedures in cases of heresy.[50] There was nothing irregular in this, although we hear secondhand reports that Jesenice was upset about Hus being examined in prison.[51] Jesenice's concern was not with procedure per se, but he knew that such interrogations indicated continued legal danger for Hus. The interrogatories do not seem to have produced evidence of new crimes. What is evident and significant from a legal point of view is that the interrogation in situ behind prison walls constitutes prima facie evidence that the Hus case was a "trial" continuing from the earlier curial processes. One may reasonably view this examination as Hus's arraignment. Summary procedure was allowed in all heresy cases from 1298 on, but evidence of its practice can be seen as early as 1255.[52] A few days later, a revised list of charges was drawn up by the commissioners of the Council.[53] This document, based on the work of Michael de Causis, also

---

46. Kaminsky, HHR, p. 53.

47. Sedlák, *M. Jan Hus*, pp. 320–322; and "Proces kostnický," in ST, vol. 2, no. 1 (1915), pp. 2–3.

48. Spinka, *Church*, p. 343.

49. Albert Hauck, *Studien zu Johann Huss* (Leipzig: Edelmann, 1916), pp. 49–50, 52.

50. Clem. 5.3.1 *Multorum querela*, in Friedberg, vol. 2, col. 1181.

51. Letter from Jan Chlum to Hus, January 4, 1415, in Novotný, *Correspondence*, p. 239.

52. Sext. 5.2.20 *Statuta quaedam*, in Friedberg, vol. 2, col. 1078; and Clem. 5.11.12 *Saepe contingit*, in Friedberg, vol. 2, fol. 1200; but see also the 1255 bull *Cupientes* of Pope Alexander IV. Paul Frédéric, ed., *Corpus documentorum inquisitionis haereticae pravitatis neerlandicae*, 5 vols. (Ghent: Vuylsteke, 1889–1902), vol. 1, pp. 123–124.

53. *Documenta*, pp. 199–204.

constituted a summary of procedures against Hus, commencing with the bull of Alexander V, thereby familiarizing the Constance commission with legal aspects of the case. This suggests that they understood their work to be a continuation of the curial process. There were factions present at the Council impatient with the deliberations of due process. For example, on December 7, the English delegation, through its representative Thomas Polton, a papal protonotary and dean of York, requested immediate judicial action against Hus.[54] At the same time, Stefano di Geri del Buono, bishop of Volterra and papal registrator, likewise pressed for swift action in the matter of the Hus heresy.[55] On behalf of Hus, Jan Chlum posted favorable public notices in Constance concerning the case, attempting to bring balance to developing public opinion. He did this on at least two occasions during the month of December.[56] After a long delay, Sigismund finally arrived in Constance at Christmas. He joined the pope in the cathedral, where "for eleven continuous hours," Pope John conducted divine worship until everyone present was wearied.[57] Initially angry that Hus had been imprisoned and the safe conduct violated, Sigismund threatened immediate retaliatory action. On the later testimony of John XXIII, the emperor was prepared to resort to violence, vowing to free Hus even if that meant breaking down prison doors.[58] Despite the bluster, Sigismund did nothing to intervene in the Hus case, and so the year 1414 came to an end with Hus a prisoner in the Dominican prison on the shores of Lake Constance.

One hundred years earlier, Philip the Fair had played a far larger role in the trial of the Templars than inquisitorial procedure normally permitted. Sigismund's role was more in line with due process in medieval heresy proceedings. On New Year's Day, 1415, Sigismund capitulated to the Council and withdrew all opposition to Hus's arrest and imprisonment.[59]

---

54. Cerretano, *Liber gestorum*, in Finke, *Acta*, vol. 2, pp. 197–198.

55. Finke, *Acta*, vol. 3, p. 41. Michael van Dussen, *From England to Bohemia: Heresy and Communication in the Later Middle Ages* (Cambridge, U.K.: Cambridge University Press, 2012), pp. 103–104, notes that representatives of the English nation were particularly keen to interrogate Hus.

56. *Relatio*, p. 42.

57. Heinrich Finke, *Forschungen und Quellen zur Geschichte des Konstanzer Konzils* (Paderborn: Ferdinand Schöningh, 1889), p. 252; Hardt, vol. 1, cols. 154–156.

58. Hardt, vol. 2, col. 253, and vol. 4, p. 26.

59. *Documenta*, pp. 609–611; and Finke, *Acta*, vol. 2, pp. 202–203.

He told the Czech barons that he had protested the action undertaken by the Council to the extent of storming out of sessions and abandoning the city altogether. The argument was put to the emperor that should he persist in hindering the prosecution of the case against Hus, there was no point for the synod to remain in session. In the face of this argument, Sigismund stood down. That procedural impediment removed, the Hus trial was declared ready to proceed without any further consideration of the safe conduct or Sigismund's preferences in the investigation of heresy. The Council took the view that in matters of faith, it could not be beholden to state affairs and had the freedom to arrest, detain, and prosecute anyone on suspicion of heresy; safe conducts were irrelevant.[60] Heresy was also grounds for canceling the imperial and papal guarantees of freedom of speech and movement extended to all who attended the Council. The safe conduct held by Hus was therefore withdrawn on the same day.[61] There is some dispute over the date of this action. According to a letter from the envoys of the University of Cologne, it occurred on January 17.[62] The Cologne envoys also noted that the safe conduct caused great commotion at Constance. The papal notary Dietrich Niem affirmed the right of the Council not only to try but also to sentence a heretic and also opined that the synod could lawfully set aside the safe conduct.[63] The hopes Hus may have pinned on the emperor were cruelly dashed on New Year's Day, when Sigismund declared that the Hus matter was of little importance in the agenda of the Council.[64] Moreover, on the same day, Sigismund forbade any further publication of notices defending Hus. Curiously, he said nothing about the posting of placards attacking Hus, which we noted earlier had been an activity undertaken rather zealously by Michael de Causis.[65]

Sometime in January, Hus was presented with formal charges.[66] These included a second examination on the "forty-five articles" of 1403, along

60. Hardt, vol. 4, p. 32.

61. Ibid., p. 26.

62. Edmond Martène and Ursin Durand, eds., *Thesaurus novus anecdotorum*, 5 vols. (Paris: Florentin Delaulne, 1717), vol. 2, p. 1611.

63. Hardt, vol. 2, col. 409.

64. Finke, *Acta*, vol. 2, p. 203.

65. Heinrich Finke, *Forschungen und Quellen zur Geschichte des Konstanzer Konzils* (Paderborn: Ferdinand Schöningh, 1889), p. 254.

66. Novotný, *Correspondence*, p. 240.

with private examination on other charges. Hus specifically claimed that he was interrogated on each of the "forty-five articles," and his replies were the same as before. Clearly, those prosecuting the case against Hus were unsatisfied with his initial replies to the December interrogatories. These accusations effectively may have been the second edition of the de Causis charges or the revised list drawn up by the commissioners of the Council. A bull was read to Hus that declared him a "heresiarch and seducer of the people." Significantly, we detect in Hus ongoing concern with perjury. This is noted often in his letters and in the *Relatio* of Petr Mladoňovice. We learn that deponents in the legal case were sworn in Hus's presence in the prison.[67] These included Johannes of Münsterberg, a Silesian doctor of theology; Peter Storch from Zwickau; Štěpán Páleč; Nicholas Zeiselmeister, a Prague canon; Jan Beroun, priest of St. Clement's in Prague; Petr of Uničov, a Dominican monk at St. Clement's in Prague; Adam of Býchory, a licentiate in canon law; and an unnamed layman. Except in the later stages of the trial, the identity of witnesses generally was not suppressed as was sometimes the case in other heresy proceedings, *inquisitio hereticae pravitatis*, that is, formal inquiries into heretical perversion.[68]

As the nonpublic aspects of the legal proceedings were unfolding in Constance, we find Michael de Causis badgering potential reluctant witnesses in December and January in efforts to secure their agreement to testify against Hus.[69] Canon law allowed judges to compel witnesses to testify.[70] To what extent the activity of de Causis remained within the spirit of the law remains debatable. Because his principal attorney, Jan Jesenice, had been excluded from the formal proceedings, Hus requested a lawyer. This was denied.[71] Commensurate with canonical legislation, in Hus's case, the denial was consistent with the ruling that since he had been excommunicated for more than a year for failing to appear, he was *de iure* considered guilty of heresy.[72] We have already noted that

---

67. *Relatio*, pp. 40–41.

68. Sext. 5.2.20 *Statuta quaedam*, in Friedberg, vol. 2, col. 1078, provides justification for concealing witness identities. This practice is discussed in Frank R. Herrmann and Brownlow M. Speer, "Facing the Accuser: Ancient and Medieval Precursors of the Confrontation Clause," *Virginia Journal of International Law* 34, no. 3 (1994): pp. 535–537.

69. *Relatio*, p. 41.

70. X 2.21.8 *Super his*, in Friedberg, vol. 2, col. 343.

71. *Relatio*, p. 41.

72. Sext. 5.2.7 *Quum contumacia*, in Friedberg, vol. 2, col. 1071.

medieval canon law forbade lawyers to act on behalf of convicted heretics. Attorneys who did so in violation of the law were punished as *infamia* and disbarred.[73] Defendants who were only under suspicion could have legal counsel.[74] Some legal statutes have been interpreted to say that lawyers were excluded altogether from heresy proceedings.[75] That line of argument is tenuous and may actually overreach the legal ruling in ultimately claiming more than what is intended by the law. However, as we have previously pointed out, summary procedure was permitted by canon law to go forward in cases of "heretical perversion" without the presence of attorneys.[76] Later, Pope Martin V ruled that suspected heretics could not have lawyers at all.[77] Strictly speaking, and based on the legal case at the Curia, Hus had already been judicially convicted of heresy and legally could be regarded as a heretic by the time he arrived in Constance. Regardless of the interpretation of law and appeals to procedural history, the ruling to disallow legal counsel to Hus did find support in specific passages of canon law and in precedent.

At the beginning of the new year, Hus was presented with forty-two articles assembled by Páleč, who had been asked by the judges to prepare these charges.[78] Hus's book *De ecclesia* seems to have been a main point of controversy. These articles constituted a series of accusations suggesting heresy, theological irregularity, and challenge to the medieval church. Páleč endeavored to take Hus to task on issues of ecclesiology, apostolic poverty, predestination, the power of the keys, papal authority, the freedom to preach, ecclesiastical obedience, and even specific charges about Hus's conduct. In many instances, Hus simply denied the validity of the allegations, in many cases pointing out that the alleged citations could not be found in his work, and in those instances, he offered the correct form of his thought as extracted from his writings. Hus was able to demonstrate the excessive sloppiness exhibited by Páleč in the construction of

---

73. X 5.7.10 *Vergentis in senium*, in Friedberg, vol. 2, col. 782.

74. X 5.7.11 *Si adversus nos*, Friedberg, vol. 2, cols. 783–784.

75. Sext. 5.2.20 *Statuta quaedam*, in Friedberg, vol. 2, col. 1078.

76. Ibid.

77. *Inter cunctas*, 1418, in Mansi, vol. 27, col. 1213.

78. *Documenta*, pp. 204–224, and referred to by Hus in Novotný, *Correspondence*, pp. 236–237.

the articles and proved beyond doubt that in many cases his statements had been taken out of context, thereby changing their intended meaning. In article 11, Hus noted that it had been Augustine, not he, who had made the point Páleč found so offensive. Nevertheless, Hus used the opportunity in reply to make essential points. For example, in responding to article 14 about the priestly power to bind and loose, Hus wrote that many Christians were mistaken in their assumption that the church could exercise arbitrary power in this area. He also criticized prelates who boasted about their ability to do whatever they wish in terms of ecclesiastical authority.[79] Elsewhere, Hus wrote long responses. Commenting on article 34, essentially a charge that priests elevated themselves in order to subjugate the laity and in doing so increased avarice, tolerated malice, and prepared the way for Antichrist, Hus wrote a short essay justifying the veracity of the charge.[80] He characterized the authors of the articles as "slanderers," "enemies," and "adversaries." On articles 41 and 42, Hus wrote, "this article is full of lies" and "this article is false in the beginning, in the middle and at the end."[81] Additionally, the Páleč articles accused Hus of inappropriately glossing a papal bull, attacking the legitimacy of indulgences and crusades, and conspiring to deceive the Council. These three matters are taken up elsewhere.[82] The interrogations were conducted in the presence of a notary, and Hus wanted his enemies punished for bringing false accusations against him.[83] In addition to charging Hus with conceit, these articles concluded that the teachings of Hus were "false, erroneous, scandalous, reckless, seditious, disturbing to the peace of the church, weakening the jurisdiction of the church, insane, against holy scripture and the universal church, in conflict with the conclusions and writings of the holy fathers and otherwise heretical."[84] Cardinal d'Ailly appointed a committee of masters to conduct an investigation of the Páleč

---

79. *Documenta*, p. 209. See also Vilém Herold, "Master Jan Hus and St. Augustine," in BRRP 8, pp. 42–51, for an important delineation of the crucial influence of Augustine on Hus.

80. *Documenta*, pp. 218–221.

81. Ibid., pp. 217, 221, 224.

82. Articles 40 and 41, in *Documenta*, pp. 222–224.

83. *Documenta*, p. 221.

84. Ibid., p. 222. The Páleč articles and Hus's replies have been analyzed by de Vooght, pp. 368–392, and Sedlák, *M. Jan Hus*, pp. 311*–317*.

articles and Hus's replies. Their findings are not extant, but it appears that significant problems were uncovered, since we later learn only eleven of the 42 articles were retained.[85] Hus was examined once again on the "forty-five articles" on January 2.[86]

That same month, ten Moravian nobles sent a letter to Sigismund—effectively a writ of habeas corpus—asking for Hus's release from an "illegal" imprisonment, insisting on a public hearing, and asking the king not to allow truth to be trampled. The nobles referred several times to the safe conduct, pointing out that its evident violation had generated considerable discussion in the Czech lands, and were the matter allowed to persist, the nobles warned Sigismund that this would besmirch his reputation and call to question the validity of any safe conduct he might issue thereafter.[87] On January 4, Jan Chlum assured Hus that Sigismund had spoken with conciliar delegates, and all agreed that Hus would have a public hearing.[88] Allegations began to be dissembled about Hus's financial capabilities. Patriarch John of Rupescissa made the putative claim that Hus held a large sum of money (January 4, 1415). An unidentified archbishop at an unspecified hearing was even more direct, asserting that Hus had seventy thousand florins at his disposal. This motivated Michael de Causis to open an inquiry into where all of Hus's money had gone and how it had been dispensed.[89] This investigation appears to fall outside the scope of discovery, but we have no information that any protective order ever limited the nature of discovery in cases of inquisitorial procedure. Prosecutorial misconduct was hardly a consideration in heresy proceedings. Exceptional crimes demanded extraordinary measures. The same letter notes that de Causis not only pried into Hus's mail but also acted centrally in interrogations, urging presiding authorities to force Hus to reply to the interrogatories. Meanwhile, Hus's health began to fail.

On January 9, after intervention by his friends, Hus was transferred to a more sanitary room in the Dominican prison.[90] He had fallen quite

---

85. Based on the witness of Peter Pulka, pp. 13–14, who represented the university of Vienna at the Council.

86. Novotný, *Correspondence*, p. 240, dated January 4, 1415.

87. *Documenta*, pp. 534–535.

88. Novotný, *Correspondence*, pp. 238–239.

89. Ibid., pp. 239–241.

90. Ibid., pp. 238–239, 248–250.

ill in the dungeon. Hus's penal treatment thus far may have constituted a violation of canon law, which specified that imprisonment in a case like this should be custodial, not punitive.[91] After all, the defendant was supposed to be presumed innocent. In this case, Hus was being held pending the completion of the legal case. The outcome of the court trial would yield a verdict in which appropriate punishment, if any, would be applied. Being remanded to prison was a guarantee that Hus would appear for the continuation of the trial. Therefore, the court had a duty to ensure that his incarceration was not a means of preemptive or retributive punishment. In terms of the trial, the possibility of bribery cannot be ruled out, since we have information that Hus apparently was told there would be no hearing of his case unless he paid the sum of two thousand florins.[92] We do not know whether Hus paid this fee. We also learn that de Causis tampered with Hus's mail.[93] Nicholas Nezero, the Prague inquisitor, was arrested in Constance sometime in February and interrogated. During his detention, he told Pierre d'Ailly that Hus had been forced to come to the Council by King Václav.[94] Was this true? Hus denied it. There is also the possibility that Nezero made the statement under duress. Wherever the truth lay, the inquisitor, once gaining his freedom, fled Constance. More important was the arrival of Jean Gerson, who entered the city sometime between February 21 and 25, bringing additional charges that were given to the Hus commission.[95] Were these new charges or simply the ones from September 1414 now formally submitted? The development on this point is somewhat muddled. Gerson's articles carried an additional but perfunctory pro forma ratification by the theological faculty of the University of Paris. The Paris theologians adjudicated the teachings of Hus as "notoriously heretical" and worthy of immediate condemnation and uprooting from among the faithful lest they "infect others." The French masters wrote that while the Hus articles appeared to correct lamentable shortcomings among the priesthood, in reality, they had another agenda, which aimed to undermine the church.[96] Following the previous advice of Dietrich Niem, noted

---

91. Clem. 5.3.1 *Multorum querela*, in Friedberg, vol. 2, col. 1181.

92. Novotný, *Correspondence*, pp. 244–245, noted sometime after January 19.

93. Noted also in ibid., pp. 240, 300.

94. *Documenta*, p. 542; and Peter Pulka, p. 15.

95. HM, vol. 1, pp. 29–30; and *Documenta*, pp. 185–188.

96. *Documenta*, pp. 187–188.

earlier, Gerson suggested that Hus be judicially condemned rather than allowed to enter debate.[97] Previously, we noted that Bernard Gui discouraged conversation with heretics, while Lucas of Túy advocated simply killing them. The following month, Hus denounced the allegations of Gerson as lies but claimed he had neither time nor opportunity to reply to them.[98] Around this same time, Hus was visited by Křišťan of Prachatice, who came to Constance sometime before March 5. Inasmuch as those who visited accused heretics after their arrest were often automatically considered suspect, Křišťan was soon denounced. At the instigation of de Causis, who continued to act in the role of a *promovens*, he was arrested, and thirty articles were leveled against him. He was examined by the patriarch of Constantinople (John of Rupescissa), he was released, and he subsequently fled Constance; we find him back in Prague by March 19.[99] From written testimony on this matter by Peter Pulka, we learn that some people feared Křišťan would only continue his wicked ways. Jesenice may also have come to Constance, but we have no reliable information about his movements or whereabouts. Czech supporters of Hus came to Constance at their own peril. Even Hus had warned them: "tell Dr. Jesenice and Master Jerome [of Prague] not to come [to Constance] for any reason, nor any of ours."[100] In other words, all those sympathetic to Hus placed themselves in harm's way.

At the request of the prison warden, Hus composed a short tract on the sacrament of the body and blood of Christ on March 5.[101] The work affirmed Hus's adherence to the doctrine of transubstantiation. Commenting further on the legal case against him, Hus referred to the massive falsehood lodged against him as a "sack of lies," which could be taken as a euphemism for Michael de Causis.[102] In a sermon on March 11, 1415, Gérard de Puy, bishop of Carcassonne, called for the condemnation of Hus and Wyclif and their heresies, which had misled many people. He also stated

---

97. Vatican Library, MS 595, fols. 55ʳ–55ᵛ. Latin text in Novotný, *M. Jan Hus*, vol. 2, p. 392; translation in Spinka, *Constance*, p. 171, n. 25.

98. Novotný, *Correspondence*, p. 256.

99. References and details in ibid., p. 249; an anonymous letter in *Documenta*, pp. 541–543; and Peter Pulka, p. 15.

100. Letter dated January 3, 1415, in Novotný, *Correspondence*, p. 236.

101. *De sacramento corporis et sanguinis domini*, in HM, vol. 1, pp. 47–52.

102. Novotný, *Correspondence*, p. 249.

that the cardinals constituted the heart of the church, while Rome (the pope) was the head.[103] These vignettes underscore the theological turmoil attending the Hus trial.

There were separate political machinations that eventually prompted Pope John XXIII to flee Constance on March 21. He was apprehended at Breisach on April 26, held prisoner in Freiburg from April 27 and thereafter at the village of Radolfzell on May 18, before being returned to Constance around the beginning of June and incarcerated in the east tower of the Gottlieben Castle fortress on June 3. The impact on the Hus trial was largely that a verdict would be handed down without papal input. Considerable uncertainty pervaded the city following John's nocturnal escape, and the unease was also felt within the Council itself. Sigismund made no move with respect to Hus. This might be regarded as nonfeasance. Because the Dominican house was situated outside city walls, and the guards were few and unreliable, Hus was transferred from the Dominican prison to the Gottlieben Castle fortress, about two and a half miles west of the city along the Rhine River, during the night of March 24, under the supervision of Otto von Hachberg, bishop of Constance, in chains, under the armed escort of 170 men, in a boat.[104] The castle of Gottlieben had been built in 1251. Hus was held in the upper portion of the west tower, manacled during the day and with one hand chained to the wall at night.

Coinciding with these momentous events in Constance, King Ferdinand of Aragon wrote to Sigismund on March 27, urging the immediate punishment of Hus and noting that despite a safe conduct, there was no such thing as breaking faith with one who did not keep faith with God.[105] Precedents for this position have been noted above. Nothing particular transpired during these weeks with respect to Hus. Elsewhere, we learn from an anonymous report, generated within Constance and dated April 2, that the Hus case had been set aside on account of what were considered other more pressing matters.[106] Meanwhile, Hus's colleague and disciple Jerome of Prague, ignoring the shrewd advice of Hus, arrived in Constance on April

---

103. Finke, *Acta*, vol. 2, pp. 403–410. See pp. 404–405 for his views on ecclesiastical headship.

104. *Documenta*, pp. 541–543; and Hardt, vol. 4, p. 66.

105. *Documenta*, pp. 539–540.

106. Ibid., p. 541.

4 and took up residence in St. Paul Street.[107] Upon assessing the situation and the prevailing mood in the city, he retired to Überlingen, a distance of twenty-five miles from Constance on the north side of the lake, and from that locale demanded a safe conduct.[108] Unsurprisingly, the request was denied.[109] We also learn that in defiance or ignorance of Sigismund's order, Jerome went around Constance posting placards defending Hus. With deliberate provocation, he especially attached notices on church doors and on entrances to places where Council dignitaries were lodged.[110] Jerome's actions contravened Sigismund's orders given on January 1 concerning the public posting of pro-Hus placards. Meanwhile, in light of the flight of John XXIII, the Council issued a statement later referred to as *Haec Sancta* on April 6, claiming authority previously held by the papacy.[111] Thus, the legal process involving Hus continued despite the fact that no pope was recognized (*sede vacante*). The departure of John XXIII and the absence of presiding pontifical authority may not be construed to suggest that established legal procedures went by the wayside. Records indicate that the papal auditor John de Thomariis of Bologna, who had previously been involved in the Hus case, took no note of Pope John's flight and deposition and continued work on other cases at Constance without deviation from established law and legal procedure.[112]

Once the Council publicly declared its superiority over the papacy, the Hus case received renewed attention. A new commission was appointed on April 6 to deal with the Hus matter. This group included Pierre d'Ailly, Cardinal Guillaume Fillastre, Bishop Stephen Coevret of Dol, and John of Martigny, abbot of Citeaux.[113] We learn, however, that d'Ailly was too busy for much involvement in the Hus case at this point.[114] Notwithstanding this, the commission was given complete authority to inquire into the

---

107. Richental, *Chronik*, p. 62; Hardt, vol. 4, p. 93. Traditionally assumed to be at the modern address of Hussenstraße 14. František Šmahel, *Život a dílo Jeronýma Pražského* (Prague: Argo, 2010), p. 72.

108. Hardt, vol. 4, p. 103.

109. Ibid., cols. 685–686; and an open letter from Czech delegates to the Council.

110. Hardt, vol. 4, p. 103.

111. Tanner, DEC, vol. 1, pp. 409–410.

112. Crowder, "Four English Cases," pp. 366–367.

113. Mansi, vol. 27, col. 592; Hardt, vol. 4, pp. 99–100.

114. Hardt, vol. 4, p. 118.

teachings of Wyclif and Hus.[115] By consequence, the prior commission appointed by John XXIII lost its authority when John left the Council and was thereafter deposed. The new commission had the ratification and mandate of the Council to proceed against Hus under a new authority structure. Before turning to those procedures, it is important to note that there remains something of a puzzle when attempting to determine how such commissions were appointed. What is apparent is that by early 1416, the Council of Constance had settled on its own unique methods for hearing legal cases. Quite separate from the established jurisdictions of the papal Camera, the Rota, the Penitentiary, and the Consistory, another less formal and controversial court existed called the *iudices generales*. Within this model, special commissions were established to deal directly with difficult or particularly complex cases. The Hus commission represented such a tribunal, which conducted preliminary hearings and formal examinations apart from the general sessions of the Council. There has been no adequate examination of the specific processes and natures of cases handled by the *iudices generales* at the Council of Constance.[116]

Among the first developments was action by Jan Náz, a diplomatic representative of King Václav, who presented a statement to the commission on April 7 in which he excoriated Hus and his disciples for anticlericalism and utraquism. He urged immediate further action against Hus, whom he characterized as a "madman" and "heresiarch" who advocated violence against wicked priests.[117] The next day, Sigismund formally revoked all safe conducts held by anyone in Constance.[118] In other words, the general protections specified in the imperial summons to the Council, along with those enumerated in the apostolic brief, were not applicable to heretics. This constituted retroactive rule making. At session 18 on August 17, 1415, the Council decreed that no safe conduct in a case of heresy could be binding and made specific reference to Hus.[119] During session 19 on September 23, 1415, the Council issued two declarations stating that any promise made that was later found to be inimical to the faith and the laws of the church, or was clearly "prejudicial to the practice

---

115. Ibid., p. 100.

116. Crowder, "Four English Cases," p. 359.

117. "Avisamentum D. Io Nasonis," FRB, vol. 8, pp. 487–488.

118. *Documenta*, pp. 543–544.

119. Mansi, vol. 27, col. 791.

of the Catholic faith or to ecclesiastical jurisdiction," or interfered with the "examination, judgment or punishment" of suspected heretics need not be maintained.[120] The controversy over the *salvus conductus* issued to Hus appears to have been the impetus for this ruling. The matter of the imperial safe conduct has remained a point of controversy in evaluating the Hus trial.[121]

Perhaps realizing the grave peril into which he had placed himself, and in the midst of discussions over the validity of safe conducts, Jerome left the vicinity of Constance on either April 8 or 9 and headed for the relative safety of Prague. There was now increased pressure to speed up the Hus case. On April 9, d'Ailly deferred procedural details to Zabarella and Fillastre, both of whom were canon law specialists.[122] This is a good indication that the legal procedures against Hus were concerned with the rule of law. At the same time, d'Ailly was ordered by the Council to be ready to submit a report on Hus when requested.[123] However, the work of the commission once again bogged down and made little progress on account of disagreements. We lack specifics. Urgency with respect to Hus now seems to have become a motivation, and a new commission was appointed during session 6 on April 17. The committee consisted of Giovanni Dominici, O.P., archbishop of Dubrovnik; John of Gudesberg, bishop of Schleswig; Master Ursin of Talavende; and Master William Corfe.[124] The Council now appeared determined to proceed to an inclusive, definitive sentence against Hus.[125] However, there was still residual dissension among those appointed to deal with the matter of the Bohemian priest. The outgoing commission was ordered to hand over its records to the new commission. It complied.[126] The new commission was required to receive the report from d'Ailly, Zabarella, and Fillastre concerning Hus.[127] The transition from

---

120. Ibid., col. 799, Hardt, vol. 4, col. 521.

121. A summary of important interpretations expressed by Novotný, Bartoš, de Vooght, and Spinka is available in Spinka, *Church*, pp. 330–337.

122. Mansi, vol. 27, col. 597.

123. Hardt, vol. 4, p. 104.

124. Jiří Kejř erroneously refers to Giovanni Dominici as "Antony." Kejř, *Husův proces*, p. 159.

125. Mansi, vol. 27, col. 610; Hardt, vol. 4, p. 118; Peter Pulka, p. 18.

126. Hardt, vol. 4, p. 100.

127. Ibid., p. 106.

one commission to another created conflict, and dissension threatened to derail the trial proceedings. In the end, the three cardinals were restored to the commission. Increasingly, the work of the new commission was dominated by Gerson, d'Ailly, and Zabarella, and this feature continued through the final hearings. It is also possible to regard Dietrich Niem as one of the principal judges, although he does not appear as prominently in the extant records.[128] On the same day, April 17, the Council formally condemned the works of John Wyclif and called for their burning.[129] This had ominous overtones for Hus.

On April 17, the Council cited the fugitive Jerome of Prague to appear within fifteen days to answer charges.[130] Michael de Causis, characterized as the instigator against Hus, personally undertook to post the notarized citation concerning Jerome on April 18 at the Franciscan Monastery and also at the churches of St. Stephen and St. Mary's in Constance.[131] One week later, Jerome was intercepted on the German-Czech border and promptly arrested in Bavaria, on April 24 or 25. Contumacy proceedings against him began on May 2.[132] Unwilling to have his voice go unheard, Ferdinand of Aragon once more contacted Sigismund by means of a short note on April 28, urging action against Hus, whom he called the servant of the Devil.[133] Demonological associations in heresy trials were expected, even routine. The Roman synodal condemnation of Wyclif dating back to 1412 and 1413 was confirmed in session 8 on May 4, 1415. The "false Christian" Wyclif was declared outside the ark of safety. His books were outlawed. No Christian was permitted to read them except for the purpose of refuting them. More than three hundred articles of his teaching were declared unsuitable and formally denounced as "heretical, seditious, erroneous, reckless, scandalous, insane, contrary to good morals and catholic faith."[134] The remains of the "notorious heretic" were ordered exhumed at

---

128. Paul de Vooght, "Jean Huss et ses juges," in *Das Konzil von Konstanz*, ed. August Franzen and Wolfgang Müller (Freiburg: Herder, 1964), pp. 172–173.

129. Mansi, vol. 27, col. 611.

130. Hardt, vol. 4, cols. 686–687.

131. Mansi, vol. 27, col. 628.

132. Hardt, vol. 4, col. 760, and p. 142.

133. *Relatio*, p. 67.

134. *Documenta*, pp. 467–469; and Mansi, vol. 27, cols. 505–508. The posthumous condemnation of Wyclif has been regarded as contrary to canon law. Vilém Herold, "Jan Hus—a

this session, because Wyclif's memory was also condemned. The order was delayed until 1428, when Richard Fleming, bishop of Lincoln, acted.[135] Each of these orders and developments had consequences for the Hus trial. Despite filing numerous writs against Hus, and determined to prevent an acquittal by lack of proofs verdict, Michael de Causis appeared before the Hus commission to testify about "that devil Jan Hus."[136] De Causis was an éminence grise who operated in the shadows of the Council rather than in the daylight of the formally appointed commissions. Still, Hus was not bereft of defenders, and on May 8, a number of Moravian barons wrote to Sigismund requesting that Hus be released from prison and provided with a public hearing.[137] A group of Bohemian nobles acted on May 12 in the same fashion. Their letter had the seals of two hundred fifty Czech lords attached.[138] The letter from the Bohemian nobles was read to Council delegates on June 12. The following day, Czech and Polish nobles present in Constance petitioned Sigismund on Hus's behalf for a public hearing.[139] Perhaps in deliberate opposition to these pro-Hus barons, the bishop of Litomyšl, Jan Železný, alleged on May 16 to the Council that serious eucharistic irregularities were being practiced in Bohemia.[140] This allegation appears to have come in immediate response to demands advanced by Czechs in the previous days. On May 18, Pierre d'Ailly and other representatives paid a visit to Hus in the airy west tower of the Gottlieben, seeking

---

Heretic, a Saint, or a Reformer?" *Kosmas: Czechoslovak and Central European Journal* 15, no. 1 (2001): 2. The claim is invalid. Posthumous condemnations were common from the patristic age to the fifteenth century, and canon law permitted it. C.24 q.2 c.6 *Sane profertur*, in Friedberg, vol. 1, col. 986–987. Inquisitorial practice allowed it. See the *Processus inquisitionis* prepared in 1248/9 by the Carcassonne inquisitors Bernard de Caux and Jean de St. Pierre, surviving in a single manuscript. Adolphe Tardif, ed., "Document pour l'histoire du processus per inquisitionem et de l'inquisitio heretice pravitatis," *Nouvelle revue historique de droit français et étranger* 7 (1883) : 669–678. Translation in Walter L. Wakefield, *Heresy, Crusade and Inquisition in Southern France 1100–1250* (London: George Allen & Unwin, 1974, pp. 256–257, for the "formula of sentence against those who died as heretics."

135. On December 9, 1427, the pope ordered Fleming to proceed against the remains of Wyclif. Odoricus Raynaldi, ed., *Annales ecclesiastici* (Bar-le-Duc: Guerin, 1874), vol. 28, p. 55. In the spring of 1428, Wyclif was disinterred, and his remains were burned and thrown into a river in accordance with X 3.40.7 *De homine*, in Friedberg, vol. 2, col. 640.

136. Mansi, vol. 27, col. 628.

137. *Documenta*, pp. 547–548; *Relatio*, pp. 69–70.

138. *Documenta*, pp. 550–552; *Relatio*, pp. 70–1.

139. *Relatio*, pp. 45–46.

140. Mansi, vol. 28, cols. 34–55; *Relatio*, pp. 47–48.

his recantation from his errors and heresies. During this effort to settle the Hus affair, the papal auditor Berthold Wildungen learned that Hus wanted to defend himself.[141] One of the delegates to Hus's prison cell was Dietrich Kerkering, a theologian from Cologne University, whose report reveals his opinion that Hus would doubtless be condemned to the fire.[142] Two years later, Robert Hallum, archbishop of Salisbury, one of the prelates involved in the Hus trial, died in the Gottlieben.[143]

Despite Sigismund's refusal to do anything, the Czech nobles once again appealed sometime before May 18 to the Council.[144] This document was read publicly that same day before Council delegates by Petr Mladoňovice. Meanwhile, having been apprehended, Jerome of Prague was returned to Constance in chains on May 23. His examination began almost immediately. He was later tortured by being hanged in a manner that excluded sitting, hands tied above his head for two days, fed only on bread and water.[145] Hus continued to lie in prison awaiting his day in court. Before that could happen, the Council turned its attention to the matter of John XXIII, another fugitive who had unsuccessfully tried to evade the Council and had also been returned in chains. Five judges, including Patrick Foxe, bishop of Cork, were appointed to pronounce sentence on John XXIII.[146] Confined at Radolfzell, John was tried on a variety of charges *in absentia* and deposed during session 12 on May 29, 1415.[147] Legally, popes were not subject to judicial proceedings unless the offense was against the faith.[148] In any other instance, medieval popes had immunity from human judgment.[149] It was generally agreed and codified in

---

141. Hardt, vol. 4, p. 428.

142. Martène and Durand, *Thesaurus novus anecdotorum*, vol. 2, pp. 1634–1638.

143. Richental, *Chronik*, p. 97.

144. *Relatio*, pp. 48–51.

145. Hardt, vol. 4, pp. 215–218. This was in the tower at St. Paul's cemetery. The modern address is Obere Laube 73. Other witnesses claim Jerome was remanded to a *sonder gemach* (special chamber) in the Gottlieben. Richental, *Chronik*, p. 63.

146. Hardt, vol. 4, cols. 279–282. Foxe, also known as Patrick Ragged, was translated to the see of Ossory in 1417 and subsequently died on April 20, 1421.

147. Ibid., pp. 237–248.

148. D.40 c.6 *Si papa*, in Friedberg, vol. 2, col. 146.

149. C.9 q.3 c.13 *Nemo iudicabit*, C.9 q.3 c.14 *Aliorum hominum causas*, C.9 q.3 c.15 *Facta subditorum*, and C.9 q.3 c.17 *Cuncta per mundum*, in Friedberg, vol. 1, cols. 610–611.

canon law that popes possessed universal power.[150] Hus previously denied such papal privilege.[151] John's trial and deposition went unchallenged and were in accordance with canonical procedure. Many of the charges in his indictment were boilerplate allegations common in late medieval legal processes involving heresy or heresy-related cases. These included allegations of perjury, simony, sexual misconduct, and murder. Notorious rumors about John circulated in Constance.[152] Dietrich Niem is largely responsible for the dreary dossier of charges advanced against John.[153] It has been suggested that he uncritically accepted all of the rumors about John told by the papal auditor John de Thomariis.[154] Be that as it may, Dietrich urged the council to remove John.[155] Based on such initiatives, a charge of heresy was advanced against the beleaguered pope but Cardinal Fillastre objected citing an absence of proof.[156] John accepted his fate. He made no effort to mount a defense. He was convicted of the dossier of charges against him, sentenced to life imprisonment, but released four years later and awarded the title Cardinal Bishop of Tusculum (Frascati). The case of John XXIII clearly slowed down the Hus trial process inasmuch as we know Zabarella spent a good part of April dealing with John. The imprisoned pope attempted to appoint Zabarella, d'Ailly, and Fillastre as his proctors.[157] Only after John was formally removed from office could the Hus case resume properly.

During the same session 12 on May 29, further action was taken with respect to Hus. He was called a heretic under suspicion of numerous errors and heresies based on his own writings and the testimony of

150. D.99 c.3 *Primae sedis* and D.99 c.5 *Ecce in prefatione*, in Friedberg, vol. 1, cols. 350–351.

151. *Contra octo doctores*, in Hus, *Opera omnia*, vol. 22, p. 427.

152. Peter Pulka, p. 22.

153. There are several relevant texts by Dietrich, including *Dialogus de modus uniendi ac reformandi ecclesiam in concilio universali* (erroneously ascribed to Jean Gerson), in Hardt, vol. 1, pt. 5, cols. 68–142, esp. cols. 127, 135; *Monita de necessitate reformationis ecclesiae* (incorrectly attributed to Pierre d'Ailly), in Hardt, vol. 1, pt. 7, cols. 277–309, esp. cols. 306–309; *Invectiva . . . Johannem XXIII*, in Hardt, vol. 2, pt. 14, cols. 296–330; *De vita . . . Papae Johannis XXIII*, in Hardt, vol. 2, cols. 336–459.

154. Eustace J. Kitts, *In the Days of the Councils* (New York: Brentano, 1909), p. 168. Kitts offers no proof for his assertion, and I have not been able to establish a connection.

155. Finke, *Acta*, vol. 3, pp. 128–129.

156. Finke, *Forschungen und Quellen*, p. 177.

157. Finke, *Acta*, vol. 2, pp. 29–33; Hardt, vol. 4, p. 167, and col. 282.

witnesses. Ostensibly, Hus agreed to abide by the decision of the Council but later refused. His objections were overruled with proof presented.[158] Hus was not present, so the action taken must refer to a report being made. Perhaps indignant at the aspersions of heresy being bandied about concerning religious practices in Bohemia, Czech barons filed a response to the statement of Bishop Jan Železný concerning the Eucharist and religious practices in Bohemia on May 31.[159] Unwilling to leave hostages to fate, the Czech nobles once more pressed their plea to Sigismund on the same day for Hus to have a public hearing.[160] This petition was incorporated into a larger document and forwarded to the emperor. The letter of recommendation for Hus was signed by eleven Czech barons and dispatched to Emperor Sigismund on June 1.[161] On behalf of the Council, on May 31, the French canon lawyer Jean Mauroux announced that a public hearing (*cognitio*) in the case against Hus had been calendared on the docket and would be held on June 5. Mauroux included in his announcement a comment that the Council continued to regard Hus as a man who could not be trusted under any circumstance.[162] The statement is as revealing as it is troubling. In preparation for a public appearance in a court of law, Hus was transferred from the Gottlieben Tower to the Franciscan house in Constance on June 3 and held there in the Franciscan prison (presumably the adjoining tower) pending the scheduled trial hearings.[163] The Franciscans had been established in Constance since around 1250. And so it came to pass that Hus finally obtained his long-held desire to present his views for judgment before all of Christendom. The trial of Jan Hus was now ready to enter the last stages.

The continuation of the legal process against Hus on charges of heresy during the Council of Constance consisted of three public hearings, which occurred on June 5, 7, and 8. Each hearing convened in the refectory of the Franciscan monastery near St. Stephen's Church in Constance. The formal charges were based chiefly on Hus's writings,

---

158. Fillastre, in Finke, *Acta*, vol. 2, p. 40.

159. *Relatio*, pp. 51–53.

160. Ibid., pp. 54–57.

161. Ibid., pp. 53–57.

162. Ibid., p. 57.

163. Hardt, vol. 4, p. 306.

which he admitted. Testimony was also heard from witnesses concerning his preaching. It seems fair to say that Hus had uneven opportunity to respond to the charges. At the first hearing, on Wednesday, June 5, the session began without the defendant being present. Once alerted to this situation by Hus's friends, Sigismund immediately objected. With the absence of official *Acta*, this procedural anomaly is difficult to explain, but the defendant soon appeared. The proceedings at the first hearing were disorderly.[164] After the first hearing, two of the articles introduced against Hus were dismissed. There are no extant sources to determine which charges these were.[165] Petr Mladoňovice was not present. This was also peculiar. He was in Constance as secretary to Jan Chlum, and the schedule of the hearing had previously been announced. Where was he? Hus says the hearing was raucous. This situation must be assessed in direct violation of rules set down by Zabarella at the first session of the Council on November 16 and in violation of summary procedure. During the proceedings, Michael de Causis shouted that Hus's books should be burned.[166] That outburst appears to have breached due process. Why the chair could not or did not establish and maintain order is a mystery. The chaotic nature of the hearing clearly violated the spirit of summary procedure, which instructed and empowered presiding judges to maintain proper order in the court.[167]

The second hearing, on Friday, June 7, was chaired by d'Ailly. Sigismund was present. Hus was accused of eucharistic heresy, principally by de Causis, who advanced "proofs" from several witnesses in Prague, especially priests and among them specifically Ondřej of Brod.[168] The testimony of witnesses was introduced.[169] Zabarella introduced procedural rules concerning witnesses, stating that "in the mouth of two or three" would constitute the basis for the evaluation of testimony.[170] Hus appealed to conscience, but d'Ailly countered by pointing out that the court could

---

164. *Relatio*, p. 74.

165. Novotný, *Correspondence*, p. 261, dated June 5, 1415.

166. Ibid., p. 261.

167. Clem. 5.11.2 *Saepe contingit*, in Friedberg, vol. 2, col. 1200.

168. Hardt, vol. 3, pt. 3.

169. Text in Sedlák, *M. Jan Hus*, pp. 338*–343*.

170. *Relatio*, p. 76.

not be guided by conscience but had to rely on testimony by witnesses.[171] D'Ailly's ruling was consistent with the view of canon lawyers and canon law, which did not enter judgment on private crimes.[172] Petr Mladoňovice was present, although it must be noted that he arrived late. We have no satisfactory explanation to account for this unfortunate tardiness. While his account is rather comprehensive, it lacks any coverage of the initial stages of the hearing, since he missed the acts of de Causis. During the second court hearing, there was discontent expressed about Hus's appeal to God. The Cambridge master John Stokes testified that while he had been in Prague in 1411, he personally saw a treatise by Hus defending remanence.[173] Both d'Ailly and Sigismund counseled Hus to submit to the authority of the synod.

At the third hearing, on Saturday, June 8, Sigismund again was in attendance, and the hearing was under the direction of d'Ailly. The examination revolved mainly around Hus's doctrine of the church based on a dossier of thirty-nine articles drawn from his books.[174] These articles constituted a revision of the forty-two allegations compiled by Štěpán Páleč and presented to Hus in prison at the beginning of the year. The more egregious inaccuracies had been removed from the accusations. In replying to article 10, Hus declared that wicked priests were truly vicars of Judas Iscariot. That comment caused much derision. During his explanation of article 17, dealing with the question of whether cardinals were the true successors of the apostles, Hus was interrupted by d'Ailly, who declared it obvious that Hus had been indiscreet in preaching to the laity. D'Ailly demanded to know the point of raising such a question when no cardinals were present. He scolded Hus with the retort, "you do a wicked thing because in this sort of preaching you sow discord within the church."[175] Implicit in this rebuke is the spirit of canon law, which clearly states that those who follow heresies cannot condemn anyone else.[176] The Council perceived Hus

---

171. Ibid., p. 76.

172. D. 32 c.11 *Erubescant impii*, in Friedberg, vol. 1, col. 120; X 5.3.33 *Sicut nobis*, in Friedberg, vol. 2, cols. 762–763; X 5.3.34 *Tua nos*, in Friedberg, vol. 2, col. 763.

173. *Relatio*, pp. 75–76.

174. *Documenta*, pp. 286–315.

175. *Relatio*, pp. 89–90.

176. C.2 q.24 p.c.4 *Si autem*, in Friedberg, vol. 1, col. 967.

in this sense. There was more commotion when it was pointed out that Hus had said those who turned an innocent man over to the secular arm before he had been convicted of heresy were no different from the chief priests, scribes, and Pharisees who delivered Christ to the Roman procurator Pontius Pilate.[177] The matter of his appeal to Christ once more was raised. Hus asked whether the fact that he may have been the first to make such an appeal was sufficient grounds for calling him a heretic.[178] On the question of whether unjust excommunications were to be feared (article 23), Zabarella interposed to say there were canons in law that decreed that even an unjust excommunication should be dreaded.[179] The articles were designed to drive Hus onto dangerous ground with respect to ecclesiastical authority. But Hus did not hesitate to affirm his conviction that a wicked pope was a "Judas, a devil, a thief, and a son of perdition."[180] Perhaps most telling of Hus's posture during these hearings is an exchange he had with d'Ailly over the legitimacy of the condemnation of the "forty-five articles" of John Wyclif. Hus declared that it appeared to him to go against conscience in consenting to an unqualified judgment against the articles. Because of this, Hus repeated his conviction that he was unwilling to give his consent.[181] The hearing went on for some time, with theological charges being laid against Hus, his efforts to respond appropriately to each of these, and occasional debates with the judges and witnesses. Given the welter of charges, allegations, and accusations being directed against the defendant, Zabarella intervened at one stage, suggesting that Hus be given a simplified version of the articles against him that he should recant. The suggestion was logical and might have served to simplify the mass of legal and theological obfuscation. At the conclusion of the proceedings, Jan Chlum rather courageously shook Hus's hand as he left the hearing. D'Ailly publicly told Hus that if he desired another hearing, it would be granted.[182] Despite that promise and Hus's eagerness for a fourth appearance, this did not take place. D'Ailly again tried to prevail upon Hus to submit to the

---

177. *Relatio*, pp. 90–91.

178. Ibid., p. 92.

179. Ibid., p. 93; and Elisabeth Vodola, *Excommunication in the Middle Ages* (Berkeley: University of California Press, 1986), pp. 11, 21, 101.

180. *Relatio*, p. 97.

181. Ibid., p. 99.

182. Ibid., p. 103; Novotný, *Correspondence*, p. 268.

Council. Petr Mladoňovice was in attendance, although once again, he was late in arriving. That unfortunate fact noted, his report is otherwise generally fulsome. An unnamed Polish bishop reminded the court that canon law was clear on how to deal with heretics and that these statutes, specifically noted as the *Clementines* and the *Liber sextus*, should be followed. Both Páleč and de Causis declared that their aim in prosecuting Hus was solely in defense of truth. Sigismund was overheard at the end of the hearing urging the burning of Hus should he not recant and going on to say that even if Hus did enter a plea of abjuration, he would not be sincere in the retraction. This constitutes a rather revealing and damning indictment of official prejudice against Hus, indicating the presumption of guilt in violation of canon law, which maintains that the accused cannot be regarded as convicted until judgment has been passed.[183] An unidentified Prussian priest asserted that Hus had written a letter in which he allegedly claimed that any forced recantation would be verbal only and not from the heart.[184] This letter, originally written in Czech, was falsified in a Latin translation with unfortunate consequences for Hus.[185] Either Michael de Causis or Štěpán Páleč might easily have pointed this out, given their knowledge of Czech, but that would not have served their interests. There is no record that they attempted to correct the misapprehension. This matter was first raised in the forty-two articles prepared by Páleč, and on that occasion, when replying to article 41, Hus dismissed the allegation as "full of lies."[186] However, in this session, Hus rather provocatively asserted that neither kings nor popes in a state of mortal sin possessed any authority. Sigismund was unpleased, and d'Ailly was outraged. It is possible that Hus was tricked into making an inflammatory statement about the king.[187] Hus appears to have backed off from earlier positions on the papal verdict concerning Wyclif handed down in 1413, and Mladoňovice seems to have apologized for this lapse, citing health issues.[188] It is beyond doubt that the protracted legal ordeal had been stressful, and Hus was surely feeling the strain.

---

183. C.15 q.8 c.5 *Sciscitantibus vobis*, in Friedberg, vol. 1, cols. 760–761.

184. October 19, 1414, Novotný, *Correspondence*, pp. 207–209; *Relatio*, p. 105.

185. Hus noted the misleading translation in letters of January 19 and one undated missive after that date, in Novotný, *Correspondence*, pp. 243, 246.

186. *Documenta*, p. 224.

187. Bartoš, *Čechy*, p. 431.

188. *Relatio*, p. 106.

The three public hearings provide ample evidence that the Hus trial would not deviate markedly from late medieval heresy procedures. In the history of law, the *stare decisis* doctrine has a long tradition of adherence among jurists. *Stare decisis* is the legal principle by which judges generally observe a practice of abiding by precedents established in prior rulings. In the matter of the medieval church versus Jan Hus, we find no evidence that judges at the Curia or at Constance were eager to deviate from prior judicial decisions on the matter of heresy. They were prepared to abide by those precedents long considered sound legal doctrine. Hus's lawyer Jan Jesenice knew this. During the court proceedings, we find considerable evidence about the virtue of using case law in the context of *stare decisis* with respect to heresy. We encounter no discussion that the *ordo iudiciarius* or legal consideration of heresy be set aside in the Hus trial. The judges were firmly committed *stare decisis et non quieta movere* (to stand by decisions and not disturb the calm). Despite the weight of legal tradition, it seems Hus fully expected his case to represent an exception to the rule. He was wrong.

Altogether, although consistent with *stare decisis*, the public hearings were irregular, deviated from legal principle, had no procedural precedent, were most likely concessions to Sigismund in return for his cooperation in the withdrawal of the safe conduct, but cannot be seen as other than advantageous to Hus, even if they accomplished little. Hus acknowledged on June 13 that he had destroyed mail delivered to the prison for fear of seizure and exploitation by the authorities and danger to the writers and to those who carried it to Hus. It would be rather impossible to know the nature and extent of this correspondence.[189] As an aside, the weather in Constance during June was exceptionally hot; Sigismund left the city on June 22 and camped in the fields, hoping to find relief from the oppressive heat.[190]

In the thirteenth session, on June 15, the Council of Constance formally condemned utraquism as "reckless, erroneous, and heretical." Those persisting in its practice were ordered subject to censure and punishment, with the help of secular authorities if necessary.[191] This was a clear verdict against the liturgical initiative of Jakoubek Stříbro and Czech religious practice, which had been gaining in strength and popularity in Prague.

---

189. Novotný, *Correspondence*, p. 275.

190. Hardt, vol. 4, p. 344.

191. Tanner, DEC, vol. 1, pp. 418–419.

Earlier, we noted that Michael de Causis formally accused Hus of promoting eucharistic heresy, especially the practice of utraquism. The argument against the cup was formulated by Jean Gerson.[192] Two years later, Gerson wrote a tract on the subject in which he advanced several arguments against the feasibility of the lay chalice.[193] First, while there were scriptural and patristic texts allowing for utraquism, there was nowhere a clear and definitive command for the laity to thus commune. Second, the doctrine of concomitance was relevant. Third, however widespread the practice may have been in the early church, it was never universal. Fourth, there was a danger that wine could be spilled and lost. Fifth, the long beards of laymen might contaminate the chalice. Sixth, wine stored after consecration might cease to be the blood of Christ on account of it becoming sour and turning to vinegar. Seventh, it was impossible to consecrate enough wine in a single chalice to suffice for large numbers of communicants. Beyond this, Gerson attacked the Hussite propensity to accept the "naked sense" of scripture without the assistance of authorized authorities, which he argued led to scandal. Although written down later, these were among the arguments propounded against the lay chalice. A commission including Patrick Foxe had been appointed to review the question of utraquism. At the same session, another special commission on the problem of heresy was formed. Membership consisted of Cardinal Giordano Orsini; Antonio Panciero, patriarch of Aquileia; d'Ailly; Zabarella; Gerson; and fourteen other bishops and theologians.[194] In response to these developments, and while at the Council, former Prague inquisitor Mařik Rvačka wrote two tracts opposing the practice of utraquism introduced by Jakoubek Stříbro.[195] More important, somewhere between June 18 and 21, Hus denounced the decision concerning utraquism as insanity.[196] He refused to be swayed by the force of argument mounted by Gerson.

On June 18, Hus received the final thirty charges against him, to which he wrote replies.[197] The list may usefully be compared with articles

---

192. Hardt, vol. 3, p. 586.

193. *De necessaria communione laicorum sub utraque specie*, in Glorieux, vol. 10, pp. 55–68.

194. Hardt, vol. 4, pp. 333–336; Mansi, vol. 27, col. 729. Panciero (1350–1431) was elected patriarch of Aquileia in 1402 and was made cardinal in 1411 by John XXIII.

195. Texts in Hardt, vol. 3, pp. 779–804.

196. Novotný, *Correspondence*, p. 289.

197. *Documenta*, pp. 225–234.

examined at the hearing on June 7. Twelve of the final charges centered on issues of ecclesiology (1, 3, 7, 9, 10, 11, 13, 21, 26, 27, 28, 29), and eight were concerned in some sense with issues of morality that Hus ostensibly raised (8, 12, 16, 19, 22, 23, 24, 30), although a number of these might be considered ecclesiological. Four articles related to ecclesiastical obedience (14, 15, 17, 18), although once again, these could easily be incorporated into Hus's doctrine of the church. Three articles had to do with predestination (5, 6, 20). The remaining three charges were connected to the "forty-five articles" of Wyclif (article 25), christology (article 4), and whether Saint Paul had ever been a member of the devil (article 2). The christological question, which goes back to the controversies discussed at the fifth-century Council of Chalcedon, was a new addition to charges against Hus, as was article 30, which affirmed that no person in mortal sin, whether secular lord or prelate, could hold legitimate authority.[198] However, this topic was at issue during the examinations in the June 8 hearing. In sum, most of the final charges were centered on the teaching of Hus concerning the church. These articles had been approved by a number of conciliar dignitaries, including Johannes Wallenrode, archbishop of Riga; Giovanni Dominici, archbishop of Dubrovnik; Dietrich Niem; Jan of Bořenice, bishop of Lebus; Peter Helburg, provost of Wetzlar; Henry Homberk, deacon at St. Peter's in Utrecht; and Peter of Mera, suffragan bishop of Utrecht. These articles were read in a general session of the Council.[199] Ultimately, Hus denied all charges of theological irregularity brought against him and maintained that any alleged disciplinary infractions on his part could not be sustained. From a legal perspective, he offered or entered a plea of "innocent." There is no evidence that Hus tried to call witnesses, invoked the canonical process of *compurgatio*, submitted other documentation in support of his plea, or had any *positiones* drawn up. Witnesses for the accused in heresy trials did run the risk of incurring personal citations themselves, but there were exceptions.[200] Of the

---

198. On this christological charge, see Helmut Riedlinger, "Ekklesiologie und Christologie bei Johannes Hus," in *Von Konstanz nach Trident: Beiträge zur Geschichte der Kirche von den Reformkonzilien bis zum Tridentinum*, ed. Remigius Bäumer (Paderborn: Ferdinand Schöningh, 1972), pp. 47–55.

199. Hardt, vol. 4, cols. 430–432.

200. A few years before the Hus trial, a heresy procedure involved more than fifty defendants, each of whom produced two character witnesses who were not accused of heresy. Gertrude Barnes Fiertz, "An Unusual Trial under the Inquisition at Fribourg, Switzerland, 1399," *Speculum* 18, no. 3 (1943): 344.

final thirty charges brought against him, Hus's replies sought to modify twenty-six. Only articles 16, 20, 25, and 27 were left as originally stated.

At this critical juncture in the legal case, around June 20, Hus received an anonymous letter from someone we know only as "pater," suggesting a means by which Hus might be lowered down the wall in a basket like Saint Paul, who escaped from Damascus that way according to the Acts of the Apostles. This was a metaphorical allusion to a solution to the legal issue.[201] As indicated earlier by Zabarella, a watered-down recantation formula was offered to Hus sometime before June 20.[202] It is tempting to nominate Paweł Włodkowicz, dean of the theology faculty at Kraków, as the "pater," but he would not have had the authority to act as he did. I cannot imagine it was d'Ailly or Jean-Allarmet de Brogny.[203] The identification of this anonymous "pater" cannot be made on the basis of any documents, but the most likely candidate is Cardinal Zabarella.[204] Perhaps sensing that the end was near, on or before June 22. Hus asked for a confessor, specifically Štěpán Páleč, but his old adversary did not appear. The prisoner was given an anonymous monk sent by the Council, who granted him absolution.[205] Evidently, the confessor did not require from Hus any proof of penitence or the preliminary abjuration. It is something of a shame that history cannot identify Hus's confessor, but the rules guarding the confessional meant that even if we did know who this anonymous monk was, we would not have any means of knowing what Hus's final confession consisted of. Páleč did visit Hus in prison sometime before June 22. Their encounter was emotional, with Páleč and Hus both weeping.[206]

Hus's other formidable enemy at Constance, Michael de Causis, later took part in the Council of Basel; on his deathbed around 1432 or 1433, he swore he had never committed any impropriety in his office.[207] Sometime

---

201. Novotný, *Correspondence*, pp. 283–284.

202. Spinka, *Constance*, p. 269, n. 18; Hardt, vol. 4, p. 329.

203. Ferdinand Seibt, "'Neodvolám!' Jan Hus před koncilem kostnickým," in *Velké procesy: Právo a spravedlnost v dějinách*, ed. Uwe Schultz (Prague: Brána, 1997), p. 96, suggests the former, while the latter is nominated by Hardt, vol. 4, col. 329.

204. Jiří Kejř, "K Husovu procesu v Kostnici," *Acta Universitatis Carolinae—Historia Universitatis Carolinae Pragensis* 48, no. 1 (2008): pp. 11–14; Brandmüller, *Konzil*, pp. 348–351; Fudge, *Jan Hus*, p. 133.

205. Novotný, *Correspondence*, p. 298; *Passio*, FRB, vol. 8, pp. 142–143.

206. Novotný, *Correspondence*, p. 298.

207. ÖNB, MS 4975, fol. 49ᵛ.

before June 23, de Causis secured an official order forbidding anyone admittance to the prison, excepting presumably prison guards and officials and those connected to the Hus inquiry. Even wives of the guards were denied entry.[208] It is a fact, based on the testimony of Hus, that some of the guards facilitated mail to and from his cell, particularly Robert, Gregory, and Jacob. The practice would certainly be frowned upon by the court and in any event violated rules for heresy prisons and guards working in them.[209] There were numerous efforts on the part of the Council or its members to persuade Hus to recant. None appears to have made any impression on Hus whatsoever. Some scholars have wondered why Hus should decline to recant when the simplified statement presented to him effectively undercut the indictment.[210] Once the formal hearings ended, the Council inexplicably delayed issuing a final verdict. This constituted irregular legal procedure. Normally, immediately after deposition, the condemned was handed over to the secular courts, and canonists such as Johannes Teutonicus noted this. Sometime in late June, possibly as an alarmed reaction to the unexpected delay of handing down a verdict, de Causis attempted to influence the Council, via a formal submission, to pass a resolution forbidding all attempts to persuade Hus to recant.[211] This fit rather well with his prohibition against prison visitors. Hus had terrorized the faith and the rules of the church, was clearly heretical, "pertinacious, obstinate and incorrigible," and without delay should be turned over to secular authorities for sentence. As the delay in announcing a decision in the Hus case turned from days into more than a week, zealous prosecutors such as de Causis must have begun to experience anxiety.

A second anonymous submission was filed with the court warning about the undesirability of a recantation, fearing that Hus's sentence might be commuted from death to a life sentence. The proposal suggested that the commission not pass sentence but instead refer the verdict to the entire Council. The brief argued that Hus should be subjected to *animadversione debita*, for he was the most "notorious heretic on earth," the disseminator of "many errors and heresies," who had attempted to

---

208. Novotný, *Correspondence*, p. 300.

209. Clem. 5.3.1 *Multorum querela*, in Friedberg, vol. 2, cols. 1181–1182.

210. Ferdinand Seibt, "Hus in Konstanz," AHC 15 (1983): 160–161.

211. Olomouc, University Library, MS II. 91, fol. 168ʳ; transcription in Novotný, *M. Jan Hus*, vol. 2, p. 447.

sway all of Christendom to his ideas. The legal penalty should be applied, for he had been "rightly convicted," and he ought to be made to abjure. Imprisonment was not a good idea (the sentence was likely to be commuted eventually), and the writer made reference to the letter Hus had left behind in Prague, before he left to attend the Council. The document warned that Hus's errors and heresies would only multiply, with the end result far worse than the beginning, for "taking seven spirits even more wicked," Hus would attack the church of God, the priesthood would be more seriously damaged, and the result would be "innumerable errors" and "great scandals" to the "destruction of the spiritual and secular estates," with sedition among the clergy and the laity. It is possible that the author was familiar with canon law glosses in which persons of higher rank were ordered punished more severely and subjected to condemnation without leniency. This document was likely authored by either de Causis or Jan Náz.[212]

In the midst of all this, Hus stated his unflattering opinion of the Council (June 26), declaring it greedy, proud, abominable, and so sinful that once it was concluded, it would require more than thirty years to clean up the city of Constance and purge the locale of the sins committed there.[213] Hus doubtlessly referred to his sense of injustice along with rumors of blatant immorality. There are stories of the Council organizing temporary brothels, and we know that Emperor Sigismund and his entourage were welcomed at brothels without charge en route to Constance in 1414.[214] In the northern part of the city near the Rhine River lay the Ziegelgraben. This may refer to a house, a series of houses, a street, or a canal, but there is fifteenth-century evidence for a red-light district in this part of Constance, and we know of contemporary songs noting that many Swiss men came to the Ziegelgraben. Moreover, chroniclers of the Council noted the preponderance of sexually available women. "It is said that one whore earned 800 florins," an enormous sum for the time.[215] There are numerous legends of prelates spending the days engaged in

---

212. The text *Avisamentum fiendum processus contra Io. Hus* has been edited in František M. Bartoš, "Z posledního zápasu o M. Jana," JSH 17 (1948): 58–59. I am grateful to Peter Morée for helping me to get a copy of this text.

213. Novotný, *Correspondence*, p. 318.

214. James A. Brundage, *Law, Sex, and Christian Society in Medieval Europe* (Chicago: University of Chicago Press, 1987), p. 527.

215. Hardt, vol. 5, col. 52.

conciliar affairs and the nights with whores.[216] One writer in the city during the Council wrote that "many pleasures . . . shine there in Constance,"
provided by women "with red lips [and] rose-colored cheeks." [There are]
"so many pretty, angelic ladies [who] have grabbed me there." Indeed,
"entertainments of all sorts you can find in Constance."[217] Oswald von
Wolkenstein remarked that "acting like a Bishop" implied having sex
with a prostitute.[218] Hus deplored all of it and also denounced the synod
itself (June 29) as a great whore and a congregation of iniquity.[219]

On July 1, Hus made his final declaration to the Council.[220] In this
statement, he feared perjury, declared he would not recant, alleged the
malignant influence of false witnesses, and suggested that the articles
extracted from his writings had been either misquoted or taken out of context. He remained defiant. On a purely technical point, with no relevance
to the Hus case, during the fourteenth session, on July 4, Pope Gregory
XII voluntarily abdicated in a statement read by Giovanni Dominici. As a
result of some behind-the-scenes politicking, Gregory was recognized by
the Council as having convened the synod, rather than John XXIII, who
had, in fact, done so. The official acts of the Council were read aloud by
the protonotary and canon lawyer Job Vener before Sigismund and other
dignitaries.[221]

A Carthusian announced to the University of Cologne on July 4 that
at the next session of the Council, Hus was likely to be condemned and
sentenced, since he had now reneged on his earlier commitment to submit to the decisions of the Council.[222] Now, at the eleventh hour, on July 5,

---

216. Beate Schuster, *Die unendlichen Frauen: Prostitution und städtische Ordnung in Konstanz im 15./16. Jahrhundert* (Constance: Universitätsverlag Konstanz, 1996), pp. 19–30; the song is noted on p. 188. An English bishop told the story of a woman in Constance who admitted that her pregnancy was the work of the Council. Poggio Bracciolini, *Facetiae*, 27, in *Opera Omnia* (Strasbourg: Knobluch, 1513), fol. 160ᵛ.

217. Albrecht Classen, *The Poems of Oswald von Wolkenstein: An English Translation of the Complete Works (1376/7–1445)* (New York: Palgrave MacMillan, 2008), p. 178.

218. Albrecht Classen, "Anticlericalism in Late Medieval German Verse," in *Anticlericalism in Late Medieval and Early Modern Europe*, ed. Peter A. Dykema and Heiko A. Oberman (Leiden: Brill, 1993), p. 96.

219. Novotný, *Correspondence*, pp. 330–301.

220. Ibid., p. 333.

221. Mansi, vol. 27, col. 730.

222. Martène and Durand, *Thesaurus novus anecdotorum*, vol. 2, p. 1639.

there was a final request for recantation during a brief appearance by Hus before representatives of the Council. This occurred outside the prison at the Minorite monastery. Hus refused to budge and remained steadfast. This delegation may have included d'Ailly; Zabarella; Jean Mauroux; Henry Scarampi, bishop of Belluna-Feltre; Bartolomeo della Capra, archbishop of Milan; Johannes Wallenrode, archbishop of Riga; Robert Hallum, bishop of Salisbury; Nicholas Bubwith, bishop of Bath and Wells; and Andreas Lascari, Bishop of Poznaň. Hus was presented with evidence and testimony, and final efforts were mounted to induce abjuration. Hus referred to his July 1 declaration, refusing to waver.[223] King Sigismund also undertook one last time to persuade Hus to submit by sending an embassy to Hus's prison cell sometime during the evening of July 5.[224] This consisted of between six and nine people, depending on the source: four bishops (unnamed in some sources), Jan Chlum, Václav of Leštno (Václav Dubá), Jindřich Lacembok, and Ludwig, Palsgrave of the Rhine. Elsewhere, we are told that Chlum, Dubá, and four bishops (among them Robert Hallum) visited Hus.[225] The prison visitation group may have included d'Ailly, Zabarella, Mauroux, della Capra, Wallenrode, Hallum, and Bubwith.[226] Ostensibly, Hus's position was that he would rather be burned a thousand times than recant.[227] That same day, Hus prepared a final statement formally refusing to recant.[228] Was Hus daring the Council to burn him? He made no reference to either of the meetings of that day. The die was cast. What remained was for the court to announce its verdict.

The prisoner had been incarcerated for 219 days, just more than seven months. The final events in the Hus trial occurred on July 6—"Saturday after [the feast of Saint] Prokop in the octave of the blessed apostles Peter and Paul"—in the cathedral at Constance.[229] Those final acts commenced

---

223. Hardt, vol. 4, cols. 431–432.

224. Anonymous report in *Documenta*, p. 560; Hardt, vol. 4, p. 386.

225. *Relatio*, pp. 111–112.

226. Hardt, vol. 4, p. 386.

227. Mansi, vol. 27, col. 764.

228. Novotný, *Correspondence*, pp. 334–335.

229. Prokop of Sázava, a Czech saint, died in 1053. He founded an Eastern Rite monastery near Prague and was its first abbot. His feast day was formerly observed on July 4. The liturgical feast of Saints Peter and Paul was observed on June 29. In the Christian liturgical sense, the octave is the eighth day after a feast.

at six a.m. The cathedral had been modified for the Council proceedings. Seats had been constructed and the high altar covered. Another altar had been built, along with several thrones. The nave had been walled in along the columns. Within the nave, extending the full length, were three rows of seats facing one another. On the highest sat the cardinals, archbishops, and princes. On the second level were the bishops and abbots. On the first level were the proctors, notaries, and theologians. Movable seats were set up at floor level, and these were filled mainly with priests and lawyers. In the midst of the nave, a pulpit had been set up.[230] Session 15 was presided over by Cardinal Jean-Allarmet de Brogny of Ostia. Odo Colonna, the future pope, was there.[231] Mass was celebrated by Mikołaj Trąba, archbishop of Gniezno. Hus and his escort, the archbishop of Riga, had to wait outside until the celebration of the Eucharist had concluded.[232] A very specific sermon (*sermo generalis*) was delivered by the Dominican bishop of Lodi, Jacob Balardi Arrigoni.[233] Ulrich Richental claims the sermon was preached by Jean d'Achéry, doctor of theology and "rector of divinity at the High School of Paris," who recently had been installed as bishop of Senlis. The attribution is quite erroneous, as is the date of July 8, that Richental supposes.[234] Hus was made to sit on an elevated seat so everyone could see him clearly.[235] The sermon delivered by the bishop of Lodi took its theme from a phrase extracted out of context from Romans 6:6: "the sinful body should be destroyed." That Pauline sentence was made to act as a proof text for arguing that heretics and heresies must be suppressed. Drawing upon patristic sources, the bishop pointed out that diseased sheep must be expelled from the fold to prevent the entire flock from becoming infected. Moreover, a small fire must be immediately extinguished to save the entire house from destruction. By implication, heretics were infected animals and uncontrollable fires. They

---

230. Richental, *Chronik*, pp. 18–19; Heribert Reiners, *Das Münster unserer lieben Frau zu Konstanz* (Constance: Thorbecke, 1955), pp. 12–20, 46–47.

231. Czech *Acta* in the Freiburg Codex, in FRB, vol. 8, pp. 259–260.

232. *Passio*, in FRB, vol. 8, p. 127; Dietrich Niem in Hardt, vol. 2, col. 408.

233. FRB, vol. 8, pp. 489–93.

234. Richental, *Chronik*, p. 64. The Czech *Acta* in the Freiburg Codex mistakenly says "6 June"; FRB, vol. 8, p. 259. Both might be attributed to scribal errors or manuscript corruption.

235. Mansi, vol. 27, col. 747.

must be contained and condemned. The first half of the sermon was a diatribe against the protracted papal schism, which had been an incubator for heresy, and heretics thereby had invaded the church. "Pits of heresies" had formed, and dwelling among the lamentable divisions was the devil. Nefarious "pirates" had conspired to cause the shipwreck of the true church.[236] The second half of the sermon lauded Sigismund as the divinely appointed instrument elected to restore the church to its former glory. The bishop of Lodi suggested that this could be accomplished in part by destroying all promoters of disobedience, "particularly this obstinate heretic here present." Although never referring to Hus by name, the bishop drew attention to Hus's wickedness, which he characterized as a "most pestilent and heretical poison," which had already infected many places. Let there be no doubt about it: Jan Hus was numbered among the "great enemies of the catholic faith."[237]

Prior to the commencement of business, a resolution of silence, issued in the name of the Council, was made that no interruptions in the proceedings, whether caused by "noise made with mouth, hands or feet," whether by "signs, words or gestures," would be tolerated. Whoever ventured to do so would be subjected to the punishment of excommunication, fines, a sentence of two months in prison, "and even more harsh punishment." This applied to everyone, including all prelates and the emperor.[238] This was consistent with the ruling noted by Zabarella the previous November and in marked contrast to the disorder that characterized the early parts of the legal proceedings, especially during the first public hearing on June 5. The *promotor iudiciis officii* (promotor) Henry of Piro read the prescribed formula, which effectively was to make a motion asking for a continuation of the trial until such time as a verdict could be reached. The papal auditor, Berthold Wildungen, then read a review of the trial from its beginnings in 1410 to Hus's declaration of July 1 up to the events of the previous day, including the final thirty articles.[239] Following this, Anthony, bishop of Concordia, whom we find described

---

236. FRB, vol. 8, pp. 491–492.

237. Ibid., p. 493.

238. Mansi, vol. 27, cols. 747–748; and the anonymous *Relatio de concilio constantiensi*, FRB, vol. 8, p. 12. The Czech *Acta* in the Freiburg Codex asserts that Anthony, bishop of Concordia, urged all present to keep silence; FRB, vol. 8, p. 260.

239. Hardt, vol. 4, cols. 429–432.

elsewhere as "an aged, bald auditor and prelate," read the definitive sentence in the legal case versus Hus.[240] This declaration characterized Hus as a disciple of John Wyclif rather than a follower of Christ. His heresies were described as "erroneous, scandalous, offensive, reckless, seditious, and notoriously heretical." The statement drew attention specifically to Hus's book *De ecclesia*, completed after the formal papal condemnation of Wyclif, which drove home the point that Hus remained impervious to correction. In the course of his career, Hus taught "many evil, scandalous, seditious and dangerous heresies" over the course of many years. The definitive sentence concluded with a five-point verdict. First, Jan Hus was a "definite heretic." Second, he "seduced the Christian people" into heresy and away from the true faith. Third, Hus was "obstinate and incorrigible" and unwilling to recant error and heresy. Fourth, Hus should be defrocked from the priesthood. Fifth, he was to be relaxed to the secular court.[241] The *culpae*, normally read out in court, formed the basis on which the defendant had been condemned. There were two versions prepared, one in the event that Hus recanted (a possibility feared by Michael de Causis) and the other scheduled to be used should the defendant refuse to submit.[242] The alternative sentence outlined that Hus must voluntarily present himself to recant and abjure all heresies, swear off allegiance to "heretical perversion," especially that connected to Wyclif, seek absolution from his excommunication, and admit his sins. Should Hus take this option, the Council decreed that because he had caused so much trouble, he was to be defrocked. Because he remained a "dangerous man to the Christian faith," the Council ordered discretionary punishment, meaning that he be immured and perpetually imprisoned. Of course, Hus declined to abjure his teachings, so the alternative sentence was never read. That reality now established, the nominated judges passing the death sentence on Hus were Patrick Foxe, bishop of Cork; Nicholas Lubich, bishop of Merseburg; Stephen Coevret, bishop of Dol; Anthony, bishop of Concordia; Vitalis Valentini, bishop of Toulon; and Berthold Wildungen.[243] The particulars of the final

---

240. FRB, vol. 8, pp. 501–503. Description of the bishop is in *Relatio*, p. 115.

241. Ibid., p. 503.

242. Sedlák, *M. Jan Hus*, pp. 351*–352*; and Hardt, vol. 4, col. 432, contain the alternative sentence text.

243. Hardt, vol. 4, col. 400; *Relatio*, pp. 112–113.

events were recorded in some detail by several sources.[244] The penalty of life imprisonment for repentant heretics had canonical support.[245] The verdict of the Council in the legal case involving Hus was unambiguous and straightforward and declared to have come by "divine inspiration."[246] In sum, Hus was an impertinent heretic inappropriately linked to the previously condemned heresiarch John Wyclif. Hus's appeal to Christ was denounced as illegal and scandalous, and the court found it an act of contempt. The verdict noted that Hus remained contumacious even after protracted instruction. During this session, two hundred sixty articles of Wyclif were condemned, fifty-eight of those enumerated.[247] Hus's books were ordered destroyed by fire.[248] The Council claimed to have established its prosecutorial case on the basis of "very many trustworthy witnesses." Some of these, such as Michael de Causis, bore *inimicitia capitalis* (mortal enmity) toward Hus and legally should have been excluded from the judicial examinations. On the other hand, since heresy was an exceptional crime, canon law permitted the testimony of other heretics in judicial proceedings, although this was limited to cases of heresy.[249] The work of Štěpán Páleč and Michael de Causis was credited with a successful prosecution.[250] With respect to Hus, Páleč was possessed by prejudice, "real hatred," and a desire to see him burn.[251] Hus was ordered deposed and defrocked. Even after the Council, Pierre d'Ailly continued to regard Hus as a "pernicious heretic."[252] Ostensibly, more than one hundred witnesses were brought to Constance to testify against Hus.[253]

---

244. *Relatio*, pp. 111–120, Richental, *Chronik*, pp. 64–66; Barbatus, FRB, vol. 8, pp. 14–24; *Passio*, FRB, vol. 8, pp. 121–149; Czech *Acta* in the Freiburg Codex, FRB, vol. 8, pp. 247–318.

245. X 5.7.14 *Excommunicamus et anathematizamus*, in Friedberg, vol. 2, col. 789; Sext. 5.9.3 *Quamvis*, in Friedberg, vol. 2, col. 1091.

246. Czech *Acta* in the Freiburg Codex, FRB, vol. 8, pp. 260–261.

247. Tanner, DEC, vol. 1, pp. 421–426.

248. Mansi, vol. 27, col. 764; *Relatio de concilio constantiensi*, FRB, vol. 8, p. 13.

249. C.2 q.7 c.26 *Si hereticus*, in Friedberg, vol. 1, col. 489; and Gratian's comment to the same canon in p.c. 26.

250. *Hussite Chronicle*, FRB, vol. 5, p. 338.

251. "M. Štěpán z Pálče a Husův proces," in Kejř, *Počátků* pp. 121–122.

252. Hardt, vol. 6, p. 16.

253. Flajšhans, *Mistr Jan*, p. 407.

Following the reading of the final charges, according to Petr Mladoňovice in his *Relatio*, along with other witnesses and sources, further allegations were leveled against Hus, accusing him of contumacy, of teaching that a priest in mortal sin could neither consecrate the Eucharist nor baptize, of holding to the remanence interpretation of the Eucharist, and of claiming to be the fourth person of the Trinity.[254] On this last point, the *Acta* says the following: "That in a particular discussion where a certain master Richard [claimed] Jan Hus conceded the point that Jan Hus was a person in the Godhead and there were more than three persons in the Godhead. This was true according to one doctor of theology from common report and rumor, by an abbot from common rumor, and also by the vicar of a Prague church who said he heard it from the mouth of Jan Hus as stated."[255] None of these witnesses was specifically identified. There was yet another attack on Hus's appeal to Christ. A legal dispute seemed to arise, with Hus being accused of performing priestly functions while excommunicated.[256] Hus defended himself, saying he had appealed to the pope, had sent lawyers to the Curia, was unable to secure a hearing; he referred to the "acts of the trial" for details and finished off by noting that he had come to the Council under the provisions of an imperial safe conduct. Sigismund is reported to have been much embarrassed at the remark.[257] Hus gave three reasons for his resolute refusal to abjure. First, he did not want to offend God; second, he feared committing perjury; and third, he did not wish to scandalize people who had heard him preach.[258] Elsewhere, we find agreement on this statement corresponding with the second and third reasons, while the first explanation has been altered to make Hus say he did not wish to go against conscience.[259] Despite Zabarella's procedural order, there was considerable disorder, with much shouting, jeering, and repeated calls for Hus to maintain silence. Nevertheless, it is overwrought and unsupported by reliable documents to claim that "although the Cardinal of Ostia [Jean-Allarmet de Brogny], who presided, endeavored to show fairness,

---

254. FRB, vol. 8, p. 114; Mansi, vol. 27, cols. 755–763.

255. Mansi, vol. 27, col. 758.

256. *Relatio*, p. 115.

257. Petr Mladoňovice, *Passio*, FRB, vol. 8, p. 135.

258. Mansi, vol. 27, col. 765.

259. *Relatio de concilio constantiensi*, FRB, vol. 8, p. 13.

the assembly at times became a howling mob with shouts of 'Burn him! Burn him!'"²⁶⁰

Hus was then degraded from the priesthood in general accord with the canonical decretal *Degradatio*.²⁶¹ He was made to wear a miter upon which demons were depicted, an unusual *poenae confusibiles*. Thus, he was defrocked from all holy orders and expelled from the priesthood. Between six and eight ecclesiastical prelates were involved. Assisting at Hus's defrocking were Bartolomeo della Capra, archbishop of Milan; Henry Scarampi, bishop of Belluna-Feltre; Albert Guttuaria d'Agliano, bishop of Asti and abbot of St. Bartholomew in Pavia; Bartholino Beccari, bishop of Alexandria; William Barrowe, bishop of Bangor; and Jean Belli, bishop of Lavaur. These were the six according to the "Acts of the Council."²⁶² Elsewhere, John, suffragan bishop of Constance, is included in some sources for a total of seven bishops.²⁶³ The *Relatio* claims seven bishops were involved but does not name them. The definitive sentence gives the seven names noted already.²⁶⁴ Richental claims a total of eight bishops and identifies the archbishop of Milan and Nicholas, prior of the Order of the Holy Sepulcher in Jerusalem, along with two cardinals, two bishops, and two bishops-elect, all unnamed.²⁶⁵ As noted earlier, one of the consequences for heretical priests according to the decretals *Ab abolendam* and *Vergentis in senium* was degradation from holy orders, which not only deprived them of *privilegium fori* (the right to be tried in an ecclesiastical court) and *privilegium canonis* (special protection) but most seriously left them without immunity from secular authorities.²⁶⁶ Stripped of those rights, privileges, and protections, Hus's soul was handed over to Satan in

---

260. As characterized by Henry Charles Lea, *A History of the Inquisition of the Middle Ages* (New York: Harper, 1887), vol. 2, p. 485.

261. Sext. 5.9.2. *Degradatio qualiter fieri debeat*, in Friedberg, vol. 2, col. 1090. See also Erwin Jacobi, "Der Prozeß im Decretum Gratiani und bei den ältesten Dekretisten," ZRG KA 3 (1913): 241–244.

262. Tanner, DEC, vol. 1, p. 429. Belli was the papal auditor assigned to the Hus case in 1412; he was elevated to the episcopacy in 1415.

263. Hardt, vol. 4, cols. 433, 437.

264. FRB, vol. 8, p. 503.

265. Richental, *Chronik*, p. 64.

266. X 5.7.9 and X 5.7.10, in Friedberg, vol. 2, cols. 780–783.

FIGURE 7.2 The burning of Jan Hus (1587). Kancionál, MS 1 A 15, fol. 305v. Library of the National Museum, Prague. Used by permission.

accordance with the law.[267] Hus demanded to know where Pilate was.[268] This implied that Hus considered the ceremony an act of betrayal and saw himself as mistreated not unlike Christ. According to canon law, excommunication jeopardized salvation only if it was ignored or condemned. In Hus's case, both had occurred, and these were regarded as aggravating circumstances.[269] Some sources suggest that Hus appeared shocked at the sentence.[270] In accordance with standard legal procedure, he was relaxed

---

267. C.11 q.3 c.32 *Omnis Christianus*, in Friedberg, vol. 1, col. 653, says "those excommunicated from the church are given to Satan."

268. *Relatio de concilio constantiensi*, FRB, vol. 8, p. 13.

269. Sext. 5.11.1 *Quum medicinalis sit excommunicatio*, in Friedberg, vol. 2, cols. 1093–1094.

270. *Relatio de concilio constantiensi*, FRB, vol. 8, p. 13.

to the secular arm for execution of sentence.[271] All of this is recounted in the *Relatio*. Normally, when a convicted heretic was handed over to the secular authorities, a boilerplate formality was appended asking for mercy and begging the condemned not be harmed. This appears absent in the Hus case except for the testimony of Richental, who said that the court asked Sigismund and the civil powers not to execute Hus but to remand him to perpetual custody.[272] Even though there is evidence for harsh prison conditions in the later Middle Ages, life imprisonment did not necessarily mean confinement to a cell, with the door walled up and food provided through a small chute.[273] This might have been implied in the call for the immuring of Hus noted in the alternative sentencing document, but life imprisonment was often commuted. The public burning of Hus's books took place in the church yard, apparently the cathedral cemetery, or in the street near the episcopal palace immediately south of the cathedral.[274]

Given the narrow streets and the throngs of onlookers, it must have taken Hus at least a quarter of an hour to reach the place of death outside the city in the Brüel Field. He was given a final opportunity at the stake to recant and live. Once convicted of heresy, the offender is subject to *animadversione debita* (the debt of hatred) under the jurisdiction of secular authority. From the publication of Gregory IX's decretal *Excommunicamus* in 1231, this normally implied death. Hus declined the opportunity to live. Death at the stake was arranged among the gardens in a meadow west of Constance, between the city and Gottlieben Fortress, between the moats and the gates of the city.[275] It is ironic that Hus came to his end in view of paradise. Between the city walls and the moats lay the suburb village of Paradise. The procession from the cathedral left the city via the Gelting Gate and ended in the Brüel Field. The penalty for impenitent heretics according to canonical legislation was capital punishment.[276] A decretal of Pope Innocent III from 1207, *Cum ex officii nostri*, mandated this principle

---

271. X 5.7.13 §1 *Excommunicamus*, in Friedberg, vol. 2, col. 787; X 5.40.27 *Novimus expedire*, in Friedberg, vol. 2, col. 924. The *res iudicatae* always prevailed.

272. Richental, *Chronik*, p. 64.

273. Flajšhans, *Mistr Jan*, pp. 436–437, understands the sentence too literally.

274. *Relatio*, p. 117; Mansi, vol. 27, col. 768.

275. *Relatio*, p. 118.

276. X 5.7.15 *Excommunicamus*, in Friedberg, vol. 2, col. 789. And Gratian previously had justified the use of force. C.23 q.5 p.c.48, in Friedberg, vol. 1, col. 945.

as perpetual law.[277] Prior to his being bound to the stake, Hus's clothes were removed.[278] These included two black coats of good cloth, a gown, stockings, shoes, an ornamented girdle, two knives in one sheath, and a leather purse with an undisclosed sum of money.[279] All of these items were burned.[280] We have noted previously the exceptionally hot weather that year in Constance. What may seem like considerable clothing for such a hot season may be put down to these being all of Hus's personal items still in his possession. There are unsubstantiated comments that the mattress in his prison cell was also burned.[281] We do know that the following year, Council officials in the case of Jerome of Prague ordered his bed, blanket, clothing, and all personal items destroyed by fire.[282] The propensity for relics to be made from the remains of heretics was no less than that within the cult of the saints. Nicholas Eymeric tells of a heresy suspect apprehended and subsequently prosecuted for collecting the bones of a burned heretic for the purpose of venerating them as relics. Bernard Gui noted that bones and ashes were gathered, preserved as relics, kissed, and venerated. Those who did so were suspected of being disciples or supporters of the convicted heretics. Examples are legion.[283] Heretics, generally, were burned in full view of the people ("igni in conspectus populi combusti").[284] With that requirement in mind and the possibility of relics collectors lurking about, Hus's body was completely destroyed deliberately to prevent the collection of relics.[285] It was later claimed that Hus's ashes were stolen by his admirers and secretly taken to Bohemia and that soil near the stake

---

277. Comment in Edward Peters, *Inquisition* (New York: Free Press, 1988), pp. 49–50.

278. *Relatio*, p. 118.

279. Richental, *Chronik*, pp. 64–65.

280. *Relatio*, p. 120.

281. Noted, for example, in Franz Lützow, *The Life and Times of Master John Hus* (London: Dent, 1909), p. 278.

282. Hardt, vol. 4, col. 771.

283. Anon., *Tractatus de haeresi pauperum de Lugduno*, in Martène and Durand, *Thesaurus novus anecdotorum*, vol. 5, col. 1787; Gui, *Practica*, p. 279; Eymeric, *Directorium*; Louisa A. Burnham, "Reliques et résistance chez les Béguines de Languedoc," *Annales du Midi* 108 (2006): 352–368.

284. Eymeric, *Directorium*, p. 499.

285. *Relatio*, p. 120; *Passio*, FRB, vol. 8, p. 147; Ludolf of Żagan, "Tractatus de longevo schismate," p. 449. One wonders how the knives were disposed of.

was dug up and spirited away, ostensibly as near-relics.[286] There is no reliable or corroborating confirmation for this. Most of the contemporary records (except the *Relatio*, Richental, and Barbatus) provide only scant details of the end of Hus. Dietrich Vrie records the judicial conviction, noting that Hus was turned over to secular authorities, and underscores the deposition of ashes in the Rhine.[287] In a display of unmitigated hypocrisy, Sigismund later claimed he could not have been any more grieved over the fate of Hus.[288] The burning of Hus technically may have been illegal. Executions, according to one scholar, were not supposed to occur on the same day as the sentence was handed down but normally took place the next day.[289] This argument is mitigated in part insofar as summary procedure implied that execution should follow swiftly after judgment and sentencing. Hesitation or delay on the part of the court officials might give cause for confusion.[290] Heresy trials and the burning of contumacious offenders were not as startling to medieval people as they doubtless would be to modern sensibilities. This may account in part for why there is a paucity of coverage of the Hus trial in the records. This is not uncommon. In the thirteenth century, a French bishop had his vicar pronounce the sentence of heresy on an old woman, who was then carried on her bed to the fire and burned alive. Once she was reduced to ashes, the bishop and the monks retired to the refectory and had lunch, giving thanks to God for the suppression of heretics and their beliefs.[291] Burning people followed by lunch helps explain why Fillastre and Cerretano were content merely to record that the heretic Hus was dead.

Bishop Jan Železný wrote a report to King Václav five days later, on July 11, noting that this past "Saturday they sentenced Master Hus and his

---

286. Aeneas Sylvius, *De rebus basiliae gestis commentarius*, in *Reject Aeneas Accept Pius: Selected Letters of Aeneas Sylvius Piccolomini (Pope Pius II)*, ed. Thomas M. Izbicki, Gerald Christianson, and Philip Krey (Washington, D.C.: Catholic University of America Press, 2006), p. 323; *Aeneae Silvii Historia Bohemica* [Fontes rerum Regni Bohemiae, vol. 1], ed. Dana Martínková, Alena Hadravová, and Jiří Matl (Prague: Koniasch Latin Press, 1998), p. 101.

287. Hardt, vol. 1, pp. 170–171.

288. March 21, 1416, *Documenta*, p. 610.

289. Lea, *A History of the Inquisition*, vol. 1, p. 393.

290. Gui, *Practica*, p. 236.

291. William Pelhisson, *Chronique (1229–1244): Sulvie de récit des troubles d'Albi*, ed. Jean Duvernoy (Paris: Editions du Centre National de la Recherché Scientifique, 1994), pp. 62–63.

Wyclifite teaching, and he was burned to death together with his books." The letter assured Václav that while Hus had been condemned, whenever the king had been mentioned as a supporter of Hus, he had been defended against the allegation by the bishop and his colleagues. Here the bishop had in mind Páleč, Náz, and other robust opponents of Hus.[292] On the same day, Železný wrote to Archbishop Konrad, claiming to have worked with all commitment at Constance to see the Czech lands rid of dangerous and poisonous heresies caused by the heresiarchs Wyclif and Hus. He argued that the Council undertook this process with the intent that "all the rigor of the law" be observed in its procedures.[293] The backlash against the persecutors of Hus in Bohemia was severe. Dietrich Niem reported that Bishop Jan "the Iron" rarely ventured outdoors after Constance and lived in fear for his life.[294] In 1416, he was appointed primate of Moravia, and he later became archbishop of Ezstergom, gradually getting farther away from Hussite territory and the bellicose climate the death of Hus engendered. Additionally, there was considerable outrage in Prague over Hus's execution. Niem claimed that households were divided, with husbands against wives and parents against children. Apparently, the destruction of properties owned by Hus's enemies occurred. Anti-Hus priests were assaulted, turned out of their livings, drowned in the Vltava River, or otherwise murdered.[295] Exaggeration must be suspected, but deep religious and social unrest followed these events in Constance. Once the trial ended, most of those who had opposed Hus were forced out of Bohemia. Štěpán Páleč was last heard of in Poland in 1422, John Peklo and Jan Protiva went abroad, Michael de Causis never returned, Ondřej of Brod spent the remainder of his life in German territories, and Mařik Rvačka vanished without a trace.[296]

Meanwhile, back at the Council venue, on July 21, Jean Gerson preached a three-part sermon known as *Prosperum iter faciat nobis*, or "may he have a good journey for us." Part one, *via pacis* (the way of peace),

292. FRB, vol. 8, pp. 9–10.

293. *Documenta*, pp. 566–568.

294. Hardt, vol. 2, col. 425.

295. Hardt, vol. 2, col. 410.

296. Prague Castle Archive, MS O 50, fols. 114^r–122^r, contains a collection of documents originating mainly in Zittau, Bautzen, and Leipzig that shed light on the fate of Hus's enemies.

focused on the *causa unionis* (cause of union) and dealt with Sigismund's trip to see the recalcitrant Benedict XIII in an effort to broker an abdication—therefore a good journey for unity. Part two, *via veritatis* (the way of truth), dealing with the *causa fidei*, was devoted to the argument that the Council had the power and the right to judge heresy; hence, the verdict on Hus was justified, and contumacious heretics ought to be burned—therefore a good journey to cleanse the church. Part three, *via morum vel virtutum* (the way of morals or virtue), on the *causa reformationis*, centered on the Council's efforts to eradicate abuses in the church, thereby effecting a thorough reform *in capite et in membris*.[297] One of the other important personalities in the trial of Hus was Pierre d'Ailly. He later went on record as saying the condemnation of Hus was entirely justified.[298] Elsewhere, Jean Gerson admitted as late as September 1418 that he had labored as diligently as anyone at the Council to secure the heresy conviction of Hus.[299] In other words, the main prosecutors in the Hus trial at Constance remained firm in their conviction that they had done the right thing in condemning Hus to death. A letter of the Council to the Czechs on July 26 provides a summary account of the trial. In broad outlines, the Council reported that a judicial procedure had opened against Hus when he arrived. This consisted of an examination of his writings and consideration of the testimony of pertinent witnesses; Hus had been given opportunity to reply to the several charges and to the testimony of deponents both via examinations *in camera* and publicly.[300] We have Hus's testimony in which he acknowledged that he had "many private hearings" during the last seven months of his life, and elsewhere, we learn that theologians visited Hus in prison every three days.[301] We must wonder if, in coming to Hus's cell so frequently, the delegates hoped to obtain an informal *confessio extra iudicialis*, that is to say, an out-of-court confession. We need not believe that the Augustinian friar Johannes Zachariae debated Hus in his cell, thereby earning the title "the scourge of Hus" (*Hussomastix*) and the papally bestowed Golden Rose traditionally

---

297. Glorieux, vol. 5, pp. 471–480; du Pin, vol. 2, pp. 273–280.

298. Hardt, vol. 6, p. 16.

299. *Dialogus apologeticus*, in du Pin, vol. 2, p. 387; Glorieux, vol. 6, pp. 296–304.

300. Mansi, vol. 27, cols. 781–783.

301. Novotný, *Correspondence*, p. 337; Richental, *Chronik*, p. 44.

blessed on Laetare Sunday (Lent IV).[302] Archbishop Konrad was ordered to proceed against the followers and teachings of Hus, and according to Dietrich Vrie, Bishop Jan Železný was instructed to deliver the letter.[303] Three weeks after the execution of Hus, the Council announced in its July 26 letter to the Bohemians that it had accomplished nothing more pleasing to God or more acceptable to the Christian people than the punishment of Hus.[304] The triumphal tone was appropriate in the context of medieval heresy trials. Pierre Cauchon, later bishop of Beauvais and chief justice at the trial of Joan of Arc in 1431, went to Constance in 1415 in connection with the Jean Petit matter and is reported to have declared the Hus trial "a beautiful process."[305] In late July, the Council of Constance sent reports to the Czech barons in Bohemia and Moravia, the nobility in Silesia, priests in the diocese of Prague, and civil authorities in the Old and New Towns of Prague. These letters presented a summary review of the legal process and defended the Council's position and decision against the stubbornness maintained by Hus. All addressees were urged to oppose the heretics in their domains and implement measures in concert with the king to eliminate those persisting in adhering to the cause of Hus.[306] Included in this missive was the report of the order to exhume the remains of John Wyclif.

Bishop Jan "the Iron" was appointed by the Council on August 31 as special legate to Bohemia, possessing extraordinary authority in terms of power to cite, excommunicate, issue interdict, and hold powers above any existing church constitution in terms of rooting out heresy.[307] He was referred to as an "obedient son" and a "brave and prudent athlete of Christ." The Council of Constance also advised clergy in the city and

---

302. Adolar Zumkeller, *Leben, Schrifttum und Lehrrichtung des Erfurter Universitätsprofessors Johannes Zachariae O.S.A. (†1428)* (Würzburg: Augustinus-Verlag, 1984), p. 66. Pope John XXIII conferred the Golden Rose on Sigismund in 1415. The latter, after a public procession, left it on the high altar in the cathedral. Richental, *Chronik*, pp. 42–43. There are tales of him giving it to Zachariae, who was later elected provincial of his order. Five sermons he preached at Constance are extant.

303. Hardt, vol. 2, col. 435.

304. Mansi, vol. 27, col. 783.

305. Noted in Jean Boulier, *Jean Hus* (Paris: Livre Club Diderot, 1958), p. 210. François Neveux, *L'évêque Pierre Cauchon* (Paris: Denoël, 1987), does not mention this.

306. *Documenta*, pp. 568–572, dated July 26.

307. Ibid., pp. 574–577.

diocese of Prague on September 2, 1415, of the appointment of Bishop Jan Železný as legate to exterminate heresy in Bohemia.[308] His powers were granted by the Council, and the letter concluded with the comment "the apostolic see is vacant." Bishop Jan returned to Bohemia sometime in October. The supporters of Hus were of no mind to take all of this passively. On September 2, 452 members of the Czech nobility sent a formal protest to the Council. Referring to Hus as "the venerable master of good memory," the barons asserted that Hus had not been legitimately charged with heresy, had not confessed to any crime, and moreover had not been lawfully convicted of heretical pravity.[309] The Czech nobility met again in Prague on September 5 and formulated a "Hussite League" aimed at implementing a defense of reformed religion.[310]

By autumn, the Council found it necessary to make a definitive statement on the matter of safe conducts. In a general sense, the synod ruled that any promise of immunity later judged inimical to the Christian faith or to the jurisdiction of the church generally had to be set aside. Those issuing such promises of safe conduct were not obligated to fulfill the provisions of the agreement. Referring specifically to the safe conduct issued to Hus, the Council denied that his safe conduct guaranteed by Emperor Sigismund had been illegally violated "contrary to the rules of honor and justice." Because Hus had attacked the Christian faith, he was ineligible for a safe conduct. Therefore, "according to natural, divine and human laws," there was no incumbent requirement to observe any promise made to him. To have done so would result in prejudice against the faith. The Council decreed that no one dare speak against this ruling, against Sigismund, or against the Council itself regarding Hus in this matter. Those who did so were ordered punished without exception, "as those who favor heretics" and "persons guilty of high treason."[311] This decision constituted retroactive rule making. By extension, the Council was simultaneously modifying the provisions of the official summons issued by Sigismund and the notarized apostolic brief, which declared that all would be protected and their freedom of speech and movement

---

308. Ibid., pp. 578–579.

309. Edinburgh, University Library, MS P.C.73. The text is in *Documenta*, pp. 580–584. The names of the barons are printed on pp. 584–590. The quotation is on p. 581.

310. *Documenta*, pp. 590–593.

311. Hardt, vol. 4, cols. 521–522.

guaranteed.[312] Suspected heretics such as Hus were exceptions to the rule. Other sources note anonymous opinion that had it not been for d'Ailly, no one at the Council could successfully have disputed with Hus.[313] Pierre of Versailles, a colleague of Jean Gerson and later bishop of Meaux, apparently made a comment during the autumn of 1415 at the Council that Hus could not have been convicted if he had been permitted legal counsel.[314] What are we to make of these assertions? In terms of the former, it would appear that only d'Ailly had a superior mind compared with Hus. But d'Ailly himself petulantly claimed that there was no more renowned mind in all of Christendom than Gerson's.[315] In light of the men involved at the synod, Pierre of Versailles's comment is no faint praise. In terms of the latter, we may suspect that there were some who felt a bit uneasy about the condemnation and execution of Hus no matter how technically legal it may have been. It is also possible to marshal this comment as evidence that at least in some quarters in the fifteenth century, it was thought permissible for men and women in Hus's position to be allowed legal counsel. While all of this continued to unfold at Constance, Archbishop Konrad placed Prague under interdict on November 1, 1415, in response to pressure from the Council.[316] Whatever opinions continued to be publicized concerning the trial and fate of Hus, an assembly of the deputies of the nations at the Council convened on December 19, 1415, and concurred that the condemnation of Hus had been just.[317] Months after it had been dispatched, the Council acknowledged receipt of the protest of the Czech nobility on April 6, 1416, which it regarded as a most "horrible and ridiculous spectacle."[318] Angrily, the Council cited each of the 452 Czech barons to appear. That decision was made on February 24, 1416, and notices to that effect were published the following month in

---

312. Note the guarantees in the edict of Sigismund, October 30, 1413, in Hardt, vol. 4, pp. 5–6; and Pope John's call, October 31, in *Documenta*, pp. 515–518.

313. Finke, *Acta*, vol. 2, p. 588.

314. Ibid., vol. 4, p. 352.

315. *Relatio* in FRB, vol. 8, p. 76.

316. *Hussite Chronicle*, FRB, vol. 5, pp. 341–342; Chronicle of the University of Prague, FRB, vol. 5, p. 580; *Documenta*, pp. 606–608.

317. Hardt, vol. 4, col. 556.

318. *Documenta*, p. 616.

Constance.[319] The barons did not respond. During a Council session on September 4, 1416, Michael de Causis reported that on that same date, he had cited 424 Czech nobles on account of allegedly maintaining Hussite beliefs.[320] De Causis had been commissioned to take action against these renegade Hussites. The reissued citations had no more power of persuasion compelling any baron to Constance than the first set. The matter was turned over to Patriarch John of Constantinople for action.[321] During this time, Sigismund urged the Czech nobility on March 30, 1416, not to accede to any religious innovations in their territories. Sigismund warned the barons that should they "defend the cause of Jan Hus," they should expect "all Christendom to unite in opposition to them," and this could result in a crusade against Bohemia.[322] One might say the comment was prophetic. Among the results of the legal proceedings against Hus culminating in the Council of Constance was a military initiative undertaken against his followers lasting almost two decades.[323]

The trial of Jan Hus continued to be a factor in a number of venues long after the legal proceedings and summary execution. For example, on November 7, 1416, Pierre d'Ailly gave an address to French delegates under the title "Protestacio." A marginal note includes the comment that "safe conducts need not be honored with heretics." Whether d'Ailly made this statement or the meeting affirmed the notion or the scribe thought it is unclear.[324] The bane of heresy persisted, bedeviling the efforts of the Council, and so Jean Gerson wrote his *Libellus articulorum contra Petrum de Luna*, attempting to show that Pope Benedict XIII was guilty of heresy.[325] On July 26, 1417, Fillastre announced during session 37 to the entire Council that Benedict had

---

319. Texts of the citations appear in Hardt, vol. 4, cols. 829–852.

320. Richental, *Chronik*, p. 80.

321. Václav Novotný, "Monitorium patriarchy Konstantinopolského Jana na uchvatitele církevního majetku v Čechách z r. 1418," *Věstník České Akademie věd a Umění* 24 (1915): 417–432.

322. *Documenta*, pp. 619–621.

323. Thomas A. Fudge, *The Crusade against Heretics in Bohemia, 1418–1437: Sources and Documents for the Hussite Crusades* (Aldershot, U.K.: Ashgate, 2002).

324. Text in D. A. Chart, ed., *The Register of John Swayne, Archbishop of Armagh and Primate of Ireland (1418–1439)* (Belfast: Government of Northern Ireland, 1935), fol. 37ᵛ. I cite from Aubrey Gwynn, "Ireland and the English Nation at the Council of Constance," *Proceedings of the Royal Irish Academy* 45, no. 8 (1940): pp. 232–233.

325. Glorieux, vol. 6, pp. 265–277.

been condemned as a heretic and deposed.[326] Complaints about the active continuation of the memory of Hus among his followers persisted. There are many allusions in the surviving sources, but among these we find a letter dated December 1416 from the canons of the Olomouc cathedral chapter in the province of Moravia to the Council.[327] In October 1417, we find a similar alarm raised in the work of the Carthusian abbot Štěpán of Dolany.[328] Some sources went further, claiming that Hus's admirers actually elevated him to a place among the gods or the saints.[329] By contrast, his detractors complained that those who opposed Hus were eventually hated by everyone.[330]

On November 11, 1417, the Council of Constance effectively solved the papal schism. On that day, the conclave gathered in the Merchants' Hall, the so-called Council Building, and elevated Cardinal Odo Colonna to the papacy. He had been involved in the Hus trial as far back as 1410. Colonna took the name Martin V. Three months later, on February 22, 1418, Pope Martin published the bull *Inter cunctus*, in which he concluded that Hus "of damnable memory" had caused much trouble and was condemned as a heretic by the Council of Constance, and the sentence was just.[331] The condemnation, therefore, was an official decision of an ecumenical council and was ratified by a pontiff whose election and reign were not in dispute. That same month, the Council published a list of twenty-four resolutions against the followers of Hus.[332] Among the resolutions was the command for everyone to agree that the condemnation of Hus's ideas and his person to the stake was correct. Defenders of Hus and those who promoted him were ordered punished. Having been appointed legate of the Council, the former bishop of Litomyšl Jan Železný took steps and on the basis of his February 18, 1418, "citation-charter" cited two dozen Hussite heresy suspects for examination.[333] In a letter to King Václav on

---

326. Fillastre, in Finke, *Acta*, vol. 2, pp. 129–130.

327. Loserth, "Beiträge zur Geschichte der Hussitischen Bewegung," pp. 386–391.

328. *Antihussus*, in Pez, vol. 4, cols. 520–521.

329. Hardt, vol. 6, col. 181.

330. John Peklo, letter to Prokop of Kladruby, 1414, in Prague Castle Archive, MS O 50, fol. 115ᵛ.

331. Mansi, vol. 27, cols. 1204–1215.

332. FRA, vol. 6, pp. 240–243.

333. Petr Elbel, "Husitské fary na Moravě ve světle citační listiny Jana Železného z února 1418: Příspěvek k poznání role šlechty v počátcích husitství na Moravé," *Časopis Matice*

December 4, 1418, Sigismund pledged to take action against the memory of the condemned heretic Hus and drown all Hussites.[334] That display of bravado not only failed, it failed spectacularly. Historical narratives written as late as 1458 reported that Hus rushed to the stake as though to a banquet and died more bravely than any philosopher ever did.[335] It does not seem too ambitious or injudicious to conclude that the trial of Jan Hus was a turning point in the ecclesiastical history of the medieval church. It was also a spark that ignited Bohemia, plunged the country into civil war, and unleashed a crusade against the followers of the convicted heretic.[336]

Moravské 124, no. 2 (2005): 395–428. Železný was elected bishop of Olomouc in late 1416.

334. *Documenta*, p. 684.

335. Aeneas Sylvius, *Historia bohemica*, chap. 36, p. 100.

336. For extensive treatments of the trial aftermath, see Frederick G. Heymann, *John Žižka and the Hussite Revolution* (New York: Russell & Russell, 1969); Kaminsky, HHR; František Šmahel, *Die Hussitische Revolution*, 3 vols. (Hannover: Hahnsche Buchhandlung, 2002); and Fudge, *The Crusade against Heretics*.

8

Assessing the Accusations
and Criminal Charges

IF WE FOLLOW the logic of Hostiensis, heresy technically is neither a way of life nor a system of beliefs but is a moment in a formal trial when the defendant decides either to submit and return to the authority of the church or to maintain his or her own views.[1] The accused who submitted to correction could not be considered a heretic.[2] Jan Hus did have options. He did not have to go to Constance. His presence may have been expected, desired, even demanded. He could have been formally subpoenaed. A specific arrest warrant could have been issued. Ultimately, he chose to attend the Council. Had King Václav ordered him to go to Germany, Hus could have resisted. There was sufficient popular support for him in Prague and in south Bohemia, where he spent two years in exile. Moreover, there was considerable support for him among Czech nobles, who could have shielded him successfully from the king and from inquisitors and papal agents.[3] We have the stout affirmation of Jan Chlum as confirmation. But the chance to appear on an international stage before all the sage men of Christendom proved compelling. The opportunity was a temptation too strong to resist. The Council of Constance was a final chance for Hus to obtain reconciliation with the Latin church. There was no court of appeal higher than a

---

1. Hostiensis, SA, 5, cols. 1532–1533.

2. *Glos. ord.* to X 5.7.9 and C.24 q.3 c.29 *Dixit Apostolus*, in Friedberg, vol. 1, col. 998 and its *Glos. ord.*

3. *Relatio*, pp. 81–82, based on testimony at the hearing of June 7. See also remarks in Ferdinand Seibt, "Hus in Konstanz," AHC 15 (1983): 160–161.

general council, and with the protection of the emperor, Hus had one last chance to face his adversaries, successfully argue his case, and defend himself against the weight of accusations and charges that had dogged him for several years. What he miscalculated entirely was the extreme prejudice arrayed against him, along with the nature of the venue in which he agreed to appear. Moreover, he failed to appreciate the full force of canon law and legal procedure that would unavoidably determine his fate.

The matter of Hus considered before ecclesiastical courts at the Curia and then again at the Council of Constance was a formal heresy trial following legal procedure and the provisions of canon law and legislation governing inquiries into the crime of heresy. It was a formal court case spanning five years. There are three main questions that emerge from this protracted legal ordeal and court case of the medieval church versus Jan Hus. These queries revolve around the nature of the accusations brought against Hus, the specific criminal charges lodged, and, of course, the question of whether he was guilty as charged. This chapter first summarizes the burden of the accusations and charges brought against Hus between 1408 and 1415. Then it takes into account, where extant, Hus's responses to the accusations, charges, and interrogatories. Once that has been done, it becomes possible to see patterns and specific emphases and to reduce the wide plethora of complaints to a series of categories that appear to form the nucleus of this medieval heresy trial. Once the specific categories have been identified, the last analysis will be to determine if there are grounds for sustaining any of the charges. Was Hus guilty of heresy? Were his doctrinal convictions contrary to established ideas espoused by the Latin church? Were his conviction and execution justified or a miscarriage of justice amounting to judicial murder? A careful consideration of the accusations and charges in light of canon law and legal procedure will provide plausible answers to these queries. It must be borne in mind that the widespread practice of extracting specific articles from the works of the suspect in heresy trials is fraught with problems and challenges.[4] By comparison, the facts of what happened and the facts judged at trial should not be assumed to be identical.[5]

---

4. This practice bears wider examination, but for calm admonition, see Thomas M. Izbicki, "The Sins of the Clergy in Juan de Torquemada's *Defense of the Revelations of Saint Birgitta,*" *Birgittiana* 20 (2005): 249–262, where he shows how the Basel articles misrepresent Birgitta and how Torquemada corrects the *articuli* from her own texts. The articles against Hus follow similar patterns.

5. Vallerani, p. 73.

Prior to the matter becoming a legal cause, there were accusations against Hus filed by an indeterminate number of Prague priests with Archbishop Zbyněk. These complaints were formalized either in August or September 1408.[6] Although falling outside the specific legal purview of the court case, these accusations form the beginning of charges laid against Hus, culminating at the Council of Constance. The Prague priests were concerned that Zbyněk needed to take immediate steps to "extinguish the small fire of scandalous preaching" that Hus had ignited.[7] The complaint alleged that this had precipitated "outrage" and led the laity to hate priests. The clerics warned the archbishop that should he not extinguish the fire, there was danger of conflagration. If the priests took matters into their own hands and attempted to put out the flames, there could be an inferno. Hus had been attacking other priests and stirring up the laity against the priesthood specifically and the church generally. Specific allegations were advanced. At Bethlehem Chapel on June 17, 1407, at three o'clock in the afternoon, Hus was said to have shamelessly spoken against the holy church and in opposition to the orders of the pope and to have caused "injustice, difficulty, indignity, insult, harm and outrage to all priests and common people."[8] What did Hus say? As it turns out, he condemned the charging of clerical fees for various functions, including confession, sacramental ministrations, christening, funerals, and so on. Ostensibly, Hus claimed that priests who practiced this sort of policy were heretics. Hus also lambasted the prevalent custom of simony. Additionally, he critiqued the memory of Petr Všerubý, a notorious pluralist who had recently died. The priests claimed that their late colleague was "a good Christian and faithful crusader for the faith," who did not disseminate heresy and was now defamed by the preacher Hus.[9] Finally, the aggrieved clerics urged Zbyněk that Hus was in violation of synodal statutes forbidding criticism of the priesthood in sermons. In defiance of that decree, on the feast of St. Vitus, Hus imprudently and slanderously spoke against the Prague priesthood. The incensed priests complained that such preaching caused "all priests to be hated by the people as they have never before

---

6. *Documenta*, pp. 153–155.

7. Ibid., p. 153.

8. Ibid., p. 154.

9. Petr Všerubý served in the papal chancery, had been canon at St. Vitus Cathedral in Prague and archdeacon of Horšov, and held positions in the cathedrals at Olomouc in Moravia and Vyšehrad south of Prague. He died in the spring of 1407.

been hated."[10] By consequence, this violation of a specific synodal statute by Hus caused the defamation of priests, the archbishop, and the church. Worse still, Hus apparently made positive public statements about John Wyclif, and the priests drew attention to the existence of the eucharistic heresy of remanence. In sum, these accusations complained about harsh preaching, slandering the clergy, and illicit connection to Wyclif and his condemned doctrines. These calumnies were attached to Hus.

The accusations were ineffectual. "They were weak, anonymous and clumsily formulated."[11] What did Hus have to say in response?[12] He claimed the charges were patently frivolous. He cut a swath across the broad thrust of the complaint by pointing out the imprecise language of the accusations, which led Flajšhans to characterize his rebuttal as "a model of sophisticated and sharpened legal analysis."[13] He did admit condemning "simoniacal heresy" and cited canon law in support.[14] Hus replied shrewdly that his detractors had greatly exaggerated his comments, taken them out of context, and generally advanced mendacious propositions. As for the comments about the deceased Petr Všerubý, Hus said he might be saved but doubted it. Hus turned the charge of remanentism back on his accusers by pointing out that the archbishop himself could not find any trace of heresy in the realm, and therefore allegations like these had to be either sustained or withdrawn. Thus, Hus concluded, the accusations were false and distorted and must therefore be denied. Where is the truth? In this case, it appears the priests were attempting to make much ado out of very little. The complaints suggest controversy and church politics, colored by personal jealousies and pettiness. All of this being true, Hus sometimes seemed less than forthright and willing to give evasive answers that are not untrue but provide him with a means of deflecting criticism.[15] We see this tendency at various stages in the legal proceedings, but in response to the 1408 accusations, it was much in focus. For example, Hus was accused

---

10. *Documenta*, p. 155.

11. Flajšhans, *Sebrané spisy*, vol. 1, p. 32.

12. *Documenta*, pp. 155–163; Novotný, *Correspondence*, pp. 30–41.

13. Flajšhans, *Sebrané spisy*, vol. 1, p. 32.

14. X 5.3.9 *Quum in ecclesiae*, in Friedberg, vol. 2, col. 751. Notably, Hus cited canon law thirteen times.

15. Joseph Rostislas Stejskal, *Le procès de Jean Huss: Étude historique et dogmatique* (Paris: Picart, 1923), p. 52; while Brandmüller, *Konzil*, vol. 1, p. 331, accuses Hus of theological equivocation.

of preaching controversy to a large congregation. Hus said the the charge was false, noting that he never preached to a big crowd. The main point of the accusation was thereby avoided.

These early accusations marked the beginning of an onslaught of charges brought against the Prague preacher. The next year, Jan Protiva filed another set of charges with Zbyněk.[16] There was a progression toward more serious allegations, including the tendency to bring Hus into confrontation with ecclesiastical authority. Such orientation proved ominous. The Protiva articles accused Hus of Donatism, of saying that an unworthy priest could neither consecrate the sacrament properly nor perform other priestly functions. Hus apparently claimed that Antichrist was in the church, and priests who exacted payment from the laity were heretics. His accusers used these points to argue that Hus was guilty of slander. Moreover, his preaching tended to exacerbate tensions between Czechs and Germans, and his sermons caused hearers to oppose priests and the archbishop. Since Hus ignored the ban on preaching and incited ordinary people against the priests, he was disobedient. Ostensibly, Hus took the view that the ecclesiastical censure of excommunication was frequently invalid. No one had the authority to exercise this sanction unless authorized by God. The other point of these accusations was connection with Wyclif. Such a relationship was ultimately fateful. Protiva alleged that Hus held Wyclif to be a "Catholic doctor" and a "magnificent man" and hoped that his soul ultimately might be wherever Wyclif was.[17] The accusations pointed out the rejection of the "forty-five articles" by the university in Prague and the Holy See. The Protiva charges could be reduced to continued moral ideas such as simony and priestly abuses, a continuation of concerns about Wyclifism, and, more important, issues of authority. With this strategy, Hus was positioned in the dangerous posture of challenging ecclesiastical power. This became the prerequisite for presenting Hus as a disobedient heretic. What did he have to say in reply? Essentially, he submitted plausible denial. Protiva advanced claims but lacked a preponderance of admissible evidence, thereby lacking incontrovertible proof to support the allegations of what Hus may or may not have said in some cases up to fifteen years earlier. In consequence, Hus plausibly denied the truthfulness of the claims. Hus said he preached the opposite of Donatism.

---

16. *Documenta*, pp. 164–169.

17. Ibid., pp. 167–168.

In fact, we can find definite statements to that effect, both before the rise of controversy and right at the end of his life.[18] Nevertheless, I think there are grounds for concluding that Hus should properly be considered a semi-Donatist.[19] In terms of some allegations in which a statement is alleged to have been made fifteen years earlier, when Hus was preaching in the Church of St. Michael, the defendant said the statement was false, for at that time, he was not even a priest. Hus admitted that he preached against the "crimes of priests" and vowed to continue doing so. As for proclaiming heresies before the provincial synod, Hus simply wanted to know if this were true, why did Adam, the vicar general, praise him, and why did Archbishop Zbyněk not object?[20] The rejoinder is significant. Much of these accusations were hearsay, and Hus simply denied he had said what he was accused of, alleged he had been misquoted, or claimed he had willfully or otherwise been taken out of context. Even without the medieval equivalent of statutes of limitations, the allegations floundered on evidentially weak arguments.

These charges, growing discontent with the papal schism, and increasing conflict with the royal house caused Zbyněk to send charges to the Curia in July 1410.[21] We do not have the text of these charges, but it appears the archbishop now considered Hus a heresy suspect and believed he should be cited to the Curia. This archiepiscopal initiative was impressed upon Zbyněk by Jiří Bor, who emerged as one of Hus's adversaries. Meanwhile, as seen previously, Hus had already appealed to the papal court. By 1410, a legal process commenced. After two relatively innocuous rounds of accusations, which were demonstrably ineffectual, the Prague priests submitted sworn depositions to Zbyněk in the autumn of 1410.[22] We begin to see a pattern in the case against Hus. For example, no one could be excommunicated unless by God, Hus was the inciter of insurrection, and he was the fulminator of anti-German rhetoric, and here we find allusions to the

---

18. Thus in his 1407 commentary on the sentences of Peter Lombard, Hus, *Super IV Sententiarum*, in *Mag. Jo. Hus Opera omnia: Nach neuentdeckten Handschriften*, 3 vols., ed. Václav Flajšhans (Osnabrück: Biblio-Verlag, 1966), vol. 2, p. 542; and in an interrogation during the last days of his life, *Relatio*, p. 97.

19. The point is succinctly argued in K. Hagen, "Hus' 'Donatism,'" *Augustinianum* 11 (1971): 541–547.

20. *Documenta*, p. 167.

21. FRB, vol. 5, p. 571; *Knížky proti knězi kuchmistrovi* in Hus, *Opera omnia*, vol. 4, p. 321.

22. *Documenta*, pp. 174–185.

controversial decree of Kutná Hora and politics leading to it, in which Hus was a key player. There were persistent connections to Wyclif, whom Hus was charged with regarding as a catholic teacher, wishing his soul to be with Wyclif and now ostensibly defending all "forty-five articles" on the assumption that they were correct, with one exception only pertaining to the body of Christ. These sworn depositions charged Hus with serious offenses, which included preaching Wyclifite heresies from the latter's books and defending Wyclif openly. There were further charges about the unworthiness of many priests, and Donatist allegations continued. There were traces of eucharistic heresy and more charges about danger-ous preaching, with witnesses claiming that Hus instructed people to obey God but not necessarily human authorities. New charges arose. Hus was accused of saying that Pope Alexander was Antichrist, and Pope Boniface was defamed by Hus, who considered him heretical.[23] Worse still, Hus claimed that a woman without mortal sin was more worthy than a pope. This led to the most serious charge of all: Hus considered the papacy unnecessary, claiming that redemption could be obtained without papal mediation. What did Hus have to say to these charges? Unlike the other lists, this one seems to have angered Hus. Since these articles were sworn depositions, Hus knew who had laid the specific charges. His responses made clear that he considered the testimonies problematic. He wrote replies to several charges for three reasons: "First, so people will not think I have taught like this or adhered to this, as these mendaciously testify, adding something or taking something away. Second, so that liars become blatant. Third, so people will know my faith on these matters."[24] At least sixteen times in his responses, Hus wrote "he lies" or similar words. The tone of Hus's rejoinders was one of indignation and general denial.

In March 1412, the next round of accusations was filed against Hus in the papal court.[25] This initiative was the work of one of Hus's most deadly opponents: "The articulation of Michael de Causis prosecutor of the case against Master Jan Hus at the Roman court." The allegations were variations on themes already advanced, but new emphases and con-cerns emerged about the case involving Hus. Nominating June 1411 as an example, de Causis said that Hus defended Wyclif and preached Wyclifite

---

23. Ibid., pp. 176, 183.

24. Ibid., p. 174.

25. Ibid., pp. 169–174.

heresy. By extension, eucharistic heresy was charged, with the elaboration that the bread remained unchanged after consecration. Sinful priests
could not consecrate. Indulgences were useless. De Causis alleged that
Hus called the pope Antichrist and denounced the Curia as belonging to
Satan. No one except those in mortal sin should be excommunicated, and
Hus claimed that his own anathema did him no harm. By defying apostolic orders, Hus showed himself specifically disobedient, and through
his sermons, he promoted general disobedience. De Causis claimed that
in preaching at Bethlehem Chapel, Hus incited people to rise up against
spiritual authority, going so far as to suggest that secular people might
divest the priesthood of property and wealth. These articles concluded that
Hus was a heretic who publicly and privately proclaimed heresies. We have
Hus's responses to these charges. He rather pointedly said that de Causis
was a liar no fewer than twelve times.[26] On the inflammatory accusations
of calling the papacy Antichrist and the Curia a "synagogue of Satan," it
is best to hear the rejoinders in Hus's own words: "I did not say this, but
I said 'if the pope is selling a prebend, if he is proud, greedy and contrary
to Christ in any other way, then he is Antichrist.' But God forbid! This
does not mean every pope is Antichrist." Moreover, with respect to the
Curia, Hus wrote, "if there are people who are pushy, greedy and haughty,
as St. Bernard says in his book to Eugenius, then it is true but this does
not mean everybody who is at the Roman Curia is wicked."[27] Technically,
the nuances were important, but the qualifications included by Hus were
subtly changed, and the inflammatory allegations indicated advantageous
points scored by the prosecution. The ecclesiastical hierarchy became
concerned over allegations that Hus was advancing arguments aimed at
encouraging the laity to take church property from priests. Hus admitted this was true, but his rejoinder placed an entirely different nuance
on the matter. Once again, his own words are instructive: "I said when
priests do not wish to live properly, but quite obviously live incorrectly
such as keeping public concubines, playing dice and when admonished by
their patron or parishioners do not wish to amend their ways then, if after
being accused at the diocese, they will not improve their lives, then tithes
may be withheld so they might improve their lives. But should they not
improve themselves, let the poor be given [the tithes] and may the declared

---

26. Ibid., pp. 170–171.

27. Ibid., p. 170.

enemies of our Lord Jesus Christ not be fed."[28] The reference to action at the diocesan level indicated a concern for due process, thus mitigating an interpretation of Hus fomenting revolt. The prosecution did not file an amended complaint or offer a rebuttal.

Admittedly, there was some obfuscation when Hus corrected de Causis by saying his parishioners at Bethlehem Chapel did not shout, in reference to the pope, "he lies," but they shouted "they lie" with reference to Prague prelates. Hus denied creating tension in Prague. He denied conflict between university masters and students on account of his preaching. He denied inciting people or creating outrage, "unless this has happened by chance," and any troubles that existed did so only because there were those refusing to accept the teaching of Christ. Here Hus appeared to hedge, wishing to excuse himself from any unintended consequences of his sermons or teaching. On the matter of heresy, Hus did not mince words: "Here the manufacturer of lies hoards and pours out many lies, but his own injustice deceives him. By the grace of God, I have never been the friend, pursuer or defender of heresies and I was not publicly considered a heretic long ago by all orthodox believers from our countries. Even many believers if they could hear what this liar Michael wrote, would say he is lying." The list of charges was dismissed by Hus as "mendacious" and manifest "lies for which Michael will be judged by the most just judge."[29]

By 1412, controversy over indulgences created more tension, and when Hus took the minority position, it gave his enemies opportunity to file another complaint. Accusations were lodged by theologians of the university, and behind these allegations we can reasonably find Štěpán Páleč, who had broken with Hus and the reform movement and now began to defend traditional church structures and teachings. The charges were filed with King Václav in June 1412.[30] In addition to despising the sale of indulgences, the allegations suggested that the preacher of Bethlehem Chapel was encouraging rebellion and advocating disobedience. Indeed, the charges alleged that Hus claimed that one need not obey the pope. Hus took no note of these complaints, and indeed, they did not represent anything new. He had already answered those accusations. Later that year, however, acting on behalf of the litigious Prague priests, de Causis

---

28. Ibid., pp. 170–171.

29. Ibid., pp. 173–174.

30. Ibid., pp. 448–450.

lodged a series of accusations with Pope John XXIII.[31] There were five themes enumerated in these accusations. First, allegations about Wyclif continued. Hus was charged with defending and promoting the heresies of Wyclif. Second, there was the matter of disobedience, mentioned in this context especially in that Hus took no note of the papal bull three years earlier. Third was the eucharistic charge that Hus held to the doctrine that consecration changed nothing in the substance of the elements. Fourth, Hus despised the keys. And fifth, Hus was responsible for the dissemination of heresy, having seduced many people into error with discernible social and political implications wherein people were grievously oppressed and in some cases actually killed. We have no record that Hus replied to these charges. At this stage, the legal case before the Curia came to a halt, and the trial was effectively suspended for two years until the Council of Constance convened. This also meant a cessation of accusations and charges against Hus, chiefly because he had been excommunicated, the aggravation of that censure had been proclaimed in Prague, interdict had been threatened, and Hus had been exiled to south Bohemia.

With the coming of the Council, new accusations and charges were filed. For Hus, the battlefield shifted from Prague and the papal Curia to the shores of the Bodensee. Here the controversies came into sharper focus. On September 24, 1414, we find a series of articles compiled by Jean Gerson, submitted to Archbishop Konrad, and delivered to the Council of Constance in February of the following year.[32] The accusations were less about dogma than implications for ecclesiastical authority. The most serious charge Gerson advanced, enumerated in at least seven articles, was Hus's claim that legitimate authority depended on the moral purity of the incumbent. Five of the accusations centered on issues of antipapalism. Once again, we see Hus accused of inciting rebellion to the extent that he encouraged the laity to critique the vices of their superiors. Connected to this, we also find a familiar theme that Hus advocated withholding monies. Hus allowed that tithes and temporal profits might be withheld from wicked priests. This was a charge he had already responded to. Gerson found it reprehensible that Hus asserted there was no such thing as unauthorized preaching and an official license was not necessary for those under holy orders. On the matter of excommunication, Hus was

31. Ibid., pp. 457–461.

32. Ibid., pp. 185–188.

represented as saying that papal excommunications might be appealed to Christ. Interestingly, we find the charge that Hus opposed capital punishment, maintaining that heretics should not be burned. Hus did not reply to these charges, all of which appear to have been extracted from his book *De ecclesia*. We do know he considered the charges filed by Gerson scurrilous and insufferable. "O, if God would give me the time to write against the lies of the chancellor of Paris, who so thoughtlessly and unjustly in the presence of such a multitude was unashamed to note errors against a neighbor. Perhaps God will prevent my writing by his death and all the better that it is decided in the trial more favorably than I could write."[33] The rest of the accusations and charges lodged against Hus were filed after the Council commenced and Hus had been arrested and remanded to prison to await the outcome of the legal proceedings.

The next series of charges came from the pen of the redoubtable Michael de Causis. Late in 1414, de Causis presented a series of charges at Constance with Pope John XXIII.[34] These charges ran the gamut from doctrinal irregularity to accusations of inciting rebellion to holding manifest heresies. In terms of the Eucharist, de Causis claims Hus favored utraquism and openly preached that the sacrament should be administered in both kinds to the faithful.[35] De Causis went on to say that the truthfulness of this charge was evident by virtue of the fact that "at this very moment," his disciples in Prague were doing this (article 1). "His disciples practice this in Prague when the holy communion is denied them, they seize the eucharist from the private chapel and communicate themselves" (article 2). From an ecclesiological standpoint, de Causis pointed out, Hus did not define the church according to its hierarchy (article 3). This suggested a lack of esteem on Hus's part for the papacy and the Curia. Wicked priests could not properly consecrate. However, de Causis claimed Hus thought it acceptable for any layperson to administer the sacrament. The church should not have temporal possessions, and in consequence, secular authorities should be allowed to divest the church of its possessions. Because of persistent sin, the church could not exercise power and authority, and therefore, the function of the keys was very much in doubt (article 5). In terms of excommunication, Hus consistently ignored it and

---

33. Novotný, *Correspondence*, p. 256.

34. *Documenta*, pp. 194–199.

35. Ibid., p. 194.

moreover continued to say Mass while expressly forbidden to do so. De Causis pointed out that Hus said Mass all the way between Prague and Constance (article 6). This became an authority issue, and once again, Hus was posited as an antiauthority personality. De Causis alleged that Hus claimed neither papal nor episcopal permission was required for appointments for the cure of souls (article 7). In terms of preaching, anyone ordained could preach and could not legitimately be restrained from doing so (article 8). Beyond this, Hus stirred up secular authorities against the church and said that tithes and offerings could be withheld. All of this indicated that one of the principal problems was Hus's disobedience. He had violated the orders of his ordinary, and de Causis claimed this could be proven by records in the apostolic see and the curial court. Alarmingly, these charges alleged that all who spoke against Hus were disadvantaged. This implied that the dissemination of heresy in Prague had become so pervasive that heretics like Hus could act with impunity. Beyond this, not only did Hus defend the outlawed and forbidden "forty-five articles," but he had also become political and deeply implicated in the events and policies leading to the decree of Kutná Hora, which inflamed racial tensions and caused a massive split within the university. Because of the unchecked activities of Hus, de Causis insisted, the entire kingdom of Bohemia was suffering. Moreover, there remained a clear and present danger that those disturbances would sweep over the German territories. Somewhat hyperbolically, de Causis suggested that the persecution of faithful Christians had no comparable parallel anywhere in the millennium preceding the advent of Hus. Not since the fourth century had a heretic done more harm to the church and the Christian faith. Hus was presented as the scion of all Christian heretics. Those offenders were qualitatively similar but quantitatively different. Hus was characterized as the worst. De Causis stated explicitly in his list of charges that "Jan Hus is dressed in the garments of a sheep but inside he is a ravenous wolf."[36]

At the same time Michael de Causis was lodging articles against Hus, the promotors of the Council of Constance were issuing their own charges.[37] These can be summarized chiefly under two main headings: Wyclifism

---

36. *Documenta*, p. 196.

37. Ibid., pp. 199–204. Promotors presented explicit requests for an inquiry against an individual pursuant to a specific crime. Vallerani, pp. 49–51, 199–200. A *promovens* functioned like a modern prosecutor in terms of drawing up charges, presenting evidence, and arguing for punishment.

and disobedience. The conciliar promotors claimed that Hus followed and taught the ideas of Wyclif, noting that he opposed the condemnation of Wyclif at Rome in 1413 and the burning of his books. In terms of disobedience, we find the reiterated charge that Hus appeared to take no note of papal bulls, had been excommunicated for contumacy, had been formally censured for nonappearance when summoned to appear in court, had ignored the *citatio*, and had refused to be in submission to his ordinary and church authorities. Hus was truculent and intractable. These constituted serious charges.

The dust had hardly settled from these two nearly concurrent rounds of accusation when Hus was served with formal charges in his prison cell. These consisted of one or both of the accusations lodged by de Causis and the promotors of the Council. Hus's replies are not among the surviving *Acta* of the legal case. Then Hus received a series of forty-two articles drawn up by Štěpán Páleč, who had submitted them to the Council of Constance around the same time as the previous two sets of accusations arrived.[38] Hus's ecclesiology came under renewed attack for claiming the church was defined by and made up of all the predestined. Those who were elected could never be lost. Hus was accused of calling for the divesting of church wealth and property. Since Christ and the apostles had nothing, their followers should also embrace poverty. Sin had impaired the proper function of the power of the keys. Popes who did not follow Christ need not be feared. The legitimacy of office came from Christ. Therefore, popes who were not of Christ were Antichrist. Hus was accused of inappropriately glossing a papal bull. The prohibitions against preaching were noted, and Hus was once more accused of saying that bans need not be obeyed. He was once more characterized as a dangerous and subversive presence, inciting rebellion by declaring that people should actively question papal directives. While it was obligatory to obey Christ, it was not necessarily binding for anyone to obey one's superiors. Mention was made of Hus's opposition to the papal crusade and the sale of indulgences. The forty-two articles alleged that Hus could not be trusted, for he told friends before leaving Prague that should he be induced to recant his positions, the retraction would not be sincere. Accusations of heresy and contumacy appeared once again, and Hus was represented as continuing in error and refusing all efforts at correction. Definite patterns had emerged. What was unique in this set of accusations was a methodological innovation. Páleč

---

38. *Documenta*, pp. 204–224.

did not construct charges from hearsay, as the Prague priests did in 1408 and 1409, nor did he depend on second- and third-hand evidence about something Hus may have said in a sermon, as de Causis did in 1412. Páleč was the first of the Czech antagonists to follow the example of Jean Gerson and draw up articles of accusation based on Hus's own written and public statements. All that was necessary was for Hus to admit that the books in question were his. The rest was interpretation.

We have answers by Hus to these charges, many of which had been drawn from his controversial book on the church. In many cases, Hus simply denied the veracity of the charges and repeatedly pointed out that they had been inaccurately cited or taken out of their original context. Often, Hus replied, "this statement is not in my book" as given and then proceeded to correct the insinuation by quoting the relevant passage. In other places, Hus made no more reply other than dismissing the accusation, saying, "this statement is not in my writing." At other junctures in response to a charge, Hus admitted it was accurate. For example, in article 23 addressing the papal ban on preaching, Hus did not deny his position as stated but ended his reply by asserting, "it is also possible to preach against the papal ban during an appeal."[39] Similarly, he replied to article 26, which accused him of saying it was improper to call the pope "holy father" if that pope acted wickedly, by saying, "I do not just deny this but I approve it."[40] Hus went further in claiming that malice underlay many of the accusations. He had already reported this to authorities. "But some enemy has fabricated it, now adding some, now taking away and now falsely attributing to me entire propositions which are not mentioned in this book. When I discovered the deceitful cunning of some articles, I showed them to the masters and commissioners how they contradicted the book which they submitted and they said to me 'your enemies have done this.' I then asked at once before a notary that they might punish my adversaries for cunningly attributing these errors and false articles to me and my book."[41] That complaint and call for redress went unfulfilled.

By June, the public hearings in the Hus case convened, and during the third of these sessions, on June 8, a series of thirty-nine articles were

---

39. Ibid., pp. 212–213.

40. Ibid., pp. 213–214.

41. Ibid., p. 221.

presented.[42] These were drawn from Hus's books on the church and two polemical writings directed in turn at his former colleagues Štěpán Páleč and the late Stanislav of Znojmo, who had expired at Jindřichův Hradec in southern Bohemia during the journey to Constance.[43] Hus's doctrine of the church once more came under attack. Predestination as the criterion for the definition of the church was nominated, along with the view that the church was better administered by Christ and the apostles and that none of the elect could be lost. There were implications for ecclesiastical authority. In terms of headship, Hus was accused of saying that Peter was never head of the church and that cardinals were not the true successors of the apostles if they failed to imitate the apostolic life. On the papacy, Hus was charged with saying that the one who followed Christ was the true vicar of Christ. The one who did not imitate the life, ethics, and teachings of Christ was by consequence Antichrist. Popes who were not ordained of God were not truly the head of the church. Moreover, sin invalidated popes, bishops, and prelates. Those who fell into wickedness and persisted therein, including popes, were not heads but devils and thieves. Further accusations included the repeated idea that popes should not be called holy simply as a matter of course, implying that popes were not necessarily holy. The priesthood was invalidated by simony and immorality. By contrast, Jean Gerson said the former offense was not heretical and preferred to minimize it by calling it the "simonian slip," as though it were an error of omission or an inadvertent mistake.[44] This attitude contrasts rather sharply with the twelfth-century canonist Simon of Bisignano, who thought that simony should be punished by death.[45] Hus agreed with neither perspective. Secular authorities had the responsibility to force church leaders to adhere to the law of Christ. Moving to the subject of obedience, Hus was charged with affirming that compelled obedience was illegitimate without scriptural basis. Therefore, the laity could disobey. Indeed, certain forms of coercive obedience were wrong and self-serving. In terms of censure, excommunication could be appealed to Christ and thereafter

---

42. Ibid., pp. 285–315; *Relatio*, pp. 83–102.

43. *De ecclesia; Contra Palecz*, in Hus, *Opera omnia*, vol. 22, pp. 233–269; *Contra Stanislaum*, in Hus, *Opera omnia*, vol. 22, pp. 271–367.

44. *De simonia*, in Glorieux, vol. 6, pp. 169–173, written at the Council of Constance.

45. Noted in Edward Peters, "*Crimen exceptum*: The History of an Idea," in *Proceedings of the Tenth International Congress on Medieval Canon Law*, ed. Kenneth Pennington, Stanley Chodorow, and Keith H. Kendall (Vatican City: Bibliotheca Apostolica Vaticana, 2001), p. 161.

had no effect. Preachers should take no heed to strictures of excommunication or bans, and interdict should not be applied. John Wyclif made an almost obligatory appearance, and Hus was accused of concluding that the condemnation of the "forty-five articles" was unreasonable. Once again, we find Hus charged with saying heretics should not be executed. These charges and accusations marked the first and only time Hus replied to his detractors in a formal and public setting. We will now look briefly at the answers Hus made to these charges.

Petr Mladoňovice pointed out in his account of the hearing that "a certain person" compared the list of accusations against the three books in question and determined that few of them coincided with what Hus actually said.[46] Many of Hus's replies were similar to his written responses. He attempted to correct and explain errors and misrepresentations. The downside of this tactic was that on occasion, the excerpt cited from the source in question caused Pierre d'Ailly, who was chairing the hearing, to remark that the corrected citation was even more erroneous and therefore even more dangerous than the version supplied in the charges.[47] Of particular importance was a crucial distinction Hus drew during the interrogation between the power invested in the priesthood and the power of jurisdiction. Hus argued that no priest or prelate truly represented Christ unless he followed him morally. It was this moral replication that allowed prelates to exercise legitimate and representative power of jurisdiction. The only ones qualified to exercise such power were those who exemplified a superior level of morality and had legal permission to do so. Popes were not the successors of Peter when they lived contrary to apostolic ideals.[48] Indeed, only the one who lived and taught properly in accordance with the law of God had the right to the *cathedra* of Moses and Peter.[49] Hus's replies to the accusations of disobedience were particularly noted by the Council, and in one instance, Cardinal Zabarella specifically instructed

---

46. *Relatio*, p. 83. Scholars generally believe this was Petr himself. Spinka, *Constance*, p. 182; Jan Sedlák, "Proces Kostnický," ST, vol. 2, no. 1 (1915), pp. 14–15. There were reasons for withholding the identity of the person in question. Other defenders of Hus, such as Křišťan of Prachatice and Nicholas Nezero, encountered grave personal danger as a result.

47. *Relatio*, pp. 83, 89, 91, 94, 99.

48. His formal reply was written in response to the final thirty articles. *Documenta*, pp. 226–227.

49. *De ecclesia*, pp. 157–173.

a notary to record Hus's words.[50] It is instructive to note Hus's answer to the charge of trivializing excommunication, in which he declared, "I will call a pretended excommunication, unjust and irregular, ordered contrary to the law of God and against the rule of law."[51] Much of the exchanges amounted to differences of interpretation in addition to the serious differences between the defendant and the court on issues of law, morals, and philosophical assumptions and the lack of agreement on matters of obedience. A Thuringian monk dressed in black advised the court that Hus was endeavoring to deceive the judges with explanations amounting to obfuscation. This anonymous religious also took credit, claiming that Hus had benefited from rejoinders made by the monk at a previous hearing.[52] Cambridge University master John Stokes weighed in, accusing Hus of simply parroting Wyclif and thereby demonstrating himself to be a disciple of the condemned heretic.[53] The point of these charges and accusations was to prove disobedience, and if Hus refused to submit to the Council, he could be adjudicated contumacious; this, together with connections to Wyclif, more than sufficed for sustaining charges of heresy. The work of the prosecutors was simplified. The hearings provided the court with an opportunity to evaluate Hus's words, how he expressed them, the sense of his responses, and his actions in doing so, and all of this confirmed to the judges the evidence they sought in assessing the central charge of heresy.[54]

The final charges against Hus, thirty in all, brought by the Council of Constance were filed on June 18, 1415.[55] These did not diverge greatly from previous accusations, but their formulation represented the apex of the legal process. There were several categories. Hus's doctrine of the church predominated. Articles 1, 3, 7, 9, 10, 11, 13, 21, 26, 27, 28, and 29 are ecclesiological in nature. The several points had already been arrayed against the defendant, some of them on many occasions. The church was defined by the predestined, none of the elect was ever lost, Peter was not the head of the church, popes were either ordained of God or they were

---

50. *Relatio*, p. 92.

51. Ibid., p. 93.

52. Ibid., p. 97.

53. Ibid., p. 102.

54. Noted by Provvidente, pp. 111–112.

55. *Documenta*, pp. 225–234.

not true popes, lifestyle legitimized authority claims, wicked popes were frauds, the papacy was not necessary and certainly not for salvation, and the church was run better by the apostles. Hus had said quite definitely that there was a difference between the Roman church and the body of Christ. "I will not say, however, the city of Rome is the Apostolic See and is necessary in order that without it the church of Jesus Christ could not stand. For if by chance Rome was destroyed like Sodom, Rome the Christian church would still remain."[56] Articles of concern surrounding Hus's insistence on morality can be located in articles 8, 12, 16, 19, 22, 23, 24, and 30. Once more, all of these were either variations of themes encountered previously or were unmodified from previous charges. Priests who lived improperly defiled the church, morals were essential, and popes should not automatically be called holy on account of their title. In terms of obedience, which turned up specifically in articles 14, 15, 17, and 18, Hus was characterized again as saying that these requirements were often contrived and self-serving. For example, no one should adhere to calls to cease preaching. Article 25 noted that Hus considered the condemnation of the "forty-five articles" unjust. Excommunication and church censures were often political and counterproductive. No secular or spiritual power was legitimate if the incumbent was in mortal sin, and the death penalty in matters of heresy was inappropriate. Hus wrote answers to these charges but noted that he was unable to do so as completely as he wished, on account of insufficient time, a shortage of paper, and unspecified danger.[57] The final comment is curious. There is no need to evaluate his responses, because they mirrored what he had said already both verbally at the third public hearing ten days earlier and in prior writings. Indeed, his replies were generally limited to adding a word or a phrase to bring nuance to the actual wording of the specific charge. Occasionally, he advanced an authority such as Augustine to support his point of view, thereby informing the court that the expressed idea was really not his at all but had been taken from Augustine, Gregory, Isidore, or another recognized source. On several of the charges, Hus elected not to offer any modification or explanation at all.[58] Therefore, it is not accurate to say that Hus declared all thirty articles without exception

---

56. *De ecclesia*, pp. 172–173.

57. Novotný, *Correspondence*, p. 279.

58. *Documenta*, pp. 227, 229.

to be erroneously formulated.[59] All of the articles from the trial proceedings had now been addressed.[60]

At the final session of the trial of Jan Hus, there were a total of four miscellaneous and ad hoc accusations advanced at the climax of the legal proceedings, on July 6, 1415.[61] Two of these had been heard before, although they were not included in the final charges. These included a return to accusations of eucharistic irregularity, with Hus ostensibly claiming that following consecration the bread remained in the sacrament. This was a final parting shot attempting to link Hus to the Wyclifite doctrine of remanence. It is curious that no allegation of eucharistic deviance was attached to Hus in the final charges. Despite the insistence of Michael de Causis and others, perhaps the Hus commission recognized the impossibility of sustaining a charge of sacramental heresy. Moreover, eucharistic irregularity was unnecessary for securing a verdict finding Hus guilty of heresy. The other outstanding allegation was Hus's position that priests in mortal sin could not adequately perform sacramental duties. Hus strongly denied allegations about the Eucharist. Petr Mladoňovice noted that Hus responded to other charges in the same manner as he had done previously in writing.[62] Two other accusations were also leveled. The first was heresy in that Hus claimed to be the fourth person of the Trinity. This charge of blasphemy seems to have upset Hus, and his emotional response asserted a strict and orthodox conception of trinitarian theology, with adamant denials that the curious thought had ever entered his mind. He demanded to know the identity of the "certain doctor" who had lodged the accusation, but the request was overruled by Berthold Wildungen, the papal auditor reading the charges. The other charge centered on contumacy, with reference to the excommunication sentence he had ignored. The charge implied that Hus was obstinate in error and heresy, obdurate in wickedness, and contumacious in heresy. Predictably, Hus denied the charge, entering a plea of innocence.

A summary of all accusations and charges against Hus appeared in the definitive sentence handed down by the judiciary, which must be taken

---

59. Matthew Spinka, "Hus' Trial at the Council of Constance," in *Czechoslovakia Past and Present*, ed. Miloslav Rechcigl (The Hague: Mouton, 1968), vol. 2, p. 1216.

60. Novotný, *Correspondence*, p. 280.

61. *Relatio*, pp. 114–116.

62. Ibid., p. 114.

as the *sententia* or the judgment of the court. This was read by Anthony, bishop of Concordia, papal auditor, and prelate, who had been selected to perform this task.[63] The first part of the summary focused on Wyclif and identified Hus as his follower: "This certain Jan Hus…is a disciple not of Christ but instead of the heresiarch John Wyclif." The language that characterizes the sentence was revealing. "With such rash daring," Hus set himself in opposition to the church, its decisions, and its authority. Rather than submitting to his ordinary, the papal court, and the hierarchy of the church, Hus chose a course of "public resistance." In defiance of directives from his superiors, Hus "asserted and publically declared" opinions in opposition to the authority of the church. When confronted, he did not yield but rather persisted in teaching what was "erroneous, scandalous, offensive to the ears of the pious, rash and seditious and notoriously heretical." Moreover, he had done this for many years. Indeed, "the said John Hus, for a long time has publicly taught many manifest errors and heresies long since damned and condemned, and many scandalous things, offensive to pious ears, rash and seditious," causing considerable damage to the church. Over many years, Hus had persisted with a "hardened mind." Flaunting due process, Hus had attempted to contravene canon law and proper legal procedure by his "excessive stubbornness" in directing an appeal to Jesus Christ, a nonexistent judicial authority.[64] All considered, the definitive sentence concluded that Hus was "obstinate and incorrigible," had no desire or intention of returning to proper obedience or fellowship with the church, and remained unwilling to recant his errors and cease and desist from publicly teaching them. Certainly, there were grave concerns about dogmatic deviation and association with condemned persons and doctrines. But of equal concern to the court was the fact that Hus appeared stubbornly committed to his point of view, unwilling to submit to external authorities. Canon law categorized this problem as contumacy.

Sustaining these accusations and charges was quite different from alleging them and lodging formal complaints with the several relevant authorities. Of course, hypothetically, being arraigned on fifty-seven counts of heresy required a finding of guilt on one count only in order to secure a conviction and a verdict upholding the initial charge. Many

---

63. Ibid., p. 115, with the text in FRB, vol. 8, pp. 501–503.

64. "Jan Hus sám o sobě," in Kejř, *Počátkŭ*, p. 35.

of the accusations were founded mainly on hearsay evidence, which may
or may not have been admissible in a medieval court of law and, even if
admissible, were not necessarily charges that could be sustained with the
necessary gravity leading to conviction. Combing the several thousands of
pages Hus wrote over the course of his lifetime does reveal that some of
the charges could have been sustained and proven beyond a modicum of
reasonable doubt. In other cases, Hus had written what was alleged, but
there remained the question of exactly what he meant, whether he had
been taken out of context, whether he had written with the intent later
alleged by his detractors. Some charges, such as the allegation that Hus
considered himself the fourth member of the Trinity, were so specious that
a reply was unnecessary. Others were questions of theological subtlety,
philosophical hairsplitting, and linguistic nuance. Canon lawyers, theologians, and specialists of the scholastic method might pore over these texts
for some time without necessarily reaching consensus. By the fifteenth
century, heresy was not so narrowly or technically defined. A means of
more fully understanding the heresy charges against Hus may be attained
by accepting that the Council understood Hus as posing a threat to the
plenitudo potestas assumed by the synod, which was considered scandalous. As representative of the universal church, the Council required obedience.[65] Unanimity on this point was as important as being doctrinally
sound.

In the more than a dozen *libelli* of accusations and charges brought
against Hus, six recurring themes emerged. These included protests and
concerns about emphases on moral issues, disobedience, ecclesiology,
connections to John Wyclif, eucharistic irregularities, and contumacy.
Accusations about morals were included in at least eleven of the fourteen lists. Disobedience appeared in thirteen of the cycles, questions about
ecclesiology turned up in twelve lists, Wyclif was represented in eleven of
the cycles (implied in others), the Eucharist was cited in six, and contumacy
was present or implied in every one of the fourteen lists. This is a telling
factor. In terms of morality, Hus was accused of "scandalous preaching,"
attacks on vices inherent in the priesthood, suspicions of Donatism, and
assumptions that wicked priests could not pronounce absolution or properly consecrate the sacraments. This concern with sin led Hus to call into
question the proper administration of the keys, which went to the heart of
ecclesiastical power and authority. Moreover, Hus evidently concluded that

---

65. Provvidente, pp. 125–126, 138.

sinful priests and superiors need not be obeyed, with the extended implication that persistent sinfulness invalidated authority claims and that this
could be applied to both secular and spiritual power. On the matter of
disobedience, Hus was accused of stirring up the laity against the church
and its representatives, especially those considered wicked or defective.
Hus openly violated papal bulls and synodal statutes, continued to preach
when effectively ordered to cease, ignored writs and proclamations of
excommunication, took the view that many anathemas were illegitimate,
defied apostolic orders, considered a preaching license unnecessary for
those under holy orders, said Mass while under strict ecclesiastical censure, openly opposed the condemnation of Wyclif at least as summarized
in the "forty-five articles," refused to appear in court when summoned,
and evidently held the view that many calls for obedience were self-serving
and illegitimate and need not be acknowledged or obeyed.

Turning to Hus's understanding of the church, we find accusations that
he thought the papacy was not essential, the institutional church could
be equated with Antichrist and the Curia with Satan, and indulgences
were ineffectual. We find accusations of Hus criticizing church authority,
refusing to define the church according to its hierarchy, advocating the
divesting of church property and wealth, advancing ideas that the church
was made up of the predestined, concluding that one had no particular
obligation to obey the orders of priests and popes who were living or acting contrary to Christ, and holding the thematic conviction that Christ
and the apostles were more appropriate to spirituality and the practice of
the faith than the current administration. Accusations of Wyclifism or a
connection to Wyclif were implied in some of the foregoing but were specifically enumerated in the eucharistic doctrine of remanence, a defense
of the condemned "forty-five articles," and general charges that Hus persisted in teaching Wyclifite doctrine even though it had been outlawed
and condemned by the church at the local, provincial, and papal levels.
In terms of the Eucharist, we chiefly find accusations that Hus adhered
to remanence, advocated utraquism, and questioned the validity of the
sacrament when consecrated by an unworthy priest. Michael de Causis
pressed these eucharistic allegations, but it is unclear according to his
accusers if Hus proclaimed these openly or merely entertained them in
his heart.[66] It is exceedingly problematic to allege the latter. Additionally,

---

66. Paul de Vooght, *Hussiana* (Louvain: Publications Universitaires de Louvain, 1960),
pp. 272–273.

there were specific allegations that Hus taught that bread and wine were unchanged after consecration. Finally, contumacy as a legal category was enumerated in terms of persistent disobedience, failure to appear at the papal court when ordered, a general refusal to be corrected or to accept the instruction and direction of his superiors, and the implications stemming from his appeal to Christ, while terms such as *obstinate* and *obdurate* were frequently used to characterize the defendant.

Considering these six categories more closely, morality drops out as a separate consideration inasmuch as it can be subsumed largely under issues of disobedience and perhaps ecclesiology. For example, one could hardly object in principle to efforts at bringing the church into more alignment with the example of Christ and the apostles. Of course, in practice there were objections. It was not the impulse for purifying the church that created problems. Instead, disagreement occurred when such reforms were advanced to extremes, pressed zealously and persistently. One might even say that moral reformers tended to exaggerate things such as clerical immorality.[67] One could argue that in order to understand many of the accusations against Hus, it is necessary to recognize the tremendous gulf between the essential purity and simplicity of Hus and the depravity of some priests, which caused such friction that the controversies that arose could only be alleviated with the destruction of the prophet who refused to retreat from his program of reform and insistence on an ethically and morally blameless priesthood.[68] However, Hus insisted on this even when it meant disobeying orders not to attack the priesthood. Moreover, the castigation of sinful priests and wicked popes sometimes resulted in Hus concluding that they were unnecessary and a detriment to the gospel and the true church. By this stage, the matter was no longer one concerned with morals but one of obedience and associated ideas in Hus's doctrine of the church. Disobedience and contumacy were obviously related. Wyclifism and alleged eucharistic irregularities were also synonyms. In any event, charges of remanentism could not be sustained, and speculations concerning what Hus might have thought about could not technically be adjudicated, were

---

67. Sedlák, *M. Jan Hus*, pp. 2, 15, 17.

68. Flajšhans, *Sebrané spisy*, vol. 1, p. 27; and the findings of an archiepiscopal visitation in the Bohemian province. Ivan Hlaváček and Zdeňka Hledíková, eds., *Protocollum visitationis archidiaconatus Pragensis annis 1379–1382 per Paulum de Janowicz archidiaconum Pragensem, factae* (Prague: Academia, 1973), with a summary of some aspects in Fudge, *Jan Hus*, pp. 23–24.

inadmissible, and furthermore were legally irrelevant.[69] This leaves the general accusations and charges against Hus reduced to three principle areas: contumacy, ecclesiology, and Wyclifism. The question remains: where did Hus stand on these accusations and criminal charges?

The first is essentially a legal category. Strictly defined, Hus had to be adjudicated guilty as charged. The force of canon law allowed for no other interpretation. Moreover, there was both considerable circumstantial evidence to support the accusation and unimpeachable cause proving the charge beyond reasonable doubt. Ecclesiastical disobedience constituted heresy, and heresy was criminal.[70] Hus and his defenders did regard his stance as justifiable and his contumacious behavior as a matter of ethics and principle. This might be taken under advisement as a mitigating factor in assessing motivation. That, however, is a secondary consideration. Legally, he was guilty. Morally, Hus may have had a case for disobedience and refusal to comply with either papal or court orders. However, the judicial procedure was concerned with law and with issues of authority and obedience. Ethics and morals did not enjoy the same currency either at the papal court or among the judges and prosecutors at Constance, any more than in a modern court of law. Situation ethics seldom prevail as a defense strategy when laws are broken. Therefore, the central issue with Hus was less doctrinal deviance than disobedience.

On the second charge, there is sustainable evidence of deviation from mainstream medieval theology, although the matter is fraught with exegetical challenges.[71] Right to the end, Hus remained adamant: "I have no doubt the holy catholic church is the congregation of all the elect on earth, in purgatory and in heaven. These are the hidden body and the head is Jesus Christ."[72] One should not underestimate the vitriolic reaction Hus's book on the church created. Dietrich Niem hyperbolically proclaimed it more inimical to the Christian faith than the Koran of Islam.[73] Jean Gerson

---

69. Fudge, *Jan Hus*, pp. 49–54; Sedlák, "Učil Hus remanenci?" ST, vol. 1 (1914), pp. 450–481, especially pp. 471–472.

70. X 5.7.10 *Vergentis in senium*, in Friedberg, vol. 2, cols. 782–783; Sext. 5.2.8 *Ut inquisitionis*, in Friedberg, vol. 2, cols. 1076–1077.

71. The fullest account of Hus's doctrine of the church in English is Spinka, *Church*. See also Fudge, *Jan Hus*, pp. 33–39.

72. *Passio*, in FRB, vol. 8, pp. 129–130.

73. Noted in *De necessitate reformacionis ecclesiae*, in Hardt, vol. 1, cols. 306–307.

judged it worthy of judicial condemnation on the grounds of "notorious and obstinate heresy," which Gerson found throughout the work and which he declared was best characterized as "manifest mischief" or "open crime."[74] On behalf of the English delegates, John Stokes denounced Hus's doctrine of the church as essentially a version of the already condemned theology of Wyclif.[75] Based on these and other evaluations, Hus's De ecclesia struck a raw nerve with some force. We must wonder why. The solution to this initially puzzling quandary is discoverable. Hus's doctrine of the church took its point of departure from the premise that it was the mystical body of Christ, made up of those divinely predestined, of which Christ was head. Membership was neither a legal right nor a matter of choice but came as a result of divine election. The church, then, was foremost a spiritual entity in the thought of Hus. By contrast, Hus's judges and the theologians arrayed against him conceived of the church as a legal corporation, represented by pope and council. The church was defined by the papacy and the appointed hierarchy. Examining Hus's native late medieval Czech context, we discover that this was a concept held by men such as Štěpán Páleč, Stanislav of Znojmo, Jan Holešov, and an otherwise unknown Benedictine monk.[76] Páleč wrote adamantly that the source of all ecclesiastical power on earth was administered by the pope as head of the church and by the cardinals as the body of the church.[77] If one wishes to understand the theological controversy, Hus's detractors must be read, especially Páleč's Antihus.[78] Stanislav of Znojmo, one of Hus's main

---

74. *Documenta*, pp. 187–188.

75. *Relatio*, p. 102.

76. Páleč wrote three relevant treatises, including *De aequivocatione nominis ecclesia*, in Sedlák, *Miscellanea*, pp. 356–363; *Tractatus de ecclesia*, in Sedlák, *M. Jan Hus*, pp. 203*–304*; and *Antihus*, in Sedlák, *Miscellanea*, pp. 366–507. Stanislav composed two important works: his 1412 essay *Tractatus de Romana ecclesia*, edited by Jan Sedlák in *Hlídka* 16 (1911): 83–95 and reprinted in Sedlák, *Miscellanea*, pp. 312–322 (I use the latter); and *Alma et venerabilis* (1413), in Johann Loserth, ed., "Beiträge zur Geschichte der Husitischen Bewegung," AÖG 75 (1889): 361–413. The third source is Jan Holešov, a Benedictine monk at Břevnov Monastery near Prague, who in 1412 wrote *An credi possit in papam*, in Sedlák, *Miscellanea*, pp. 522–542. There are useful analyses of the latter in Spinka, *Church*, pp. 151–157; and de Vooght, *Hussiana*, pp. 116–123. The fourth source, *Hic tractatus editus est contra Huss hereticum et contra eius tractatum, quem "de ecclesia" appellavit*, was written around 1414 and survives in the twelfth-century Benedictine Seitenstetten Abbey Library, MS 262, fols. 235ʳ–246ᵛ. See comments in Sedlák, "Anonymův spis proti Husovu traktátku 'ecclesia,'" ST, vol. 1 (1914), pp. 312–318, with an edition on pp. 319–348.

77. Štěpán Páleč, *Tractatus de ecclesia*, in Sedlák, *M. Jan Hus*, p. 219*.

78. "Pálčův Antihus," in Sedlák, *Miscellanea*, p. 201, expressing a view I endorse.

detractors, articulated the official doctrine rather succinctly. He wrote that the one holy catholic and Roman church was permanent and ordained of Christ. The head of the church was the pope, and the body was made up of the college of cardinals. This structure descended from Peter, the chief of the apostles, and the rest of the existing manifest successors of the apostles of Christ. The truth embedded in this office brought light to Christians throughout the world, and the ecclesiastical authority therein was diffused over all the earth. The church had been structured in this fashion in order to properly and authoritatively enlighten the world in all matters of faith and to define truth against error, to instruct and correct, and all Christians must hold this to be true.[79]

Other theologians agreed.[80] Supreme authority was held by the prelates, for this was the will of Christ.[81] The "fullness of power" was retained by the pope and the cardinals, and the church did not exist apart from this composite. Therefore, this properly constituted church was immune to the pollution of error; it remained ever holy and impervious to "all pernicious error concerning the faith or morals."[82] Therefore, everything taught by the pope was true and incapable of error.[83] This did not mean that popes and cardinals were sinless or perfect, but it did guarantee the rule of Christ.[84] The papacy possessed "the sacrament of anointing or unction," and this gift was not degraded by virtue of sinfulness or malice, for the anointing was not forfeit because of wickedness.[85] It likewise prevented the proliferation of "endless errors and endless separations."[86] This was because the Roman church thus constituted had never erred in matters of faith.[87] This "sacrament of unction" prevented heresy and error from taking hold of the papacy by means of the Holy Spirit, which provides

---

79. Articulated in his *Tractatus de Romana ecclesia*, p. 318.

80. Páleč, *Tractatus de ecclesia*, p. 240*.

81. Stanislav, *Tractatus de Romana ecclesia*, pp. 312–313.

82. Ibid., p. 315. One finds the same sentiment expressed in *Alma et venerabilis*, where Stanislav claims it is impossible for the church to be infected with heresy.

83. Holešov, *An credi possit in papam*, pp. 531–532.

84. Stanislav, *Alma et venerabilis*, pp. 370–371.

85. Páleč, *Antihus*, in Sedlák, *Miscellanea*, pp. 414–415.

86. Stanislav, *Tractatus de Romana ecclesia*, p. 317.

87. Páleč, *Tractatus de ecclesia*, p. 228*.

infallible direction.[88] Thus, the prelates governed the entire church in the same manner as the human body was regulated by the soul.[89] The anointing possessed by popes guaranteed that the repository of supreme sacerdotal authority resided in the papal office, and this also extended to the social and political spheres.[90] By contrast, Hus "and his party consider themselves an evangelical clergy of the free spirit who wish to judge all things and be judged by no one."[91] This was considered improper and dangerous. Hus's detractors considered it foolish and madness to turn away with contempt from the Roman church. It was contrary to scripture, reason, the sacred canons, the saints, and the sacred doctors. This was precisely what Hus had done, Páleč argued, for he was unwilling to defer to the church and refused to recognize the pope as the head and the cardinals as the body. He would not consent and under this illusion erred most seriously, and he and his followers would find themselves eventually cast into hell.[92] Stanislav commented that it was "extremely erroneous" to suggest that the church was made up chiefly of those who were righteous and elected by God, and it was "foolish to say this."[93] Hus's doctrine was judged subversive and injurious to the ecclesiology maintained by the Council. It contravened traditional authority claimed by the papacy, the Curia, and the episcopate. Should Hus's theology be applied broadly, this theoretically could spell the end of the church as a legal entity, along with its universal coercive powers. Medieval theology held inviolable that prelates (including popes, cardinals, bishops, and priests) constituted the essence of the "congregation of the faithful."[94] More than this—and here is where Hus encountered the stiffest resistance—the church defined by popes and cardinals possessed jurisdictional power over the world, with absolute authority to pass judgment as a legal entity on all causes relating to the faith. The binding authority of the church included jurisdiction over both theological and legal matters, and the prelates retained

---

88. Holešov, *An credi possit in papam*, pp. 539–540.

89. *Hic tractatus editus est contra Huss hereticum*, p. 340.

90. Páleč, *Tractatus de ecclesia*, pp. 217*–218*.

91. Stanislav, *Alma et venerabilis*, p. 394.

92. Páleč, *Tractatus de ecclesia*, pp. 222*–223*, and 245*.

93. Stanislav, *Tractatus de Romana ecclesia*, p. 317.

94. Holešov, *An credi possit in papam*, p. 537.

ultimate authority to make judgments and render verdicts. This had been recognized for more than a thousand years.[95] The anonymous Benedictine monk wrote his opinion: "This is against the heretical treatise which was published in opposition to Hus' treatise which he called 'concerning the church,'" because in these "modern times," some considered the church more properly identified other than by pope and cardinals.[96] A marginal note in the manuscript says that this problem relates directly to Hus's error concerning the church as the congregation of the predestined.[97] The very identity of the church was at issue, along with its authority. The primacy of the Roman church extended to all ecclesiastical cases but could also encompass many civil causes.[98] The church could "correct and purge" the faithful of error. It had authorization to judge, but it could not be judged by its members or by a lower court or authority.[99] Whenever there was doubt, Rome provided certainty.[100]

Summarized in this fashion, Hus could not agree. Canon law defended and protected the authority and jurisdictional prerogatives of the institutional church. If the Latin church decided to operate on a strict predestination model, this would have shifted the essence of the church away from its hierarchy and sacerdotalism. The implications were even more striking and immediate in the sense that popes, prelates, and priests might not, in fact, be members of the true church and therefore might possess no real spiritual power and might be irrelevant. The possibility of that conclusion, of course, rendered the institutional and legal church entity without meaning or merit. The practical implications were unthinkable. Páleč convinced the court at Constance that Hus's doctrine of the church nullified the medieval institution as most Christians knew it.[101] Not even the conciliarists were prepared to pursue that model or run the risk of a Hussite ecclesiastical matrix challenging the *Romana ecclesia*. Even sympathetic modern scholars have identified the critical idea in

---

95. Stanislav, *Tractatus de Romana ecclesia*, pp. 314–316.

96. *Hic tractatus editus est contra Huss hereticum*, p. 328.

97. Seitenstetten, Benedictine Monastery Library, MS 262, fol. 237ᵛ.

98. Páleč, *Tractatus de ecclesia*, p. 217*.

99. Páleč, *De aequivacatione nominis ecclesia*, pp. 360–362.

100. Expressed by John Peklo in a letter of 1424 to Prokop of Kladruby, in Prague Castle Archive, MS O 50, fols. 117ᵛ–118ʳ.

101. Páleč, *Tractatus de ecclesia*, pp. 203*, 241*, et al.

Hus's ecclesiology as predestination.[102] Hus dismissed the ecclesiology of his opponents as based on principles "according to philosophy and vain deceit."[103] Hus wanted the law of God and scripture to prevail as the ultimate court of appeal. His detractors considered that hopelessly subjective and ultimately problematic.[104] They demanded that everyone submit to the authority of the church.[105] Here we see once more the perennial conflict over issues of authority. These theologians struggled to some extent with the balance between a fossilized scriptural emphasis that ignored tradition and the wholly arbitrary beliefs resulting from traditional practices that had little or no anchor in scripture.[106] Páleč characterized the defendant as "the fox-like Hus with his babbling Wyclifites howling like wolves," who used deceit, many errors, and an evangelical voice to contradict the sacred canons. This was judged contrary to the rule of faith, and salvation, and deviant from the established paths of the church fathers.[107] The implications the court drew from Hus's doctrine of the church were sufficient to warrant the condemnation of his ideas. He may have been misquoted and taken out of context, but the judges were not so benighted as to miss the broad thrust of his theology. His concept of the church was different from that of the theologians with whom he clashed, and there is no argument that he opposed the idea that everything ordered by the church in matters of faith must be obeyed.[108] This reflects the language of intensity with which Hus was consistently presented as a veritable terror to the faith. His detractors claimed that the authorities he advanced to support his ideas proved nothing.[109] Another of Hus's Czech contemporaries who uncritically supported papal primacy was Štěpán of Dolany. In his writings, there is prima facie acceptance of fact and law that the papacy is the highest

---

102. Paul de Vooght, "Eglise et corps mystique: Les erreurs de Jean Huss sur les prédestinés," *Irénikon* 26 (1953) : 237–255, especially p. 250.

103. *Contra Stanislaum*, in Hus, *Opera omnia*, p. 286.

104. Stanislav, *Tractatus de Romana ecclesia*, p. 317.

105. *Hic tractatus editus est contra Huss hereticum*, p. 341.

106. Articulated succinctly in Paul de Vooght, *Les sources de la doctrine chrétienne d'après les théologiens di XIVᵉ siècle et du début du XVᵉ* (Bruges: Desclée de Brouwer, 1954), p. 262.

107. Páleč, *Tractatus de ecclesia*, p. 231*.

108. Páleč, *De aequivacatione nominis ecclesia*, p. 362.

109. In a 1424 letter to Prokop of Kladruby, John Peklo argues this, referring to inscriptions Hus placed on the Bethlehem Chapel walls in 1413. Prague Castle Archive, MS O 50, fol. 117ᵛ.

authority in Christendom. The Carthusian abbot based his assumptions on scriptural texts, especially in the gospel of Matthew. Since Peter was the rock, he was the leader, implying that he held supreme power, which is necessary. Applied in practice, all controversy must be subordinated to papal authority, and heretics must be silenced, for there can be no question about the source of power and authority in the church.[110] Štěpán wrote vociferously against both Hus and his followers.[111]

Štěpán Páleč, Stanislav of Znojmo, Jan Holešov, and the anonymous Benedictine monk accurately represented the traditional late medieval doctrine of the church, especially as understood in the Bohemian province. Hus clashed rather dramatically with that model. By the time his trial shifted to the Council of Constance, the ecclesiology of conciliar thinkers such as Jean Gerson, Pierre d'Ailly, Francesco Zabarella, and Dietrich Niem presented another doctrine that must be taken into account in order to understand properly the strong reservations engendered by Hus's *De ecclesia*, which contributed to his designation as a capital offender and his subsequent conviction as a felon.[112] Their theological convictions are relevant in assessing the validity of the second categorical criminal charge lodged against Hus throughout his legal ordeal culminating at the ecclesiastical court in Constance. Conciliarism emerged in force in the early fifteenth century. But its roots extend to the twelfth century. This was a movement aimed at modifying the direction and extent of papal development and power.[113] In brief, the conciliar theory advanced the idea that

---

110. *Antihussus*, in Pez, vol. 4, pp. 362–430, esp. p. 367; *Antiwikleffus*, in Pez, vol. 4, cols. 276–277, 296; *Dialogus*, in Pez, vol. 4, cols. 471, 479; *Liber epistolaris*, cols. 605–607.

111. The only study of note is Johann Loserth, "Die literarischen Widersacher des Huß in Mähren: Mit zwei noch ungedruckten Briefen Stephans von Dolein," *Zeitschrift des Vereines für die Geschichte Mähren und Schlesiens* 1, no. 4 (1897): 1–16.

112. De Vooght, *Hussiana*, pp. 186–208, for an overview. On d'Ailly's ecclesiology, see Louis Pascoe, *Church and Reform: Bishops, Theologians, and Canon Lawyers in the Thought of Pierre d'Ailly, 1351–1420* (Leiden: Brill, 2004). Gerson's doctrine of the church has been assessed in John B. Morrall, *Gerson and the Great Schism* (Manchester, U.K.: Manchester University Press, 1960); and Louis Pascoe, *Jean Gerson: Principles of Church Reform* (Leiden: Brill, 1973). For Zabarella, see Brian Tierney, *Foundations of the Conciliar Theory: The Contribution of the Medieval Canonists from Gratian to the Great Schism* (Leiden: Brill, 1998); and Thomas E. Morrissey, "Franciscus Zabarella (1360–1417): Papacy, Community and Limitations upon Authority," in *Reform and Authority in the Medieval and Reformation Church*, ed. Guy Fitch Lytle (Washington, D.C.: Catholic University of America Press, 1981), pp. 37–54.

113. The classic study is Tierney, *Foundations of the Conciliar Theory*, which popularized what Walter Ullmann pioneered in *Origins of the Great Schism* (London: Burns Oates, 1948), pp. 191–231.

the community of faith was more important than any prelate, and a pope should truly and properly be *servus servorum dei*, the "servant of the servants of God," rather than a dictator.[114] Applying this to the practice of church government, thinkers such as John of Paris, Marsiglio of Padua, and William of Ockham (to mention but three) held that a general council possessed greater authority than a pope. It can be demonstrated that conciliarists such as Gerson and d'Ailly were in some sense disciples of Ockham, while Zabarella was certainly under the influence of John of Paris.[115] The central conviction held by these men had implications for the doctrine of the church. More specific, however, was the concept of authority that underlay the main thrust of conciliarism.[116] Investigations into the intellectual history of medieval Christianity reveal that on issues of ecclesiastical or spiritual authority, there were two main schools of thought. The first subscribed to the idea that scripture was the highest source and criteria of faith. This did not necessarily mean a doctrine of *sola scriptura*, but the emphasis was clear. The second trajectory allowed that scripture, along with tradition and canon law, represented the highest court of authority but not in isolation from tradition, ecclesiastical rulings, and canon law.[117] The first idea found representatives from Augustine to Thomas Bradwardine to Wyclif and Hus. The other point of view was espoused by Ockham, Gerson, and d'Ailly. This helps to explain why the latter theologians were so sharply opposed to Hus. Nevertheless, it is impossible to define precisely the borderline between the two hermeneutics when applied to the contrasts between papalism and conciliarism.[118]

D'Ailly agreed with Hus in principle on the reform of morals. Despite being a cardinal, he took the view that a general council might be convened without a pope, indeed, even in opposition to one, on the grounds that conciliar authority was derived from Christ and not from the papal office. The fullness of power resided first in the papacy but also in the council as a representative of the universal church. It may be argued that d'Ailly's articulation on this theme constituted a basic summary of conciliar

---

114. Tierney, *Foundations of the Conciliar Theory*, p. 5.

115. Pointed out in ibid., pp. 199–200.

116. See the essay in Spinka, *Constance*, pp. 3–22.

117. Heiko Oberman, *The Harvest of Medieval Theology: Gabriel Biel and Late Medieval Nominalism*, rev. ed. (Grand Rapids, Mich.: William B. Eerdmans, 1967), pp. 361–412.

118. Ibid., p. 375.

theory.[119] Applying this principle to heresy condemnations, we find a stark contrast. Jean Mauroux, for example, called for condemnation of heresy in the name of the pope, with approval by the Council, since he argued that the Council possessed no independent authority. D'Ailly countered by asserting that such judgments might be made in the name of the Council because the pope was part of the synod and the Council possessed greater authority collectively than the pope individually.[120] In terms of philosophical disputes over metaphysics, Jean Gerson was committed to nominalism, and this brought him into conflict with Hus, who adhered to the realist perspective. Agreeing with d'Ailly, Gerson believed that the general council must be obeyed. He affirmed that a council had the authority to adjudicate all matters of faith and morals. It had the responsibility to pass judgment on cases brought within its purview, and it could do so even though the council might not have specific support from scripture.[121] Here we see starkly the basis for disagreement with Hus. Moreover, Gerson said nothing about the moral quality of the council, a matter Hus believed was of seminal importance when it came to matters of jurisdictional power. In terms of the papacy, Gerson believed popes would come and go, but the papacy would continue. "Popes pass, the papacy endures."[122] This remark is rather similar to one made by the anonymous Benedictine monk whose work survives at Seitenstetten Abbey in Austria. Our nameless monk wrote that the universal authority of the bishops in Rome is constant. A pope might die but is replaced by another. This can be expressed by way of analogy. The Vltava River in Prague or the Tiber River in Rome is always there, but the current of water may change. So it is with ecclesiastical authority.[123] Gerson was not antipapal, but he was committed to principles of conciliarism by which a Council had the duty to limit papal power if the latter threatened the integrity of the church. Gerson, d'Ailly, and Zabarella

---

119. Francis Oakley, ed., "The 'Propositiones Utiles' of Pierre d'Ailly, an Epitome of Conciliar Theory," *Church History* 29 (1960): 398–403.

120. Finke, *Acta*, vol. 3, pp. 48–50.

121. *Tractatus de potestate ecclesiastica*, in du Pin, vol. 2, cols. 225–256, especially cols. 247, 249.

122. Comment in "Propositio facta coram Anglicis," in du Pin, vol. 2, pp. 123–130; and Glorieux, vol. 6, pp. 125–135.

123. *Hic tractatus editus est contra Huss hereticum*, pp. 341–342. The phrase reads, "Patet a simili, quia semper eadem manet Multava in Praga et Tiberis in Roma, continue aquis defluentibus et affluentibus."

regarded the Council as the representative of the church as *congregatio fidelium*, or the community of baptized Christians.[124] It is among the ironies of the trial that Hus was censured for declaring that a sinful pope need not be obeyed by conciliarists such as Gerson and d'Ailly, who had just taken part in the deposing of a pope for alleged gross misconduct. The canon lawyer Zabarella was opposed to Hus, because Zabarella conceived of the church as a legal entity governed by the papacy and a general council. Hus's views subverted that paradigm. Dietrich Niem held similar views to Hus's on matters of morality (although he kept a concubine) and also called for a limitation of papal power, especially a curtailing of the legal provisions governing papal authority. The church therefore should "limit the misused papal power contained in the *Decretum* and the *Decretales* and the pretended power in the *Sext* and *Clementines*, not to mention other papal constitutions."[125] All of these men were reformers. Why were they so opposed to Hus? Štěpán Páleč underwent a complete volte-face in his own theology and outlook on authority once he reached Constance but nevertheless persisted in his belief that Hus was guilty.[126] Unresolvable controversy over acceptable definitions of the church and the nature of spiritual authority between Hus and representatives of the Latin church remained acute. The legal process concluded that Hus's perspective was insubordinate and subversive. The finding was guilty as charged. Theories of power and authority separated those involved on crucial points, as did the conflict between nominalism and realism when applied to theology. For example, nominalists such as Gerson and d'Ailly could not understand why a realist like Hus logically did not repudiate the doctrine of transubstantiation. Inexplicably, Hus defied logic and continued to adhere to the traditional and official view of the Eucharist to the very end.

Hus was judged guilty on charges of contumacy and maintaining a deviant doctrine of the church. On the third charge, espousing certain condemned doctrines of John Wyclif, Hus admitted he held opinions expressed by Wyclif to be correct not because they were Wyclifite but on

---

124. Scott Hendrix, "In Quest of the *Vera Ecclesia*: The Crises of Late Medieval Ecclesiology," *Viator* 7 (1976): 347–378; and for implications, Heiko Oberman, ed., *Defensorium obedientiae apostolicae et alia documenta* (Cambridge, Mass.: Belknap Press, 1968), pp. 3–55.

125. *De modis uniendi ac reformandi ecclesiae*, in James Kerr Cameron, "Conciliarism in Theory and Practice, 1378–1418," 2 vols., PhD dissertation, Hartford Seminary Foundation, 1953, vol. 2, p. 262.

126. De Vooght, p. 503.

the grounds that Hus considered them supported by scripture and reason. If there were errors, he repudiated them.[127] Right or wrong, persisting in a public defense of Wyclif was a dangerous course of action. When confronted and admonished, Hus refused to distance himself adequately from the controversial aspects of doctrines advanced by Wyclif. The practice exposed Hus to misunderstanding and left him open to all sorts of allegations, ranging from a decided lack of wisdom to theological irregularity to gross impertinence. It might be said that if Hus had not insisted on publicly defending the "forty-five articles" or parts thereof, it would mainly be the Wyclifite implications for Hus's doctrine of the church, with its commensurate effect on questions of power and authority, that would have been at issue. Wyclif had been condemned and outlawed, and at least one priest claimed to have seen a vision of Wyclif in hell.[128] Hus took no note of any of that and continued to defend some of Wyclif's ideas. He could not be judged guilty as charged on this point, full proof (*plena probatio*) was lacking, but a verdict of guilt on modified Wyclifism was not difficult for the court to sustain, and indeed, that finding ultimately was unavoidable. This did not de facto make Hus a Wyclifite in terms of the slavish disciple some studies have labored to show.[129] "Hus was not a blind epigone of Wyclif."[130] It is dangerous to accept the conciliar presentation of Hus as Wyclif revived.[131] Therefore, we can reduce the categories of criminal charges to the accusations against Hus's doctrine of the church, broadly defined, and contumacy and conclude that there was a preponderance of legitimate evidence to sustain these charges. Those accusations were neither contrived nor inaccurate, and as criminal charges, in a medieval court trial operating within the *ordo iudiciarius* of an inquisitorial process, they were quite justly sustained.

---

127. *Contra Palecz*, in Hus, *Opera omnia*, vol. 22, p. 267.

128. University master Jan Jičín reported that John Peklo, rector of St. Giles Church in Prague, claimed this. Included in the former's defense of Wyclif's *Pro tractatu materiae et formae*, ÖNB, MS 4002, fol. 38ʳ.

129. Johann Loserth, *Wiclif and Hus*, trans. M. J. Evans (London: Hodder and Stoughton, 1884), is a notorious example.

130. Jiří Kejř, "Jan Hus jako právní myslitel," in *Jan Hus mezi epochami, národy a konfesemi*, ed. Jan B. Lášek (Prague: Česká Křesťanská Akademie, Husitská Teologická Fakulta Univerzity Karlovy, 1995), p. 199.

131. Sebastián Provvidente, "Inquisitorial Process and Plenitudo Potestatis at the Council of Constance (1414–1418)," in BRRP 8, (2011), p. 99.

Hus was no more willing to accept conciliar theology than he was to defer to strict papalism. He maintained doubts about the legislative authority of a general council almost to the same extent and degree that he was convinced that the papacy, buttressed by canon law, practiced illegitimate coercive powers. "Who made these books, the *Sext* and the *Clementines* which demonstrate in every way arrogance, pride, the usurpation of the rights of ordinaries...and many other things fabricated with evil intent and a persistent lust for power to the detriment of spiritual and secular well-being? This is evil."[132] Hus did not write these words, but he concurred. His position left him adrift in the perilous seas between the forces of papalism and conciliarism, and he was reluctant to drop anchor in either harbor and alight upon either shore. Hus was not amenable to either dominant ecclesiastical force in the later Middle Ages. He refused to retreat from his position that while sin did not interfere with the *potestas ordinis*, the power of the priest to function sacerdotally, sinfulness did invalidate *potestas iurisdictionis*, the jurisdictional authority claimed by prelates. When behavior was contrary to the law of God, the perpetrator might be publicly resisted.[133] Hus practiced that conviction. The conciliarists could not abide it. The absolute sticking point was Hus's willingness to circumvent papal authority, the powers claimed by a general council, the provisions of canon law, and the obligations of legal procedure. This was nowhere better expressed than in Hus's decision to take his case outside the purview of the late medieval judicial and ecclesiastical systems. "Therefore, since my appeal from one pope to his successor was of no benefit, and to appeal from the pope to a council involves a long process and means calling for uncertain help, therefore I finally appealed to the head of the church, which is the Lord Jesus Christ. For he is above the pope in every way in judging a cause. He cannot err nor deny justice to requests properly made, and he cannot condemn a man by his own law who is not without merit."[134]

The court case of Jan Hus at the Council of Constance, convened at the end of the Middle Ages, was heard in a context shaped by a three-hundred-year-old tradition of legal development and the formation of canon law. That inheritance led authorities to deal defensively with

---

132. Dietrich Niem, *De modis uniendi ac reformandi ecclesiae*, p. 239.

133. Hus, *De ecclesia*, p. 177.

134. Ibid., pp. 165–166.

heresy investigations. This was chiefly on account of the fact that heresy was regarded as a serious attack on the official structures of religion and the established categories of doctrine. In the later Middle Ages, it was impossible to challenge the church without also engaging in provocation with the state, and vice versa. That accurately implies that heresy was both a religious issue and a social problem. In Hussite Prague, this was entirely the case. Since it implied challenge to established authority, heresy became a legal issue.[135] Therefore, accusations of heresy and even procedure in heresy trials were adopted and adapted according to a number of variables subject to prevailing authorities. Medieval heresy was neither immutable nor absolute. The medieval legal world regarded heresy as an offense against God, to whom the heretic owed repentance, and also against the secular authorities to whom compensation was due. Drastic and severe punishment—perpetual incarceration or death—was thought to ameliorate both. Heresy was a new type of crime, and from the twelfth century onward, it was dealt with partly by forcing it to conform to existing legislation and legal process. This might be regarded as the politicizing of heresy.[136] Hus was a schismatic convicted largely on the grounds that he rejected the proper authority of the Latin church. He was judged heretical because he persisted in that rejection, even after receiving the requisite instruction. The Council could not afford to ignore canon law when it involved heresy. Despite intensive efforts to spare his life, the conciliar fathers sacrificed Hus on the altar of expediency, according to the letter of the law, in hopes of gaining some benefit. The execution of Hus ran the risk of causing scandal greater than the alleged crime, thereby violating the spirit of the canonical admonition to balance punishment with justice.[137] "The statute is not a closed text, but is in continuous evolution, often contradictory and the result of heated contrasts."[138] After all, there was a measure of latitude within canon law. "There are many to be

---

135. Noted by Herbert Grundmann, *Ketzergeschichte des Mittelalters*, vol. 2, in *Die Kirche in ihrer Geschichte: Ein Handbuch*, ed. Kurt Dietrich Schmidt and Ernest Wolf (Göttingen: Vandenhoeck & Ruprecht, 1963), passim.

136. Othmar Hageneder, "Die Häresie des Ungehorsams und das Entstehen des hierokratischen Papsttums," *Römische Historische Mitteilungen* 20 (1978): 29–47.

137. C.23 q.4 cc.18–19 *Quidam vero*, in Friedberg, vol. 1, cols. 781–782. Judges were encouraged to follow the more humane path. *Glos. ord.* to C.23 q.4 and X 1.36.11 Ex parte *tua*, in Friedberg, vol. 2, cols. 204–205.

138. Vallerani, p. 237.

corrected, like Peter; many to be tolerated, like Judas; and many who are unknown, until the Lord comes, who will bring to light the hidden things of the darkness."[139] Nevertheless, within a climate of turmoil and uncertainty, the church had no wish to be characterized as soft on heretics.[140] The spirit of Hus and the Bohemian reform movement came into sharp conflict with the canon law mentality of the Council. This collision proved an overwhelming challenge.[141]

The repression of Hus stemmed from several motivations, all of which dovetailed, especially during the latter stages of his trial at Constance. There was a commitment to protect orthodoxy. That legitimate impulse on the part of some should not be dismissed. There was also a desire to maintain social and religious order. In the unsettled and unsettling times of the fifteenth century, there existed significant umbrage at challenges to tradition and established cultures of power. Moreover, there were manifestations of general aversion to heresy and dissent. The papal schism presented one of the most ominous dangers to the medieval church. The Hus problem was perceived as an obstruction impeding the repair of that controversy. Finally, Hus seems to have possessed the unenviable ability to rouse jealousy and malevolence in the hearts of others. The conduct of Michael de Causis and Štěpán Páleč is an unarguable example. Consequently, when Hus refused the authority of his ordinary (Archbishop Zbyněk), and by extension the prerogative of the Latin church, he defined himself as a heretic within the religious and legal climate of late medieval Europe. On account of his prominence at the university in Prague and in the pulpit of Bethlehem Chapel, he was by extension an heresiarch—the leader of heretics. Canon law defined the heresiarch as one who defended the errors of others but in so doing was worse than those who simply erred. The heresiarch erred but also confirmed the errors of others, compounding the problem. Therefore, the one who taught error was both heretic and heresiarch.[142] Hus matched that legal profile. It is absolutely correct to argue that the identification of a heretic by definition was a political act,

---

139. C.2 q.1 c.18 *Multi corriguntur*, in Friedberg, vol. 1, col. 382.

140. Hefele and Leclercq, vol. 7, part 1, pp. 330–331. The observation is Leclercq's.

141. The argument relates to the Hussite appearance at the Council of Basel in 1433, but the observation is valid for Constance. Paul de Vooght, "La confrontation des thèses hussites et romaines au concile de Bâle (Janvier–Avril 1433)," *Recherches des Théologie Ancienne et Médiévale* 37 (1970): 282.

142. C.24 q.3 c.32 *Qui aliorum errorem*, in Friedberg, vol. 1, col. 999.

since it demanded that the accused submit to obedience and required that he or she unequivocally refuse.[143] The heart of the matter in the Hus case was ecclesiastical authority. The medieval heretic was the sort of person, like Hus, who privileged personal integrity over the unity and authority of the church. The Council demanded that the defendant set aside personal convictions and individual judgment and exercise obedience. Hus's failure to comply with that value made accusations of heresy inevitable and ultimate conviction unavoidable. That was not the only conclusion. Hussite perspectives explained Hus's death as intimately connected to his insistence on speaking the truth. From this point of view, Hus was burned on account of his faithfulness to Christ, not because of dogmatic error but rather in steadfast defense of the gospel.[144] The language surrounding accused or convicted heretics is revealing. Context and predisposition determine vocabulary, shape nomenclature, and fold themselves into separate dictions describing common events.[145] Political and ecclesiastical authorities referred to the condemnation of Hus. His supporters called it persecution. The definitive sentence of the Council against Hus referred to punishment, and he was burned. The Hussites spoke of these events as suffering and martyrdom. To the Latin church, Hus was an offender, a manifest heretic, a convicted felon. For those regarding him as a "gift of God" and a "faithful champion" of the Lord, martyrdom enabled him to be "clothed with the garments of glory," becoming a source of inspiration for others in bearing witness to truth. The dean's book at the university in Prague for 1396 includes the name Jan Hus, while a later hand has added the comment "a holy martyr of Christ and a faithful Czech" (*sanctissimus Christi martyr et verus Boemus*).[146] For those opposed to the outcome of the trial, Hus was both martyr and saint.[147]

---

143. R. I. Moore, "Heresy, Repression, and Social Change in the Age of Gregorian Reform," in *Christendom and Its Discontents: Exclusion, Persecution, and Rebellion, 1000–1500*, ed. Scott L. Waugh and Peter D. Diehl (Cambridge, U.K.: Cambridge University Press, 1996), p. 41.

144. Sermon by Jakoubek Stříbro in 1416 at Bethlehem Chapel. NK, MS VIII E 3, fol. 70ᵛ.

145. Stanislaw Byłina, "*Martires Gloriosi*: Le martyre et la souffrance chez les contesteurs franciscains en Languedoc au XIVᵉ siècle," *Les Cahiers de Varsovie* 14 (1988) : 76–77.

146. *Liber decanorum facultatis philosophicae Universitatis Pragensis ab anno Christi 1367 usque adannum 1585*, 2 vols. (Prague: Joan. Nep. Gerzabek, 1830–1832), vol. 1, p. 309.

147. Mikuláš Pelhřimov, *Chronicon causam sacerdotum thaboritorum continens*, in Höfler, vol. 2, pp. 477, 567–568; and Ulrich of Znojmo's speech at the Council of Basel, in František M. Bartoš, ed., *Orationes* (Tábor: Jihočeské Společnosti, 1935), p. 133.

Because Hus was perceived as posing a threat to the priests of Prague, Archbishop Zbyněk, King Václav, the papacy, the Latin church, and general ecclesiastical authority and as an obstacle to overcoming the papal schism, he came under withering criticism from many quarters. His refusal to denounce the teachings of John Wyclif, together with some of his own ideas that renegotiated the boundary of acceptable doctrine, provided his detractors with sufficient ammunition to question his loyalty to the church and brought him into the orbit of heresy. Political motivations are apparent in the case of Hus. The formal accusations lodged against him over the course of seven years formed the basis for his protracted legal ordeal and resulted in his execution as the pertinacious "Judas the traitor."[148] The medieval church preferred to characterize him as a man "of damnable memory," who caused much trouble and was justly condemned as a heretic by the Council of Constance.[149] The central aim in the trial of Hus from the point of view of the prosecution was to bring Hus into obedience to the authority of the church. His work in Prague clearly took Hus outside the orbit of conformity to the *magisterium* of the Latin church and jurisdictional obedience to his ordinary. The accusations and charges brought against him over a number of years were largely an exercise in conclusively demonstrating that he was disobedient. Hus was *auctor schismatis* (the author of schism) because he persisted in disobedience. That was the growing assumption. In an age characterized by papal schism, internecine ecclesiastical conflict, the flourishing of dissent, and challenges to the nature of authority itself exemplified in the conciliar movement, continued refusal to remain within traditional expectations of obedience was regarded as intolerable and a detriment to the task of securing ecclesiastical unity. In short, Hus's allegiance to personal conviction and subjective principles of conscience was simply not as important as the unity of the Western church and the challenges facing the Council of Constance.

Many of the accusations brought against Hus were retained to the very end. Numerous other charges were dropped because of insufficient

---

148. The phrase appears in an eyewitness account of the last stages in the Hus trial. *Passio etc. secundum Iohannem Barbatum, rusticum quadratum*, FRB, vol. 8, p. 16. See Fudge, "Jan Hus at Calvary: The Text of an Early Fifteenth-Century Passio," *Journal of Moravian History* 11, no. 3 (2011): 45–81.

149. Pope Martin V's bull *Inter cunctus* (February 22, 1418), in Mansi, vol. 27, cols. 1204–1215.

evidence, clear spuriousness, or myriad other reasons. It is indisputable that some of the evidence brought against Hus was false and deliberately contrived.[150] Indeed, in another system of legal procedure, some of the witnesses in the Hus case would be tried on charges of perjury. It appears that some of the witnesses in the Hus case had the intention (*mens rea*) of committing a perjurious act and in the course of the trial did, in fact, commit that act (*actus reus*). We need not believe claims advanced at his funeral in 1433 that Michael de Causis was an honorable man who strove with selflessness to protect the faith.[151] There is little doubt that de Causis engaged in subornation of perjury when he attempted to induce others to perjure themselves in testifying against Hus.[152] In modern Western legal systems, that behavior itself is a crime. Canon law and medieval legal procedure did have provisions for dealing with perjury, which was considered as grave an offense as homicide, with parallel punishment.[153] That lawyers in the Hus case did not pursue those irregularities, that neither the papal court nor the church court at Constance elected to prosecute those suspected on these grounds, cannot be marshaled as evidence to invalidate the Hus trial. An appellate court may have been interested in such assertions, but the fact remains: Jan Hus was convicted on two counts of heresy. False witnesses, prejudiced testimony, and perjury were not needed for the court to return a verdict of guilt. It appears evident that there was never any real effort actually to prove or disprove the veracity of all accusations and charges by means of due process and legal procedure. It is improper to suggest that because the court did not prove that Hus was in error, this demonstrates the illegality of the process. Such claims are unjustified.[154] The papal Curia and the Council of Constance had sufficient cause to hold hearings and try Hus. Procedure was not the issue at Constance, and it was not what convicted Hus. The issue was less a matter of total consistency on every point of theology than it was a matter of bringing Hus by whatever means into general conformity. Once Hus became an antiauthority figure, the Latin church had to ignore him, co-opt his negative

---

150. Kejř, *Husův proces*, pp. 202–203.

151. "Collectio in exequiis Magistri Michaëlis de Praga procuratoris de causa fide," in ÖNB, MS 4975, fols. 49ʳ–53ᵛ.

152. *Relatio*, p. 41.

153. C.22 q.1 c.17 *Predicandum est*, in Friedberg, vol. 1, col. 866.

154. A point noted in "Jan Hus sám o sobě," in Kejř, *Počátků*, pp. 20–21.

influence by promoting him to a position of power and authority, or force him into subjection. His popularity and influence were too significant to ignore, and in light of the grueling task of regaining ecclesiastical unity, it seemed imprudent to permit such a disrupting presence to go unopposed in the Bohemian province. Therefore, the first option was never considered. Occasionally, in the history of the church, troublesome priests have been elevated into positions of prestige whereby the empowering rather benignly eliminates the prior threat. But no one seems to have thought of offering Hus a cardinal's hat, and it remains doubtful that Hus would have accepted in any event. The second option never gained traction. Church authorities elected to take up the third option and secure the obedience of this recalcitrant priest by means of coercion and the traditional defensive approach. It took five years, but in the end, that approach was successful, although it meant eventually relaxing Hus to the secular authorities as a convicted felon for execution of a capital punishment sentence. The Council of Constance had no other option. *Haec Sancta* declared that all people were obligated to obey the Council in matters pertaining to the faith.[155] Disobedience could not be tolerated. Dissent had to be crushed. When John XXIII attempted to circumvent the authority of the Council, the synod did not hesitate in arresting, prosecuting, and deposing him. He wound up in prison. When Hus refused to recognize the authority of the Council, he had to be destroyed. The consolidation of conciliar authority in the decree *Haec Sancta* did not affect the development of heresy trials at Constance. The Hus process, for example, was already in place. The flight of John XXIII created a dilemma. The Council solved that problem via *Haec Sancta*, and the Hus trial continued. He had already been censured by provincial synods, by the papal court, by two popes before the convocation of the Council, and by Martin V afterward, and it would be unwise to dwell on the technicalities of the administration of ecclesiastical power and by this means attempt to invalidate the heresy proceedings at Constance.

Once the matter of Jan Hus reached the papal court in 1410, it was no longer simply a case of assessing Hus on questions of theology only. Concerns about his strict orthodoxy were always at issue, but these were increasingly secondary. The legal proceedings, although characterized by points of theology from beginning to end, as evident in the numerous

---

155. "Cui quilibet cuiuscumque status vel dignitatis, etiam si papalis exsistat, obedire tenetur in his quae pertinent ad fidem." Tanner, DEC, vol. 1, p. 409.

cycles of accusations and charges, were not an exercise in sustaining a preponderance of evidence or probable cause in terms of doctrinal deviance. Certainly, there were powerful men arrayed against Hus, motivated by desire to eliminate all trace of deviance and doctrinal difference. The legal procedures against Hus at the papal court and then before the Council of Constance were more concerned with eliminating all evidence that might sustain reasonable doubt that Hus was contumacious and therefore make him legally innocent of being a heretic. The process in Prague failed to secure that conclusion. The legal procedures at the papal court reached an impasse when Hus refused to appear, refused to recognize the jurisdiction of the court, and was then excommunicated for contumacy but almost completely disregarded the implications of that legal verdict. Then Hus inexplicably appealed to Jesus Christ as the arbiter or mediator in the conflict. Once the trial venue shifted to Constance, Hus thought he had the legal right to dictate the nature of the proceedings and believed he was legally entitled to enter into discussions with his judges, and he expected that he had to submit to the authority of the court and by extension to the *magisterium* of the Latin church only if and when he was proven wrong by the criteria he selected and defended. No court procedure in the medieval world operated on principles like this. The behavior of the constituency of the court, although viewed askance by the modern eye, is reflective of the incompatibility of men who gathered to seek submission from a defendant in a court of law but who encountered a man who considered himself above the technical letter of the law, for he had subordinated that human code to the law of God. Indeed, the reforms Hus desired were predicated on subjective concepts of truth and justice, and these changes that Hus demanded had to follow the law of God.[156]

Ultimately, it must be recognized that Hus and Wyclif articulated a theological definition of the church that was neither novel nor especially revolutionary had it been considered in another context. The ecclesiology of Augustine utilized by both reformers was well known. However, Hus shifted purely abstract theological terms into concrete models at a time when conciliar and papal leadership were locked in a power struggle. An otherwise innocuous idea was thereby exacerbated by a context of crisis. The uses of Augustine were now regarded by conciliarists and papalists

---

156. Robert Kalivoda, *Husitská ideologie* (Prague: ČSAV, 1961), p. 172.

alike as lethal. Beyond this, Hus seems to have possessed a natural talent for irritating his detractors, and this abrasiveness put a sharp point on his ecclesiology. The conciliar threat altered theological discourse at the end of the Middle Ages. It was in this volatile environment that Hus embarked on his attempt to establish a reformed doctrine of the church and practice of the faith. The fact remains that in an earlier period, Hus's concept of the church would not have created the furor it did in the fifteenth century. In those theologically unsettled times, the Latin church experienced a sense of desperation in the face of dissent and conciliar challenge. It chose to respond by playing the law-and-order card. One of the results of that strategic policy was the politicizing of Hus's theology and the associated conviction that his doctrine of the church threatened the future of the community of faith. In conciliar Europe, Hus's ideas caused alarm bells to sound.

It is not accurate to conclude that Hus's conviction on charges of heresy can only be sustained if one accepts the final thirty charges as accurately representing his teaching. It is also incorrect to assume that Hus had the right in a medieval court of law following the *ordo iudiciarius* in a heresy proceeding to expect to be able to demand instruction and correction by his own chosen standard. It is also not a persuasive argument to submit that the conception of the church as held by the trial prosecutors and judges was somehow inferior to Hus's doctrine or to imply theological superiority on the part of the defendant. These are subjective evaluations driven by confessional predispositions. It is also a mistake to claim that proving Hus guilty of heresy meant demonstrating that his scriptural and patristic bases were incorrect. Finally, it is inappropriate to argue that Hus's conviction was valid only if one accepts conciliar theory as codified in the decree *Haec Sancta*. The appeal that Constance was not a legitimate court misses the point of heresy in the later Middle Ages, criminal procedure as set forth in canon law, and the nature of legal cases before ecclesiastical authority.[157] In matters of heresy, popes wielded absolute jurisdictional authority. After the deposition of John XXIII, the Council of Constance functioned under the mandate *Haec Sancta*. However, pursuant to *sede vacante*, when the papacy was vacant, jurisdiction was delegated to the power of the chapter, and the church through its bishops retained the authority to judge people

---

157. The third point is rather ably established by examining other cases heard at Constance. C. M. D. Crowder, "Four English Cases Determined in the Roman Curia during the Council of Constance, 1414–1418," AHC 12 (1980): 315–411, and 13 (1981): 67–145.

in matters of heresy.[158] Moreover, the argument that Constance was illegitimate is fatally flawed inasmuch as it ignores more than eighty-five percent of the Hus trial, which chronologically took place between June 1410 and November 1414. Focusing on the final months and last acts of the court case as witnessed at the Council of Constance presents at best a truncated perspective and a caricature.[159] Whereas the trial of Joan of Arc in 1431 began with a month and a half of procedural motions and investigations, the trial of Jan Hus spanned several years before it resumed at Constance. This cannot be ignored.

By modern, Western, democratic, legal standards, the trial of Jan Hus was unfair and unjust. This is beyond dispute. However, modern, Western, democratic, legal standards have no relevance in a discussion of medieval heresy, criminal procedure in the Middle Ages, or the trial of Jan Hus. We must neither evaluate nor judge a fifteenth-century trial by comparing it with court procedures and legal standards in our own time. The trial of Jan Hus invokes in many people the same sort of sympathy instinctually felt for Joan of Arc. This results in a firmly held belief that any trial proceeding or court convicting such people must surely be invalid.[160] Such opinion forgets that medieval canon law was unequivocal that persons advancing improper teachings, refusing correction, persisting in their own points of view, and remaining contumacious were regarded as heretics.[161] Neither must one forget that Saint Jerome considered heresy worse than sin, indeed, according to Bishop Lucas of Túy, the greatest sin.[162] Thus, the final verdict in the Hus case—the *sententia*—comes as somewhat shocking to those who insist on evaluating other ages and events by means of postmodern theoretical approaches, politically correct guidelines, and gentle ecumenical applications, all of which are plain and simple anachronism when applied to the trial of Jan Hus. Utilizing such methodology, it is not difficult to provide a careful demonstration for why Hus should

158. X 3.9.1–3 *Ne sede vacante*, in Friedberg, vol. 2, cols. 500–501. The pursuit and punishment of heresy cannot be regarded as an innovation.

159. Spinka, *Constance*, pp. 73–76.

160. Daniel Hobbins, *The Trial of Joan of Arc* (Cambridge, Mass.: Harvard University Press, 2005), pp. 2, 18.

161. C.24 q.3 c.31 *Qui in ecclesia*, in Friedberg, vol. 1, col. 998.

162. "Against the Pelagians," in PL, vol. 23, cols. 544–548; Lucae Tudensis, *De altera vita*, ed. Emma Falque Rey [Corpus Christianorum Continuatio Mediaevalis, vol. 74A] (Turnhout: Brepols, 2009), bk. 2, ch. 9.

not have been burned. But this is hardly what is required. A careful examination of the nature of medieval heresy and legal procedure in the early
fifteenth century also yields an entirely reasonable explanation—perhaps
even a justification—for why the defendant in this case was executed. The
truth is, by the strict application of medieval law and legal procedure in
heresy trials, Jan Hus got what he deserved.

Closing Arguments

THE TWELFTH-CENTURY CANONIST Stephen of Tournai once pointed out the differences between religious thought and legal statutes. He proposed inviting a theologian and a lawyer to an intellectual dinner but struggled to find an appropriate menu for people with such opposite tastes, one preferring something sweet, the other favoring what is bitter. Stephen assumed rightly that if he stressed legal matters, the theologian would be unhappy, but if he concentrated on theology, the lawyer would curl his nose in disgust and tear his hair out. He concluded that each party should make allowances and be tolerant of the other.[1] The idea was salutary, but the result was predictable. In practice, the trial of Jan Hus failed to solve the predicament. There were similar medieval suggestions. "It is necessary to love them both, that is, those whose opinions we follow and those whose opinions we reject. For both have devoted themselves to seeking the truth and both have helped us in finding it."[2] This ideal is seldom achieved. The past is indeed a foreign country, and things are done differently there. We need not agree, but it is imperative that we understand. Jan Hus was a casualty of the ethos characterizing the late Middle Ages. He was subject to antiheresy law, political intrigue, the urge to purge the church of dissent, bellicose controversies over indulgences, the protracted papal schism, disputes over the imperial and Czech crowns, fallout from the decree of Kutná Hora, and a host of other factors. Few people today, regardless of political or confessional persuasion, would take delight in the Hus trial or its outcome. The severity of the court had its foundation

---

1. Stephen of Tournai, *Die summa über das Decretum Gratiani*, ed. Johann Friedrich von Schulte (Aalen: Scienta, 1965), pp. 1, 5.

2. Thomas Aquinas, *Sentencia super Metaphysicam*, 12, 9, 2566, in *Sancti Thomae Aquinatis, doctoris angelici, ordinis praedicatorum Opera omnia* (Parma: Petri Fiaccadori, 1866), vol. 20, p. 643.

in a commitment to law and order and a conviction of its own divine mandate. The sentence of death was not too steep a cost in defense of God. Throwing stones at the Council is an almost involuntary reaction, but "seldom do we reflect that we who are aghast at the burning of one man to ashes for religion do not hesitate for the preservation of our culture to reduce whole cities to cinders."[3]

There will be objections that canon law and a legal approach are sterile, pedantic, and inflexible, while the practice of law and order represents a different reality. The assertion requires demonstration. The trial of Jan Hus, in its general process, was legal. The careful work of Jiří Kejř and this book prove that. In his memoirs, Kejř reiterated that "the criminal process was performed according to the norms of canonical procedure and was supported...by all the relevant regulations of canon law."[4] Hus was charged with heresy. Certainly, his enemies, such as Michael de Causis and Štěpán Páleč, were motivated by malice, and the series of accusations were sometimes little more than ad hominem attacks. There is plenty of evidence of unworthy conduct during the public hearings (and we might also surmise that this extended to the *in camera* conferences), which cannot be characterized as other than disgraceful disorder, disruption, and dishonor. Not only were these incidents shameful, but they were also contrary to the rule of law as outlined in the *ordo iudiciarius*. The presiding judges should have been subject to judicial sanctions. The sessions on June 5 and July 6, especially, displayed conduct that tended to defeat the administration of justice to the extent of bringing the court and the legal profession into disrepute in violation of canon law and the principles of the *ordo iudiciarius*. One might even critique the court for its unswerving commitment to the *stare decisis* doctrine and find fault with the inflexibility of medieval canon law, criminal procedure as practiced by the judiciaries that heard the Hus case, and the entire antiheresy initiative. But none of this constitutes proper legal analysis. There is no question that the trial and court procedures were marked by irregularities. Contextually, every trial is different.[5] On this, there is room for dispute and interpretation. However, this is where subjective assessments, emotion, anachronism,

---

3. Roland H. Bainton, *Hunted Heretic: The Life and Death of Michael Servetus* (Gloucester, Mass.: Peter Smith, 1978), p. 215.

4. Kejř, *Žil jsem ve středověku* (Prague: Academia, 2012), p. 190.

5. Vallerani, p. 42.

and irrelevant nonlegal factors intrude, yielding wholly unsustainable conclusions. Returning to the construct of the medieval haunted house of the heretics, it is possible to see Hus through eight of the nine windows. Hus stood askance of the understanding of heresy as determined in canon law.[6] He did choose his own theological conclusions; he publicly declared his ideas and, despite admonition, persisted in holding those views. His continuation in this rendered him notoriously suspect of heresy. Deviation from established doctrine and church law placed one in a precarious position as a heretic. The canonists were clear on this. On the matter of contumacy, it is impossible to portray Hus as obedient. We have his own public testimony of active disobedience. Neither the curial nor the conciliar courts erred in returning a guilty verdict on this point. While many accusations lodged against Hus were questionable, the charge of contumacy was accurate. Hus himself once defined heresy as contumacy.[7] Moreover, his ecclesiology did deviate in terms of Latin Christendom, and he refused to distance himself from the teachings and influence of John Wyclif, a condemned heresiarch. There were theological differences, and Hus found himself in a minority position. Beyond this, the naiveté of the defendant cannot be overlooked. Hus insisted on maintaining his own views, was truculent in personal convictions, and refused to stand down unless convinced by his own nominated criterion. No amount of pressure or persuasion could pry him loose from a strident unwillingness to compromise, negotiate, or plea-bargain. For Hus, it was all or nothing. He demanded acquittal or death.

More than a century after the Hus trial, Martin Luther held his infant son Martin in his hands and was heard to say aloud, "If you become a lawyer, I'll hang you on the gallows myself." Luther said this because he was convinced that canon lawyers were bad Christians (*juristen böse Christen*).[8] Critics of the Hus trial argue that it was immoral to try him. One must wonder by what definition or criterion that position can be maintained. Surely, the medieval church had the rights of discipline and self-definition. *Qualiter et quando* makes the essential point that prelates

---

6. C.24 q.3 c.26 *Inter heresim*, in Friedberg, vol. 1, col. 997.

7. *Super IV Sententiarum*, in *Mag. Jo. Hus Opera omnia: Nach neuentdeckten Handschriften*, 3 vols., ed. Václav Flajšhans (Osnabrück: Biblio-Verlag, 1966), vol. 2, p. 616.

8. *D. Martin Luthers Werke. Kritische Gesamtausgabe. Tischreden*, 6 vols. (Weimar: Hermann Böhlaus Nachfolger, 1912–1921), vol. 2, p. 96, for the remark about baby Martin; vol. 5, p. 307, for the comment about lawyers.

had a duty to prosecute crimes.[9] Other thinkers believed that "judgments rooted in church law are good because the judge and the advocates are pious" and are devoted to concerns for "the body and the soul" of the parties involved.[10] It is doubtful that Hus agreed with this sentiment expressed by his Czech predecessor Tomáš Štítný. The late medieval church found itself at risk from division and dissent. One might argue that the Latin church was rather poorly equipped to weather the storms generated by the crises of the later Middle Ages. Borrowing a maritime analogy, the church was a grand institution but more or less unseaworthy. Its timbers were decidedly rotted in places and elsewhere barnacled by all manner of corruption. The superstructure of the ship had sustained severe damage from fires started by its numerous enemies. Many of the ship's crew were bitter and spiteful, others divided, and there were those plotting outright mutiny. Some of the watchmen high on the masts either suffered from poor eyesight or were unschooled in meteorological prediction. Among the officers, we find an appalling lack of navigational skill. If in this situation, crew members still committed to a safe voyage elected to take action against another perceived threat, many of those faithful to the survival of the church were more likely to applaud than object.[11] Rightly or wrongly, Hus was charged with creating disturbances in the Bohemian province. His refusal to adhere to his ordinary prompted papal action. The matter escalated into a full-blown legal process. Reaching the climax of the court case, it is plausible to consider the legal ordeal a blot, among many in the history of Christianity, perhaps as a consequence of the systemic failure to follow the teachings and example of Jesus. The medieval church had the finest buildings in the Middle Ages and the worst record on what we might call human rights. The Latin church possessed the best-organized social and political structures in Europe but no constructive means of dealing with difference and diversity. The houses of worship were luxurious edifices, but prelates failed to use them successfully to attack social

---

9. X 5.1.17, in Friedberg, vol. 2, cols. 738–739.

10. In 1376 (and revised several times, the last being in 1400), Tomáš Štítný wrote his *Books of Christian Instruction.* Antonín Jaroslav Vrťátko, ed., *Thómy z Štítného Knihy naučení křestanského* (Prague: Nákladem Musea Království českého, 1873), bk. 4. For a larger contextualization, see Emil Ott, "Das Eindringen des kanonische Rechts, seine lehre und wissenschaftliche Pflege in Böhmen und Mähren während des Mittelalters," ZRG KA 3 (1913): 1–106, especially 102.

11. I adopt the metaphor from A. G. Dickens, "The Reformation in England," in *The Reformation Crisis,* ed. Joel Hurstfield (London: Edward Arnold, 1965), p. 48.

injustice. These same buildings were too often characterized by a reluctance to publicly condemn political and religious corruption or decidedly anti-Christ policies and practices. The initiatives proposed by Hus were out of step with medieval church priorities.

Nevertheless, the church has often been sustained and preserved throughout history by the dissenters and the heretics. What is still required is "an impartial history of the church and heretics," which means dealing with heretics on their own terms.[12] This has seldom been achieved. Almost five hundred years after the Hus trial, another dissenter was expelled from the Christian community. When asked to recant and retreat from his convictions, he had this to say: "Whether these beliefs of mine offend, grieve, or prove a stumbling-block to anyone, or hinder anything, or give displeasure to anybody, or not, I can as little change them as I can change my body.... I loved Christianity more than my Church, and now I love truth more than anything in the world."[13] The stance was not dissimilar to the one taken at the Council of Constance. For this reason, Leo Tolstoy was excommunicated and Jan Hus burned. On account of this basic incompatibility, Pope John Paul II would not, indeed could not, rehabilitate Hus in 1999.

My conclusion about the heresy conviction of Hus and the legal verdict reached at the conclusion of the five-year court case will provoke hostility, astonish, and consternate. It will cause distress and be denounced as betrayal. Others will grumble and disagree in silence. However, refutation can only be achieved by means of an even more careful legal exegesis than I have been capable of. One of the basic tenets of legal argument is *affirmanti non neganti incumbit probatio*, which is to say, the burden of proof is incumbent upon the one affirming, not the one denying. Many of the assessments of the Hus trial, produced on both sides of the Atlantic, have been characterized by a common inability to read the relevant texts objectively apart from modern opinions of what one thinks the court should have done. That this observation applies to many capable and intelligent scholars is surprising and troubling. Even in otherwise reputable scholarship, the trial of Hus is often treated according to philosophical, psychological, and sentimental types of arguments. It is rare to find sustained

---

12. A pioneering effort is Gottfried Arnold, *Unparteyische Kirchen- und Ketzer-Historie*, 3 vols, (Frankfurt: Thomas Fritsch, 1699–1700).

13. Leo Tolstoy, *My Reply to the Synod's Edict of Excommunication* (Christchurch, Hants: Free Age Press, 1901), p. 12.

analyses of canon law, criminal procedure, or judicial approaches to the topic of heresy and its repression in relation to Hus.[14] It is essential to recognize precisely those points that distinguish modern justice from the core of law and legal practice in the fifteenth century. Those differences are at the heart of understanding the trial of Hus. With the notable exception of the work of Kejř, most scholarship on the subject has lacked the necessary grasp of canon law to make possible a thorough analysis of the breadth and complexity of the topic. None of the previous work in English provides a comprehensive legal analysis. Instead, too many evaluations of the Hus trial have been hobbled by either political or confessional bias or further by a selective approach to medieval canon law. Many other examples of scholarship on the Hus trial are little more than the pious longings of their evaluators, who demonstrate, involuntarily perhaps, that their work ultimately is a projection of their own ideas and desires. This is a rather severe judgment but one that must be pointed out, especially to the neophyte. One of the great misunderstandings of the Hus case is that the defendant was denied due process, subjected to an illegal court, convicted of offenses he was innocent of, and subsequently murdered. On what basis does such a widely accepted view rest? Certainly not on any clear understanding of canon law, criminal procedure, and the nature of medieval heresy. This book has endeavored to remedy that deficiency. It has been an exercise in unmasking a persistent historical misrepresentation.

None of this should be read as an indictment of Jan Hus or his character, ideas, or memory. Although a fervent follower of Jesus Christ, Hus died more like Socrates than like Jesus. According to Plato, the former was composed and peaceful, without the terror of death.[15] The latter was distressed, his body trembled, and his soul was troubled. There is evidence from earliest Christian witnesses of the dread of death. Jesus begged his disciples to stay with him. Socrates made no such request of his followers. Jesus pleaded for deliverance. Socrates embraced death as friend. Jesus cried aloud, asking God why he had been abandoned. Socrates calmly

---

14. The most influential Western studies of Hus are those by de Vooght and Spinka. While, for example, they routinely list Friedberg in bibliographies, in four books on Hus, Spinka refers to canon law about twenty times but only thrice to elements relating to heresy or criminal procedure. In two large tomes, de Vooght cites canon law slightly more (about twenty-eight times) but not once anything relative to a legal analysis. By contrast, this book refers to legal sources more than three hundred fifty times.

15. Plato, *The Trial and Death of Socrates*, ed. G. M. A. Grube (Indianapolis: Hackett, 2000).

drank the hemlock. Hus was passionate for God, for Christ, for the gospel, and for his own concept of truth. Moreover, he was convinced of the Christian teaching of resurrection. His commitments were incompatible with the legal and doctrinal standards of later medieval Europe. Bested in a power struggle that he simply could not win, Hus committed himself to Jesus but died in the manner of Socrates.[16] His passion transformed a nation and became part of the collective Czech consciousness. One example must suffice. In 1416, in Hus's own Bethlehem Chapel, the Hussite priest Jakoubek Stříbro preached a sermon in which he recounted the gripping scene of Hus's final moments:

> Then he was handed over to the secular authorities who led him to the place of his execution and death. On the way he shouted that false and twisted testimonies were submitted and that no one should believe that he advocated any heretical article. When he arrived at the place of execution, he knelt down and prayed with a joyful heart and a bright countenance. Then they stripped him down to his shirtsleeves, chained and roped him to a stake and piled wood around him to such a height that his head was barely visible—I omit other details. When the strong flames blazed up, he stopped singing and praying. But his spirit as we devoutly believe, reached with the flames to heaven, to the company of angels, just as Elijah did.[17]

Among many Hussites, Hus was made a saint. There is no history without tragedy, but both are shaped by the politics of memory.

I believe the evidence shows conclusively that Jan Hus was a heretic. I am also convinced that a careful investigation of canon law and medieval criminal procedure demonstrates that, despite identifiable irregularities, the trial was legal. Even some of the most strident critics of the trial concede that the process conformed to current court practices.[18] At the same time, it is important to articulate my parallel conviction. Hus was a good man, a person of virtue and integrity, a faithful priest who strove for

---

16. An eyewitness account of the execution of Jerome of Prague on May 30, 1416, draws similar parallels. Critical edition of the Poggio Bracciolini letter in *Poggii Epistolae*, ed. Tomaso de Tonellis (Florence: L. Marchini, 1832), vol. 1, pp. 11–20.

17. The text of the sermon appears in FRB, vol. 8, pp. 231–242, with the citation on p. 240.

18. Spinka, *Constance*, p. 68.

honesty, conviction, and truth in the practice of his faith. Heretics may be heroes. Convicted felons are not void of humanity, goodness, and courage. Some may even be worthy of admiration. I believe Hus to have been such a man. The past is a foreign country, and those dwelling there do things differently. This applies to Hus and to his judges, prosecutors, and opponents. Attempting to change the world of the past or condemning their practices from the safe distance of six centuries indicates a failure to comprehend that past and further suggests a form of condescension manifested by a posterity that seeks to control rather than participate in history.

All said, it is the trial of Jan Hus, especially its culmination at the Council of Constance, that has consistently attracted the most interest, generated the greatest indignation, and prompted the widest range of response. This is evident in practically every consideration of the life and work of this medieval priest. The legal ordeal is the most compelling chapter in this gripping adventure of faith, reform, dissent, and martyrdom. It is a tale of crime and punishment, a drama with implications for the ages.

Dramatis Personae in the Trial of Jan Hus

The legal proceeding involving Jan Hus ranks among the most important heresy trials of the later Middle Ages. The sheer numbers involved and the span of time it commanded, to say nothing of the political and religious fallout from its conclusion, support this claim. The following list presents the names of 106 individuals involved in the prosecution of Hus and his formal legal ordeal. There is, further, an indeterminate number whose names have not survived. A few are described in the sources as the "certain monk wearing a black cape on which something shiny black is draped," or the priest wearing a "green garment with red silk lining," or the "old, bald Polish bishop," or the "fat priest who looked like a Prussian." There are many others who played roles in the curial and/or conciliar aspects of the trial of whom we know nothing. Of the 106 individuals named here, many filled several different roles, but I have listed their names only once. Similarly, some of these had different titles but are identified by one. In general, I have followed their designation in the sources, which at times introduces multiple terms for the same function. The accompanying abbreviations key indicates a principal role played by each one. The codefendants, Wyclif and Jerome, appear only because the case against Hus was in some sense an extension of the church's hostility to Wyclif, and the subsequent procedure involving Jerome (one of Hus's disciples) is to some degree linked with Hus.

Defendant	Jan Hus (p)
Codefendants	John Wyclif (m) (posthumous), Jerome of Prague (m)
Defense Attorneys	Lead counsel Jan Jesenice; assistant lawyers Marek of Hradec and Mikuláš Stojčín; associate counsel Peter of Ancharano, Giovanni Scribanis (or Scrivanis), Augustinus, Marcus of Caniculo, and Ardicin

Prosecutors	Michael de Causis (l), Mařik Rvačka (i), Zbyněk Zajíc (ab)
Judges	Pierre d'Ailly (c), Odo Colonna (c), Francesco Zabarella (c), Rainaldo Brancacci (c), Antonio Caetani (b), de Veneficiis (?), Ursin of Talavende (m), William Corfe (m), Stephen Coevret of Dol (b), John of Martigny (abb), Giovanni Dominici (ab), John of Gudesberg (b), Jean Gerson (ch), John of Rupescissa (ph), Jan of Bořenice (b), Bernard of Castellamare (b), Peter delgi Stephaneschi (c), Guillaume Fillastre (c), John XXIII (P), Antony of Pereto (r), Leonard of Florence (r), Johannes Wallenrode (ab), Peter Helburg (pv), Henry Homberk (d), Peter Mera (b), Dietrich Niem (n)
Jury	[none per se] Council of Constance, the Hus Commission
Witnesses	Štěpán Páleč (m), Jan Protiva (p), John Peklo (p), Beneš (pr), Pavel (pr), Ondřej of Brod (m), Mikuláš of Podviní (m), Mikuláš of Všetaty (p), Václav of Voděrady (pn), John Stokes (m), Stanislav of Znojmo (m), Jan Cifra (cn), Johannes of Münsterberg (t), Peter Storch (m), Nicholas Zeiselmeister (cn), Jan Beroun (p), Peter of Uničov (r), Adam of Býchory (lc), Konrad of Vechta (ab), Nicholas Nezero (i), anonymous layman, unidentified Prague priests
Court Officials	John de Thomariis of Bologna (a), Berthold Wildungen (a), George Fleckel (a), Konrad Conhofer (a), Anthony of Concordia (b), Henry of Piro (pro), Patrick Foxe (b), Nicholas Lubich (b), Vitalis Valentini (b), Bartolomeo della Capra (ab), Henry Scarampi (b), Albert Guttuaria d'Agliano (b), Bartholino Beccari (b), William Barrowe (b), John of Constance (b), Nicholas of Milan (ab), Jean Belli (b)
Prison Embassies	Robert Hallum (b), Nicholas Bubwith (b), Andreas Lascari (b), Jindřich Lacembok (k), Jean Mauroux (l)
Execution Associates	Sigismund (e), Ludwig of the Palatine (dk), Hans Hagen (l), Hoppe of Poppenheim (im), anonymous executioners
Amicus Curiae	Jan Náz (l)
Others	Jan Železný (b), Jacob Balardi (b), Jan Chlum (k), Václav Dubá (k), Petr Mladoňovice (sb), Wenceslas Tiem (d), Štěpán of Dolany (r), Jiří Bor (l), John of Lisbon (pl), Václav Králík (b), Giacomo Cerretano (n), Ferdinand of Aragon (kg), Dietrich Kerkering (t), Stefano di Geri del Buono (b), Thomas Polton (d), Peter Pulka (ue), Gérard de Puy (b), Ulrich Schorand (p), Ulrich Richental (sb), Jean-Allarmet de Brogny (c), Henry of Bavaria (dk), Friedrich of Brandenburg (dk)

Abbreviations Key

a	auditor
ab	archbishop
abb	abbot
b	bishop
c	cardinal
ch	chancellor
cn	canon
d	dean
dk	duke
e	emperor
i	inquisitor
im	imperial marshal
k	knight
kg	king
l	lawyer
lc	licentiate in canon law
m	master
n	notary
P	pope
p	priest
ph	patriarch
pl	papal legate
pn	public notary
pr	preacher
pro	promotor
pv	provost
sb	scribe
r	religious
t	theologian
ue	university envoy

Glossary of Legal Terms

There are numerous technicalities in legal practice and its Latin nomenclature. The terms below appear or are implied in this book in specific relation to the Hus process and generally in legal proceedings involving heresy cases. Most of these have been translated within the text, or their meaning can be understood from the context, but the glossary provides a concise reference.

accusatory procedure (*accusatio*)	Prosecution based on the accusation of a private citizen
actiones	Specific legal procedure
actor	Private accuser
actus reus	Wrongful commission of an offense
advocatus	Legal counsel who appears with a defendant in court (see also *procurator* and *defensorius*)
affirmanti non neganti incumbit probatio	Burden of proof rests on the party making the allegation
aggravatio	Implementation of legal sanction
amicus curiae	Friend of the court
anathema	Major excommunication
animadversio debita	Due punishment, but often meaning capital punishment
apostoli	Formal response by a judge to an appeal
appellatio (appeal/appellate)	Formal request for review of a decision or action of a lower court
arraignment	Formal reading of criminal complaint or indictment of charges

audiencia causarum sacri palatii	Delegated authority of the church, also known as the *Rota*
auditores generales	Auditors or general hearing officers
auxilium brachii secularis	Aid of the secular arm, means utilizing the power of the state, especially to impose a death penalty
brief	Written arguments
canonica monitione	Specific admonition or warning
capitulum	Canon
carcere perpetuo	Life imprisonment
carcere perpetuo irremissibile	Noncommutable life sentence
causa	Case
causae haereticorum	Formal cases of heresy
citatio	Summons to a court
clamosa insinuatio	Notorious suspicion
cognitio	Hearing or judicial examination
compurgatio	Witnesses swearing to the innocence of the defendant (see also purgation)
confessio extra iudicialis	Out-of-court confession
consistory	Bishop's court
consuetudo	Customary law or tradition
contumacia	Stubborn disobedience or defiance of authority (see also *pertinacia*)
contumacia crescente	Increasing stubbornness
contumax	One suspected or convicted of contumacy
crimen exceptum	Extraordinary crime (i.e., heresy or witchcraft)
crimen mere ecclesiasticum	Offenses reserved exclusively for judgment by the church
culpae	Formal writ of judicial guilt
Curia	Papal court
defensorius	Legal defender (see also *advocatus* and *procurator*)
degradatio	Specific canon and procedure for defrocking priests
denunciatory procedure (*denunciatio*)	Court convened by a public official to deal with an offense
deposition	Sworn testimony
dictum	Comment

discovery	Procedural device aimed at revealing pertinent information
error intellectus	Intellectual mistake
exceptio	Formal objection
exceptio criminis	Procedural device to disqualify a hostile witness
excommunication	Minor excommunication means being barred from receiving the sacraments, while major excommunication indicates expulsion from the community of faith altogether (see also anathema)
ex parte	Legal procedure or contact made by one side with the court in a case without the knowledge or presence of the other side
extra ordinem	A legal procedure that is out of order
facti evidentia	Factual evidence
fama publica	Rumor, common report, or public reputation
habeas corpus	A writ requesting a court hearing or the release of a person subjected to unlawful detention
heretica pravitas	Heretical depravity
immuratio	Walled-up incarceration
in absentia	Hearing at which the defendant is not present
in camera	Private, nonpublic hearing or proceeding
indicia	Circumstantial evidence of an offense
indictment	A formal written accusation (see also *libellus*)
infamis	Legal status of infamy or dishonor (see also *mala fama*)
inimicitia capitalis	Mortal enmity
in limine	Pretrial motions
inquisitio generalis	Preliminary inquest, often directed at groups or communities, or a process to determine if a crime was committed
inquisitio hereticae pravitatis	Legal procedure in which a judge handles discovery of facts, convenes, and presides over the court
inquisitio specialis	Investigation of a specific individual or examination of evidence connected to a particular suspect
interdict	Suspension of formal religious activities in a specified location for a determined length of time

interdictum ab ingressu ecclesiae	Personal interdict
interlocutory rulings	Provisional ruling by a trial court
interrogatories	Formal written or oral questions
item quilibet presumitur innocens	
nisi probetur nocens	Innocent until proven guilty
iudex generalis	Judge specially commissioned by a superior authority
iudicis recusatio	Removal of a presiding judge
ius commune	Common law
ketzerei	(German) heresy
latae sententiae	Automatic excommunication without the requirement of a trial
lèse-majesté	Treason
lex talionis	punishment in kind (see also *pena talionis*)
libellus (pl. *libelli*)	Formal petition inaugurating a legal process or written accusation (see also indictment)
litis contestatio	Procedural step in which matters preliminary to proof are advanced and the defendant contests the litigation
magisterium	Teaching authority (of the church)
mala fama	Evil reputation (see also *infamis*)
malfeasance	Commission of an illegal or wrongful act
mens rea	Criminal intent
misfeasance	A legal act performed improperly
motion	Written or oral application requesting a court ruling on a particular issue
nonfeasance	Failure to perform a required duty
ordo iudiciarius	Standard legal procedure (also known as *ordo juris*)
peine forte et dure	Severe and hard punishment, used at times to force the accused to answer
pena talionis	Retaliatory punishment (see also *lex talionis*)
Penitentiary (apostolic)	Tribunal of the Roman Curia with jurisdiction over writs of excommunication and other spiritual matters
pertinacia	Stubbornness (see also *contumacia*)
pertinacia voluntatis	Willing stubbornness
plena probatio	Full proof
poenae confusibiles	Forms of degrading penance
positiones	Formal arguments drawn up for the court
potestas iurisdictionis	Jurisdictional power
presentment	Indictment

privilegium canonis	Right to special protection, usually reserved for the clergy
privilegium fori	Right to trial in a church court
procurator	Legal counsel (proctor) who appears on behalf of the defendant (see also *advocatus* and *defensorius*)
promotor	Either an independent prosecutor or a judge's assistant in a legal process
promotor iudiciis officii	Judicial assistant appointed ad hoc in specific cases (see also promotor)
promovens	Individual initiating and prosecuting charges (see also promotor)
purgation	Defendant swearing his or her innocence under oath (see also *compurgatio*)
quaestio	Question
redirect	Reexamination of evidence or witnesses
remand	Appellate finding referred back to a lower court
res iudicatae	Binding court verdict
reus	Defendant
Romano-canonical	Court procedure adopted by medieval church courts, rooted in Roman law procedures (see also *ordo iudiciarius*)
Rota	Highest appellate court of the church (see also *audientia*)
salvus conductus	Formal guarantee of safe passage and protections
sede vacante	The episcopal see of a particular locale is unoccupied
sententia	Judicial sentence or judgment of the court
sermo generalis	Formal addresses (sermon) delivered at the conclusions of heresy trials
stare decisis	Legal procedure based on precedent
summary procedure	Abbreviated legal process limiting objections
suspectus	Person suspected of heresy
talio	(See *lex talionis* and *pena talionis*)
validus clamor	Strong outcry
voir dire	Preliminary oral examination of prospective jurors
writ of mandamus	A mandatory order issued by a superior court addressing a lower court

References to Canon Law

Selected Bibliography

A fuller listing of sources for the study of Jan Hus appears in Thomas A. Fudge, *Jan Hus: Religious Reform and Social Revolution in Bohemia* (London: I. B. Tauris, 2010), pp. 323–350. It seemed redundant to duplicate that list here when many of the sources are not particularly relevant in terms of the legal process. Part of this book relies on the writings of Hus, and these have been drawn principally either from the modern critical editions in *Iohannis Hus Opera omnia* where available or from the older collections in the *Historia et monumenta Ioannis Hus atque Hieronymi Pragensis*. Although some manuscript sources were consulted, these have not been listed, as the main sources for the study of the trial have been edited and printed. In terms of canon law, the Friedberg edition has been adequate, while the fragmentary *Acta* of the legal process have been drawn from various sources.

PRINTED PRIMARY SOURCES

Buck, Thomas Martin, ed. *Chronik des Konstanzer Konzils 1414–1418 von Ulrich Richental*. Ostfildern: Jan Thorbecke Verlag, 2010.

Dobiáš, František M., and Amedeo Molnár, eds. *Sermon de pace—Řeč o míru*. Prague: Česká Křesťanská Akademie, 1995.

Du Pin, Louis Ellies, ed. *Joannes Gersonii Opera Omnia*, 5 vols. Antwerp: Sumptibus Societatis, 1706.

Eymeric, Nicholas, *Directorium inquisitorum*. Venice: Simeonis Vasalini, 1595.

Finke, Heinrich, ed., *Acta concilii Constanciensis*, 4 vols. Münster: Druck und Verlag der Regensbergschen Buchhandlung, 1896–1928.

Firnhaber, Friedrich, ed. "Petrus de Pulka, Abgesandter der Wiener Universität am Concilium zu Constanz." *Archiv für Kunde Österreichischer Geschichts-Quellen*, 15 (1856): 1–70.

Flajšhans, Václav, ed. *Mag. Io. Hus Sermones in Capella Bethlehem, 1410–1411*, 6 vols. Prague: České Společnosti Nauk, 1938–1945.

————. *Mag. Jo. Hus Opera omnia: Nach neuentdeckten Handschriften,* 3 vols. Osnabrück: Biblio-Verlag, 1966.

————. *Spisy M. Jana Husi,* 3 vols. Prague: Vilímek, 1904–1908.

Fowler-Magerl, Linda. *Ordo iudiciorum vel ordo iudiciarus.* Frankfurt: Klostermann, 1984.

Friedberg, Emil, ed. *Corpus iuris canonici,* 2 vols. Leipzig: Tauchnitz, 1879–1881.

Fudge, Thomas A. "Jan Hus at Calvary: The Text of an Early Fifteenth-Century Passio." *Journal of Moravian History* 11, no. 3 (2011): 45–81.

Glorieux, Palémon, ed. *Jean Gerson Oeuvres Complètes,* 10 vols. Tournai: Desclée, 1960.

Goll, Jaroslav, et al., eds. *Fontes rerum bohemicarum,* 8 vols. Prague: Nákladem Nadání Františka Palackého, 1873–1932.

Gui, Bernard. *Practica inquisitionis heretice pravitatis,* ed. Célestin Douais. Paris: Picard, 1886.

Hardt, Hermann von der, ed. *Magnum oecumenicum constantiense concilium,* 7 vols. Leipzig: Genschii, 1699–1742.

Hlaváček, Ivan, and Zdeňka Hledíková, eds. *Protocollum visitationis archidiaconatus Pragensis annis 1379–1382 per Paulum de Janowicz archidiaconum Pragensem, factae.* Prague: Academia, 1973.

Höfler, Konstantin von, ed. *Geschichtschreiber der Husitischen Bewegung in Böhmen,* 3 vols. Vienna: Hof- und Staatsdruckerei, 1856–1866) [= Fontes rerum austriacarum, vols. 2, 6, 7.]

Hostiensis. *Commentaria in Decretales Gregorii IX.* Venice: Apud Juntas, 1581.

————. *Summa aurea.* Venice: Iacobum Vitalem, 1574.

Illyricus, Matthias Flacius, ed. *Historia et monumenta Ioannis Hus atque Hieronymi Pragensis,* 2 vols. Nürnberg: Montanus and Neuberus, 1558; 1715.

Kadlec, Jaroslav V. "Synods of Prague and their Statutes 1396–1414." *Apollinaris* 54 (1991): 227–293.

Klicman, Ladislav, ed. *Processus iudiciarius contra Jeronimum de Praga habitus Viennae a. 1410–1412.* Prague: Česká Akademie Císaře Františka Josefa Pro Vědy, Slovesnost a Umění, 1898.

Krofta, Kamil. "Z Geschichte der husitischen Bewegung: Drei Bullen Papst Johanns XXIII. aus dem Jahre 1414." *Mittheilungen des Instituts für österreichische Geschichtsforschung* 23 (1902): 598–610.

Loomis, Louise R., ed. *The Council of Constance: The Unification of the Church.* New York: Columbia University Press, 1961.

Loserth, Johannn, ed. "Beiträge zur Geschichte der Husitischen Bewegung: Gleichzeitige Berichte und Actenstücke zur Ausbreitung des Wiclifismus in Böhmen und Mähren von 1410 bis 1419." *AÖG* 82 (1895): 327–418.

Mansi, Giovanni Domenico, ed. *Sacrorum conciliorum nova, et amplissima collectio…,* 53 vols. Graz: Akademische Druck- u. Verlagsanstalt, 1960.

Martène, Edmond, and Ursin Durand, eds. *Veterum scriptorum et monumentorum amplissima collectio*, 9 vols. Paris: Boudot, 1724–1733.

Migne, Jacques Paul, ed. *Patrologiae Latina*, 221 vols. Paris: Migne/Garnier, 1844–1865.

———, ed. *Patrologiae Graeca*, 161 vols. Paris: Migne/Garnier, 1857–1866.

Mladoňovice, Petr. *Relatio de Mag. Joannis Hus causa in Fontes rerum bohemicarum*, vol. 8, ed. Václav Novotný. Prague: Nákladem Nadání Františka Palackého, 1932.

Molnár, Amedeo, and František M. Dobiáš, eds. *Husova výzbroj do Kostnice*. Prague: Kalich, 1965.

Nicolaï, Jean, and François de Bois, eds. *S. Thomae Summa Theologiae*. Bar-le-Duc: Guérin, 1874.

Novotný, Václav, ed. *M. Jana Husi Korespondence a dokumenty*. Prague: Nákladem Komise pro Vydávání Pramenů Náboženského Hnutí Českého, 1920.

Palacký, František, ed. *Documenta Mag. Joannis Hus vitam, doctrinam, causam in constantiensi concilio actam et controversias de religione in Bohemia annis 1403–1418 motas illustrantia*. Prague: Tempsky, 1869.

Palacký, František, ed. *Scriptores rerum bohemicarum*, vol. 3. Prague: JSP, 1829.

Pez, Bernard, ed. *Thesaurus anecdotorum novissimus seu veterum monumentorum*, 6 vols. Augsburg: Philippi, Martini & Joannis Veith Fratrum, 1721–1729.

Ryba, Bohumil, ed. *Betlemské texty*. Prague: Orbis, 1951.

Ryšánek, František, et al., eds. *Magistri Iohannis Hus, Opera omnia*, 27 vols. Prague: Academia and Turnhout: Brepols, 1959–.

Schaff, David S., trans. *The Church by John Huss*. New York: Scribner's, 1915.

Schmidtová, Anežka, ed. *Sermones de tempore qui Collecta dicuntur*. Prague: Academia, 1959.

Sedlák, Jan, ed. *Studie a texty k životopisu Husovu*, 3 vols. Olomouc, Czech Republic: Matice Cyrilometodějská, 1914–1925.

Šimek, František, ed. *Staré letopisy české z vratislavského rukopisu novočeským pravopisem*. Prague: Historické Spolku a Společnosti Husova Musea, 1937.

Šimek, František, and Miloslav Kaňak, eds. *Staré letopisy české z rukopisu křižovnického*. Prague: Státní nakladatelství Krásné Literatury, Hudby a Umění, 1939.

Spinka, Matthew, ed. *John Hus at the Council of Constance*. New York: Columbia University Press, 1965.

Tanner, Norman P., ed. *Decrees of the Ecumenical Councils*, 2 vols. London: Sheed & Ward, 1990.

Thomson, S. Harrison, ed. *Magistri Johannis Hus Tractatus De Ecclesia*. Boulder: University of Colorado Press, 1956.

Wakefield, Walter L., and Austin P. Evans, eds. *Heresies of the High Middle Ages*. New York: Columbia University Press, 1991.

Wyclif, John. *John Wyclif's Latin Works*, 20 vols. in 33 parts (1883–1922). New York: Johnson Reprints, 1966.

SECONDARY SOURCES

Asad, Talal. "Medieval Heresy: An Anthropological View." *Social History* 11, no. 3 (1986): 345–362.

Bartoš, František M. "Apologie de M. Jean Huss contra son apologiste." CV 8 (1965): 65–74.

———. *Čechy v době Husově 1378–1415.* Prague: Laichter, 1947.

———. *Co víme o Husovi nového.* Prague: Pokrok, 1946.

———. *Literární činnost M. Jana Husi.* Prague: ČSAV, 1948.

———. "Z posledního zápasu o M. Jana." JSH 17 (1948): 57–60.

Bartoš, František M., and Pavel Spunar, eds. *Soupis pramenů k literární činnosti M. Jana Husa a M. Jeronýma Pražského.* Prague: ČSAV, 1965.

Becker, Hans-Jürgen. *Die Appellation vom Papst an ein allgemeines Konzil.* Cologne: Böhlau Verlag, 1988.

Brandmüller, Walter. *Das Konzil von Konstanz 1414–1418,* 2 vols. Paderborn: Ferdinand Schöningh, 1991–1997.

———. "Hus vor dem Konzil." In *Jan Hus: Zwischen Zeiten, Völkern, Konfessionen,* ed. Ferdinand Seibt, pp. 235–242. Munich: Oldenboug, 1997.

Brundage, James A. *Medieval Canon Law.* New York: Longman, 1995.

———. *The Profession and Practice of Medieval Canon Law.* Aldershot, U.K.: Ashgate-Variorum, 2004.

———. "Proof in Canonical Criminal Law." *Continuity and Change* 11 (1996): 329–339.

Buck, Thomas Martin. "Fiktion und Realität: Zu den Textinserten der Richental-Chronik." *Zeitschrift für die Geschichte des Oberrheins* 149 (2001): 61–96.

Carraway, Joanna. "Contumacy, Defense Strategy, and Criminal Law in Late Medieval Italy." *Law and History Review* 29, no. 1 (2011): 99–132.

Clarke, Peter D. *The Interdict in the Thirteenth Century: A Question of Collective Guilt.* Oxford: Oxford University Press, 2007.

Coulton, G. G. *The Death Penalty for Heresy.* London: Simpkin, 1924.

De Vooght, Paul. *Hussiana.* Louvain: Publications Universitaires de Louvain, 1960.

———. "Jean Huss et ses juges." In *Das Konzil von Konstanz,* ed. August Franzen and Wolfgang Müller, pp. 152–73. Freiburg: Herder, 1964.

———. *L'Hérésie de Jean Huss,* 2nd ed. Louvain: Publications Universitaires de Louvain, 1975.

———. *Les pouvoirs du concile et l'autorité du pape au concile de Constance: Le décret "Haec Sancta Synodus" du 6. avril 1415.* Paris: Édition du Cerf, 1965.

Diehl, Peter. "Ad abolendam (X 5.7.9) and Imperial Legislation against Heresy." *Bulletin of Medieval Canon Law* 19 (1989): 1–11.

Doležalová, Eva, Jan Hrdina, František Šmahel, and Zdeněk Uhlíř. "The Reception and Criticism of Indulgences in the Late Medieval Czech Lands." In *Promissory*

Notes on the Treasury of Merits: Indulgences in Late Medieval Europe, ed. R. N. Swanson, pp. 101–145. Leiden, Neth.: Brill, 2006.

Dondaine, Antoine. "Le manuel de l'inquisiteur (1230–1300)." *Archivum Fratrum Praedicatorum* 17 (1947): 85–194.

Dossat, Yves. "La repression de l'hérésie par les évêques." *Cahiers de Fanjeaux* 6 (1971): 217–251.

Drda, Miloš, František Holeček, and Zdeněk Vybíral, eds. *Jan Hus na přelomu tisíciletí*. Tábor: Hussite Museum, 2001. (= *Husitský tábor*, supplement 1).

Evans, G. R. "Notoriety: A Mediaeval Change of Attitude." *Ecclesiastical Law Journal* 4, no. 20 (1997): 629–638.

Flajšhans, Václav. *Mistr Jan řečený Hus z Husince*. Prague: Vílimek, 1901.

Fraher, Richard M. "Conviction according to Conscience: The Medieval Jurists' Debate concerning Judicial Discretion and the Law of Proofs." *Law and History Review* 7, no. 1 (1989): 23–88.

Frenken, Ansgar. *Die Erforschung des Konstanzer Konzils (1414–1418) in den letzten 100 Jahren*. Paderborn: Ferdinand Schöningh, 1993.

Fowler-Magerl, Linda. *Ordines iudiciarii and libelli de ordine iudiciorum: From the middle of the Twelfth to the end of the Fifteenth Century*. Turnhout: Brepols, 1994.

Fudge, Thomas A. "'Ansellus deï' and the Bethlehem Chapel in Prague," *CV* 35, no. 2 (1993): 127–161.

———. *Jan Hus: Religious Reform and Social Revolution in Bohemia*. London: I. B. Tauris, 2010.

———. *The Magnificent Ride: The First Reformation in Hussite Bohemia*. Aldershot, U.K.: Ashgate, 1998.

———. *The Memory and Motivation of Jan Hus, Medieval Priest and Martyr*. Turnhout, Belgium: Brepols, 2013.

———. "Obrana 'Kacířství': Teoretické pojednámí." *Medievalia Historica Bohemica* 9 (2003): 295–314.

———. "O Cursed Judas: Formal Heresy Accusations against Jan Hus." In *Political Uses of the Accusation of Heresy*, ed. Thomas M. Izbicki. Forthcoming.

———. "Picturing the Death and Life of Jan Hus in the Iconography of Early Modern Europe." *Kosmas: Czechoslovak and Central European Journal* 23, no. 1 (2009): 1–18.

Gilmour-Bryson, Anne. "L'eresia e i Templari: 'Oportet et haereses esse.'" *Ricerche di Storia Sociale e Religiosa* 24 (1983): 101–114.

———. "The Templar Trials: Did the System Work?" *Medieval History Journal* 3 (2000): 41–65.

Given, James B. *Inquisition and Medieval Society: Power, Discipline, and Resistance in Languedoc*. Ithaca, N.Y.: Cornell University Press, 1997.

Graus, František. "Der Ketzerprozeß gegen Magister Johannes Hus (1415)." In *Macht und Recht: Große Prozesse in der Geschiche*, ed. Alexander Demandt, pp. 81–102. Munich: Beck, 1990.

Grundmann, Herbert. *Religious Movements in the Middle Ages*, trans. Steven Rowan. Notre Dame, Ind.: University of Notre Dame Press, 1995.

Haberkern, Phillip Nelson. "The Presence of the Past: History, Memory, and the Making of St. Jan Hus." PhD dissertation, University of Virginia, 2009.

———. "What's in a Name, or What's at Stake When We Talk about 'Hussites'?" *History Compass* 9, no. 10 (2011): 791–801.

Hefele, Karl Joseph von, and Henri Leclercq. *Histoire des Conciles*, 9 vols. Paris: Letouzey and Ané, 1907–1952.

Heirbut, Dirk. "Rules for Solving Conflicts of Law in the Middle Ages: Part of the Solution, Part of the Problem." In *Boundaries of the Law: Geography, Gender and Jurisdiction in Medieval and Early Modern Europe*, ed. Anthony Musson, pp. 118–129. Aldershot, U.K.: Ashgate, 2005.

Helmholz, R. H. "The Early History of the Grand Jury and the Canon Law." *University of Chicago Law Review* 50 (1983): 613–627.

———. "Excommunication as a Legal Sanction: The Attitudes of the Medieval Canonists." ZRG KA 68 (1982): 202–218.

———. "The *litis contestatio*: Its Survival in the Medieval *ius commune* and Beyond." In *Lex et Romanitas: Essays for Alan Watson*, ed. Michael Hoeflich, pp. 73–89. Berkeley: University of California Press, 2000.

Herrmann, Frank R., and Brownlow M. Speer. "Facing the Accuser: Ancient and Medieval Precursors of the Confrontation Clause." *Virginia Journal of International Law* 34, no. 3 (1994): 481–552.

Hilsch, Peter. *Johannes Hus (um 1370–1415): Prediger Gottes und Ketzer*. Regensburg: Verlag Friedrich Pustet, 1999.

Hoke, Rudolf. "Der Prozeß des Jan Hus und das Geleit König Sigmunds: Ein Veitrage zur Frage nach der Kläger—und Angeklagtenrolle im Konstanzer Proceß von 1414/1415." AHC 15 (1883): 172–193.

Holeček, František J. "The Problems of the Person, the Life and the Work of Jan Hus: The Significance and the Task of a Commission of the Czech Bishops' Conference." BRRP, vol. 2 (1998), pp. 39–47.

Holeton, David R. "The Celebration of Jan Hus in the Life of the Churches." *Studia Liturgica* 35 (2005): 32–59.

Jacobi, Erwin. "Der Prozeß im Decretum Gratiani und bei den ältesten Dekretisten." ZRG KA 3 (1913): 223–343.

Kaluza, Zenon. "Le chancelier Gerson et Jérome de Prague." *Archives d'Histoire Doctrinale et Littéraire du Moyen Age* 51 (1984): 81–126.

Kaminsky, Howard. *A History of the Hussite Revolution*. Berkeley: University of California Press, 1967.

Kelly, Henry Ansgar. *Inquisitions and Other Trial Procedures in the Medieval West*. Aldershot, U.K.: Ashgate-Variorum, 2001.

Kejř, Jiří. *Husitský právník: M. Jan z Jesenice*. Prague: ČSAV, 1965.

———. *Husův proces*. Prague: Vyšehrad, 2000.

————. "Husova Pravda." *Theologická Revue* 77 (2006): 232–243.

————. *Husovo odvolání od soudu papežova k soudu Kristovu.* Prague: Albis International, 1999.

————. "Das Hussitentum und das kanonische Recht." *Proceedings of the Third International Congress of Medieval Canon Law* 4 (1971): 191–204.

————. "Jan Hus jako právní myslitel." In *Jan Hus mezi epochami, národy a konfesemi,* ed. Jan Lášek, pp. 197–207. Prague: Česká Křesťanská Akademie: Husitská Teologická Fakulta Univerzity Karlovy, 1995.

————. *Jan Hus známý a neznámý.* Prague: Karolinum, 2009.

————. "K Husovu procesu v Kostnici." *Acta Universitatis Carolinae—Historia Universitatis Carolinae Pragensis* 48, no. 1 (2008): 11–18.

————. *Z počátků české reformace.* Brno: L. Marek, 2006.

Kéry, Lotte. "Inquisitio—denunciation—exceptio: Möglichkeiten der Verfahrenseinleitung im Dekretalenrecht." ZRG KA 87 (2001): 226–268.

Klener, Pavel, ed. *Miscellanea husitica Ioannis Sedlák.* Prague: Katolická Teologická Fakulta Univerzity Karlovy, 1996.

Knox, Ronald. "Accusing Higher Up." ZRG KA 77 (1991): 1–31.

Kopičková, Božena, and Anežka Vidmanová. *Listy na Husovu obrana z let 1410–1412: Konec jedné legendy?* Prague: Karolinum, 1999.

Krzenck, Thomas. "Johannes Hus—ein 'halsstarriger Ketzer'? Der böhmische Reformator und sein Leben im Dienste der Wahrheit." *Arbeitsberichte des Kultur- und Museumsvereines Thaya* 3–5 (1997): 703–717.

Kuttner, Stephan. "The Date of the Constitution 'Saepe,' the Vatican Manuscripts and the Roman Edition of the Clementines." In *Mélanges Eugène Tisserant,* vol. 4, pp. 427–452, *Archives Vaticanes Histoire Ecclesiastique,* pt. 1 [*Studi e testi,* 234]. Vatican City: Biblioteca Apostolica Vaticana, 1964.

————. "Ecclesia de occultis non iudicat: Problemata ex doctrina poenali decretistarum et decretalistarum a Gratiano usque ad Gregorium PP. IX." In *Acta Congressus iuridici internationalis Romae 1934,* vol. 3, pp. 225–246. Rome: Apud Custodiam Librariam Pont. Instituti Utriusque Iuris, 1936.

————. *Kanonistische Schuldlehre von Gratian bis auf die Dekretalen Gregors IX. Systematisch auf Grund der handschriftlichen Quellen dargestellt.* Vatican City: Biblioteca Apostolica Vaticana, 1935.

Lambert, Malcolm. *Medieval Heresy: Popular Movements from the Gregorian Reform to the Reformation,* 3rd ed. Oxford: Blackwell, 2002.

Lášek, Jan B., ed. *Jan Hus mezi epochami, národy a konfesemi.* Prague: Česká Křesťanská Akademie: Husitská Teologická Fakulta Univerzity Karlovy, 1995.

Lenfant, Jacques. *The History of the Council of Constance,* 2 vols. London: Bettesworth, 1730.

Litewski, Wiesław. *Der römisch-kanonische Zivilprozeß nach den älteren ordines iudiciari,* 2 vols. Kraków: Jagiełłion University Press, 1999.

Lützow, Franz. *The Life and Times of Master John Hus.* London: Dent, 1909.

Maisonneuve, Henri. *Études sur les origines de l'inquisition*, 2nd ed. Paris: J. Vrin, 1960.

Marin, Olivier. *L'archevêque, le maître et le dévot: Genèses du mouvement réformateur pragois années 1360–1419*. Paris: Honoré Champion Éditeur, 2005.

———. "Hus et l'eucharistie: Notes sur la critique hussite de la *Stella clericorum*." BRRP, vol. 3 (2000), pp. 49–61.

Molnár, Amedeo. *Jan Hus: Testimone della verità*. Turin: Claudiana, 1973.

Moore, R.I., *The War on Heresy: Faith and Power in Medieval Europe*. Cambridge, MA: Belknap Press of Harvard University Press, 2012.

Nechutová, Jana. "M. Štěpán von Páleč und die Hus—Historiographie." *Mediaevalia Bohemica* 3 (1970): 87–122.

Novotný, Václav, and Vlastimil Kybal. *M. Jan Hus: Život a učení*, 2 vols. in 5 parts. Prague: Laichter, 1919–1931.

Odložilík, Otakar. "The Bethlehem Chapel in Prague: Remarks on Its Foundation Charter." *Studien zur Älteren Geschichte Osteuropas* 2, no. 1 (1956): 125–141.

Ott, Emil. "Das Eindringen des kanonische Rechts, seine lehre und wissenschaftliche Pflege in Böhmen und Mähren währen des Mittelalters." ZRG KA 3 (1913): 1–106.

Parmeggiani, Riccardo. "Un secolo di manualistica inquisitoriale (1230–1330): Intertestualitè e circolazione del diritto." *Rivista Internazionale di Diritto Comune* 13 (2002): 229–270.

Patschovsky, Alexander. *Die Anfänge einer Ständigen Inquisition in Böhmen ein Prager Inquisitoren-Handbuch aus der ersten Hälfte des 14. Jahrhunderts*. New York: Walter de Gruyter, 1975.

———. "Ekklesiologie bei Johannes Hus." In *Politik—Bildung—Naturkunde—Theologie*, ed. by Hartmut Boockmann, Bernd Moeller, and Karl Stackmann, pp. 370–399. Göttingen: Vandenhoeck & Ruprecht, 1989.

Paul, Jacques. "La mentalité de l'inquisiteur chez Bernard Gui." In *Bernard Gui et son monde*, ed. Marie-Humbert Vicaire, pp. 279–316. Toulouse: Privat, 1981.

Pennington, Kenneth. "Due Process, Community and the Prince in the Evolution of the *Ordo iudiciarius*." *Rivista Internazionale de Diritto Comune* 9 (1998): 9–47.

———. "Innocent until Proven Guilty: The Origins of a Legal Maxim." *Jurist* 63, no. 1 (2003): 104–124.

———. *The Prince and the Law, 1200–1600: Sovereignty and Rights in the Western Legal Tradition*. Berkeley: University of California Press, 1993.

———. "*Pro Peccatis Patrum Puniri*: A Moral and Legal Problem of the Inquisition." *Church History* 47, no. 2 (1978): 137–154.

———. "Torture and Fear: Enemies of Justice." *Rivista Internazionale de Diritto Comune* 19 (2008): 203–242.

Peters, Edward. "*Crimen exceptum*: The History of an Idea." In *Proceedings of the Tenth International Congress on Medieval Canon Law*, ed. Kenneth Pennington,

Stanley Chodorow, and Keith H. Kendall, pp. 137–194. Vatican City: Bibliotheca Apostolica Vaticana, 2001.

———. "The Prosecution of Heresy and Theories of Criminal Justice in the Twelfth and Thirteenth Centuries." In *Vorträge zur Justizforschung*, ed. Heinz Mohnhaupt and Dieter Simon, vol. 2, pp. 25–42. Frankfurt: Klostermann, 1993.

Plöchl, Willibald M. *Geschichte des Kirchenrecht*, 5 vols. Vienna: Verlag Herold, 1953–1969.

Pořízka, Aleš. "Listy na obranu Husova ze 12. září až 2. října 1410: Konec druhé legendy?" *Český Čaposis Historický* 99, no. 4 (2001): 701–723.

Provvidente, Sebastián. "Factum hereticale, representatio et ordo iuris: Le procès contre Jean Hus au Concile de Constance (1414–1418)." *Temas Medievales* 17 (2009): 103–138.

———. "Inquisitorial Process and *Plenitudo Potestatis* at the Council of Constance (1414–1418)." BRRP, vol. 8 [= Filosofický časopis, Supplementum 3] (2011), pp. 98–114.

Schaff, David S. *John Huss: His Life, Teachings and Death after Five Hundred Years.* New York: Scribner's, 1915.

Sedlák, Jan. *M. Jan Hus.* Prague: Dědictví sv. Prokopa, 1915.

———. *Miscellanea husitica Ioannis Sedlák*, ed. Pavel Klener. Prague: Katolická Teologická Fakulta Univerzity Karlovy, 1996.

Seibt, Ferdinand. *Hussitenstudien: Personen, Ereignisse, Ideen einer frühen Revolution.* Munich: Oldenbourg, 1987.

———, ed. *Jan Hus: Zwischen Zeiten, Völkern, Konfessionen.* Munich: Oldenbourg, 1997.

———. "'Neodvolám!' Jan Hus před koncilem kostnickým." In *Velké procesy: Právo a spravedlnost v dějinách*, ed. Uwe Schultz, pp. 84–97. Prague: Brána, 1997.

Šmahel, František. *Die Hussitische Revolution*, 3 vols. Hannover: Hahnsche Buchhandlung, 2002.

Smolík, Josef, "Truth in History according to Hus' Conception." CV 15 (1972): 97–109.

Spinka, Matthew. *John Hus: A Biography.* Princeton, N.J.: Princeton University Press, 1968.

———. *John Hus' Concept of the Church.* Princeton, N.J.: Princeton University Press, 1966.

Stump, Phillip H. *The Reforms of the Council of Constance (1414–1418).* Leiden: Brill, 1994.

Thijssen, J. M. M. H. "Master Amalric and the Amalricians: Inquisitorial Procedure and the Suppression of Heresy at the University of Paris." *Speculum* 71 (1996), pp. 43–65.

Tierney Brian. *Foundations of the Conciliar Theory: The Contribution of the Medieval Canonists from Gratian to the Great Schism.* Leiden: Brill, 1998.

Torquebiau, Pierre. "Contumacia, Contumax." In *Dictionnaire de droit canonique*, 7 vols., ed. Raoul Naz, vol. 4, cols. 507–525. Paris: Librairie Letouzey et Ané, 1935–1965.

Trusen, Winfried. "Der Inquisitionsprozeß: Seine historischen Grundlagen und frühen Formen." ZRG KA 74 (1988): 168–230.

Ullmann, Walter. "Some Medieval Principles of Criminal Procedure." *Juridical Review* 59 (1947): 1–28.

Vallerani, Massimo. *Medieval Public Justice,* trans. Sarah Ruben Blanshei. Washington, D.C.: Catholic University of America Press, 2012.

Vernay, Eugène. *Le "Liber de Excommunicatione" du Cardinal Bérenger-Frédol précédé d'une introduction historique sur l'excommunicatione et l'interdict en droit canonique, de Gratien à la fin du XIIIe siècle.* Paris: Rousseau, 1912.

Vodola, Elisabeth. *Excommunication in the Middle Ages.* Berkeley: University of California Press, 1986.

Waugh, Scott L., and Peter D. Diehl, eds. *Christendom and Its Discontents: Exclusion, Persecution, and Rebellion, 1000–1500.* Cambridge, U.K.: Cambridge University Press, 1996.

Werner, Ernst. *Jan Hus: Welt und Umwelt eines Prager Frühreformators.* Weimar: Böhlaus, 1991.

Wetzstein, Thomas. *Heilige vor Gericht: Das Kanonisationverfahren im europäischen Spätmittelalter.* Cologne: Böhlau Verlag, 2004.

Index

Entries for Jan Hus, Bohemia, canon law, the Council of Constance, criminal procedure, legal statutes, and heresy law, are selective on account of the fact that these subjects form the fabric of the book and as such are very numerous. Popes, councils of the church, and specific churches are listed alphabetically under those headings. Abbeys, convents cloisters, monasteries, and priories are noted under the heading of religious houses. Unless otherwise noted, the churches and religious houses specifically identified are in Prague. Medieval people are generally listed under places of origin. Lesser known figures have been identified according to their chief role in connection with the subjects under investigation. Czech proper names have generally been given in their native form. The main exception is Prague rather than Praha.